Fragmented Vision

FRAGMENTED VISION
Culture and Politics in Contemporary Malaysia

Editors

JOEL S KAHN
FRANCIS LOH KOK WAH

UNIVERSITY OF HAWAII PRESS
Honolulu

Published in North America by
University of Hawaii Press
2840 Kolowalu Street
Honolulu, Hawaii 96822

First published in Australia by
Allen & Unwin in association with
the Asian Studies Association of Australia

Library of Congress Cataloging-in-Publication Data

Fragmented vision : culture and politics in contemporary Malaysia /
    Joel S. Kahn and Francis Loh Kok Wah, editors.
        p.   cm.
    Includes bibliographical references and index.
    ISBN 0-8248-1461-4
    1. Malaysia—Politics and government. 2. Malaysia—Civilization.
I. Kahn, Joel S. II. Loh, Francis Kok-Wah. 1951–
DS597.2.F72 1992   91-39532
959.5—dc20   CIP

Typeset by Vera-Reyes Inc., Manila
Printed in Singapore by Fong & Sons Printers

Contents

1

Introduction: Fragmented Vision

Francis Loh Kok Wah
Joel S Kahn

Malaysian society has undergone sweeping changes in the last two decades. Indeed the pace of change has been so rapid that each new development seems to catch the observer and analyst of Malaysian economy and polity unawares. Two kinds of transformation have drawn the most attention. These are the emergence of authoritarian structures and tendencies in the apparatus of the Malaysian state on the one hand, and the vastly accelerated rates of economic growth and a restructuring of the Malaysian economy on the other.

As Crouch (this volume) suggests, 1969 marks a significant shift in the mode of government, from a modified democracy to "a form of authoritarianism in which an entrenched elite takes whatever steps necessary to ensure its continued control of government." This authoritarian tendency is manifest in the increasingly wider use of the Internal Security Act (1960) and other forms of detention without trial, the Societies Act (1966), the Sedition Act (1971), the Universities and University Colleges Act (1971), the Official Secrets Act (1972), the Printing Presses and Publication Act (1988), most of which have been amended in the 1980s, to place tight restrictions on the activities of individuals and groups who would seek to challenge the legitimacy of the powers that be. In 1983 the Malaysian government, under Prime Minister Dr Mahathir Mohamed, also amended the constitution with regards to acquiring Royal Assent for the declaration of a State of Emergency. More recently in 1988, Mahathir began to undermine the doctrine of separation of powers between the executive, legislative and judiciary with yet another constitutional amendment. In this regard, the increasing inclusion of ouster clauses in new legislations is especially noteworthy. It marks a significant break with the policies of earlier governments.

At the economic level, the last two decades have witnessed relatively high rates of growth, prompting at least some recent observers to characterise Malaysia as the next NIC.[1] This economic growth has been achieved in the context of the development of new kinds of relations between political

---

[1] See, for example, *Far Eastern Economic Review* 7 September 1989.

instrumentalities and the economy. The State itself has played a more and more influential role, not just in economic planning, but it has also become more directly involved in financing and organising production. New circumstances have given rise to what in Malaysia has come to be called "Money Politics". This term covers a range of practices whereby the benefits of State economic sponsorship and protection are channelled to individuals, groups and private companies associated with the ruling political parties, in particular UMNO (the United Malays National Organisation). Consequently, the rise of Money Politics has resulted in the blurring of State and UMNO business interests and the increasing dominance of UMNO and UMNO associated enterprises in the economy (for some examples see paper by Khoo Kay Jin, this volume, and Gomez 1990).

These transformations in Malaysia's economy have contributed to the emergence of a more differentiated society which has been accompanied by, and interrelated with significant changes in civil society as well—in the nature of gender relations and the way in which these relations are perceived; in the lives of small-scale rural cultivators; in the composition, delineation and dominant symbols of the major ethnic groupings; in the circumstances of minority groups such as the Orang Asli and the indigenous peoples of East Malaysia; in the religious life of the nation (most clearly manifest in the rise of a new Muslim fundamentalism, but also in non-Muslim religious changes); in national and local cultural life—the list is potentially a very long one indeed.

What has, perhaps, most baffled observers is that the political and economic developments have occurred simultaneously. Analysts of liberal persuasion have, for example, been prepared for Malaysia's ability to stage economic recovery and yet often been at a loss to account for the activities of a state which contradict the ideals of classical liberalism. More radical critics have been less surprised by the authoritarian turn in Malaysian political life, but unable to account for the fact of sustained economic growth.

But analyses of what might be termed the *structure* of Malaysian economy and polity, as well as of the relationships between them, have only had limited reference to the cultural dimensions of social change in Malaysia. Two noteworthy exceptions are Muzaffar (1987) and Ackerman and Lee (1988). Apart from marking a significant gap in our understanding of contemporary Malaysia, this lack of attention to culture undermines those very structural analyses which predominate. Liberal analysts, for example, have failed to appreciate the extent to which culture, in this case the culture of democracy, must intervene between the terms of their standard equation, economic growth-political liberalism. And radical critics, by all too frequently relegating culture to the dustbin of false consciousness, fail to appreciate the unique features of the Malaysian social formation.

While we do not claim to have resolved these issues, our intentions in putting together this collection of papers on culture and politics in contemporary Malaysia are twofold: first, to document some of the significant cultural developments which have accompanied the political and economic changes in Malaysia over the last couple of decades; and second to demonstrate ways in which an understanding of these developments promotes understanding of some of the enigmas of Malaysian development over the same period.

If the formation of contemporary Malaysian political economy has its origins partly in the years after 1970, then 1969 is also a watershed in Malaysian cultural history. For all Malaysians memories of the traumatic events of 13 May 1969, when communal violence broke out on the streets of Kuala Lumpur, continue to loom large. When, almost twenty years later, a Malay soldier ran amok in Kuala Lumpur, shooting several innocent bystanders, rumours that racial disturbances had broken out spread rapidly among the residents of Malaysia's capital city. Large numbers of them rushed to the shops to stockpile essential foodstuffs, and refused to allow their children to go to school, fearful of the impending disintegration of Malaysian society into warring groups and factions. Such a fear was further fuelled by another rumour that a mammoth UMNO rally that was planned to be held in the city at about the same time was aimed at precipitating another outbreak of communal violence.

The feared immediate social disintegration did not eventuate, the rumours died down, and daily routines resumed. In the eyes of ruling elites, disaster was only averted by the government's use of the Internal Security Act in a mass arrest exercise in October and November 1989 under the codename "Operation Lallang".

Altogether 106 citizens were arrested. They included leaders of the opposition parties, church social workers, human rights activists, Chinese educationalists, environmentalists, trade unionists, Muslim religious teachers and several evangelical Christians, most of whom the government conveniently accused of contributing to rising racial and religious tensions in the country. In fact, the majority of those arrested were government critics and on a number of issues, government ministers and members of the ruling coalition had been responsible for playing up and aggravating the tensions.

At any rate, those tensions were real and Malaysia did come to the brink of another outbreak of communal violence. But the circumstances which allowed those tensions, fears and anxieties to take place have not disappeared, a fact clearly captured in the contributions to this volume. The strongest impression generated by this collection, reflecting accurately the symposium held at Monash University in November 1988 when they were first delivered, is that at least at the level of culture broadly conceived, contemporary Malaysia is characterised by a very fragmented vision. By this we refer in fact to a number of related phenomena which, taken together, have resulted in the proliferation of discourses and/or cultural practices which are either implicitly or explicitly particularistic, and which seek to replace or resist the imposition of universalistic value systems generally assumed to accompany modernisation.

This fragmentation is most immediately evident in the political sphere, characterised as it is by splits and conflicts between existing parties and extra-official political groupings; between government and opposition; between parties in the ruling coalition; and, most recently, even within the coalition's dominant party, UMNO.

An admirably clear exposition of this political landscape is to be found in the contribution by Harold Crouch. And, as several of our other contributors demonstrate, these splits and conflicts run deeper than normal political rivalry and factionalisation, representing as they frequently do fundamentally different visions of Malaysian society in the future and/or constituencies which are themselves culturally diverse. An example of the former is the division within UMNO. That this split is more than a reaction to the challenge of political rivals in search of power, but instead revolves around contrasting cultural visions is nicely documented in the paper by Khoo Kay Jin.

Khoo Kay Jin provides both a detailed summary of recent economic and political developments as well as setting up a framework for the subsequent analyses of cultural/political movements by focussing on the specific nature of the Prime Minister's vision of "modernisation". He contends that Dr. Mahathir, the Prime Minister and leader of UMNO Baru, has gone beyond interpreting the goals of the NEP purely in terms of transfering equity and positions to the Malays as most Malay leaders were wont to do in the 1970s. For Mahathir, the Malays are also required to be efficient, hardworking and disciplined capitalists and workers. But Khoo notes that the pursuit of Mahathir's vision of modernity has been accompanied by an erosion of democratic principles and practices in the society writ large. Given such developments, authoritarianism appears to be an integral part of Mahathir's "grand vision". The splits in Malay society and within UMNO itself, therefore, should be understood not in terms of factionalisation and personal rivalries but in terms of Mahathir's modernist, but undemocratic discourse and those visions opposed to it too.

Part Two of the volume contains four articles which focus on links between developments in Malay culture and recent political and economic changes. The first piece by Ahmad Shabery Cheek and K.S. Jomo focuses on the various Islamic movements, in particular ABIM and PAS. They discuss the origins, social composition and organisation, and activities of each of them. It is clear from the survey that the interests of ABIM and PAS do not converge at this juncture. Hence the Islamic movement cannot and should not be seen in monolithic terms. The next paper by Halim Salleh captures nicely an emerging conflict between the Federal Land Development Authority (FELDA) authorities on the one hand and the Malay settlers on FELDA resettlement schemes, specifically in Pahang, on the other. Guided by a modern bureaucratic vision demanding continual rationalisation of all operations in resettlement schemes so that investments can be recouped, the FELDA officials have instituted various impersonal and rigid regulations to ensure that the settlers become a disciplined, frugal and hardworking work force and they have taken a decision to postpone issuance of land titles to individual settlers until a later point in time. However, the settlers have come to feel that the regulations are overly restrictive and that they are unnecessarily burdened with having to maintain an over-sized bureaucracy. For Halim Salleh this amounts to "proletarianisation" to which they object. Consequently, they have demanded greater control over their labour, finances and land; in the last case that individual land titles be issued to them. In pursuit of this goal, as individuals and as groups of settlers, they have first protested against the authorities, turned to UMNO and even the opposition parties, and sometimes resorted to various forms of "everyday resistance". Significantly the struggle for their rights is fragmented.

A different sort of Malay vision is taken up in Clive Kessler's analysis of Malay political culture. His paper analyses the ways in which ideas of Malay tradition based on idealised relations between raja and subject are interwoven in much of modern Malay political culture. Using the notion of the "invention of tradition" purveyed in an influential volume by Eric Hobsbawm, Terrence Ranger and others (Hobsbawm and Ranger, 1983), Kessler shows how constructions of Malayness are manipulated in the discourse of at least a fraction of the ruling Malay elite. At the same time we might suggest that this particular Malay vision is more than a cloak to conceal some hidden agenda. There is certainly evidence to suggest that, for different reasons, Malay leaders and large numbers of their supporters are fully committed to a future which is Malay rather than Malaysian, and "traditionalised" rather than modernist.

In the final piece in Part Two Joel Kahn explores some of the reasons why these Malay visions should resonate among at least one group, the emerging Malay middle class. He is struck by how Malaysia is currently awash with the symbolism of "traditional Malay culture". He notes that the makers of these images as well as the consumers, are overwhelmingly part of a growing Malay middle class of civil servants, educators and professionals. Paradoxically, he observes, this revived interest occurs at a time when there is a massive decline in what is considered to be the real nexus of traditional Malay culture, the Malay peasant community. (We may ponder, in passing, just how much faster this decline would occur if Mahathir's "grand vision" had its way). By so locating this cultural revivalism, he suggests that the development of what it means to be a Malay is both changing and fragmenting at the same time.

In all these examples of the Malay vision for Malaysia's future we are struck by three things. First unlike Mahathir's image of modernity which is based on a universalistic understanding of what it is to be modern, Malay visions are based on particularistic and exclusive views of the distinctiveness of Malay culture. Second, at the same time as the Malay vision is by definition restrictive, it is also fragmented. In other words there are substantial differences among Malays both as to what constitutes the essence of Malayness and what a future Malay (and for many hence Malaysian) society should look like. For some it is Islam which is the key to Malay identity, for others it is attachment to a leader/patriarch, and for others it is a tradition of egalitarianism and democracy. Ironically, perhaps, the supposedly authentic bearers of the Malay tradition, the peasants, are—at least in the case of Halim's FELDA settlers—the least "traditional" of the lot, struggling as they are for a non-communalistic future characterised by small scale capitalist agriculture. A third feature of these Malay visions is the extent to which they can be seen to be cultural artefacts which are in the process of construction, rather than a mere carryover from the past. All the contributors show in different ways how "Malayness" is currently being worked and reworked in conditions given by the present. If one wishes to maintain, as we certainly do, that Malaysia is in the throes of a modernising process, then we shall have to rethink earlier attempts to characterise cultural modernisation as an inexorable dissolution of so-called primordial loyalties and the emergence of universalistic values.

But of course the constitution and fragmentation of particularistic visions is restricted neither to the Malays, nor indeed to ethnic groups alone. Part Three of the volume brings together the remaining six articles. Tan Liok Ee traces the history of the *Dongjiaozong* (the Chinese education movement). She shows that the movement was initially led by big businessmen and Chinese school teachers who commonly articulated an alternative vision of a democratic multiethnic nation wherein minority languages and cultures are given equal rights. On the basis of this alternative vision, the *Dongjiaozong* has challenged the legitimacy of State policies on language, education and culture. Although it broke with the Malayan Chinese Association (MCA), the major Chinese party in the ruling coalition, the movement has continued to win popular support. This was perhaps because its struggle on behalf of mother-tongue education and for the preservation of Chinese culture has been couched in moral terms. But Tan notes that the nature of Malaysia's polity and economy has changed dramatically since 1970. Hence an exploration of the movement's success since 1970 must take into account the changing composition of its leadership (which today comprises mid-level businessmen and professionals who are less susceptible to government pressures); the re-organisation of the independent Chinese schools so that mother-tongue education also has utilitarian, not merely moral, value; and the adoption of new strategies, ranging from participation in a component-member of the ruling coalition to joining non-communally based citizens' organisations in the struggle for democracy. Hence the *Dongjiaozong's* vision for the Chinese in the 1980s was not only different from that of the MCA's, it was also quite dissimilar to that of the same organisation in the 1950s and 1960s. Francis Loh Kok Wah next investigates the background to the success of the Kadazan dominated PBS in Sabah. He argues that modernisation, especially rapid educational development in the 1970s and 1980s, spawned the emergence of a Kadazan intelligentsia. However, they soon became disaffected with both the state as well as the Federal governments. In the eyes of these intellectuals, the Kadazans constituted the largest indigenous group and the "definitive people" of Sabah. Yet they perceived that their state was being "colonised" by the Federal government, the Kadazan people neglected and discriminated against in the allocation of benefits, and as a result of the national culture policy, subjected to Malay Muslim hegemony. Consequently, they initiated a Kadazan cultural revival focused around the celebration of the Harvest Festival. This fostered Kadazan ethnic consciousness and unity in spite of the novelty of a so-called Kadazan identity. With solid support from the village Kadazans, a counter-hegemonic movement emerged.

The article by Muhammad Ikmal Said traces how ethnicity has plagued the visions of both the Malay and non-Malay left in Malaysia. Basically there was an absence of agreement on what he terms the "fundamentals of national integration". Specifically, this refers to the questions of the right to citizenship, the right to one's culture and the preservation of vernacular schools, and the right to equal socio-economic opportunities. Whereas as "sons of the soil" (bumiputera), the Malay left insisted upon Malay "special rights" and the preservation of the historical character and original Malay sovereignty of the land, the non-Malay left demanded equal rights in keeping with the notion of popular sovereignty (this recalls Tan Liok Ee's discussion of the "alternative vision" articulated in the *Dongjiaozong* but also the Kadazan intellectual's rejection of the extension of this sense of Malay sovereignty over Sabah). In this regard a potentially strong but equally universalistic challenge to the hegemony of modernisation, the discourse of socialism, has similarly been subject to fragmentation. Ikmal ends with a proposal of what a common vision for the left might entail.

But as we have suggested, Malaysian visions are not fragmented solely along so-called "ethnic" cleavages. Maila Stivens, in the penultimate article, discusses the reception that universalising western feminism has had in Malaysian academic women's writing on gender. She suggests that much of this writing has not embraced western feminist agendas in a wholehearted way, in spite of growing feminist action in local women's organisations and that this caution is far from surprising, given the conditions under which knowledge about women has been produced in postcolonial societies such as Malaysia. Feminist scholarly projects operate within an external frame of reference (Lazreg 1988: 81), while constrained by an economistic discourse of 'relevance' produced by involvement in academic consultancies. Finally, Tan Sooi Beng discusses how the Malaysian State has tried to centralise and control the performing arts and how various individuals and groups have responded. She notes that most of the latter have declared their independence of the government's national culture policy. This includes individuals and groups who are more concerned with challenging the policy's emphasis on a core of Malay-Muslim attributes; those who are more socially aware and concerned with human rights abuses, rising consumerism and environmental issues; or those simply against government curtailment of their individual creativeness. Given this disparate set of artistes, she notes that no common vision of an alternative culture policy can be attributed to them. Indeed, very little co-operation and/or artistic exchange occurs among them at this stage: perhaps the best illustration of fragmentation without the vision or possible evolution of a consolidated counter-hegemonic position. Instead these individuals and groups serve as "counterpoints".

This coverage of cultural developments in Malaysia is, unfortunately, far from exhaustive; we had to be guided by the interests and on-going research of our participants. There is, as a result, no chapter on the Orang Asli peoples, and the growing movement intended to promote their culture and politico-economic concerns. Nor is there a chapter on the cultures and politics of Malaysia's Indian communities. These are serious omissions for which we apologise.

But the volume is in no sense to be treated as a comprehensive survey of cultural and political development in Malaysia. Instead by means of the examples we have been able to include, we hope to go beyond documentation, to draw some tentative conclusions about the ways rising authoritarianism, rapid economic growth and the cultural landscape in Malaysia intersect. In so doing we hope to address not only academic but political concerns as well, for example: how can we best understand, and hence combat, the increasingly authoritarian actions of the current regime? Do the demands for democratisation articulated by at least some government critics really go to the heart of the problem, or do the real problems lie elsewhere? Should the activities of the "middle class" dominated pressure groups, often concerned with single issues, be discounted, or do they provide a genuine way forward? Is the struggle for cultural freedom really significant, or does it represent a diversion from more fundamental struggles—for higher wages, for example, or for popular control of the whole political process?

How are we to reconcile the aims of Malaysia's women's movement with those of groups seeking to challenge other forms of inequality? What attitude should we take towards the new developments in ethnic consciousness, as in the case of the Kadazans? What should we make of current attempts to use, and indeed rework, the symbolic meanings of the ideas of "Malayness"? What about the varied and competing claims of religious groups? What about the nature and significance of those aspirations advanced by, and in the name of, Malaysia's peasantry? What significance should be attached to developments in popular culture, and the challenge of youth, particularly in their passion for new forms of popular music?

We cannot pretend to be able to offer definitive answers to all these questions. Before articulating our own perspective let us first investigate the so-called liberal consensus by which Malaysians were ruled in the first decade of independence and, second, why and how that consensus collapsed in the years after 1969.

Consensus, Universalism and the Elite: 1957–1969

Although they may disagree on how to characterise it, most observers of the Malaysian political scene have described the situation from 1957 up to the late 1960s as marked by an ideological unity on the part of the elite on the one hand, with widespread 'communalism' among the masses on the other. In the cultural sphere we therefore have to do with a shared commitment to a more or less universalist discourse (deriving also more or less directly from classical European liberalism) at least among the ruling elite, but one which is maintained in the face of the cultural particularism (here termed "ethnicity") of the masses. This characterisation has its origins in an approach often labelled "plural society" theory. Following the anthropologist M. G. Smith in particular, many such commentators claimed that they had discovered a new type of social organisation, qualitatively different from the caste or estate systems. The plural society was said to be divided vertically into different "communal groups" which were in turn conceived as homogeneous entities capable of acting corporately. This view was based on the premise of shared values and institutions. There was a general assumption that rising tensions and conflict would quite inevitably occur in a plural society. Hence there was special concern to explain how the plural society was being maintained in spite of the lack of widespread consensus in the society.

Consequently, much of this writing has been orientated towards exploring how "political development' could be achieved through formulation of a national identity (in turn often based on the development of a national language, educational system and culture), and/or how the elites of the various communal groups were able or unable to reach some measure of consensus to maintain political stability, preferably within a democratic framework.

In a majority of these works it was concluded that the Malaysian government's efforts towards achieving political development were praiseworthy. For although the creation of a national identity might be based upon the cultural attributes of a particular group, the political and economic interests of the other groups were being catered for. This was all made possible by what were termed the "consociational" attitudes and practices of moderate and responsible elites of whatever "ethnic" background represented in Malaysia's governing alliance (a coalition of ethnically based parties). This view is most clearly articulated in the works of Gullick (1964), Ratnam (1965), Milne (1967) and Ratnam and Milne (1967).

This approach of course had its problems. Advocates were for example forced to explain away the electoral success of opposition parties like the Chinese based People's Progressive Party and the Malay-based Pan Malayan Islamic Party (PAS) as "chauvinistic" or "extremist" without investigating the social bases for their popularity (Gullick 1964: 213; Milne 1967: 278–9; Ratnam and Milne 1967: 48–50; and Means 1970: 216ff). The divisions and cleavages internal to ethnic entities were also ignored. Moreover, instead of exploring the process by which an ethnic section or category became a group/community, and the purposes which led such ethnic entities to act corporately (Strauch 1981), advocates of the plural society approach merely took the existence of ethnic groups as given, that is as inevitable products of a pre-existing cultural differentiation of the masses. This, as we shall see, has serious implications for analyses of later developments.

Accordingly, there was little consideration of Cohen's (1969: 24) insights into the nature of ethnicity as an "idiom" continually being interpreted and re-interpreted; in other words, something situational and dynamic. Although many works on Malaysian ethnicity, adopting Cohen's approach, are now available (Nagata 1979; Strauch 1981; Lee 1986), nonetheless, for many plural society theorists, culture continues to be regarded as an immutable given in any situation. Here culture tends to be treated like other features of the supposedly objective environment within which social processes are enacted. This means that the plural society approach is precisely unable to analyse cultural phenomena and cultural development.

That said, the important contribution of plural society theorists was to warn us against being too complacent about ethnic cleavages. As Geertz argued, governments cannot wish primordial sentiments out of existence, but need instead to domesticate them by means of an "integrative revolution". In this way such sentiments will be "divested of their legitimate force with respect to government authority", and "discontent arising from their dislocation [will be channelled] into properly political rather than parapolitical forms of expression" (see Geertz, 1963). In the context of Malaysia, a coalition at the level of the elite of ethnic based grou s was seen to be capable of engendering this integrative revolution.

It is interesting to note that although they have reached quite different conclusions by means of different concepts, so-called political economists and other critical observers have nonetheless characterised the pre-1969 mode of governing in similar ways. In their terms, it was in the interest of the competing factions of capital and other dominant classes to forge alliances among themselves. They view the practice of consociationalism in this light, namely as a strategy employed by the dominant classes not because they (in contrast to the lower classes) are imbued with some sense of altruism, but because it is in their interest to prevent any threat to the process of continued capital accumulation (Kieve 1981). Hence an investigation of the role of the State in this period revealed both the adoption of policies in favour of the dominant classes (for instance regressive tax laws, tax exemption schemes for investors, anti-labour laws, absence of minimum wage legislation, and so on) as well as repression against those who were adjudged to be promoting ethnic extremism (Brennan 1982: 204 and 210). Again, however, the picture which emerges is of a society characterised by high levels of cultural fragmentation being held together by a multi-ethnic elite committed to a universal liberal rationality. The difference between this view and that of the plural society theorists is that the political economists characterise that rationality as an ideology of domination.

After 1969: A Revolt of the Masses or Elite Fragmentation?

It seems reasonable to suggest that the picture painted by both plural society theorists and political economists, a system of roles revolving around a commitment, more or less, to a discursive universalism, itself derived from a variant of western liberalism, is an accurate one. The difficulties with both approaches lie in their characterisation of the culture of the masses. This comes out most clearly in their respective diagnoses of the situation after 1969, when that liberal consensus (or ruling ideology) began to fragment. Here the prevailing view is that this fragmentation took place largely as a consequence of pressures from below—either the pressures of ethnicity (for the pluralists) or of class conflict (for political economists). We shall conclude our introduction by proposing an alternative, one which in our view allows us to make much more sense of the situation described by our contributors. Our alternative is based on the view that the post-1969 period is characterised by and large not by a renewed challenge from the masses, but instead by a fragmentation of the Malaysian elite and middle classes. Before spelling out this conclusion in more detail, let us look briefly at existing accounts of what happened after 1969.

Plural society theorists see 1969 as marking the breakdown of the Malaysian liberal consensus, taking the view that existing consociational arrangements and/or efforts to promote national identity were inadequate to prevent the outbreak of communal violence in May 1969. Comparing the legislative to the administrative elites these observers have argued that consociational attitudes and practices were more widespread among the latter. The reasons for this, however, lie less with the elites themselves than they do with a presumed attachment to primordial values on the part of the masses. Thus it is assumed that politicians were more inclined towards breaking the rules of the consociational game in order to gain electoral support. Consequently, insofar as the management of communal conflict was the major problem, it was not only necessary to maintain a coalition government (in which parties representing the different races were involved) but to ensure the predominance of executive institutions (the cabinet and administration) over participative ones (Esman 1972: 6). Such a view has now become commonplace. Although the plural society theorists would deny it this, in effect, suggests the need to curtail some aspects of democratic participation—by strengthening the executive institutions, the pursuit of development goals will be enhanced allowing the government to be responsive (Milne 1984; Mauzy 1982; Ismail Kassim 1979; Esman 1972). Hence the view of democracy that is presented by plural society theorists amounts to the regular holding of elections and government being responsive to pressures. Yet even this limited view of democracy has come into contention in recent times. According to this approach, then, post-1969 cultural fragmentation represents an eruption of mass cultural particularism into the politics of the elite, an eruption which forces the breakdown of liberal consensus. Authoritarianism is, in this view, seen to be a (sometimes justified) response to this state of affairs, especially when it is coupled with the need to sustain rapid economic growth.

Critical scholars, of course, have characterised post-1970 developments differently, maintaining that the collapse of liberal consensus was inevitable given that it was a thinly veiled ideology to prop up the ruling class. Some theorists like Abraham (1977) and Cham (1975) have argued that rising communalism was largely a result of "false consciousness" on the part of the peasants and proletariat, which was in turn a result first of the "divide and rule" policies of the British, and, since Independence, ideological manipulation by a Malaysian ruling class intent on perpetuating their political power. Following this line of analysis, the resolution of the communal problem would follow from the realisation by the peasants and proletariat of their genuine class interest regardless of ethnicity. The coming to power of a socialist government would help facilitate the resolution of the problem and the achievement of national unity in plural Malaysia.

This approach has been criticised by a new generation of scholars who now regard ethnic consciousness among the lower classes as a rational response to their predicament, given the peripheral nature of the Malaysian social formation (see, for example, Brennan 1982; Hing 1984; Lim 1988).

Like plural society theorists, then, political economists have also pinpointed the breakdown of liberal consensus as a significant turning point, and have attributed the breakdown at least implicitly to an eruption from below, although this time the emphasis is somewhat different. The pressures from below tend to be described as more or less "rational", i.e. class-based, and as a consequence the authoritarian response is characterised negatively. Nonetheless plural society theorists and political economists have produced surprisingly similar explanations of authoritarianism on the one hand and the fragmentation of vision on the other.

Fragmented Vision, the Middle Class and Authoritarianism

In a very different context Frederic Jameson (1984) has described a phenomenon at least ostensibly similar to this one of cultural fragmentation as a characteristic of "postmodernism" and, further argued that postmodernism represents the "cultural logic of late capitalism". One reason he offers for the proliferation of competing visions is that they have been allowed to develop largely, perhaps, because the late capitalist State no longer requires a dominant and pervasive discourse or ideology for its own reproduction. Being no longer a threat to the viability of State power, particularistic visions can now be allowed to proliferate.

But one should be wary of too quickly transplanting at least this vision of postmodernity into the Malaysian context. For whether or not it can be argued that Western States have abandoned universalistic discourses, and whether or not this can be said to have given rise to a democratisation at least at the level of culture as the postmodernists understand that term, such has quite clearly not been the case in Malaysia. One need only look at the developments in the cultural sphere narrowly defined to demonstrate this point. At a national conference organised by Malaysia's Ministry of Culture, Youth and Sports in 1971, the Malaysian government took (what in the eyes of Westerners must be) the unusual step of formulating what was to become a national cultural policy based on the following principles:

1 The national culture of Malaysia must henceforth be based on the cultures of the people indigenous to the region
2 Elements from other cultures which are judged suitable and reasonable may be incorporated into Malaysia's national culture
3 Islam will be an important element in the national culture (see Tan Sooi Beng, this volume)

In the period since its implementation, Malaysia's national culture policy has become one important point of vigorous debate and political conflict. Numerous examples are provided by the contributors to this volume (see in particular Tan Sooi Beng, Tan Liok Ee and Loh).

In the years since the formulation of a National Cultural Policy, and particularly in the late 1980s, the Malaysian government has been concerned to implement its basic principles by intervening directly and across the board in the cultural field, though as Tan Sooi Beng (this volume) notes, it has not been altogether successful.

Not surprisingly, and perhaps because it has not been altogether clear and efficient about its task, government intervention in the cultural field has produced a response on the part of a variety of non-Malay groups who feel that their cultural freedom has been curtailed. For example, at a meeting of the Chinese guilds and associations of Malaysia held in March, 1983, delegates passed a series of resolutions which were compiled in a joint memorandum to the Ministry of Culture, Youth and Sports. In April 1984, a group of the best-known Indian cultural, social and religious organisations submitted a similar memorandum. Both memoranda accused the government of having formulated a cultural policy which was Malay-centric and undemocratic, and requested that a new policy on national culture be established which was more clearly multi-ethnic and democratic (see Kua 1987: 15).

While earlier generations of modernisation theorists, plural society theorists and political economy theorists all in different ways anticipated either a decline in the variety of cultural identity, or at least the retention of existing ones, recent Malaysian cultural history manifests just the opposite tendency, not because the State has chosen to relinquish control of the cultural field as has been argued for the West, but precisely because the State has chosen to impose a single set of cultural values for all.

However, such an explanation cannot account for the proliferation of new cultural activities and visions on the part of Malays whose culture, presumably, is not being threatened by the National Culture Policy. At this point the contributions by Khoo, Jomo and Shabery, Kessler, Kahn and Halim come into their own. They show that Malay ethnic identity is being reworked by means of emphasising new cultural symbols both narrowly and more broadly defined. In fact, the contributions by Loh on the Kadazans and Tan Liok Ee on the Chinese also suggest that the discourses on non-Malay identities are being reconstructed too.

Likewise, by solely referring to the formulation and implementation of the National Cultural Policy, we are also at sea in trying to explain the active non-communally based performing arts scene in Malaysia today, and the cultural activities and visions, broadly defined, of women's groups, environmentalists, human rights activists, the Bar Council, consumerists, and other special interest groups. For all of them, the point of departure is not the National Culture Policy.

This brings us to consider how, over the past twenty years, quite apart from giving rise to Money Politics and effecting the restructuring of the economy, rapid economic growth has also resulted in a more differentiated Malaysian society. In particular, a substantial middle class has emerged. The contributions to this volume take note of this development. This is by no means a novel observation. However, few observers of the Malaysian landscape have investigated the cultural implications thereof, and further, when the few do, the middle class is either seen as potential modernisers or as the source of rising ethnic tensions, arising from their competition with one another. While rising ethnic tensions might be explained in terms of inter-ethnic middle class rivalry, it cannot account for intra-ethnic splits.

We suggest that we need to consider both the rise of the middle class, and how fractions of that middle class are involved in a process of reworking their ethnic as well as social identities. In other words, structure and agency must be considered. It is in this manner that we explain the fragmented cultural scene, narrowly and broadly defined, and the new *alliances* and splits within as well as across ethnic blocs which are so different from those which existed before 1969.

All this leads us to conclude that 1969 marks a watershed in Malaysian history, but not because it represents the beginnings of a mass based struggle against elite domination or a reassertion of traditional, primordial sentiments in the political arena. Instead the Malaysian political arena, both official and unofficial, has become the battleground for different fragments of Malaysia's elite and middle classes, groups that can no longer be controlled and hence brought in under the shared consociational vision of the years before 1969. Yet clearly these new movements sometimes penetrate beyond their initially middle class constituencies. Indeed were any of them to achieve overwhelming success in acquiring a mass base they would no doubt pose an even greater threat than they currently do. And no, the fact that they are elite or middle class movements led by intellectuals does not make them either by definition impotent or "merely reformist", although more attention needs to be given to the, at least in certain circumstances, coincidence of interests between the middle class and mass components of these movements.

At any rate, increasing authoritarianism in Malaysia in the late 1980s is not a response to an eruption of mass cultural particularisms, based on given primordial sentiments, into the politics of the elite. Neither is it a response to a mass based struggle threatening the ruling elites. It is in part related to the growing role of the State in promoting and creating capitalist development from above (on this see Saravanamuttu 1987 and Higgott and Robison 1985). Ultimately, however, increasing authoritarianism is a response on the part of the ruling elites to a fragmented cultural and political situation. Such fragmentation is a manifestation of the arrival of the middle class and their challenge to the cultural vision of the ruling elites.

This explanation of the current cultural and political landscape in Malaysia is incomplete. But it does reorient current discussions in potentially interesting ways, and raises important topics for further investigation. Why, for example, was Malaysia's ruling elite no longer able to contain and control its erstwhile supporters beginning in the early 1970s? To what extent has this loss of control of the elite and middle classes also been a factor in rising authoritarianism in Indonesia and Singapore? How effective can these groups be in countering such authoritarian trends? Are at least some of their visions equally totalitarian? Answering these questions also means developing a better empirical and theoretical understanding of the elites and new middle classes in the region.

Bibliography

Abraham, C. E. R., 1977. "Race Relations in West Malaysia with Special Reference to Modern Political and Economic Development". D. Phil. Thesis, Oxford University.

Ackerman, S. and Lee, R., 1988. *Heaven in Transition: Non Muslim Religious Innovation and Ethnic Identity in Malaysia*, Honolulu: University of Hawaii Press.

Brennan, M., 1982. "Class, Politics and Race in Modern Malaysia", *Journal of Contemporary Asia*, 12 (2), pp. 188–215.

Cham, B. N., 1975. "Class and Communal Conflict in Malaysia". *Journal of Contemporary Asia*, 5 (4), pp. 446–61.

Cohen, A., 1969. *Customs and Politics in Urban Africa*, Berkeley and Los Angeles: University of California Press.

Esman, M. J., 1972. *Administration and Development in Malaysia*, Ithaca: Cornell University Press.

Geertz, C., 1963. "The Integrative Revolution". In C. Geertz (ed), *Old Societies and New States*, New York: Free Press, pp. 105–57.

Gomez, E. T., 1990. *Politics in Business: UMNO's Corporate Investments*, Kuala Lumpur: Forum.

Gullick, J., 1964. *Malaya*, London: Longmans.

Higgott, R. and R. Robison (eds), 1985. *Southeast Asia: Essays in the Political Economy of Structural Change*. London: Routledge.

Hing Ai Yun, 1984. 'Capitalist Development, Class and Race'. In S. Husin Ali (ed) 1984, pp. 296–328.

Hobsbawm, E. and Ranger, T. (eds), 1983. *The Invention of Tradition*, Cambridge: Cambridge University Press.

Ismail Kassim, 1979. *Race Politics and Moderation*, Singapore: Times Books International.

Jameson, F., 1984. "Postmodernism or the Cultural Logic of Late Capitalism", *New Left Review*, No. 146 July–August.

Kieve, R., 1981. "Pillars of Sand: A Marxist Critique of Consociational Democracy in the Netherlands". *Comparative Politics*, 13 (3), pp. 313–37.

Kua Kia Soong (ed), 1987. *Defining Malaysian Culture*, Petaling Jaya: K. Das Ink.

Lazreg, M, 1988. "Feminism and Difference: The Perils of Writing as a Woman on Algeria" *Feminist Studies* 14(1), pp. 81–107.

Lee, Raymond (ed), 1986. *Ethnicity and Ethnic Relations in Malaysia*, De Kalb, Illinois: Centre for Southeast Asian Studies, Northern Illinois University.

Lim Mah Hui, 1980. "Ethnic and Class Relations in Malaysia", *Journal of Contemporary Asia*, 10 (1/2), pp. 130–54.

Lim Teck Ghee and A. Gomes (eds), 1990. *Tribal Peoples and Development in Southeast Asia*, Kuala Lumpur: Department of Anthropology and Sociology, University of Malaya.

Mauzy, D., 1982. *Barisan Nasional: Coalition Government in Malaysia*, Kuala Lumpur: Marican and Sons.

Means, G., 1970. *Malaysian Politics*, London: Hodder and Stoughton, 2nd edition.

Milne, R. S., 1967. *Government and Politics in Malaysia*, Boston: Houghton Mifflin.

16

Milne, R. S., 1984. "Ruling the ASEAN Countries" in D. Mauzy (ed), *Politics in the ASEAN States*, Kuala Lumpur: Marican and Sons, pp. 264–93.

Muzaffar, Chandra, 1987. *Islamic Resurgence in Malaysia*, Petaling Jaya: Fajar Bakti.

Nagata, J., 1979. *Malaysian Mosaic*, Vancouver: University of British Columbia Press.

Ratnam, K. J., 1965. *Communalism and the Political Process in Malaya*, Singapore: University of Malaya Press.

Ratnam, K. J. and Milne, R. S., 1967. *The Malayan Parliamentary Elections of 1964*, Singapore: University of Malaya Press.

Saravanamuttu, J., 1987. "The State, Authoritarianism and Industrialisation: Reflections on the Malaysian Case", *Kajian Malaysia*, 5(4), pp. 43–76.

Smith, M. G., 1960. "Social and Cultural Pluralism". *Annals of the New York Academy of Sciences*, 83 (5), pp. 763–77.

Strauch, J., 1981. "Multiple Ethnicities in Malaysia". *Modern Asian Studies*, 15 (2), pp. 235–60.

I

Authoritarianism, Money, Politics and Modernity

2

Authoritarian Trends, the UMNO Split and the Limits to State Power

Harold Crouch

The mainstream studies of Malaysian politics present a picture of modified democracy (von Vorys, 1975; Means 1976; Milne and Mauzy, 1977; Bedlington, 1978; Mauzy, 1983). An essentially democratic political system in the 1960s had to adjust itself to the communal tensions of the 1970s and 1980s by modifying its own democratic character. In the context of a multi-communal society, it is argued that Malaysian democracy cannot be the same as democracy in the West but has to accept restraints in the interests of political stability and inter-communal harmony. But these writers stress that, whatever the restraints, Malaysia still maintains its democratic constitutional structure and the government continues to be responsible to a legislature elected in regularly held elections.

While this perception of the Malaysian political system had a certain credibility in the early 1970s following the racial upheaval of 1969, the steady erosion of democratic characteristics which continued into the 1980s raised not only the question of whether the modified-democracy model was still appropriate but indeed suggested, with the benefit of hindsight, that it may in fact have never provided an adequate framework for understanding political developments since 1969. Instead it could be argued that the post-1969 system might be best seen as a form of authoritarianism in which an entrenched elite took whatever steps were considered necessary to ensure its continued control of the government. In this interpretation, apparently democratic practices were permitted only as long as they did not actually undermine the power of the ruling elite while they were quickly modified or abolished when elite interests were threatened. It would indeed be possible to take this interpretation back to cover the whole period since 1957 by arguing that the relatively open democratic quality of the pre-1969 system was possible only because it did not threaten the domination of the established elite and was quickly modified when it did.

By the mid-1980s, therefore, a modified authoritarian model seemed to offer a more plausible explanation than the modified-democracy model of

Malaysian politics during the previous decade and a half. But political developments since 1986 can hardly be explained merely in terms of authoritarian response to popular challenge. Following the split in the United Malays National Organisation (UMNO), open competition between rival parties for popular support in elections became increasingly important and the search by rival factions for allies outside the Malay elite provided opportunities for both non-Malay elements in the government and the opposition parties to make demands which might otherwise have been ignored. While the authoritarian controls remained in place, the government found itself forced to become more responsive to outside pressures.

In 1990 the Barisan Nasional (National Front—BN) government faced the strongest electoral challenge that it had experienced since its formation in the early 1970s. In 1988 the UMNO dissidents were finally excluded and in 1989 they formed a new party, Semangat 46 (The Spirit of 46), which claimed to represent the true spirit of UMNO, harking back to its foundation in 1946. Semangat 46, realising that it had no hope of electoral success if it stood alone against the multi-communal BN coalition, set about forming its own multi-communal front based on separate alliances with the two main opposition parties, the non-Malay-based Democratic Action Party (DAP) and the Malay-based Parti Islam Se-Malaysia (Pan-Malaysian Islamic Party—PAS). The BN therefore was challenged for the first time by a rival front in which all the main opposition parties were represented and it seemed possible that some kind of two-party system, based on rival multi-communal coalitions, might evolve.

The 1990 election results, however, were ambiguous in their significance. Once again the BN won an overwhelming majority of seats in parliament and almost all the state elections. But in contrast to the past when it had always held more than four-fifths of the seats in parliament and attracted between 57 and 61 per cent of the votes, this time its share of the seats fell to 71 per cent and of the votes to 53.4 per cent while it lost control of two state governments. From one point of view the election could be interpreted as a vote for continuity despite reduced support for the BN, but from another perspective it could be seen as something of a turning point in that the opposition was able for the first time to form itself into a multi-communal semi-alliance which, together with independent candidates, boosted the anti-BN vote to almost half of the total.

The 1990 election, therefore, returned a strong BN government but with a significantly reduced majority. It did not, however, constitute the unambiguous breakthrough toward the emergence of a two-party system for which the opposition had hoped. Whether the 1990 election will be seen in the future as a watershed or just a minor aberration in Malaysia's political development remains an unanswered question.

The Post-1969 Authoritarian Trend

Although the Malaysian political system moved in an authoritarian direction following the racial conflict in 1969, it nevertheless retained significant democratic features. The government continued to be responsible to a parliament elected at least every five years. Although the ruling coalition always won at the national level and almost always at the state level, elections could not be dismissed as mere formalities as they were vigorously contested by opposition parties which usually won around forty per cent of the votes although a much smaller proportion of seats. In addition, vigorous, more or less open, contests took place from time to time within political parties, including the major parties in the government. The only political party to be formally banned was the Communist Party of Malaya which was involved in an armed insurgency.

Nevertheless authoritarian controls increasingly limited the scope for opposition after the 1969 race riots. The government justified authoritarian measures on the grounds that they were necessary to prevent a recurrence of racial conflict. Following the 1969 upheaval the government had introduced the New Economic Policy (NEP), a far-reaching plan to restructure society in order to tackle the economic inequalities which were seen at the root of racial conflict. But the implementation of the plan would inevitably benefit the Malay community at the expense of the non-Malays and therefore lead, at least in the short run, to increasing racial polarisation. The implementation of the NEP, it could be argued, needed stricter authoritarian controls.

The government's most powerful authoritarian weapon was the Internal Security Act (ISA) which had been adopted in 1960 immediately following the lifting of the emergency declared by the British in 1948 to fight the communist insurgency. Under the ISA the Minister of Home Affairs has power to detain without trial anyone considered to be likely to act "in any manner prejudicial to the security of Malaysia" (Internal Security Act, Article 8). Between 1960 and 1981 more than 3000 people were detained under the act although most were eventually released (NST 17 November 1981). In the late 1970s there were some 900 detainees but the number had fallen to 586 when Dr Mahathir became Prime Minister in 1981 (NST 5 July 1982). Under Mahathir the number fell rapidly to only 40 at the end of 1986 (Letter from Mahathir's press secretary, FEER, 28 January 1988) before increasing again with the sudden arrest of 106— including the Leader of the Opposition, Lim Kit Siang, and another thirteen DAP members of parliament or state assemblies as well as PAS activists—following a sharp rise in racial tensions in October 1987. However, all 106 were gradually released over the following eighteen months. Nevertheless in 1989 about seventy detainees continued to be held under the ISA (NST 16 March 1989).

In the 1960s the government justified the introduction of the ISA as being necessary for the continuing fight against communist insurgency;

but later the main stress was placed on the preservation of inter-communal harmony. In practice, however, the ISA has also been used to block political challenges and intimidate critics. Among the critics of the government who were detained under the ISA during the 1970s were the University of Malaya anthropologist, Dr Syed Husin Ali, the Malaysian People's Socialist Party (PSRM) leader, Kassim Ahmad, and the Muslim youth leader, Anwar Ibrahim. Local leaders of the Muslim opposition party, PAS, were detained after peasant demonstrations in Kedah in 1980 and leaders of the Airlines Employees Union were arrested after industrial action taken by MAS workers in 1978–79. Members of the government itself were not exempt from the provisions of the act as two deputy ministers, Datuk Abdullah Ahmad and Abdullah Majid, together with the editor of the New Straits Times, Samad Ismail, discovered when they found themselves on the wrong side in a factional struggle in 1976 (Crouch 1980).

During the 1980s the ISA was used less freely until the arrest of the 106 in October and November 1987 (See CARPA 1988). Again the government claimed that the arrests had been necessary to prevent the outbreak of communal conflict but the list of detainees was not restricted to leaders of the DAP and Chinese educational bodies who had been debating emotional issues involving Chinese education while many UMNO leaders who had also been raising such issues were not detained. Among those arrested were critics of the government like the Aliran president, Dr Chandra Muzaffar, members of environmental groups, Christian social welfare activists and many others who were clearly not involved in activities contributing to heightened communal tensions. But even among those involved in activities which may have increased communal tension, it was not clear that these activities constituted the main reason for their arrest. The DAP leaders, Lim Kit Siang and Karpal Singh, for example, had brought a legal suit against government leaders, including the Prime Minister, who had awarded a huge public works contract to a company in which they themselves had direct interests as trustees for UMNO. The DAP's suit had resulted in the High Court issuing an injunction against the project early in October, only a few weeks before the arrests (AWSJ 18 January 1988, 21 March 1988).

Other laws restricted the scope of public debate. The Sedition Act proscribes the discussion of issues having "a tendency . . . to promote feelings of ill-will and hostility between different races or classes of the population of Malaysia" and specifically made it an offence to question the sovereignty of the Malay sultans, the position of Malay as the national language, the "special rights" of Malays and conditions for citizenship in the case of non-Malays (Sedition Act, Article 3(1)). While a case might be made that something along the lines of the Sedition Act is needed in a society like that of Malaysia and is indeed preferable to the ISA, in practice the act operated to limit public discussion. Although the government argues that the act does not prevent the questioning of the "implementation" of policies but only the policies themselves, the distinction is a fine one with the result that critics feel inhibited in raising issues which might come within the scope of the act. In practice the act has been used sparingly and only a few cases, the most important involving the DAP, have gone to court. Public debate has also been deterred by the Official Secrets Act which covers the unauthorised publication of information in the hands of the government. The act is very broad in scope and, until amended in 1986, applied to all government information even when the information was already public knowledge. Although, like the Sedition Act, it has been used sparingly, in practice it has the effect of deterring the exposure of abuses where the ultimate source of information could only be an unauthorised "leak". In 1986, after two cases involving journalists, the act was strengthened to provide for mandatory gaol sentences.

Public criticism in the mass media has also been restricted. While radio and television are effective government monopolies (the "private" television channel being controlled by UMNO), the main newspapers are owned by party-affiliated companies. The main English-medium newspaper, the New Straits Times, and its Malay-medium sister publication, Berita Harian, are both owned by the UMNO-owned Fleet group (Gomez 1990: 61–66). UMNO also owns the other major Malay-medium newspapers, Utusan Malaysia and Utusan Melayu, and a Chinese newspaper. The second major English-medium newspaper, Star, is owned by a company controlled by the Malaysian Chinese Association (MCA) which also owns a Chinese-medium newspaper while the Tamil press is closely tied to various factions in the Malaysian Indian Congress (MIC). Although owned by one of the BN parties, the Star had increased its circulation in competition with the New Straits Times by giving prominence to concerns in the Chinese community and also by publishing a regular column by the disaffected elder statesman, Tunku Abdul Rahman. After receiving warnings from the government, the Star was eventually suspended for several months at the end of 1987 together with a Malay weekly, Watan, and a Chinese newspaper. Nevertheless the government continued to permit the circulation of several critical journals such as the DAP's Rocket, PAS's Harakah and the Penang monthly, Aliran, but their readership remained quite limited. In the case of the foreign press, the Far Eastern Economic Review and the Asian Wall Street Journal have at times suffered from deliberately slow censorship procedures which have meant their late arrival in the hands of readers, a particularly effective tactic against a daily such as the Asian Wall Street Journal.

Despite the increased resort to authoritarian methods since 1970, the judiciary had retained much of its independence although it never had a reputation for deep commitment to democratic values and human rights. Most judges were in fact part of the conservative Malay elite from which the UMNO leaders and the senior officials of the bureaucracy were also drawn. Nevertheless they occasionally delivered judgements unfavourable to the government. In the mid-1980s several judgements seem to have particularly rankled the Prime Minister. In 1986 an attempt to expel journalists from the Asian Wall Street Journal was disallowed and in 1987 a judge found that the Home Affairs ministry had erred in refusing to allow the critical journal, Aliran, to publish in Malay (for a summary of some of these cases see Asiaweek, 16 October 1987). The Prime Minister seemed especially outraged when a judge ordered the release of a DAP leader detained under the ISA on the grounds that the detention order was "made without proper care, caution and a proper sense of responsibility" (AWSJ 18/19 March 1988). While previous prime ministers had either accepted unfavourable judgements or responded with new, sometimes retrospective, legislation, Dr Mahathir decided to amend the constitution itself in March 1988 with the intention, as he put it, that "judges apply the law made by parliament and not make their own laws as is happening now" (FEER 31 March 1988). Then, in May, the Yang di-Pertuan Agung, acting in close co-operation with the Prime Minister, laid charges of "gross misconduct" against the Lord President (Chief Justice) who was dismissed in July following a judicial inquiry. In a related case similar charges were brought against five more Supreme Court judges resulting in the dismissal of two. The background to these cases is extremely complex and cannot be separated from the factional split in UMNO, especially a crucial court challenge by the anti-Mahathir group which was due to be heard in mid-June but was postponed after the suspension of the Lord President (see Tun Salleh Abas and K. Das 1989; Lawyers Committee for Human Rights 1989; Williams 1990). Developments during 1988, therefore, reduced the effectiveness of the judiciary as a check on government power.

The gradual trend toward the increased use of authoritarian controls took place in the shadow of the constitutional provision enabling the government to issue a Proclamation of Emergency if "the security or economic life of the Federation or of any part thereof is threatened" (Federal Constitution, Article 150(1)). The first emergency, which had been introduced by the British to repress communist insurgency, had been lifted in 1960 but another proclamation was issued to allow the government to deal with the racial rioting of 1969. Although "normalcy" was restored when parliament was re-convened in 1971, the emergency proclamation was never in fact lifted so that the government could, if it so desired, re-activate its extensive emergency powers without issuing a new proclamation. Detentions without trial under the Emergency (Public Order and Crime Prevention) Ordinance, for example, are still made under powers derived from the 1969 proclamation. While many would accept that democratic governments need reserve emergency powers to deal with major crises threatening the continuity of the state and public order—such as insurgency or communal rioting—the routine use of emergency powers at a time when "the security or economic life of the Federation" is not under particular threat is another matter. Further, emergency proclamations have been used twice in the past to overthrow opposition controlled state governments—in Sarawak in 1966 and Kelantan in 1977.

It could be argued, therefore, that Malaysia's democratic institutions have been little more than a facade disguising effective authoritarian rule. The ISA, various restrictions on public debate, effective control of the press, intimidation of the judiciary and the emergency provisions combined to block the emergence of an effective opposition, thereby enabling the Malay-dominated elite to rule continuously. In this context, elections provided little opportunity for opposition parties to effectively challenge, let alone replace, the government. Critics were tolerated only to the extent that they did not actually pose a political threat to the ruling elite.

UMNO Dominance

Increasing authoritarianism reinforced the pre-eminence of UMNO which had formed the backbone of the government since independence, first dominating the three-party Alliance and then the multi-party BN. UMNO has always presented itself as the champion of the Malay community from the time of its formation in 1946 when it successfully opposed British constitutional proposals which would have deprived the Malays of their special status. In the negotiations leading to the 1957 constitution UMNO insisted on provisions which symbolised the Malay nature of the state—the office of Yang di-Pertuan Agung, Islam as "the religion of the Federation", Malay as the national language and the guaranteed preponderance of Malays in the elite class of the civil service. And in the 1970s, following the shock of 1969, UMNO emphasized its Malay nature even more strongly, most notably through the NEP which provided a huge increase in business, educational and employment opportunities for Malays, and the language policy which gradually converted the language of administration and English-medium educational institutions to Malay.

But in addition to its image as champion of the Malays, much of UMNO's appeal in fact lay in its patronage dispensing function. In the 1960s UMNO was able to provide its supporters with access to land and government employment while the distribution of timber licences was of importance to aspiring businessmen. But in the 1970s the scope for patronage distribution increased enormously. The introduction of the NEP was accompanied by a huge expansion of the state role in the economy both in terms of controls over the private sector and active participation in business. In control of the government at all levels, UMNO was well positioned to provide material benefits to its supporters whose loyalty to the party was thereby strengthened.

One of the main goals of the NEP was the creation of a Malay business class. Malay businessmen were given preference in obtaining licences, credit and government contracts. At the same time the state sector expanded rapidly under the control of Malay bureaucrats and politicians. As part of the strategy to increase Malay participation in the modern economy, the government forced established Chinese and foreign enterprises to "restructure" in such a way that at least 30 per cent of their shares would be owned by Malays—either government agencies acting "on behalf of" the Malay community or private Malay businessmen. Enterprises which failed to restructure found it difficult to renew necessary licences or to obtain contracts with the expanding state sector. The normal way for large companies to restructure was through the issue of new shares which were made available for purchase by Malays at below par prices. In the 1970s the actual allocation was in the hands of the Department of Trade and Industry which kept a list of potential Malay shareholders who were given the option to buy such shares before they came onto the market although by the 1980s, while part of the shares were still reserved for companies on the Ministry's list, it was common for at least some shares to be distributed by open ballot. The Ministry of Trade and Industry also played a big role in finding local partners for foreign investors and in the appointment of local agents and distributors for imports. The implementation of the NEP and the economic expansion of the 1970s and 1980s thus provided enormous scope for patronage distribution as licences, contracts, concessions and undervalued shares were awarded to Malay businessmen and others who normally had UMNO connections.

Patronage distribution was important at the middle and lower levels as well. Evidence of support for UMNO was helpful for applicants for a taxi licence, for example, or a permit to run a lorry or to set up a rice mill. Loans from government bodies, such as the Majlis Amanah Rakyat (MARA) were also more easily available to those with political backing. The government's programme of building low-cost houses for the poor provided another avenue for patronage distribution. In Johor, for example, it was the practice to reserve twenty per cent of low-cost houses for those described as "pillars of the Government", that is "staunch members of UMNO, MCA and MIC" (NST 24 December 1980, 12 June 1984).

At the village level, government patronage was used blatantly to win support for UMNO. Relatively well-off farmers affiliated with UMNO almost always controlled local Village Development and Security Committees and the government-sponsored Farmers' Associations through which government aid was channelled in principle to the village as a whole or to the very poor but in reality to UMNO supporters (Scott 1985: 220–231) Moreover, applications by villagers for title to land were considered by committees dominated by UMNO stalwarts, often including the local state assemblyman (NST, 9 February 1990). Often authority to distribute assistance in the form, for example, of fertilizer, seedlings or livestock was delegated "to local ketua kampung (village heads) who are, more often than not, the chairmen of UMNO branches in their respective villages" (Shamsul 1986: 220).

UMNO's dominance was also due to its superior political strategy in the context of a multi-communal society. Although UMNO was formed in 1946 as a communal party concerned exclusively with the protection of Malay interests, it soon learned that political power could be best secured by forming the multi-communal Alliance with parties representing the Chinese and Indian communities. The basic concept was extended with the formation of the BN in 1974 which included not only the original three parties representing the three main peninsula communities but several former opposition parties in the peninsula and the main parties of Sabah and Sarawak. While the BN brought together parties representing different communities under the same banner, the main opposition parties, the DAP and PAS (although PAS was part of the BN for a few years until expelled in 1977) tended to fight for the separate interests of particular communities. While the compromises within the BN strongly favoured the Malay community, enough was offered to the non-Malays for the BN to mobilise a substantial share of the non-Malay vote as well. In contrast, before 1990, the opposition parties were never able to cross the communal barrier and form their own counter-alliance.

The BN's electoral strategy was of course assisted by an electoral gerrymander which effectively guaranteed Malay domination of the parliament. The electoral system was heavily weighted in favour of the predominantly Malay rural constituencies and against the mainly non-Malay urban constituencies. Under new electoral boundaries drawn up for the 1974 election the largest urban constituency in the peninsula was almost three times larger than the smallest rural constituency. By 1982, however, the largest urban constituency was almost five times larger than the smallest rural seat. The new electoral boundaries introduced for the 1986 election resulted in Malays making up absolute majorities in 92 (70 per cent) of the 132 peninsula seats despite constituting only 56.5 per cent of the population. Moreover, until the defection of the Kadazan-based Parti Bersatu Sabah (Sabah United Party—PBS) in 1990, UMNO could assume that the Malay majority in the peninsula would be reinforced by the bumiputera representatives from East Malaysia where many of the 48 constituencies are even smaller than the smallest peninsula seats.

UMNO was also able to use its control of the government to win votes by mobilising the machinery of government on the BN's side during election campaigns. Of particular importance were the Information Ministry (which controlled television and radio) and Kemas (Community Development). The Kemas programme involved adult education classes in civics and various other useful skills like cooking, nutrition, hygiene and so on. But in practice Kemas officers were full-time propagandists for the government during election campaigns. Moreover, UMNO leaders regularly made it clear that village officials identified with the opposition would be dismissed while villages voting for the opposition would be in danger of losing development funds.

Until the mid-1980s, therefore, UMNO's dominant position was virtually unchallenged. UMNO's deep roots in the Malay community were reinforced by its adroit use of patronage, its alliance with non-Malay parties in the BN, a gerrymandered electoral system and a range of authoritarian controls while the opposition remained divided along communal lines. But the open split in UMNO threw Malaysia's political future into uncertainty and raised the possibility of far-reaching change. While UMNO

was united, democratic institutions tended to atrophy but, especially since
1988, Dr Mahathir's opponents increasingly used the formal democratic
machinery in their challenge to the Prime Minister. It was not that the
dissidents were confirmed democrats while Mahathir's supporters were
ideological authoritarians. It was rather that the challenge was so strong
that it was not easy to suppress by blatantly authoritarian means. The
battle shifted from within the confines of UMNO to parliament and the
electoral system.

The UMNO Split and its Implications

The increasingly authoritarian nature of the government during the 1970s
and 1980s had been greatly facilitated by the almost unchallenged predominance of UMNO as the backbone of the government. During the
1960s and 1970s factionalism had been common enough in UMNO but,
in contrast to some of the other BN parties, never developed to the point
where the essential unity of the party itself was at stake. By the mid-
1980s, however, Dr Mahathir's leadership was being openly opposed by
senior UMNO leaders and in 1987, for the first time ever, an incumbent
prime minister faced a serious challenger for the post of party president.
Finally, in 1988 the party split in two.
    Ideological and policy differences seem to have played almost no part
in the UMNO split.[1] Certainly the dissidents criticised some of Mahathir's
policies such as his expensive industrialisation drive (especially the
"Malaysian car" project), his "Look East" policy, and, in some circles at
least, his "Islamisation" policy. And when the ISA was strengthened in
1988, the dissidents voted against the amendments in parliament. But
Mahathir was able to point out in reply that his critics were all part of
the government which adopted the policies which they now disowned.
Mahathir was also criticised for alleged favouritism toward certain big
businessmen, as well as his own sister-in-law's contracting firm (see FEER
2 April 1987). But the distribution of favours to businessmen was not, of
course, Mahathir's invention. It is particularly interesting to note the
reluctance of both sides to exploit the damaging revelations about various
leaders which emerged in evidence presented to a Hong Kong court case
dealing with the massive Bank Bumiputra scandal, presumably because it
tarnished the images of both Mahathir's supporters and his critics.[2]
    The UMNO split can be largely understood as a struggle for power and

---

[1] For a different view, see Khoo Kay Jin's chapter in this book.
[2] Mahathir, Musa and Razaleigh all received adverse mentions in the case (AWSJ,
15 January 1987). However, apparently in desperation, UMNO used its control of
the mass media to publicise "documents" linking Razaleigh to the affair during the
last week of the 1990 election campaign.

position revolving around the question of succession to Mahathir (See Shamsul 1988). When Mahathir backed his long-time friend and ally, Datuk Musa Hitam, for the deputy presidency of the party and deputy prime ministership, Musa was challenged by Tengku Razaleigh in two hard-fought struggles which divided the party into two camps in 1981 and 1984. Although Musa was victorious on both occasions, he was unhappy with Mahathir's unwillingness to remove Razaleigh from the cabinet after the second challenge. Meanwhile the former Muslim youth leader and prominent critic of the government, Anwar Ibrahim, had not only been recruited into UMNO in 1982 but rapidly moved up the party hierarchy. Anwar's rapid rise and his growing influence with the Prime Minister disturbed Musa and his supporters who had begun to envisage the possibility that Anwar, who was in his late 30s, might eventually displace Musa, who was in his early 50s, as the heir apparent if Mahathir stayed on too much longer. The tension between Mahathir and Musa culminated in Musa's resignation in early 1986 and his alliance with his erstwhile foe, Tengku Razaleigh, in 1987. The Razaleigh-Musa challenge at the 1987 party assembly was narrowly defeated by Mahathir and his new deputy, Ghafar Baba, who earlier had been a close ally of Razaleigh's. As a result of the Razaleigh-Musa challenge, the party was divided into the so-called teams A and B which continued to spar with each other until the unexpected court decision in February 1988 declaring UMNO, on the basis of a technicality, to be an illegal organisation. In response to the court decision, Mahathir stymied an attempt by the dissidents to register a new party to be called UMNO Malaysia and succeeded in having his own UMNO Baru (New UMNO) registered. Without a registered party of their own the dissidents remained in UMNO Baru for several months before deciding in the middle of 1988 to sit in parliament and contest elections as independents, and in 1989 to set up a new party, Semangat 46.

The UMNO split had occurred in a society which had undergone extraordinary change during the previous fifteen years of rapid economic growth and social restructuring under the NEP. UMNO had been founded at a time when a small aristocratic and bureaucratic elite exercised great influence over a largely subservient rural Malay society, but by the 1980s old stereotypes had to be abandoned. In 1970 some 62.3 per cent of the Malay work-force was still engaged in agriculture, but by 1985 this had fallen to 41.3 per cent while those employed in the middle class occupational categories (professional and technical, administrative and managerial, clerical, sales) had increased from 12.9 per cent in 1970 to 24.1 per cent in 1985 (calculated from Fourth Malaysia Plan: 59 and Mid-term Review of the Fifth Malaysia Plan: 66).[3] The growth of the Malay middle class reflected an enormous expansion in secondary and tertiary edu-

---

[3] Note that the 1970 figures refer to Peninsular Malaysia while the 1985 figures refer to Malaysia as a whole.

cational opportunities for Malay students. At the time of independence in 1957 only 16,000 Malay children attended high schools but by 1967 the number had grown to 219,000 (Tan 1982: 2) and by 1985 to 732,750 (calculated from Mid-Term Review of the Fifth Malaysia Plan: 274). At the same time the number of Malay students enrolled in degree courses in universities grew from 3,084 in 1970 (Mid-Term Review of the Third Malaysia Plan: 203) to 29,875 in 1985 (Mid-Term Review of the Fifth Malaysia Plan: 277).

Government policies designed to foster the emergence of a new Malay business class had also begun to bear fruit towards the end of the 1970s and in the 1980s. The main asset of the new Malay business class was its links with UMNO and the bureaucracy and it was this which made Malay businessmen attractive to Chinese and foreign investors as business partners. The new Malay business class, however, was heavily dependent on its access to government patronage and therefore tended to become an appendage to the government rather than a significant check on its power. But Malay businessmen soon became an important force in the internal politics of UMNO and made a major contribution to the factional rivalries within the dominant party which grew in importance in the 1980s.

The factional struggle within the UMNO leadership took place in the context of growing competitiveness within the party as a whole since the 1970s. In the past, as a rural-based organisation, UMNO usually gave almost automatic support to its leaders. It was common for local meetings to be held in the friendly atmosphere of the house of one of the members while wives provided light refreshments. As a former party leader said, "In those days, almost everyone was reluctant to hold posts, still less to contest against their friends for any post, for fear of offending or hurting the feelings of others. They had to be coaxed or even forced to hold posts. But now it is different" (UMNO secretary-general, Datuk Mustafa Jabar, quoted by Zainah Anwar in NST, 30 April 1984). In the past many local office-holders were Malay schoolteachers who in the 1970s usually made up around forty per cent of the delegates to the annual assembly at the national level. By the late 1970s and 1980s, however, the composition of the party was undergoing substantial change as the schoolteachers and other local leaders were increasingly pushed aside by a new generation of businessmen and university-educated professionals who had been produced by the NEP and the associated education policy. The new leaders usually resided in Kuala Lumpur or the state capitals but regularly returned to their home kampungs in order to consolidate political support. Party meetings were no longer held in members' homes but often in big hotels with expenses met by aspirants for party position.

NEP-produced business opportunities inevitably increased the stakes in the struggle for power in UMNO. Victory in a local party election meant a chance to become a member of parliament or a state assembly with all the attendant commercial opportunities. Huge sums were spent on local UMNO elections and Dr Mahathir himself expressed concern at reports about candidates offering supporters all-expenses-paid trips to Tokyo or Medan or, for those so inclined, Mecca. Mahathir mentioned the case of one leader who was said to have spent $600,000 in his campaign to head a local division in 1985 (NST 20 May 1985). While still Deputy Prime Minister, Datuk Musa Hitam had complained that "if an analysis of this question is made today, it will reveal that many had joined the party to acquire more wealth" (NST 30 November 1980) while the future secretary-general of the party, Sanusi Junid, got to the essence of the problem when he said "These people are 'investing' money to reap material gains when they are in power" (NST 21 May 1985). In the past timber concessions, import permits, bank licences and so on had gone to Chinese businessmen but now they went to Malays and, in order to gain such opportunities, a businessman had to have UMNO connections. The intensifying rivalry in the party's national leadership, therefore, became interlinked with local factional struggles.

The struggle for the spoils of political office was aggravated by the general economic downturn in 1985. The rapid economic expansion of the 1970s and early 1980s had provided vast resources to reward aspiring Malay businessmen so that even those who failed to win top political positions could still receive consolation prizes. But in the economic circumstances of 1985 and 1986 the government had much less patronage to distribute and many UMNO-connected businessmen faced problems in repaying bank loans. Having political influence, therefore, was not just a help but for many was vital for survival. The struggle for influence within UMNO took on an increasingly life-or-death quality.

Given the importance of patronage, it was not surprising that most party leaders remained with Mahathir's UMNO Baru (Team A)—or, perhaps more aptly, did not commit themselves to Team B. All the state Menteri Besar stayed with Mahathir while only 16 of UMNO's 83 MPs openly sided with the dissidents. It is not unlikely that some had outstanding loans or other obligations which made it difficult for them to join the dissidents and some who initially aligned themselves with Team B eventually returned to Team A. The cases of Adib Adam and Marina Yusuf, both leading dissident supporters who were subjected to legal action over loans (NST 10 June 1988, 11 August 1988), served as a warning to all and a few days before a by-election for a vacant seat in the Johor state assembly in October 1988, it was revealed that Bank Bumiputra was taking action to recover $689,397 from the dissident UMNO candidate, who had stood in 1984 as a guarantor for an UMNO-owned company which later went bankrupt (NST 17 October 1988).[4]

Following their formal exit from UMNO Baru, the dissidents turned to the electoral system by contesting a series of by-elections. In August 1988

---

[4] Nothing more was heard of this case after the candidate narrowly lost the by-election. He rejoined UMNO a few months later.

a leading dissident and former minister, Datuk Shahrir Samad, won an overwhelming victory over UMNO Baru when he recontested the Johor Baru parliamentary seat from which he had resigned the previous month. Not only did it appear that Shahrir won a majority of Malay votes in a constituency which is evenly divided between Malays and non-Malays, but for the first time ever an "UMNO" candidate was able to enter an informal alliance with the DAP which then delivered a large majority of the Chinese vote to Shahrir. The opposition's euphoria, however, was not to last. In the next parliamentary by-election, in January 1989, for the Ampang Jaya seat on the outskirts of Kuala Lumpur, the Semangat candidate, Datuk Harun Idris, probably won a majority of Malay votes but failed to win Chinese support and was defeated. Datuk Harun was indelibly associated in the popular Chinese mind with the 1969 riots which had begun near his official residence as Menteri Besar of Selangor at that time. Then in May the Semangat failed to deliver significant support to the DAP in a by-election for the Bentong seat in Pahang which was easily retained by the MCA.

Meanwhile the dissident challenge had been complicated by continuing rivalry between its two main leaders, Tengku Razaleigh and Datuk Musa Hitam, who had been "enemies" until 1987. During 1988 several supporters of Musa had been enticed or pressured back into UMNO, including three who were reappointed to the party's Supreme Council. Finally, Musa himself and his ally, Datuk Shahrir, decided to rejoin the party at the beginning of February immediately after the loss of the Ampang Jaya by-election and, coincidentally or not, the sudden hospitalization of the Prime Minister for an emergency heart operation.

The by-elections of 1988 and 1989 showed that even when the UMNO dissidents won a majority of Malay votes they could still be defeated if non-Malays voted against them. When they had Chinese support, as in Johor Baru, they won comfortably but when the Chinese gave their votes to the BN, as in Ampang Jaya and several by-elections at the state level, the dissidents lost by fairly narrow margins. It was clear therefore that the UMNO dissidents needed to work out some sort of electoral understanding with the DAP. But it was no easy matter to win support from, or to deliver Malay votes to, a party which all UMNO leaders had branded as "chauvinist" and "anti-Malay" in the past. On the other hand, in the overwhelmingly Malay areas of the northeast, the dissidents needed to reach an understanding with PAS. Without such an understanding it seemed likely that PAS would emerge as the main beneficiary of three-cornered contests. But like the DAP, PAS had long been villified by the ex-UMNO leaders of Semangat. In particular, the Semangat leader, Tengku Razaleigh, while still in UMNO, had been the architect of the overthrow of the PAS-dominated government in Kelantan in 1977.

Political realities, however, prevailed. An opposition front offered not just the prospect of more opposition seats in parliament but even the glittering possibility of winning control of government. The Semangat 46 therefore worked hard to set up an opposition front which would include both the DAP and PAS. Not only was it difficult for the Semangat leaders to ally with one or other of their former bitter rivals but even more difficult simultaneously as the DAP and PAS had been no less strongly opposed to each other. In the middle of 1989 Semangat succeeded in forming the Angkatan Perpaduan Ummah (APU—Muslim Unity Movement) with PAS and two small Islamic parties, Berjasa and Hamim, but it was not until just before the election in October 1990 that it was able to establish a separate alliance with the DAP together with the small, largely Malay, socialist party, the Parti Rakyat Malaysia (PRM—Malaysian People's Party) and another small party of MIC dissidents. In exchange for support for a Semangat-led government at the national level, the Semangat leaders promised to support a DAP-based state government in Penang and PAS-based state governments in Kelantan and Terengganu.

While Tengku Razaleigh seemed reasonably comfortable with both his major allies individually, they were not comfortable with each other. The DAP leaders declared that they could not accept the PAS goal to establish an Islamic state in Malaysia and would not be able to co-operate with that party if it did not abandon that aim (statements by DAP vice president, Karpal Singh, NST 11 December 1989, and secretary-general, Lim Kit Siang, NST 6 May 1990). PAS, of course, had no intention of abandoning its fundamental ideological goal. Its leaders denied that the party had any association with the DAP and its treasurer, Haji Mustafa Ali, declared that "PAS has never and will not work with DAP as long as it remains a secular party and opposes PAS' aspirations for the creation of an Islamic state" (NST 12 April 1990). PAS's pact with the Semangat in APU, however, had avoided the term "Islamic state" and instead referred to the aim of "upholding Islam as a way of life based on truth, justice, freedom and good values" (NST 13 October 1990). Thus the Semangat maintained two separate electoral pacts, one based on its alliance with PAS in the Malay-majority areas, and the other with the DAP in the west-coast states. The obvious conflict between the Semangat's two most important allies was of course fully exploited by the BN in its efforts to show that the coalition led by Tengku Razaleigh was unfit to govern.

The 1990 Election

Despite contradictions between its components, the two overlapping alliances led by Tengku Razaleigh offered an unprecedented challenge to the BN. The election was eventually held on 20 and 21 October for the federal parliament and all the state legislative assemblies except those of Sabah and Sarawak where state elections had been held earlier. Of 180 parliamentary constituencies, 132 were in the peninsula and 48 in East Malaysia—27 in Sarawak, 20 in Sabah and one in Labuan.

The linked electoral pacts between the main opposition parties in the peninsula resulted in a drastic decline in the number of opposition candidates. In the past it was common for several opposition parties to contest in the same constituencies. But in 1990 only one major opposition candidate was nominated in all but one of the peninsular parliamentary constituencies although in several state constituencies the DAP and PAS both nominated candidates. The main opposition party, Semangat 46, contested 59 peninsula seats, the DAP 34, PAS 31 and PRM three. Only seventeen—of which seven were in Kelantan—of the 132 peninsula constituencies were contested by more than two candidates.

The opposition was dramatically strengthened several days after nominations closed when the PBS, the Kadazan-based ruling party in Sabah, announced its withdrawal from the BN. The BN had nominated PBS candidates in fourteen of Sabah's twenty seats. By withdrawing after nominations had closed, the PBS deprived the BN of the opportunity to put up new candidates, virtually ensuring fourteen seats for the opposition. The relationship between PBS and the central government had in fact never been warm and it was no secret that UMNO preferred to work with fellow Muslims in the United Sabah National Organisation (USNO) rather than the Christian Kadazans who were predominant in PBS. Before the Sabah state election in July the PBS had rejected pressure from the central government to form a coalition with USNO which was a member of the BN at the federal level but an opposition party at the state level. Even while still in the BN, PBS had insisted on using its own election symbol rather than the BN symbol.

On the eve of the election the combined opposition fronts had been confident that they would at least deprive the BN of the two-thirds majority that it claimed was necessary to govern effectively while some leaders, especially after the defection of the PBS, seemed to believe that victory was not completely out of reach. However, the BN once again scored an overwhelming victory in terms of seats in parliament, winning 127 of the 180 seats, seven more than needed to retain its two-thirds majority although 21 less than in the 177-seat parliament elected in 1986. However, its performance in terms of votes was less impressive, falling to 53.4 per cent of the valid votes compared to 57.3 per cent in 1986. Moreover, the BN suffered a devastating defeat in the state election in Kelantan and won only narrowly in Penang. Further, the defection of the PBS meant that it no longer controlled Sabah. In the new parliament the opposition parties occupied 49 seats and another four seats were won by independents. The DAP continued to be the largest opposition party with twenty seats while Semangat had eight, PAS seven and PBS fourteen. In the peninsula the BN's share of the votes fell from 61.3 to 55.7 per cent. Support for the DAP and PAS also declined—from 21.4 to 17.6 per cent of the peninsula votes for the DAP and from 17.5 to 7.8 per cent for PAS—but this was not a setback because both parties had nominated fewer candidates under the opposition agreement. Although the new opposition party, Semangat 46, attracted 17.4 per cent, it is likely that a substantial part of its votes in fact came from DAP and PAS supporters who voted for common opposition candidates (For election statistics see I & J Sdn Bhd 1990).

The opposition's most spectacular success was in Kelantan where APU was able to establish a PAS-led state government after it won all seats for both parliament and the state assembly. But in neighbouring Terengganu it was less successful, winning only two of eight parliamentary seats and ten of 32 state seats, while in the other Malay-majority states it won only a solitary state seat in Kedah. As expected, PAS's strength was concentrated in the Malay-majority states of the northeast where it won seven parliamentary seats, six from Kelantan and one from Terengganu. However, its partner, Semangat 46, which had national aspirations, was also largely confined to those states, seven of its eight seats in parliament being from Kelantan and the other from Terengganu. At the state level, Semangat won 14 seats in Kelantan and two in Terengganu while it managed only one seat in each of Pahang, Selangor and Johor and none in the other states.

The victories of the other opposition front, based on Semangat's alliance with the DAP, therefore, were almost entirely achieved by the DAP which won eighteen parliamentary seats in the peninsula, taking six of eleven in Penang and four of seven in Kuala Lumpur as well as seats in Perak, Selangor and Melaka. In addition the DAP won another two seats in Sarawak. At the state level, however, the DAP failed in its bid to take over the state government in Penang. Although it clearly had the support of a majority of non-Malay voters and its leader, Lim Kit Siang, defeated the long entrenched Chief Minister, Dr Lim Chong Eu, the DAP's Malay partners in the Gagasan Rakyat—Semangat and PRM—as well as PAS lost in all their contests with UMNO. The DAP won fourteen seats, three short of a majority in the state assembly. Although the Gerakan had been reduced to seven and the MCA eliminated altogether, Gerakan was able to head the state government with UMNO support. Outside Penang, the DAP was able to win more than one-third of the state seats in Perak as well as seats in all the other west-coast states of the peninsula.

In Eastern Malaysia, where the election was limited to parliamentary seats, the sudden withdrawal of PBS from the BN meant that it was not opposed by the BN in the fourteen seats which had been allocated to it while the BN was not opposed by PBS in the six seats allocated to USNO. Both PBS and USNO won all the seats that they contested. In Sarawak, the BN won 21 of the 27 seats, the DAP captured two and four were won by independents, three of whom seem to have been unofficially supported by BN parties against official BN candidates.

In the election support for the non-Malay opposition seems to have remained more or less at its old level, the DAP winning eighteen peninsula seats compared to nineteen in 1986. Although its share of the peninsula vote dropped from 21.4 per cent to 17.6 per cent, this was largely due, as explained above, to the channelling of DAP votes to common opposition candidates. In contrast to UMNO's continued domination of the Malay vote, the Chinese BN parties were, as usual, less successful. The MCA won only 18 of the 32 parliamentary and 34 of the 69 state seats that it contested, and suffered the loss of all parliamentary and state seats in predominantly Chinese Penang. Gerakan won five of nine parliamentary seats and eleven of 21 state seats. On the other hand, the MIC won all six of the parliamentary seats that it contested and twelve of thirteen state seats.

The Malay opposition, however, failed to match UMNO in attracting Malay votes except in Kelantan. The outcome of the parliamentary election once again depended on the contest for the 91 Malay-majority seats in the peninsula and once again UMNO proved its supremacy. Of the 85 peninsula parliamentary seats that it contested, UMNO won 70, the lost seats all being in Kelantan (13) and Terengganu (2) while non-Malay BN parties won in the other Malay-majority seats with UMNO backing.

Although earlier by-election results had suggested that Semangat 46 may have been supported by as many as half the Malay voters in some areas, its performance was poor in the general election. In the Malay-majority states of the north and the northeast it had been assumed that PAS would maintain its usual share of the Malay votes ranging from about forty to fifty per cent to which would be added a substantial share of the votes previously won by UMNO but which would now be directed to Semangat. This is indeed what happened in Kelantan where virtually half the Malay voters were already committed to PAS while it seems that about forty per cent of UMNO's old supporters switched to Semangat[5]. In the other states, however, the defections from UMNO were much fewer and not sufficient to boost the opposition vote substantially. In the Malay-majority states of the northeast and north, the vote for UMNO candidates fell only marginally compared to 1986. In Terengganu it dropped by only seven percentage points and in Perlis by one while in Kedah the BN's share actually increased. In the absence of substantial defections from UMNO, it would seem that in these states much of Semangat's votes must have come from PAS supporters following party directions to vote for APU candidates. Similarly, in the states with substantial non-Malay populations on the west coast and in the south, support for Semangat candidates was boosted by DAP as well as PAS voters. One possible indicator of the degree of support for Semangat—as opposed to the opposition alliance—in these states can be seen from UMNO's performance in the same seats that it contested in 1986. In Negeri Sembilan support for UMNO candidates declined by thirteen per cent of the 1986 UMNO vote, in Selangor by seven per cent and by less than three per cent each in Johor, Pahang and Perak while UMNO candidates actually won higher percentages in Penang, Melaka and Kuala Lumpur.

---

[5] This rough estimate is reached as follows. The share of the BN (i.e. UMNO) in the total votes for parliament in Kelantan declined from 54 per cent in 1986 to 33 per cent in 1990, a decline of 21 percentage points or 39 per cent of the BN vote in 1986.

Why did Semangat fail to live up to expectations? Part of the answer lies in the nature of patronage politics in UMNO. The Semangat's supporters had all been part of the UMNO patronage network before the UMNO split. Indeed, the split itself had revolved to a large extent around control of the patronage machine. In the 1987 contest for the presidency of UMNO, the two sides were evenly balanced and in the by-elections of 1988 it seemed that the Semangat was attracting around half of Malay votes. The patronage network was in disarray as a result of the split and it was still not clear which side would come out on top in the end. If the general election had been held in 1988 or early 1989 the result might have been much more favourable for the opposition. But the advantages of incumbency made themselves felt during 1989 and 1990 with the result that dissidents at all levels gradually moved back to UMNO. Businessmen who were dependent on government licences, credit or contracts, politicians with big personal loans from banks, schoolteachers who did not want to be transferred to Sabah or Sarawak, and villagers who were applying for land all felt that they had no choice but to return to UMNO. After all, many had joined UMNO in the first place in order to get access to the patronage network and they had supported Semangat because they thought that the dissidents were about to take control of it. Now that it seemed clear that Semangat's chances were not so bright, it was safer to return to UMNO.

Nevertheless, in the weeks before the election it still seemed that the opposition would do well and many observers predicted that the government might lose its two-thirds majority. However, the opposition could not match the resources of the government, particularly its effective monopoly of the English and Malay daily newspapers and television. In an extraordinary propaganda campaign following the PBS defection from the BN, the government turned Razaleigh's weapon back on him by suggesting that he was supporting Christianity against Islam. On a visit to Sabah, Tengku Razaleigh had been photographed wearing a traditional Kadazan headdress which was decorated with what looked like a cross! The photograph of Razaleigh wearing what appeared to be a bishop's mitre was used to telling effect by the mass media and was believed by the opposition to have swayed many Malay voters at the last moment. At the same time government-provided sermons read in mosques on the Friday before the election played up the danger of Christianisation, and in Penang, the threat to the Malays if the DAP gained control of the state government.

Democracy and Authoritarianism

Although the democratic constitutional framework was maintained, the Malaysian political system had become increasingly authoritarian during the 1970s and 1980s. Elections were held in circumstances which guaranteed government victory while parliament, opposition parties and the press had little capacity to act as checks on government power. But the formal democratic framework became relevant again in the wake of the split in UMNO. The dissidents quickly made use of the electoral system in their challenge to the government and once again parliament became a forum of significant political debate. While the regime remained under the control of the established Malay elite and continued broadly to serve its interests, the political struggle within that elite made the system more flexible and uncertain.

Unlike earlier challenges which had been met with the ISA or declarations of emergency, this time the government avoided resort to drastic authoritarian measures. The UMNO dissident movement was too strong to be easily controlled through straightforward repression, especially as it was not impossible that a significant number of Malay civil servants, police and military officers sympathised with them. The revival of democratic practice, however, was still only partial and most of the authoritarian controls remained in place. Although the ISA and the emergency provisions were not used against the dissidents, the opposition's scope for mobilising popular support continued to be restricted, especially because of the government's effective monopoly of the main mass media.

Backed by its authoritarian powers, the government also relied on its control of patronage to undermine the opposition challenge. By winning back supporters of the Semangat 46, UMNO was able to weaken the key component of the opposition front. Without a strong Semangat to act as a bridge between PAS and the DAP, it seemed unlikely that co-operation between the opposition parties would be strengthened. Indeed, if UMNO were to succeed in enticing a few more Semangat members of parliament to cross to the government's side in the future, the opposition would in effect return to its pre-1990 condition when it consisted of a Malay party and an essentially non-Malay party which were rivals rather than partners.

In the long run, however, it could be expected that Malaysian society will continue to change in a way that would favour the growth of political checks and balances. During the 1970s and 1980s Malaysian society was transformed as a result of rapid economic growth. In particular an extraordinary expansion took place in the urban middle class while the restructuring programme ensured that Malays were increasingly represented in the modern sector of society. By the late 1980s the urban, educated middle class constituted a large part of a society in which Malay peasants and non-Malay labourers no longer made up the majority.

The emergence of the middle class had ambiguous political consequences. As beneficiaries of government policies, the middle class—both Malay and non-Malay—had reason to be grateful to the government but at the same time they were more inclined to oppose and criticise particular policies and leaders. Moreover, while some members of the middle class adopted a non-communal political perspective, most continued to stress communal identity. The new Malay members of the middle class owed their rising social mobility to the government's restructuring policy while non-Malay members of the middle class felt discriminated against. The 1970s and

1980s were therefore characterised by continuing racial polarisation in the middle, as well as in other, classes, with non-Malays much more inclined to support the opposition.

Although the rise of the Malay middle class provided the government with an expanding base of support, it also had disruptive consequences. While the major non-Malay parties in the government had always been plagued by factionalism, the peasant-based UMNO had in the past given strong support to its aristocratic and semi-aristocratic leaders. But the huge influx of educated middle-class leaders, often from humble rural backgrounds, led to increased rivalries in the party and eventually contributed to the party split in 1988. Although the BN scored an impressive victory in the 1990 election, it faced the strongest opposition it had ever encountered. But the performance of the new Semangat 46 fell below expectations and the degree of co-operation between the opposition parties was still limited. The implications for the future were still ambiguous.

Bibliography

Cited books, articles

Bedlington, S. S., 1978. *Malaysia and Singapore: The Building of New States*, Ithaca: Cornell University Press.

CARPA, 1988. *Tangled Web: Dissent, Deterrence and the 27 October 1987 Crackdown in Malaysia*, Haymarket, Australia: Committee Against Repression in the Pacific and Asia.

Crouch, H., 1980. "The UMNO Crisis: 1975–1977" in Harold Crouch, Lee Kam Hing and Michael Ong, (eds), *Malaysian Politics and the 1978 Election*, Kuala Lumpur: Oxford University Press.

Gomez, E. T., 1990. *Politics in Business: UMNO's Corporate Investments*, Kuala Lumpur: Forum.

I & J Sdn Bhd, 1990. *Malaysian General Election 1990* (An Analysis Presented at a Forum held on October 25, 1990 at Maktab Kerjasama Malaysia, Petaling Jaya).

Lawyers Committee for Human Rights. 1990. *Malaysia: Assault on the Judiciary*, New York: Lawyers Committee for Human Rights.

Mauzy, D. K., 1983. *Barisan Nasional: Coalition Government in Malaysia*, Kuala Lumpur: Maricans.

Means, G. P., 1976. *Malaysian Politics* (2nd ed.), London: Hodder and Stoughton.

Milne, R. S. & D. K. Mauzy, 1977. *Politics and Government in Malaysia*, Singapore: Federal Publications.

Salleh Abas (Tun) with K. Das. 1989, *May Day for Justice*, Kuala Lumpur: Magnus Books.

Scott, J. C., 1985. *Weapons of the Weak: Everyday Forms of Peasant Resistance*, New Haven: Yale University Press.

Shamsul, A. B., 1986. *From British to Bumiputera Rule*, Singapore: Institute of Southeast Asian Studies.

Shamsul, A. B., 1988. "The 'Battle Royal': The UMNO Elections of 1987" in Mohammed Ayoob & Ng Chee Yuen (eds), *Southeast Asian Affairs 1988*, Singapore: Institute of Southeast Asian Studies.

Tan Tat Wai, 1982. *Income Distribution and Determination in West Malaysia*, Kuala Lumpur: Oxford University Press.

Von Vorys, K., 1975. *Democracy Without Consensus*, Princeton: Princeton University Press.

Williams, P. A., 1990. *Judicial Misconduct*, Petaling Jaya: Pelanduk Publications.

Malaysian Government Publications

Mid-Term Review of Third Malaysia Plan 1976–1980.
Fourth Malaysia Plan 1981–1985.
Mid-Term Review of Fifth Malaysia Plan 1986–1990.
Federal Constitution.
Internal Security Act
Sedition Act.

Newspapers, Periodicals

New Straits Times (NST)
The Star
Asiaweek
Far Eastern Economic Review (FEER)
Asian Wall Street Journal (AWSJ)

3

The Grand Vision: Mahathir and Modernisation

Khoo Kay Jin

It started as a couple of smaller eruptions, beginning in 1981, before exploding in dramatic fashion with the April 1987 UMNO elections. It then temporarily receded into behind-the-scenes manoeuvres, interrupted and obscured in October 1987 by "Operation Lalang", the mass arrests and detention under the Internal Security Act of over a hundred persons. A stunning climax came in February 1988 with the court declaration that UMNO was an illegal party. There followed a year of pitched battles and shifting alignments which continued right up to January/February 1989 before receding once again into behind-the-scenes activity, but not before it had counted among its victims the judiciary, in general, and the Lord President, in particular.

"It" was the UMNO split.[1] It had been threatening since 1981 when the timing of the resignation of the Prime Minister, Hussein Onn, and the initial public reluctance of his successor, Mahathir Mohamed, to indicate his preference for a deputy, ostensibly threw open the question of succession to that post. As is well-known, the then Minister of Finance since 1976, Tengku Razaleigh, ran for the Deputy Presidency against the then Minister of Education since 1978, Musa Hitam, in a bitterly fought, no-holds-barred contest. Musa Hitam, it turned out, was Mahathir's preferred candidate. Musa won with over 55 percent of the vote, only to have Razaleigh challenge him again in the next General Assembly in 1984.[2]

---

[1] UMNO is Malaysia's dominant political party, the dominant partner in all coalitions governing the country since independence in 1957, and putative representative of the majority Malay population. By tacit agreement, its President and Deputy President become the country's Prime Minister and Deputy Prime Minister, while the other holders of high office within the party generally also end up as Cabinet ministers in the Government. Thus, position within the party carries with it position in Government. For this reason, it is often commented that the real elections in Malaysia are the UMNO elections, held once every three years.

[2] A fascinating, almost blow-for-blow account of the 1981 fight and its ramifications up till mid-1983 can be found in A. Ghani Ismail (1983). See also, Gale (1982:

Musa won a second time, only to resign as Deputy Prime Minister and Deputy President in February 1986, but was "persuaded" to stay on as Deputy President.

Following the general elections and as 1986 drew to a close, rumours abounded of a possible Razaleigh-Musa front to contest the Presidency and Deputy Presidency of UMNO in the next General Assembly in 1987. Thus was born "Team A" comprising Prime Minister Mahathir, and his supporters, and "Team B" comprising Razaleigh, Musa and their supporters, both equally matched, each having the support of an almost equal number of UMNO cabinet ministers and deputy ministers. 1987 saw an even more bitter, winner-takes-all contest. Mahathir's "team" won; the challengers, including those elected to the positions they contested, either resigned or were removed from the Cabinet. In the course of the year, a series of ancillary events, primarily organized by non-UMNO critics or opponents of the Government,[3] provided a temporary rallying point for both UMNO sides around the issue of Malay honour and sovereignty, if not dominance.[4] The ensuing escalation of ethnic tensions provided an opportunity for the executive to impose control, at least upon non-UMNO critics and dissidents thus permitting it to concentrate its attention upon the UMNO dissidents. This took the form of a mass crackdown under the country's Internal Security Act which permits detention without trial.

Meanwhile, a group of "Team B" supporters contested the validity of the 1987 UMNO elections in court, only to have the court rule that the party was illegal because it had contravened sections of the relevant act governing societies.[5] As outrage, anger, fear and panic set in amongst broad sections of the Malay public, and the stunned and worried non-Malay public waited for the next move, Mahathir used the power of incumbency and control of the media to strengthen his hand.

So began a scramble to register a new party to be heir to the old

---

Chapters 8 & 9) and Chamil Wariya (1988: Chapter 5). For a good summary and more, see Shamsul A. B. (1988).

[3] Some, particularly those involving ethnic concerns, involved the non-Malay parties, particularly the Malaysian Chinese Association (MCA), in the ruling coalition. This was especially so in the immediate period prior to the crackdown. Note, however, that a number of these events were non-ethnic in concern. This included events, such as the seminar on the constitution organized by the social reform movement ALIRAN, which UMNO leaders chose to interpret in ethnic terms.

[4] It was simultaneously a point of competition between the two sides. Thus, Ibrahim Ali, a "lieutenant" of Tengku Razaleigh, and Najib Tun Razak, the youth division leader, a minister and an ambitious politician who had aligned himself to the Mahathir camp but whose loyalties were suspect, were both prominent actors.

[5] According to the Asian Wall Street Journal (4 February 1988), it was the lawyer representing UMNO, i.e., Team A, who maintained that the dissidents' arguments against the validity of the elections should be seen in the context of another provision in the relevant law which would require that the court find the party

UMNO. Given the advantages of state executive power, it was a foregone conclusion as to who would be able to set up a reconstituted and "purified" UMNO. Razaleigh's grouping, after losing a series of legal battles, assumed the name "Semangat '46", or "The Spirit of '46", a reference to the year in which UMNO was founded, and continued the battle, crisscrossing the country and holding a series of gatherings. The reconstituted UMNO did the same, via the state machinery. Simultaneously, the state executive sought to ensure its ascendancy over the judiciary, the site of a series of skirmishes not only between the UMNO combatants but between the Government and the Opposition, critics and dissidents. The Constitution was amended in March 1988 followed by the institution of tribunal proceedings against the Lord President of the Supreme Court, resulting in his dismissal from office in August 1988.

Finally, the battle was extended into a series of by-elections, the most dramatic being the August 1988 Johor Baru by-election which Mahathir's side lost by a humiliating margin. But by January 1989, the new UMNO had won two other by-elections, the first narrowly, and the second by a fairly comfortable margin.

In February 1989, Musa Hitam joined the new UMNO. In March, the "hero" of the Johor Baru by-elections, ex-Minister of the Federal Territory Shahrir Samad, applied for membership.[6] Meanwhile, some middle ranking members of the Razaleigh camp had also defected. The Razaleigh group found itself on the defensive, and entered into an alliance with the Islamic party, PAS. Efforts to form at least an electoral pact with other opposition parties continued, as the prospect of general elections drew near. The war was not yet over.

Tweedledum and Tweedledee?

But what, if anything, is or was the war about? Is it, as widely believed, little more than a fight over an economic pie between rival patronage networks and factions? Are there no policy issues at stake?

Popular attention has naturally focused upon the shifting fortunes and stances of the major personalities. To a large extent, the participants themselves cast the split in terms of personalities, personal styles[7] and personal greed, and of nebulous notions such as "political culture" and the "spirit of '46" and, unavoidably in Malaysia, in terms of "Malay unity", "Malay

---

illegal. The dissidents' lawyers reportedly urged the court to take, not the broad view, but the narrow view, and rule only on the legality of the elections.

[6] By March 1989, the majority of Musa's big-name supporters had joined the new UMNO.

[7] Although Musa Hitam, for one, attempted to give some political content to the notion of "style". See, for example, *The Correspondent* (November 1988), or the videotape released during the campaign for the Johor Baru by-election of August

interests" and "Malay sovereignty and dominance".

Obviously, the faction holding power has found it convenient to take advantage of the power of incumbency and to portray the split as essentially one of personalities and of personal greed for power on the part of the challengers as well as to cast aspersions on the current financial status of the opposition, many of whom suffered serious losses in the last recession.[8] However, the opposing faction, too, has tended to cast its grievances in terms of issues such as "leadership style", "cronyism" in the award of government contracts, mismanagement, corruption, absence of Cabinet and inner-party democracy, and other failings of Mahathir. But their formulations do not so much spell out a difference over policy as imply a deviation on the part of Mahathir from a common policy.[9]

Even well-informed academic observers saw the fight in terms of factions fighting for the levers and benefits of patronage and the lucrative spoils of office. Thus, one such observer viewed it as factional fighting within the Malay middle class as "both camps, in essence, did not really differ in their overall philosophy, policy and approach to many important national issues" (Shamsul A.B. 1988 179; see also Gale 1981: 200–201).

It is the contention of this paper that underlying the conflict is a real difference in policy which has been obscured by the alliances that were formed by the coalescence of varied, even conflicting, interests around each of the two sides. As was pointed out more than ten years ago (Business International 1977),[10] in the context of another, relatively more contained, split within UMNO,[11] to see the split only, or even primarily, as one of personalities and factional power struggles would obscure the fact that there are "major policy issues directly at stake, with important ramifications for the future direction of economic development" (BI 1977: iii).

The difficulty perhaps arises from the fact that almost everyone in

---

1988. A transcript of the tape was printed in the Malay edition of the Democratic Action Party (DAP) paper. See *Roket*, October 1988.

[8] Mahathir's presidential speech to the reconstituted UMNO's First General Assembly on 28 October 1988 provides an example of such a portrayal. For the first time too, he labelled them a "splinter group". See the full text in *Utusan Malaysia*, 29 October 1988; translated excerpts in *The Star* 29 October 1988.

[9] The terms in which the conflict has been expressed appear to be part of the contemporary idiom of Malaysian politics.

[10] Hereafter cited as BI (1977). This much neglected report, despite some glaring blunders, is remarkable for its insightful and novel approach.

The report observed that "ironically, discussions with many senior government leaders involved in the struggle reveal that they themselves are not aware of some significant aspects of the struggle (and) tend to see the current UMNO struggle simply as a clash of personalities or personal ambitions . . ." (BI 1977: iii).

[11] The split referred to is that which occurred in 1975–1977. Perhaps the most insightful account of that split is to be found in BI (1977). See also Crouch (1980).

[12] The New Economic Policy (NEP) was formulated in the aftermath of the 1969 riots, and has since been the underlying ideology of national development. It is due

Malaysia publicly avows support for the New Economic Policy (NEP),[12] but differs over its implementation. But the NEP is not so much a policy as a statement of objectives. Thus differences in implementation are crucial and relate to goals and policy orientations.

This paper brings together a few obvious facts pertaining to the political economy of Malaysia since 1970, especially the developments of the 1980s, and suggests that the split, in particular its timing, should be viewed in that light. This is not to suggest that politics is an epiphenomenon of economics, nor that the split was "inevitable". But it is to suggest that the split would not be as deep and wide as it evidently is if not for certain fundamental strains within Malaysian, particularly Malay, society. These strains resulted as much from an evident policy shift as from underlying economic fundamentals. In effect, political and policy decisions and actions interacted with underlying economic fundamentals to create a climate in which a split could occur when and if the personalities were available to take up the cudgels, irrespective, to a certain extent, of what those cudgels represented. That such a personality was available in the person of Tengku Razaleigh[13] may well have derived from a possible difference in policy

---

to terminate in 1990. Representing a consensus of sorts, it contains two goals: (i) the eradication of poverty irrespective of race; (ii) the restructuring of society to eliminate identification of economic function and race. See Malaysia (1971).

[13] It is asserted without discussion that Musa Hitam's alliance with Tengku Razaleigh was primarily motivated by a combination of personal political circumstances and ambitions and a real difference with Mahathir over matters of "leadership style" reflected perhaps most acutely by their different responses to the events leading up to the trouncing of Parti Berjaya by the Parti Bersatu Sabah (PBS) in Sabah in 1984–86. Another possible area of difference might have to do with the form of the party's involvement in business, which clearly embroils it in patronage problems. Musa, it appears, would prefer to see the party's businesses run independently by professionals, and not by politicians or politically associated persons. See his speech to the 1986 UMNO Women and Youth General Assembly, as reported in *Asiaweek*, 28 September 1986.

That Musa might be more averse to blatant patronage politics appears to be indicated by an account of the disappointment felt by a number who had given their support to Musa (A. Ghani Ismail 1983: 48).

[14] This possible policy difference is not discussed in any depth in this paper. The argument does not require that Razaleigh personally has a different policy, simply that those who support him tend towards a different policy from that being pushed by Mahathir.

That Razaleigh may have different policy commitments is suggested by the view of the Business International consultants that Razaleigh "believes in aggressive bureaucratic means to shift more resources into Malay hands, even at the cost of serious economic dislocations and inefficiencies" (BI 1977: 90). Funston (1980: 258–9) noted Razaleigh's economic nationalism, directed generally to the foreign sector. Razaleigh headed the newly created UMNO Economic Bureau in 1970, supervised the committee drafting the Second Malaysia Plan, and became the

commitments[14] as from personal ambition. More critically, it is because the policy shift was identified with and was so much the result of Mahathir's ideological commitments, virtually obsessions, that the conflict came to centre upon him.

Basic Facts

In 1969, Malaysia experienced its crisis of decolonization, nation-building and development in the form of the post-election race riots of May 13th, 1969. In 1970 the New Economic Policy (NEP) was launched, reflecting the triumph of then Deputy Prime Minister Tun Abdul Razak's, and the younger intelligentsia's,[15] analysis of the causes of the May 13th race riots over Prime Minister Tunku Abdul Rahman's.[16]

It is common belief that the NEP virtually adopted the programme advanced by then recently expelled UMNO Executive Committee member, Dr Mahathir Mohamad, in his then recently banned book, *The Malay Dilemma* (Von Vorys 1975). But there were some differences that came to play an important part in Mahathir's subsequent assessment of the NEP in the form it assumed, in execution if not in design.[17] That form differed somewhat from the underlying philosophy of Mahathir's book, a

---

director of PERNAS, one of the most ambitious public enterprises set up for NEP purposes. On PERNAS, see Gale (1981: Chapter 4); also Jesudason (1988: 86–98 *passim.*)

[15] "Intelligentsia" as used here refers to a category of persons with at least upper secondary education, often inducted into the middle and upper ranks of government service, and professionals/salariat.

[16] See, Malaysia (1969) and Tunku Abdul Rahman (1969).

The Tunku's book was published in September, while the National Operations Council (NOC) report, i.e. Malaysia (1969), with a foreword by its Director, Tun Razak, was published in October.

The Tunku's view was that the riots were essentially the result of subversive and communist agitation. The NOC's report intimated that the clash was the culmination of over a decade of mis-development which had paid insufficient attention to Malay backwardness. The New Economic Policy and, more so, the Second Malaysia Plan (1971–75) was to make this explicit. But the most explicit statement of this line of thought was to be found in Mahathir Mohamed (1970). However, the economic proposals in Mahathir's book and in the Second Malaysia Plan had been voiced earlier in economic congresses organized by Government bureaucrats and billed as Bumiputera Economic Congresses. See, e.g., Kongres Ekonomi Bumiputera (1965).

[17] Indeed, the BI noted that "it is known that the Deputy Prime Minister (Mahathir) himself does not agree with some of the policies, but he has had to go along with them" (BI 1977: 8).

[18] A comparison with his collection of essays first published in 1976 under the title "Menghadapi Cabaran", and his speech at the first General Assembly of the reconstituted UMNO in October 1988 will bear this out, as will portions of his

philosophy that the author has held to consistently over the years.[18] This
helps explain the attempt at re-orientation that came with Mahathir's ascendancy. This re-orientation derived at least partly from his perception of the
gulf between the social changes wrought by the NEP and his view of what
needed to be done and of the desirable society.

Whatever the sources of inspiration for the NEP, it spelled a new phase
in Malaysia's development, overturning the relationship between state and
economy and re-casting the balance of power within the "pact of domination". The NEP spelt the end of an alliance between the Malaysian state
and private capital in which the state was content to support the efforts of
private accumulation, both local and foreign, restricting itself to limited
programmes aimed at ameliorating rural discontent and the frustrations of
a rising Malay intelligentsia. Instead, the roles were to be reversed with
the state playing the leading role and laying down the agenda with private
capital in tow (BI 1977: 45–50). The choice of this particular alternative
expressed primarily the demands of the Malay business and intelligentsia
network, many of the latter being in bureaucratic positions, who wanted
the state to be interventionist in favour of "Malay" interests. To the degree
that state power depended upon its ability to command votes in the country-
side where poverty levels were atrocious, the policy also expressed incorporating intentions towards such strata, primarily the peasantry. In power
terms, it spelled a shift of power to technocrats and bureaucrats. In implementation, it was geared towards the utilization of state resources to
sponsor a Malay capitalist class. In realization, it assumed in large part the
form of public corporations acquiring assets for and on behalf of Malays,
and run by political appointees and bureaucrats.[19]

A combination of economic circumstances, particularly in the latter half
of the seventies, gave the state sufficient room for manoeuvre when faced
with the reluctance of say, domestic capital, to play along or when confronted with demands from below. Generally favourable international
circumstances, including the commodities boom and the worldwide reorganization of capital investment, state led demand and investment[20]

---

interview with *Malaysian Business* in January 1988 (Jayasankaran 1988a). See
also the various interviews with Mahathir in 1981, 1982 and 1983, reprinted in
Rosnah Majid (1985). Also, his speech to the Women and Youth wings of UMNO
in June 1981, translation in Morais (1982: 223–232), original in A. Ghani Ismail
(1983: Appendix D).

[19] For an interpretation of the NEP as bureaucratic power, see Jomo Kwame
Sundaram (1986: Chapter 10; also 1978). For a more straightforward characterization
of the NEP as a policy by and for a technocratic-bureaucratic strata, see BI (1977:
Chapter 2). Also, Funston (1980: Chapter 9) who concluded that "the new changes
strengthened the hand of the bureaucracy" (*ibid.*: 282). For NEP as the expression
of the demands of the Malay business stratum and the intelligentsia, see Lim Mah
Hui (1985). See also Mehmet (1986).

[20] Development expenditure grew from $9.8 billion for the 1971–75 period to
$24.9 billion in the 1976–80 period. As a percentage of GDP, development

primarily via public enterprises now known as Non-Financial Public Enterprises (NFPEs), and the discovery of off-shore petroleum resulted in an exemplary growth rate. Real GDP averaged 7.6 per cent for the 1970–80 period, and 8.6 percent for the 1975–80 period. Per capita income increased from M$1,100 in 1970 to M$3,700 in 1980. Given that the country was awash with cash including, importantly, petroleum revenues, this impressive performance was achieved without undue stress on the budget and on the balance of payments.[21]

In contrast, or, perhaps, as a result, the 1980s, up until mid-1987 with reverberations into 1989, have been unaccustomedly lean years. Beginning in 1980/81, the economy started slipping into recession despite heavy counter-cyclical spending. It picked up somewhat in late 1983, only to fall into an even worse recession in 1985, without the cushion of counter-cyclical measures and of easy petroleum revenues.[22] This lasted well into 1987. Per capita GNP, after hitting a high of just over $4,800 in 1984, fell to $4,600 in 1985 and to $4,100 in 1986, before pulling back to $4,500 in 1987.[23]

Midway through the period, in July 1984, a change of Finance Minister, enabled by Razaleigh's second loss to Musa Hitam, consolidated a change in fiscal policy signalled shortly after the 1982 elections. Not only were counter-cyclical measures spurned, state expenditure actually contracted. This contraction, coupled with increased financial disciplining of public enterprises (the NFPEs), accelerated greatly after 1984. The ostensible reason for this was the precarious state of the country's finances, particularly the ballooning external debt of the early 1980s, and the threat of bunched repayments falling due after 1985. This precarious financial state was seen in the twin deficits in the balance of payments and the budget.[24]

---

expenditure grew from 8.5% in 1971 (6.1% in 1970) to 14.4% in 1980. The massive expansion of public enterprises can be gauged from the increased expenditure on them which went from about 37% of the total annual federal budget in 1970 to 56% in 1974. In this paper, all currency figures are cited in the Malaysian *ringgit* (dollar).

[21] A necessary caveat to this is that the impressive performance, while it brought down the poverty rate in the country, also resulted in increased disparity in intra-ethnic, specifically intra-Malay, income distribution. See for example Jomo Kwame Sundaram & Ishak Shari (1986). Khor Kok Peng (1983a) detected basic structural weaknesses behind this impressive performance.

[22] Petroleum prices started falling in 1981/82 and then took a nose-dive in 1985/86 to a level well below one half of its peak values in 1980.

[23] Real GNP growth between 1981 and 1988:

1981	1982	1983	1984	1985	1986	1987	1988
7.5	4.6	3.9	6.7	−1.2	2.6	4.8	8.6

Source: *Treasury Economic Report 1988; Bank Negara Annual Report 1988.*

[24] For details, see Jomo (1987); Khor (1983b; 1987); the Annual Reports of Bank Negara for the early 1980s, especially the 1983 Annual Report. Just one indicator: by the mid-1980s, the cost of servicing the federal debt accounted for close to 30

Increases in Government operating expenditure were held down, partly by means of a job- and wage-freeze.[25] Development expenditure was halved between 1983 and 1987. By means of such austerity measures, a budget deficit amounting to 20 percent of GNP in 1982 was turned around, with assistance from an improved international economic climate, to under 7 percent of GNP in 1987. While the external debt burden continued to rise, with the total, inclusive of the private sector, external debt servicing ratio approaching 19 percent (one-third of it due to NFPEs) in 1987 (IMF, 1987), borrowing was restrained and the Government's outstanding external debt was actually reduced. Simultaneously, there was a loosening of NEP constraints with regards to equity and other encouragements to private, particularly foreign, investment.

Serious controls upon NFPEs were instituted beginning in mid-1982.[26] The NFPEs had been a crucial component of the NEP (Gale, 1981), consuming a major share of development expenditure. In the Third Malaysia Plan period (1976–80), 14 large public enterprises consumed just under one-fifth of the development budget of the Federal and State Governments. A survey of the largest 27 such enterprises in 1983 revealed that they consumed nearly two-thirds of net Federal Government development expenditure (Bank Negara, 1983: 9). As a result of these controls, spending has been curbed. Some enterprises have had to fold[27] while others,

---

percent of the operating expenditure. Indeed, in 1986 and 1987, the Federal Government's operating expenditure exceeded revenue. See Treasury Economic Report, v.y.

[25] The significance of such a job-freeze can be gauged from the fact that government services, comprising public administration, health, education, defence and public utilities but excluding public corporations, accounted for almost 14% of total employment in 1980, up from 12% in 1970. In absolute terms, this averaged an additional 30,000-plus public sector jobs per annum in that ten year period. Its absorptive capacity was only topped by the manufacturing sector. This rate of public sector job creation accelerated over the next two years to 1982. Something of the order of 100,000 new jobs were added so that by 1982, the public sector accounted for 14.8% of total employment. But over the next five years, 1983–1987, the average net new jobs created in the public sector fell precipitously to around 6,500 per annum. This occurred over the worse years of the recession when jobs elsewhere were hard to come by, as unemployment soared from under 6% in 1980 to just under 9% in 1986, before falling back to around 8.3% in 1987 and 8.1% in 1988. See, *Treasury Economic Report*, v.y. Cf. *Bank Negara Annual Report*, v.y.

[26] According to Gale (1981: 179–184), there was increasing concern over the performance of public enterprises in the latter half of the 1970s, but no effective controls had been effected by the end of the decade.

A caveat here on the controls of NFPEs. A point of apparent contention was the spending on HICOM, *the* NFPE of the early 1980s, and generally seen as a brainchild of Mahathir himself.

[27] There will apparently be further closures of some 300+ NFPEs from a total of

including the Prime Minister's pet project, HICOM or the Heavy Industries Corporation of Malaysia, have been reorganized. This has been coupled with a privatization programme.

There was even talk of a reconsideration of subsidy payments, including those to the sensitive padi sector, and there have been noises made about the possibility of freeing controls on the rice market.[28] Measures have been taken to reduce the padi subsidy bill by abandoning the long standing, although never seriously pursued, goal of rice self-sufficiency. Peasants in marginal padi areas have been encouraged or pushed into cultivating other commercial crops on the grounds that this gives better returns.

Beginning in 1985/86, wage increments were kept under control with the Government showing the way.[29] This was coupled with attempts to further reduce the average wage by floating the idea of a lower starting salary for new Government employees as well as by new labour legislation.[30]

Nevertheless, mindful of the need to keep the largest component of Government employees quiescent, a 6 percent wage increment was granted to about 800,000 Category C & D[31] workers in 1985. But allowances for

---

over a 1,000. Meanwhile, profitable NFPEs as well as profitable shares held by NFPEs in other companies have been and are being transferred to the National Unit Trust Fund for Bumiputera run by the Permodalan Nasional Berhad (PNB), or National Equity Corporation. This has led to some conflict between those running the NFPEs and the PNB.

[28] Domestic prices for padi are kept "artificially" high by a guaranteed price. They are substantially higher than the world market price. On the average, some 50% of farm incomes of padi farmers derive from subsidy payments. A freeing of price controls could have a widespread impoverishing effect.

[29] Cf. the IMF's view: "Wage increases have outpaced the rate of inflation, and certain fringe benefits have almost become contractual. Consequently, the structure of labor costs has become rigid, resulting in increasingly higher labor costs . . . . . . Recently the Government has enacted legislation that provides for reducing overtime premia by between 10 percent and 50 percent . . . . . Wage increases in the public and private sectors are also likely to be monitored and restrained for a period of three years" (IMF 1987: 17).

[30] Minister of Finance, Daim Zainuddin, in his 1988 Budget Speech recalled the promise in the 1987 Budget Speech (following upon previous calls for a wage freeze) that the government "would review the labour laws in order to make changes to lower the cost of production". *The Treasury Economic Report 1988/89:* "In the past, there has been a tendency for real wages to keep ahead of labour productivity, thereby causing an increase in wage costs . . . However, the present review of existing labour laws has attempted to rectify this situation . . . . With the introduction of the proposed changes it is anticipated that the new labour laws will contribute to lower labour costs" (p. 155).

[31] The public sector is organized in four main salary schemes, A through D, with C and D being the lower schemes.

senior employees were reduced by 10%, even as salaries were held to a scale established in 1980. For the upper and middle levels of the bureaucracy was added the ignominy of being scorned for low productivity and inefficiency. They were reined in and subjected to a number of irksome, albeit inconsequential, measures, including clocking in and out, required attendance at refresher courses, and so on. In addition, those running public enterprises were publicly rebuked, told to resign if they could not do the job and sometimes replaced.

These measures have naturally won the approval of the International Monetary Fund (IMF). It might indeed be suggested that they were undertaken under pressure from the IMF (Jomo 1987), and that Government had little choice but to comply. However, the initial push for these measures apparently came from the technocrats in Bank Negara (see Bank Negara, 1982; 1983). Most likely, there was some convergence of thought on the part of the Prime Minister. Then a Finance Minister was appointed who, while widely believed to be guilty of all manner of conflicts of interest, worked the country's finances like the businessman he was. The country was run like a company, albeit allowing for what many believe to be insider trading, with the executive quite firmly in charge, even to the extent of challenging the Governor of Bank Negara in 1985 when the latter refused to assent to looser monetary policies—basically easier loans for the purposes of share purchases.[32]

The turnaround has been remarkable (Bank Negara, 1988), albeit aided by the good fortune of a tremendous recovery in commodity prices. Some see the country as having been brought back from the brink of financial disaster; that the bitter medicine has forestalled deepening of the ill-effects of the commodities boom and petroleum wealth of the later 1970s, coupled with the NEP as interpreted by bureaucrats and politicians.[33]

But the medicine has been indeed bitter for virtually everyone, except a fortunate few. Unemployment shot up from a low of under 5 percent in 1982 to a high of around 8.6 percent in 1987, with total unemployed more than doubling between 1982 and 1986 and crossing the half million mark. Youth unemployment in the 15–24 age group is believed to have been very much higher, "about three times that of the overall rate" (Malaysia 1986: 140). For the first time since the massive expansion of the universities under the NEP, severe graduate unemployment became a fact of life.[34] Bankruptcies and near insolvency, involving some of the biggest

---

[32] The then Governor, Aziz Taha, resigned.
[33] This boom made possible all sorts of public enterprises without clear goals and accountability, increasing state presence in the economy, easy contracts, and a shift in levels of private consumption and expenditure, met by imports and not by domestic production.
[34] A substantial number of the unemployed graduates are Malays who would otherwise have been absorbed by the public sector.

names in business, became a commonplace. Smaller bumiputera business-men, many of them contractors,[35] have been particularly badly hit by the almost total collapse in the construction and property market in the mid-1980s, partly due to over-supply and partly brought about by contraction of Government expenditure. For many, if not most, Government contracts constituted their main source of business.[36] The urban middle classes experienced declining real incomes. They, as well as lower income groups, also had to shoulder a major part of the burden of Government cut-backs as well as Government attempts to make up for loss of revenue, either due to economic conditions or to concessions to high income earners and cor-porations, by more indirect taxation.

The commercial sector contracted as private consumption took a nose-dive. The tin industry all but collapsed, with mines reopening only in 1988. FELDA settlers also experienced tremendous falls in their levels of income as palm oil fell to $579 per tonne in 1986, having averaged close to $1,300 for the ten years from 1975–85. Rubber faced a depressed market, even in the early 1980s. As a result, estate workers and, by implication, rubber smallholders, one of the major poverty groups in the country, experienced a substantial decline in income.[37] At the same time, the manufacturing sector, which had been growing at a rate considerably higher than the national average, contracted, particularly in 1985–86. Between 1983 and 1987, over 50,000 workers, or more than one-half of the total workers retrenched, came from this sector (*Star*, 2 July 1987). While an upturn began to be seen in 1987, it was not until 1988 that it began to be felt, particularly as commodity prices took off again. But as of 1989 the fall in unemployment was marginal, as current investments appear to have lower labour absorption capacity.[38]

In brief, the main engine of growth and patronage in the 1970s stopped to function as such. Indeed, the state even spurned some of those cor-

---

[35] In terms of the direction of bank lending to the bumiputra community, loans for real estate and construction are the most important, accounting for approximately 1/3 of all bumiputra loans. The proportion would be even higher if housing loans were excluded. See Bank Negara, *Annual Report*, v.y.

[36] A point recognized by Mahathir in an interview: "Malay contractors can never get contracts other than from the Government . . . . Now that the Government is cutting back . . . . A lot of them are bankrupt because they borrowed money" (Jayasankaran 1983a).

[37] Estate rubber tappers experienced a fall in monthly income from $259 in 1980 to $216 in 1984 (Malaysia 1986: 140). In virtually all other sectors, the early 1980s actually saw a rise in wages, some of a substantial order. Since 1984–85, most sectors would have experienced a decline in real, if not nominal, incomes, until 1987–88.

[38] According to the 1988 *Bank Negara Annual Report*, while private investment grew by 14.5 percent in real terms in 1988, unemployment fell by a marginal 0.1 percent to 8.1 percent.

porations that it had itself spawned, demanding that they conform to commercial criteria. At the same time, private sector investment, both local
and foreign, stagnated.[39]

For better or worse, the period coincided with Mahathir's assumption
of the Prime Ministership and the worst, at least the most publicised,
financial scandals in post-independence Malaysia. While acknowledging
that not much could be done about the downturn in commodity prices,
many attributed the severity of the problems to Mahathir's stewardship,
that it was his obsessions, and mismanagement, that created the mess in
the first place.[40]

The widespread perception was of favouritism to certain pet projects of
the Prime Minister which were seen as extravagant and foolhardy, and to
favoured individuals. This was compounded by a series of scandals: the
Prime Minister's official residence, the attempt to corner the tin market,
the use of EPF (the Employees' Provident Fund, a social security scheme
for wage earners) funds to prop up the stock market and to cover up the
losses incurred in the attempt to corner the tin market, the BMF[41] affair,
the North-South Highway[42] and, in general, the activities of his finance
minister and associates.[43]

In the context of a shrinking pie, the present leadership was perceived

---

[39] Percentage change in gross fixed capital formation in constant prices for
1981–1988 were:

	1981	1982	1983	1984	1985	1986	1987	1988
Public	41.5	20.7	15.2	−8.5	−10.4	−20.7	−14.6	15.7
Private	4.1	−2.3	0.8	16.0	−8.6	−16.3	4.1	14.7

Source: *Treasury Economic Report, 1988/89, Appendix* Table 2.1.

[40] However, the current boom has undoubtedly muted criticism. In the context of
the split, it has also given the group holding power breathing space and the resources
with which to quell, or at least to buy off, the opposition.

[41] Bumiputera Malaysia Finance, a subsidiary of Bank Bumiputera operating in
Hong Kong, was caught very badly by the collapse of the Hong Kong property
market because of the size of loans, over $2 billion, made improperly to one client,
Carrian. There was widespread belief in Malaysia that the client had links with
powerful persons in Malaysia.

[42] The contract, carrying with it concessionary toll-collection rights, for construction
of this highway was awarded to a virtually bankrupt company, United Engineers
Malaysia, which had been taken over by UMNO shortly prior to the award. This
company has since become a "blue-chip" in the Kuala Lumpur Stock Exchange.

[43] The most publicized were those relating to the United Malayan Banking
Corporation deal, which resulted in PERNAS, the National Corporation, losing
control. PERNAS subsequently bought up shares at considerably higher prices
from companies that were connected with Daim. This was justified as part of
Daim's divestment effort. See, *Asian Wall Street Journal* 30 April 1986; *Business
Times* 25 Sept. 1986.

This became one of the issues used in the run-up to the April 1987 UMNO
elections. See *Star* 21, 23, 25 March 1987.

and believed to be guilty of excessive "cronyism". There developed a sense of gross injustice that a few had become extremely well-off while so many found themselves in tremendous financial difficulties. The largest projects, the big money spinners, were seen to be given either to foreigners or to a select few.[44] To this was added a belief of increasingly widespread corruption, perhaps heightened and highlighted by the general penury.

The About Face

The redirection of political economic policy must be credited to Mahathir himself. Economic fundamentals alone cannot be said to be that much of a deterrent to political leaders, especially when the policy changes would clearly hurt sectors whose political support counted, and would put paid to perhaps the single largest resource, namely Government development expenditure and jobs, with which political support and quiescence had been bought.

Furthermore, the policy change was couched in such "radical" and ideological terms that one has to conclude it was not simply an adjustment to economic realities. The changes were "radical" in putting forth drastically different measures for the achievement of a reinterpreted NEP, measures amounting to an about-face with respect to the understanding of the NEP that had developed through the latter half of the 1970s and the early 1980s—an understanding that may be summarized crudely as Government largesse to prop up a growing stratum of Malay businessmen.

But what basis is there for suggesting that it must be credited to Mahathir? After all, as already noted, the NEP as formulated and practised is widely believed to have come out of his "Malay Dilemma". The

---

[44] The Dayabumi building in Kuala Lumpur, originally owned by the Urban Development Authority (UDA), a public enterprise, but since sold to the national oil corporation PETRONAS after it incurred major losses, is often cited as an example. The contract was awarded to Zenecon, a company in which Mahathir's sister-in-law held substantial interests. It was then subcontracted to Japanese contractors.

Another example would be the privatization of Jalan Kuching-Jalan Kepong interchange, the major route into Kuala Lumpur from the north, to a company in which Finance Minister Daim Zainuddin's brother and one of Daim's business associates had interests. This company, Seri Angkasa, founded in 1981, had never contracted any business prior to being awarded the project which carried with it a toll concession. Apparently it was the only company, of seven, to submit proposals that fitted the bill. The company subsequently subcontracted the whole project to Mitsui Construction of Japan. The toll concession is now held by Kamunting, which Seri Angkasa purchased from the state mining corporation in a reverse take-over in 1987. See, *Asian Wall Street Journal* 31 May 1988.

most convenient evidence for this lies in the Mid-Term Review of the Fourth Malaysia Plan (MTR), released in March 1984. Confirmation can be found in his writings published in 1976 under the title "Menghadapi Cabaran" (translated into English as "The Challenge"). They reveal a consistency of thought persisting down to today as exemplified by the latter part of his speech to the 1st General Assembly (*Utusan Malaysia*, 28 October 1988) of the reconstituted UMNO.

The MTR is symptomatic of Mahathir's thinking. The first chapter, a sharp contrast to the corresponding chapter in the Fourth Malaysia Plan itself, repays close reading. It's title "New Directions in Development and Implementation of Strategies" is indicative. Its language and the logic of its argument might well have come out of "The Challenge". In it are to be found the "hobby-horses" of the Prime Minister—the need for a new man with new values, centrally hard work and thrift, under firm leadership in an ordered hierarchy in which all know their place and accept their role, playing their part towards the realization of a grand vision—Malaysia's and the Malays' rightful place in the sun—in which politics would be administration and there would be little room for "destructive" criticism.

Using the undeniably bleak economic fundamentals as the reason "for a rethinking of the current development strategies", the MTR set out the new directions. It called for "changes in the existing working and institutional arrangements" and for "new values" to be adopted in order "to build a better society which will be united, self-reliant and progressive" (Malaysia 1984: 11).

It inveighed against the "subsidy mentality" amongst farmers, businessmen and in general, and extolled the virtues of thrift, hard work and individual self-reliance. With almost touching faith in private enterprise and competition, it preached the virtues of accumulation via enterprise, not get-rich-quick schemes through sales of assets and tribute.

With a penchant for things big—large farms, large enterprises, large population, urbanization, heavy industry—the programme also called for "responsible, strong and firm leadership with clear policies and instructions at all levels of society . . ." (*ibid.*: 30), and "leadership by example" supported by a clean and efficient Government administration.

And towards all of this, Islam was to play its part: "With Muslims forming the majority of the population in the country, aspects of the religion, particularly for accelerating economic development, receptiveness and readiness to utilize advancements in knowledge, especially scientific knowledge, and toleration of diversity in religious practices will have to be harnessed for the good of the nation" (*ibid.*: 28–9).[45]

---

[45] It was repeated in his speech to the crucial 38th UMNO General Assembly of April 1987 (translation in *The Star* 25 April 1987) and again at the 1st General Assembly of the new UMNO (*Utusan Malaysia* 30 October 1988).

As has been pointed out, this amounts to a latter-day "Protestant Ethic" (Mauzy

The same set of ideas has been presented time and again, with almost religious fervour: a latter-day Samuel Smiles' philosophy of rugged individual endeavour and of lifting oneself by one's own bootstraps. The primary policy manifestations of this initiative were curtailment of public expenditure, control over bureaucratically managed public enterprises, deregulation of the economy coupled with regulation of labour, and privatization.

While a superficial reading of the "Malay Dilemma" might suggest an incongruity of thought, there is really no contradiction between this and the underlying analysis of that work. In brief, and very crassly put, the "Malay Dilemma" portrays the Malays as weaklings. The solution then accepted was protection. But the protection was meant to breed a stratum of Malay capitalists who would be capable of standing on their own feet. Instead, in Mahathir's view, that protection had largely served to create a dependent Malay business community, with some exceptions.[46]

Furthermore, the protection was intended against non-Malay, specifically Chinese, capital. To the extent that Chinese capital, although benefitting in no mean way from the growth generated by the NEP, has been put in its place, and there is now a significant Malay economic presence, such protection may no longer be absolutely necessary, even if political and other considerations mean it cannot be done away with.[47] Government, after all, directly or indirectly controls the commanding heights of the

---

& Milne 1986: 87). Mauzy and Milne use the term in connection with the "Look East" policy, being somewhat uncertain about the Islamization policy. They present a good discussion of the ambiguities of the latter.

The ambiguities do not lie only with Mahathir, but with the very nature of such a policy in the context of Islam in Malaysia. Thus, while some large capitalists would find themselves in broad agreement with most of the planks of Mahathir's policy, they feel discomfited by the Islamization drive. See, e.g., Malek Merican (1987).

[46] Symptomatic of Mahathir's view is his assessment of the NEP in an interview with *Malaysian Business* (Jayasankaran, 1988a). Also his opening speech to the April 1987 UMNO General Assembly (*Star* 25 April 1987).

[47] In an interview in July 1983, Mahathir said: "Previously there were no bumiputera companies or agencies which could participate (in privatization) . . . . . But now we have many bumiputera companies including PNB which owns Guthrie, Sime Darby, Boustead and as well as bumiputera individuals who are capable of participating in the privatization programme . . ." (Rosnah Majid 1985: 258; my translation).

In June 1981, at the general assembly of UMNO Women and Youth, after attributing the colonization of the Malay states to laziness, he added: "If Malay workers and students are over-protected, they will bring adverse consequences to their people, the nation, religion and to themselves . . . . We must guard against over-indulging the Malays because there is nothing more destructive than pampering . . . . When the Malays become conceited and arrogant because of the power in their hands, when they do not want to pursue knowledge because power can

economy,[48] in particular, the financial sector (as members of the UMNO opposition have been finding out much to their dismay). The economic environment of the mid-1980s saw Chinese capital, except for the largest, generally lose ground. At the same time, large Chinese capitals are more than happy to take on Malay partners and there are now significant linkages between large Chinese and Malay capital. The Chinese response to NEP, a string of holding companies and companies to mobilise capital culminating in Multi-Purpose Holdings, is in tatters. The party behind it, the MCA, even had problems meeting payments for its headquarters building. Finally, in April 1989, it had to face the ignominy of a takeover-bid upon Multi-Purpose Holdings. In contrast, UMNO has been able to reorganize its stable of companies and is now one of the country's most important corporate players (Gomez 1990).

Given the situation, Malays and aspiring Malay capitalists needed not so much protection as prodding, and Mahathir was the man for it.[49] Such a consideration dove-tailed ideology with economic fundamentals, namely, the precarious financial situation of the state. In addition, as already noted, the existence of well-established large bumiputera capitalists and firms, including UMNO's, provided assurance of a continued significant bumiputera presence in the economy. To the extent that Malays still could not go it alone, the solution was to be found in partnership with the appropriate capital, to provide the skills and the technology. Non-Malays could, if they wanted to, join in, but still subject to NEP constraints. In any case, Mahathir places no great faith in them, seeing them as naturally footloose. The main thing was that the umbrella of the state was to shrink: the state would help those who helped themselves. Inevitably, those most capable of helping themselves were the large capitalists and the large corporations.

In the context of the developments since 1970 and the depressed economic circumstances, stresses and strains were inevitable. Even in the best of circumstances, they would have required adroit government

---

control other people's knowledge, when the Malays do not want to work or carry arms to defend themselves, these are signs that the Malays are half-way down the road to destruction. Initial symptoms of these destructive values among the Malays are discernible" (Morais pp. 227; 230. Translation modified according to the original text as reprinted in A. Ghani Ismail 1983: Appendix D).

[48] The bulk of this is now held by Permodalan Nasional Berhad (PNB), the National Equity Corporation, set up in 1978 to take over assets acquired by the state on behalf of bumiputera. It has been given the choice pickings and has added to them. PNB is headed by Tun Ismail Ali, the well-respected former Governor of Bank Negara and Mahathir's brother-in-law. For a convenient source on PNB see, *Asiaweek*, 20 May 1988. See also, Gale (1981: 189–193); Jesudason (1988: 86–98 *passim*.)

[49] Musa Hitam characterized Mahathir in the following terms: ". . . the current prime minister . . says like the good doctor that he is, 'this is good for you, take it' . . . . The problem with Dr Mahathir is he is crass, rough and hard. This man pushes things down your throat . . . . ." (*The Correspondent* November 1988).

management. In the event, given Mahathir's conservative, authoritarian political outlook—his fears of "individualism" and "individual freedom" are all too well-known, as are his views regarding political participation and expression,[50] labour unions,[51] and inequality, aside from ethnic inequalities[52]—and his general impatience with challenges to his agenda, the slide towards executive hypertrophy and the arrogation of greater executive powers was perhaps predictable, particularly as the challenges mounted. Progressive centralization of power in the Executive, finally in the Prime Minister himself, had occurred under Mahathir's predecessors, but accelerated when he came to office. Deemed essential to launching Malaysia into NIC status, it took a relatively benign form initially, only to transform into what many see as a qualitative and dangerous change to the political order as the challenges became more intractable.[53]

Stresses and Strains

A brief examination of the lines of stress may help unravel some of the complex knot of alignments,[54] as well as help account for some of the actions taken. The lines of stress were essentially a consequence of the social structure and commercial culture created by the first dozen years of

---

[50] His short essay, "Pressure Group Dalam Demokrasi", on pressure groups in a democracy in Mahathir (1976) is typical.

[51] See, Mahathir (1970: 108). See also his speech to the UMNO Women and Youth divisions on 25 June 1981 (Morais 1982: 223-232; original text in A. Ghani Ismail 1983: Appendix D).

[52] On inequality, his views are typically conveyed by an article in Mahathir (1976) entitled "Yang Miskin Bertambah Miskin, Yang Kaya Bertambah Kaya!" ("The Poor Get Poorer, The Rich Get Richer!") which is a sustained invective against the slogan.

[53] See, for a representative sample of Mahathir's views, Jayasankaran (1988a; 1988b).

With respect to centralization of decision making in the Prime Minister himself and his personalization of all critical comments, we have Musa Hitam's testimony, particularly the video-tape that was circulated at the time of the Johor Baru by-election in August 1988. There is little reason to doubt Musa's account, just as there is little reason to question Mahathir's riposte that if cabinet or UMNO Supreme Council dissidents don't speak out then that's their problem. Malaysians will be quite familiar with the atmosphere of meetings conducted in the manner that Musa describes

This sense of a growing authoritarian state is analysed from a different perspective, that of the bureaucratic-authoritarian state, by Johan Saravanamuttu (1987).

[54] There can never be any single explanation for the complex alignments which, as already noted, are a consequence of multiplex individual considerations, both of a short- and long-term nature. Besides the sorts of considerations mentioned earlier, one should add the fact that Malaysia participates in a world culture, one aspect of which tends towards increasing consciousness of democratic values, human

NEP coupled with the economic boom.[55]

For the purposes of this paper, the relevant aspect of the social structure resulting from the NEP was the creation of a more differentiated Malay community, in particular the rise of a differentiated capitalist stratum and of a differentiated bureaucratic elite. The capitalist stratum came to comprise two broad categories. One consisted of large capitalists[56] some of whom may originally have obtained their start through state sponsorship or political patronage but had grown to the point where they were increasingly independent of such sponsorship or patronage and indeed viewed them as market distortions and obstructions to growth.[57] To this group, restructuring goals, in the sense of equity targets, do not have much meaning, particularly in the context of a slowing down of growth.[58] Their own interests dictate the maximum growth possible and meaningful measures towards that end. Generally staying out of the political arena, but having channels to make their views known, they maintain an independent view

---

rights, etc. Thus, many who might have remained neutral in the UMNO conflict turned on Mahathir and, for lack of a better choice, cheered on the Razaleigh side, because of a series of actions and legislation that represented a serious slide towards greater authoritarianism.

[55] While the important aspect of the social structure created by the NEP pertains primarily to the Malays, the commercial culture it has spawned cuts across all ethnic groups. The series of spectacular commercial failures in the 1980s bears ample testimony to the speculative, gambling, get-rich-quick style that set in. But this may be an aspect of the culture of late capitalism. See, *Business Week's* 16 September 1985 issue's cover story entitled "The Casino Society".

[56] The term is used loosely to include not just owners of capital, but senior managerial personnel. Such a usage is justifiable given the community of interest between owners of capital and the managerial personnel who actually oversee the use of this capital.

[57] Robison (1987) provides what may perhaps be considered as parallel developments in Indonesia.

[58] Thus, Mokhzani Rahim, speaking at a seminar on the NEP after 1990 suggested that bumiputera should get rid of the idea of owning 30% of every venture, that "ownership of corporate wealth does not matter". Instead of being constrained by the "old idea of corporate ownership", he advised bumiputera to go for growth and the creation of new industries which bring employment opportunities; restructuring would follow upon this. Mokhzani was formerly a professor of economics at the University of Malaya and is now President of the Malaysian Employers' Federation as well as Executive Chairman of Innovest, holder of the Kentucky Fried Chicken franchise and other fast food chains. See, *The Star* 27 March 1987.

These views were partially repeated by another speaker, Malek Merican, at the same seminar. Malek proposed scrapping the NEP and replacing it with a National Growth Policy, which would differ from the NEP mainly by doing away with "forced restructuring". In his view, "to put the emphasis permanently on restructuring, the provision of cheap minority shares from non-Bumi companies, will only mislead the Bumis to a path of national economic stagnation" (Malek Merican 1987: 20). Malek Merican was an official in the Malaysian Treasury from

on Government actions, approving or disapproving as the case may be.[59]

The other category in the capitalist stratum consists primarily of small and medium capitalists, many of them contractors, highly dependent upon state and political patronage for their very survival. The small and medium capitalists are precisely the ones active in UMNO, vocal in their complaints about patronage abuses and privatization to allegedly favoured persons. At the same time, public sector involvement in the economy is bothersome to them as it provides yet another competitor, and they wish for direct transfer of state acquired assets to themselves rather than to trust agencies. In that sense, the equity aspect of restructuring remains an important goal to them. This category is also precisely the one that was hardest hit by the recession, the tightening up of credit, the cutbacks in Government expenditure and the centralization of economic assets in fewer public enterprises or trust agencies.[60]

UMNO itself or, given the centralization of power within it, the UMNO

1959–1974, rising to the position of deputy secretary-general. He then went on to become managing director of Aseambankers Malaysia, before becoming managing director of Arab-Malaysian Merchant Bank, AMMB, the merchant banking arm of Azman Hashim's conglomerate. On Azman Hashim, see Jesudason (1988: 106–107).

Daim Zainuddin, another large capitalist before becoming Minister of Finance, at least partially shares these views, restraining demands to up the equity percentage and shifting the question to poverty eradication. Talk of poverty eradication appears to be code for downplaying the equity aspect of restructuring. See the interview with Daim in 1984 in Rosnah Majid (1985: 285–305); also *Asiaweek*, 20 May 1988. Compare these views with Mahathir's, as discussed above. See also Mahathir's opening speech at the above-mentioned seminar as reported in *Star* 25 March 1987.

[59] Thus, they would disapprove of the national car project, and the wisdom of other HICOM investments, but approve of measures to curb wage increases, or deregulation. See for example *The Star* 13 August 1987, for Mokhzani's views on escalating wages.

Cf. Jesudason's (1988: 100-109) assessment of this category of persons.

[60] The relatively more anonymous and disperse nature of this category makes it harder to collate secondary sources. But one could for instance take the reactions of Moehamad Izat Emir to Malek Merican's views, set out earlier, as partially representative of this category. Moehamad Izat is the president of the Federal Territory Malay Chamber of Commerce and Industry. As with its Chinese counterpart, it comprises a majority of small and medium capitalists. In his view, "the NEP must complete its course within the specified period" but added that there may be "no choice but to extend the NEP for a longer period". While expressing agreement with Malek Merican's forcefully stated view that giving cheap shares to bumiputera is not the solution, he added, "but if there is an opportunity for a bumiputera candidate to buy one-third of the shares of a non-bumiputera company because he is capable, has talent and is qualified, then the financial institutions should finance his purchase and hold the shares until he pays back the loan through his salary, director's fees, bonus and other dividends" (*The Sunday Star* 10 May 1987.

executive, is actually a large capitalist capable now of standing on its own feet,[61] even though it continues to be a beneficiary of state awards. Thus how UMNO's economic empire is run is relevant to the interests of the other groups.

The other relevant aspect of social structure derived from the increasingly interventionist posture of the state with respect to the economy. This produced a more complex bureaucratic formation, not only as between branches but also between federal and state bureaucracies. Without going into details, one might suggest, minimally, a distinction between the branches with primarily control functions, such as the Treasury Department in the Ministry of Finance, the Economic and Planning Unit (EPU) or the Implementation-Coordination Unit (ICU) of the Prime Minister's Department, the Ministry of Public Enterprises or the Ministry of Trade and Industry or even Bank Negara itself, and those with primarily implementation functions such as the public enterprises. Public enterprises are divided between federal and state enterprises, each jealous of its own turf even while trying to enlarge it.[62] As already mentioned, the NEP, whatever other interests it served, enhanced considerably the power of bureaucrats, particularly control bureaucrats who obtained a wide range of discretionary powers which could be converted into other resources, not least through corruption. Public enterprise bureaucrats also benefitted from the NEP. But the changes in policy—deregulation, privatization—in the 1980s have affected them negatively, although in different ways. Bureaucrats with control functions have been disciplined, their discretionary powers curtailed except, perhaps, with respect to public enterprises.

See also, *Far Eastern Economic Review*, 13 March 1978, for some views on the disadvantaged position of the smaller businessmen in the face of large public enterprises, or of enterprises set up by such as royalty. Again, it may be useful to compare the situation to that in Indonesia where the Muslim petty-capitalists have also been disadvantaged by the setting up of large public enterprises and monopolies involving the MNCs, the generals and the Chinese towkays (Robison, 1987: Ch. 10).

[61] For UMNO's economic empire, see *Far Eastern Economic Review* 10 October 1988; 6 October 1988; Gomez 1990. There are some caveats to the statement that UMNO as a business corporation can stand on its own. First, there is a close tie-up between public enterprises and trust agencies, including some of the companies held by PNB, and the UMNO corporate empire, and between that and certain other private sector companies. This derives from the blurring of the distinction between party and Government resulting from the extended period over which UMNO has been the major party of Government. Secondly, there appears to be a tendency, deriving probably from the need for cash for party political purposes, a need which escalated with Government cutbacks and the open rift in UMNO, to engage in all sorts of financial manipulations, mainly through the stock exchange (*Far Eastern Economic Review*, 6 October 1988).

[62] See Gale (1981) for some discussion of the tensions between public enterprises *per se* and between federal and state public enterprises. A specific articulation of tensions between federal and state enterprises and between control and

There are complex linkages, both of tension and cooperation, within and between these various formations. For instance, there has been long standing tension between small and medium, and even large capitalists, and some of the larger public enterprises, as there are tensions between control bodies, public enterprises and private sector capitalists. Such linkages become even more complicated when interests become lodged within some or all of these bodies or groupings.

Turning to the commercial culture created in the context of the NEP, there are two aspects to be considered. The first is what might simply be referred to as a gambling, speculative style of business. It is characterized by short time horizons, quick profits, and jumping on the bandwagon, whether it be construction, the stock market or the retailing market. Its instruments were easy credit and financial "wizardry". For some of the larger capitalists, the easy credit and booming stock market allowed them plenty of room for financial "wizardry" in the form of using share issues or flotations to realise a quick profit and to raise capital for takeovers and rapid expansion. The recession, the stock market collapse and Government cutbacks resulted in many being left high and dry when the economic crunch came.

The other aspect is the "subsidy mentality", the expectation of hand-outs and bail-outs. This was perhaps most highly developed in the public sector. An example of this was the stance of the director and general manager of Perwaja, the $1.2 billion flagship steel mill of state-owned HICOM. Queried about the length of protection he desired as an "infant industry", he responded: "If possible we want to be protected forever" (*Malaysian Business*, 16 May 1987). Finally, he suggested that the government should take over all of Perwaja debts, amounting to 41 billion yen, saying, "If Perwaja could shift the entire burden to the government, then it would be viable overnight, and the company could really be the flagship of the heavy industry thrust" (*ibid.*).[63]

Hitherto, public enterprises were often seen, politely, as "social enterprises", viz., they might not be profitable and the state would have to keep pouring money into them, but they were necessary to achieving NEP equity goals and the price of providing experience, jobs and skills. Partly because of the shortage of Malay management personnel, the enterprises were managed by political appointees or seconded senior bureaucrats who

---

implementation branches can be found in Mohamed Ali bin Hj Hashim (1987). Mohamed Ali is the Executive Director of the Johor State Economic Development Corporation, one of the most successful state-level public enterprises, as well as the former president of the association of public enterprises.

[63] In mid-1988, there was a reorganization of HICOM, including Perwaja and Proton, the national car company. Japanese management consultants and managers were brought in as well as local private sector entrepreneurs such as United Motor Works' (Chinese) chairman, in an attempt to turn the corporation around and make it self-sustaining (*Asian Wall Street Journal* 27 June 1988).

often saw them as an extension of the bureaucracy or, worse, as personal sinecures. Both management and workers assumed that their jobs were relatively safe, much as in the civil service. Opportunities for such appointments have shrunk and will probably continue to shrink. Furthermore, with the institution of controls, even if partial and limited, these formerly plum appointments have become uncomfortable ones. There was bound to be resentment against the controls and the withdrawal of support, particularly in the case of ailing companies.

Resentment of another sort came from those public enterprises that were relatively successful. They found Government interference and changes in regulations irksome. In addition, they felt short-changed when their choice holdings or companies were transferred to PNB at book rather than market value, or were put up for privatization. This meant that they were left with the less profitable concerns which, they feared, would be the basis of assessment. PERNAS, for instance, was one of the most ambitious of NEP federal level public enterprises, and for long associated with Tengku Razaleigh, its first chairman. PERNAS was the source of sponsorship for budding small and medium Malay capitalists in construction and retailing, although it sometimes came under attack for unfair competition from, for example, Malays attempting to enter the securities market or to break into larger projects (Gale 1981: 186). In the middle and later 1970s PERNAS became a major symbol of Malay economic strength and a focus of Malay economic nationalism, when it embarked on a series of takeovers of British-owned plantation and mining companies, the most publicised being the takeover of London Tin (which resulted in the formation of corporate giant MMC, the Malaysian Mining Corporation) and Sime Darby.[64] Following upon the formation of the national unit trust, ASN, under the control of PNB whose chairman is responsible only to the Prime Minister, PERNAS had to transfer over $1 billion of its holdings, including both MMC and Sime Darby, to the former. As a result of the transfer, PERNAS reported a substantial loss in 1982 (Mehmet 1986: 109).

About such transfers, state-level public enterprises have an additional complaint: that they are a net loss to the particular state, depriving it of assets and thus stunting growth. Such enterprises argue that if they are to be assessed on commercial criteria, they should be allowed to function as commercial ventures without Government interference (Utusan Malaysia, 7 September 1988). In brief, they wish to function as private sector enterprises but with public funds (Mohamed Ali bin Hj Hashim 1987).

---

[64] It was in the context of the controversy over the London Tin takeover attempt, involving Haw Par of Singapore, that Tengku Razaleigh was proposed for the title of "Father of the Bumiputera Economy" (*Bapa Ekonomi Bumiputera*) subsequently amended to "Father of the Malaysian Economy" (*Bapa Ekonomi Malaysia*) by the Association of the Malay Chambers of Commerce. On PERNAS, see Gale (1981: Chapter 4).

Their view is that the PNB or any such trust agency should take out equity in the state-level public enterprises, taking the risks and sharing the profits and, possibly, contributing management expertise. Alternatively, only federal-level enterprises should be required to transfer their assets to PNB (*Utusan Malaysia* 7 September 1988).[65] But some opinions go even further to reject transfers of shares, whether between public enterprises and trust agencies or between other enterprises and public enterprises and trust agencies, as the way forward. Instead, they hold that restructuring which only involves transfers of assets should not be encouraged if the capital can be invested in new activities as this would contribute more to growth in production, job opportunities and national competitiveness (Mohamed Ali bin Hj Hashim 1987: 24–25).

This social-commercial structure and culture, in the context of the economic recession and the shift in Government policy, threw up the main social forces that found expression in UMNO in the form of a deep-seated factionalism. Simultaneously, the increased differentiation of society and the continuing presence of ethnic issues, given the economic situation and the local political context of democratic authoritarianism, resulted in a variegated series of challenges to Government, ranging from civil liberties to, of course, the NEP itself, at a time when Government was attempting to reconstitute the social, economic and political order.

The Split

The above provides some pointers to the broad social dimensions of the UMNO conflict and the broad alignments involved. One estimate of the

---

[65] While this illustrates the centrality of patronage politics and the resistance of state-level power holders to surrender control of resources which can be used to secure their power bases, it is also true that these enterprises have acquired interests of their own, even if they do have to accomodate the patronage politics of state-level politicians, which they oppose at another level. For a well-considered statement of such interests, see Mohamed Ali bin Hj Hashim (1987).

As an instance of opposition to patronage, Mohamed Ali suggested that the criteria for appointment and termination of services should be purely commercial and based upon performance (*ibid.*: 28). He urged Government to *reject* both the view that they should be protected under all circumstances and the view that the restructuring programme should be implemented on a trusteeship principle which gives priority to distribution, subsidies and patronage (*ibid.*: 30). In this light, he argued that privatization was irrelevant, that the meaning of "entrepreneur" should be broadened to include executive officers in public enterprises, that all business opportunities should be allocated on a commercial and competitive basis, that control bodies such as the ministries should avoid all measures that will restrict growth, that the 30 percent goal need not be in all sectors, and that public enterprises will have to accept competition as the basis of business and entrepreneurship as the basis of growth (*ibid.*: 30–36 *passim*).

composition of the delegates to the 1987 UMNO General Assembly is revealing. According to this estimate, businessmen made up 25 percent of the delegates, civil servants 23 percent, Members of Parliament and State Assemblymen 19 percent, community development officers 5 percent, teachers 19 percent and professionals and others 1 percent (Shamsul A.B. 1988: 180).[66] The businessmen were generally small and medium capitalists, while the civil servants were more likely to be middle-ranking bureaucrats—precisely two categories which, by the account above, had reason to be unhappy with Mahathir. Members of Parliament and State Assemblymen, on the other hand, would, in many instances, be beholden to the executive for their seats and, given the associated perks, would tend to be cautious and go with the incumbent.[67] Teachers, the traditional base of UMNO, would again generally go with the incumbent. But their position had been eroded over the years: in 1981, they formed 40 percent, and in 1984, 32 percent, of the delegates. Is it coincidental that the sum of businessmen and civil servants come up to 48 percent, just slightly short of the percentage that Tengku Razaleigh actually received in 1987, or is it the case that a significant proportion of them formed the solid base from which Tengku Razaleigh campaigned, aided, this time, by the 1985–87 recession?

But as in any conflict of this nature, one cannot expect lines to be clearcut: power bases, immediate interests, perceived or real advantages, patronage, loyalties, commitments, etc. all serve to blur the picture.[68] What is important is the admixture of the policy directions, the socio-cultural, economic and political situation resulting from the NEP itself and the worst recession since the Great Depression. All it needed was a match. Mahathir's personality ("leadership style"), the unsettled and unsettling question of who was to succeed Mahathir leading to power plays in the upper reaches of Government, and Tengku Razaleigh's and Musa Hitam's decision to challenge Mahathir, provided that match.

---

[66] That leaves another 8 percent unaccounted for.

[67] One such, legal, "perk" is the pension, with gratuity, given to members of parliament, a point of friction between civil servants and politicians. A member of parliament gets a pension of $750 for life after serving three years, or $1,500 for life after six years, together with a gratuity. In addition, a person who has served as both a state assemblyman and a member of parliament (and as a minister) has his or her pension calculated on the combined salaries. Hence, the fights for selection to be a candidate for political office. This, incidentally, gives great leverage to the executive, which has the final, if not the first, say on candidates.

[68] A reader interested in details of who is who and how they may be linked together is directed to Chamil Wariya (1988). Shamsul A.B. (1988) provides a good account of the 1987 UMNO General Assembly, including some details of who voted with whom and who switched sides at the last minute. A. Ghani Ismail (1983) provides a longer view of the 1987 conflict.

That there were policy issues at stake should be evident, at the very least in the negative form of opposition to the policy direction adopted by Mahathir. But it was also as much an implicit push for continuing with the old policies. This was understandable; as practical policy had been that of patronage, a departure (in the sense of a narrowing of such patronage) was characterized as "cronyism". This was articulated as the issue of "party controlling Government", that is, who should determine policy.

That there were and are policy issues involved was cogently characterized by Malek Merican (1987).[69] He outlined two polar types representing the limiting options on the NEP. These polar types he labelled "Group A" and "Group B".

In his characterization, "members of Group A argue about the ultimate proportions of corporate equities the Bumis should own; whether the NEP restructuring effort should be pushed more vigorously or implemented more slowly" (Malek Merican 1987: 5). In contrast, "Group B worries about the need for a fundamental modification or replacement of the NEP restructuring exercise as presently conceived because . . . this programme in itself will cause the Malaysian economy to stagnate" (*ibid.*). Hence, he observed, Group B "seeks to formulate other ways of promoting the interest of Bumis so as to be consistent with the need to promote faster development of the Malaysian economy" (*ibid.*).

Within Group A, Malek identified "militant" and "moderate" groups. "Militants" demand more vigorous implementation of the 30 percent target in view of its likely non-attainment by 1990, indeed demand that the percentage should be raised, whereas "moderates" essentially argue for the setting of percentage, but not time, targets.

Group B members were not divided into sub-groups but viewed as having a set of concerns, of varying importance for different members: the impact upon growth, the negative effects of NEP such as corruption resulting from restrictive regulations, and Islamization.[70]

The concern over growth derived from the fear that the "eagerness to assist the Bumis" and "Malaysian nationalism" may have "driven away more investments than we should" (*ibid.*: 8; Cf. Jesudason, 1988). In this

---

[69] The ensuing draws from this paper. It is one of the most coherent statements of the various options on the NEP and deserves to be more widely known. Press reports concentrated on his proposals for a National Growth Policy, on which see note 58.

[70] Malek's discussion of Islamization clearly derived from observation of actual results of the programme. This is indicated by his statement that the programme "implicitly questions the need to refashion Bumi individuals to make a success of the NEP programme" (Malek Merican 1987: 6). As has been noted above, Islamization is precisely directed at refashioning bumiputera individuals. That the programme carries with it great ambiguity has already been remarked on.

[71] The ICA was first put up in 1975 requiring all firms employing more than 50 workers and with paid-up capital exceeding $100,000 to take out a licence to

regard, he noted that relaxations on foreign investments, equity conditions and the Industrial Coordination Act (ICA),[71] the "strong undertaking to promote economic growth came as a major shock to members of Group A, who continue to hanker to require all firms to sell at least 30 percent, if not more, to Bumis" (*ibid.*: 10).

As for the negative effects of the NEP, Group B is characterized as concerned that "Bumis and non-Bumis are beginning to believe that they should aim to become power brokers and influence pedlars rather than dedicate themselves to become the most efficient managers, producers and manufacturers" (*ibid.*: 11).

There should be little doubt as to who broadly belongs to Group A and Group B in the above analysis. This may be compared with another, more personalized, analysis made in the context of the 1975–1977 UMNO conflict. That analysis (BI 1977) drew an interesting distinction between Mahathir and Razaleigh, both of whom were located within the bureaucratic-technocratic side in that conflict.[72] It contended that "Mahathir is identified with the technocrat group that would like to see tighter controls on public enterprises and a reduction in the degree of direct competition with Malay businessmen", whereas "the other contender in the bureaucratic camp for the prime ministership, Tengku Razaleigh . . . . believes in aggressive bureaucratic means to shift more resources into Malay hands,

---

manufacture one or more products for each location or manufacturing activity, i.e., it affected mainly small and medium Chinese capitalists. Such a licence was subject to conditions which the licensing officer deemed expedient and necessary, giving the licensing officer, a bureaucrat in the relevant controlling body, great discretion. The Chinese Chambers of Commerce protested against it. It was then amended to cover firms employing more than 25 workers with paid-up capital of more than $250,000. In this form, the Act held till 1985, despite years of protests, when it was amended to cover firms with more than 50 employees and more than $1 million paid-up capital. It was amended again in 1986, this time to cover firms with more than 75 employees and $2.5 million paid-up capital.

After the ICA was first passed, there was reportedly great bureaucratic resistance to amendments, "despite pressure from Deputy Prime Minister Mahathir, who has privately stated his dissatisfaction with the bureaucratic obstructionism and has even publicly stated that the government is on the verge of revoking the act entirely" (BI 1977: 98).

In this regard, it is one of the ironies of politics that in the 1981 and 1984 contest for the Deputy Presidency between Tengku Razaleigh and Musa Hitam, Tengku Razaleigh was tarred with being pro-Chinese. See, A. Ghani Ismail (1983).

[72] In brief, the consultancy group characterized the conflict then as one between "party-crats" who drew their power base from within the party, and technocrats-bureaucrats whose power, enhanced by the NEP, resided within the bureaucracy. The analysis attempted to disentangle the components of this technocrat-bureaucrat coalition, distinguishing between different segments and suggesting that these segments had different policy orientations, submerged temporarily by the need to survive the onslaught by the "party-crats". See, BI (1977: 2 & 3).

even at the cost of serious economic dislocations and inefficiencies" (BI 1977: 90). It thus predicted that "if Deputy Prime Minister Mahathir remains in power . . . there will be a tendency toward tighter controls over the bureaucracy", but "if the political power of Razaleigh Hamzah increases, there will be a tendency to acceleration of bureaucratic expansionism" (ibid.: 101). If this reckoning is correct, Razaleigh was the natural leader of the opposition to Mahathir.[73]

Conclusion

By no means comprehensive, and in many ways tentative, this attempt to delineate the basic parameters of the UMNO conflict argues that it is more than just a factional struggle between two blocs, both marriages of convenience, each trying to get a larger piece of the economic pie. It is that, but it is also more than that and the outcome, as the conduct of it, has borne and will bear serious implications for the Malaysian society and polity. The tragedy is that neither of the two main outcomes is particularly palatable in the short- to medium-term. One outcome apparently leads to bureaucratic hypertrophy, hand-outs, potential economic stagnation and financial crisis. The other outcome, to even be an outcome, means an administered and increasingly authoritarian society and polity under a hypertrophied executive with greatly reduced space for popular partici-pation, except as a disciplined work-force.

But there is another outcome which, although unlikely, might still be possible. Pushed against the wall, the Razaleigh faction has increasingly adopted the stance of an opposition as a consequence of experiencing the treatment meted out to the opposition. If an opposition coalition were to be formed out of this, then Malaysia would have a two-party system, each a coalition of ethnic parties. That outcome might at least have the possible merit of reducing the level of ethnic "politicking", thus allowing other issues to emerge.

But this seems a remote possibility, not least because the Razaleigh faction remains entrapped within the ideological strait-jacket that UMNO is the party of the Malays; that the Malays will never accept any other party except UMNO. Their reluctance to formalize their opposition status, the contradictions within which they are caught—on the one hand, cam-paigning against candidates from the ruling coalition, on the other, insist-ing that they subscribe to the principles of the ruling coalition—in all likelihood means their eventual marginalization.

---

[73] See also note 17. To repeat, there is no real necessity to assume that Razaleigh represents a different policy option. The BI analysis is given because it is rare to find social science predictions that even come out half right. But it might be dead wrong on Razaleigh.

The final and most likely outcome is a partial return to the *status quo ante*, which simply brings us back to a consideration of the original two outcomes mentioned above. Many of the UMNO dissidents will switch their overt alignment according to the dictates of prudence. This has been encouraged by the Mahathir side.[74] Thus, much-publicized applications to join the new UMNO by erstwhile supporters of Tengku Razaleigh only mean that the conflict is being reimported into what was intended to be a "purified" UMNO. Such shifts will, in all probability, accelerate given the increased opportunities available with the present and foreseeable healthy state of the economy and in the event, widely expected, of a convincing Mahathir win, at the level of parliamentary seats, in a snap general elections.

Postscript

The above was written in early May 1989, and intellectual honesty dictates that the argument should not be amended to incorporate the wisdom of hindsight. However, it is pertinent to point out that the major development since then has been the formalization of the Razaleigh faction as an opposition political party. Adopting the same name as had been assumed by the faction, namely Semangat '46, it laid claim to being the true heir of the original UMNO and defined as one of its major goals, should it come to power in the impending general elections, the legalization of the old UMNO.

The formation of this party meant that the contest with the new UMNO essentially acquired a new form. The removal of Mahathir could no longer be an internal UMNO affair, to be brought about by UMNO members and delegates. Instead, it had to be done through the national electoral process, and the party had to convince the electorate that it could become the party of government. To do so, it had to project an image of difference, that is, be an opposition party, with an alternative platform.

Given the ethnic equation, it had to be, first of all, a Malay party. To distinguish itself from the new UMNO, it projected itself as standing for the unity of all Malays, and this found expression in an alliance with the Parti Islam (PAS) and other smaller Malay-Muslim parties, formalized as the Angkatan Perpaduan Ummah (APU). Subsequently, alliances were concluded by Semangat '46 with the Chinese based opposition Democratic Action Party (DAP), and the Malay based Parti Rakyat Malaysia (PRM), formerly the Parti Sosialis Rakyat Malaysia (PSRM). Thus, an ostensible opposition coalition materialized, holding out the possible development of two-party politics, each a coalition of primarily ethnic parties.

---

[74] Originally, the new UMNO was meant to exclude the dissidents. But the depth of feeling, which they misgauged, caused a change and an opening of the doors.

Semangat '46 projected the new UMNO as careless of the interests and needs of the Malay masses, and as subverting the intent and thrust of the New Economic Policy. In particular, it cast Mahathir as not paying sufficient attention to rural development in his quest for industrialization and urbanization.

To the wider audience, in concert with its allies, it attempted to project what might be described as a rudimentary social democratic policy of caring government. It also took up the issues that the opposition had been hammering at through the 1980s: corruption, abuse of power, authoritarianism and the erosion of democratic rights, the undermining of the independence of the judiciary, and so on. The examples used in illustration of such arguments were the ones made familiar by the opposition. It even promised to re-open consideration of the contract for the North-South Highway given to UEM, and to amend, perhaps even abolish, the Internal Security Act.

For a while, the possibility of a change of government appeared to capture the imagination of the public and the rallies organized by Semangat '46 and their allies drew mammoth crowds. However, the new UMNO's counter-attack, coupled with the booming economy and the absence of fundamental ideological, despite policy, differences between the Malay supporters of Semangat '46 and of the new UMNO started to turn the tide. As state largesse increased—a result of the conflict—in the greatly improved economic climate, economic exclusion proved too much for many of Semangat '46 supporters.

In addition, the new UMNO, by virtue of its command of government, was able to utilise state resources for party-political ends and thus exchange of economic goods for political support, if only out of a deep-rooted cultural sense of gratitude. Command of power also allowed the new UMNO to acquire the vast assets of the old UMNO, via the mechanism of corporate re-structuring.

Thus, by August 1990, Semangat '46 appeared to have past its peak and headed towards electoral defeat. Some observers believe that no matter what happens to Semangat '46, the conflicts of the past few years have changed the face of Malay and Malaysian politics for good. However, one may well doubt this. True, this paper has argued that the conflicts were themselves a consequence of the altered social structure of Malay society. In that sense, it signals a change in Malay politics, albeit within certain ideological parameters. But if the idea of a change in Malay politics means that the Malay party of government, UMNO (old or new), will no longer be the central axis of Malay politics and the arena in which conflicts are fought out, then it must be pointed out that historical memory in the modern world is not only extremely short but also rather malleable. In the event of a convincing Barisan Nasional, hence UMNO, victory, Semangat '46 will be quickly forgotten, dismissed as an unpleasant and alien irruption fermented by the base ambitions of one man, suitably assimilated to any number of other events in Malay history and consigned to the dustbin of Malay historical memory. UMNO will once again set the definitive tone and texture of Malay, thus Malaysian, politics, and its power to do so will have been enhanced, in the medium term, by the state powers acquired over the last few years.

Bibliography

A. Ghani Ismail, 1983. *Razaleigh Lawan Musa: Pusingan Kedua 1984*, Taiping, Perak: IJS Communications.

Bank Negara Malaysia (various years), *Annual Report*.

Business International, 1977. *Malaysia to 1980: Economic and Political Outlook for Business Planners*, Hong Kong: Business International.

Chamil Wariya, 1988. *UMNO Era Mahathir*, Kuala Lumpur: Penerbit Fajar Bakti.

Crouch, H., 1980. "The UMNO Crisis: 1975–1977" in H. Crouch, Lee K.H. & M. Ong (eds), *Malaysian Politics and the 1978 Elections*, pp. 11–36, Kuala Lumpur: Oxford University Press.

Funston, J., 1980. *Malay Politics in Malaysia: A Study of UMNO and PAS*, Kuala Lumpur: Heinemann.

Gale, Bruce, 1981. *Politics and Public Enterprise in Malaysia*, Petaling Jaya, Selangor: Eastern Universities (M) Press.

Gale, Bruce, 1982. *Musa Hitam: A Political Biography*, Petaling Jaya, Selangor: Eastern Universities (M) Press.

Gomez, Edmund T., 1990. *Politics in Business: UMNO's Corporate Investments*, Kuala Lumpur: Forum.

IMF (International Monetary Fund), 1987. *Malaysia - Recent Economic Developments*. Background paper SM/87/163 for the 1987 Article IV consultations with Malaysia.

Jayasankaran, S., 1988a. "Interview: Premier in Power", *Malaysian Business*, January 1.

Jayasankaran, S., 1988b. "Mahathir: The Man and the PM", *Malaysian Business*, January 1.

Jesudason, J., 1988. *Ethnicity and the Economy: The State, Chinese Business, and Multinationals in Malaysia*, Singapore: Oxford University Press.

Johan Saravanamuttu, 1987. "The State, Authoritarianism and Industrialization: Reflections on the Malaysian Case", *Kajian Malaysia: Journal of Malaysian Studies*, 5(2).

Jomo Kwame Sundaram, 1978. "Restructuring Society: The New Economic Policy Revisited". Paper presented at the *Fifth Malaysian Economic Convention*. Penang, 25–27 May 1978.

Jomo Kwame Sundaram, 1986. *A Question of Class: Capital, the State, and Uneven Development in Malaya*, Kuala Lumpur: Oxford University Press.

Jomo Kwame Sundaram, 1987. "Economic Crisis and Policy Response in Malaysia", in R. Robison, K. Hewison & R. Higgott (eds), *South East Asia in the 1980s: The Politics of Economic Crisis*, Sydney: Allen & Unwin, pp. 113–148.

Jomo Kwame Sundaram & Ishak Shari, 1986. *Development Policies and Income Inequality in Peninsular Malaysia*, Kuala Lumpur: Institute of Advanced Studies, University of Malaya.

Khor Kok Peng, 1983a. *The Malaysian Economy: Structures and Dependence*, Kuala Lumpur: Marican and Sons.

Khor Kok Peng, 1983b. *Recession and the Malaysian Economy*, Penang: Institut Masyarakat.

Khor Kok Peng, 1987. *Malaysia's Economy in Decline*, Penang: Consumers' Association of Penang.

Kongres Ekonomi Bumiputera, 1965. *Kertas-Kertas Kerja*, Kuala Lumpur: Government Printers.

Lim Mah Hui, 1985. "Contradictions in the Development of Malay Capital: State, Accumulation and Legitimation", *J. Contemporary Asia*, 11 (2).

Mahathir Mohamed, 1970. *The Malay Dilemma*, Singapore: Donald Moore Press.

Mahathir Mohamed, 1976. *Menghadapi Cabaran*, Kuala Lumpur: Pustaka Antara. (Available in English translation as *The Challenge*).

Malaysia, 1969. *The May 13th Tragedy, A Report*, Kuala Lumpur: National Operations Council.

Malaysia, 1971. *Second Malaysia Plan, 1971–75*, Kuala Lumpur: Government Printers.

Malaysia, 1984. *Mid-Term Review of the Fourth Malaysia Plan, 1981–85*, Kuala Lumpur: Government Printers.

Malaysia, 1986. *Fifth Malaysia Plan, 1986–1990*, Kuala Lumpur: Government Printers.

Malaysia Ministry of Finance (various years), *Treasury Economic Report*.

Malek Marican, Dato', 1987. "The NEP from a Private Sector Perspective". Paper presented at *Dasar Ekonomi Baru Selepas 1990: Peranan Sektor Korporat Awam*, Kuala Lumpur, 24–26 March 1987.

Mauzy, D.K. & Milne, R.S., 1986. "The Mahathir Administration: Discipline through Islam", in B. Gale (ed), *Readings in Malaysian Politics*, Petaling Jaya, Selangor: Pelanduk Publications.

Mehmet, Ozay, 1986. *Development in Malaysia: Poverty, Wealth and Trusteeship*, London: Croom Helm.

Mohamed Ali bin Hj Hashim, Dato', 1987. "Sektor Korporat Awam Sebagai Teras Pencapaian Matlamat Dasar Ekonomi Baru Selepas 1990". Paper presented at *Dasar Ekonomi Baru Selepas 1990: Peranan Sektor Korporat Awam*, Kuala Lumpur, 24–26 March 1987.

Morais, J. Victor, 1982. *Mahathir: A Profile in Courage*, Petaling Jaya, Selangor: Eastern Universities (M) Press.

Robison, R., 1986. *Indonesia: The Rise of Capital*, Sydney: Allen & Unwin.

Rosnah Majid, 1985. *Koleksi Temuramah Khas Tokoh-Tokoh*, Kuala Lumpur: Utusan Publications.

Shamsul, A.B., 1986. *From British to Bumiputera Rule*, Singapore: ISEAS.

Shamsul, A.B., 1988. "The Battle Royal: The UMNO Elections of 1987", in M. Ayoob & Ng Chee Yuen (eds), *Southeast Asian Affairs 1988*, Singapore: ISEAS.

Tunku Abdul Rahman, 1969. *May 13: Before and After*, Kuala Lumpur: Utusan Melayu Press.

Von Vorys, Karl, 1975. *Democracy Without Consensus*, Princeton: Princeton University Press.

Newspapers and News Periodicals

Asiaweek	*New Straits Times*
Far Eastern Economic Review	*Roket*
Malaysian Business	*The Star*
Mingguan Malaysia	*The Sunday Star*
Mingguan Kota	*The Correspondent*

II

Constructing Malayness

4

Malaysia's Islamic Movements

K S Jomo and Ahmad Shabery Cheek

Most political observers would agree that Malaysia's Islamic resurgence since the early seventies has undergone three phases. The beginning of an Islamic revival in the early seventies among young Malaysian Muslims mainly trained in a secular Western educational system, coupled with the growing political assertion by governments of Muslim nations, especially with the first 'oil shock' of 1973, and the renewed interest in religion generally can be said to mark the first phase. Later, the apparent alliance between ABIM (the Malaysian Islamic Youth Movement) and PAS (the main Islamic opposition party), and Iran's Islamic Revolution in the late seventies drew renewed interest to the phenomenon and its implications. More recently, the Malaysian government's Islamisation drive, ex-ABIM leader Anwar Ibrahim's switch to and rapid rise within UMNO, and the radical change in the PAS leadership since the early eighties have sustained interest in the almost enigmatic role of the contemporary Islamic resurgence in Malay, and hence Malaysian politics.

The Islamic resurgence in Malaysia is, of course, a cultural response, or more precisely, the sum of various cultural responses, to the times Malaysian Muslims live in, of which the political dimension is crucial in many (but not all) cases. While there is a vague nebulous consensus that 'Islam is the best', what this actually means varies considerably, not only across movements, but within movements over time as well. The account which follows is a largely impressionistic description focusing primarily on the public profile of the dominant tendencies, in order to draw out political implications. As we shall show, Islam is indeed a significant religious, cultural as well as political force in Malaysia today (as it has indeed been at different times in the past).

However, we wish to draw attention to three features which seem to mark the current relation between Islam and politics as historically distinctive. First, it has become increasingly difficult to speak of Malaysian Islam as a unitary force and/or set of discourses. Rather, like the general religious and cultural landscape of which it forms a part, Malaysian Islam is characterised by disagreements, debate and fragmentation. Second, while Islam has experienced periods of resurgence from the time of its first introduction in the region, in terms of the nature of both beliefs and practices, the contemporary resurgence—or better, resurgences—of Islam are distinctive to their historical circumstances. Finally, and in part as a consequence of these characteristics of the situation in which Malaysian Muslims find themselves, Islamic movements in the 1970s and 1980s have experienced some success, but also numerous difficulties in developing their programmes and maintaining momentum and credibility in the face of the competing claims of a disparate collection of movements, groups and individuals (including the governing elite itself), all claiming to speak for and on behalf of Malaysia's Muslims as a whole.

Several sociological studies have gone over similar terrain. But they have tended to come to somewhat different conclusions. The main such studies have argued that the major forces underlying Islamic resurgence have been either ethnic (e.g. Nagata 1984; Chandra 1986), or arising from underlying class contradictions (e.g. Kessler 1980; Shamsul 1983). While we appreciate the significance of class and the centrality of the ethnic dimension of Malaysian society, in this review of the development of some of the major Islamic movements, we assume also that religion cannot be completely reduced to external and supposedly more objective dimensions of social and cultural existence, and that it therefore deserves also to be treated in its own terms. For reasons of space and time, therefore, we have in this paper not attempted to set the contemporary Islamic resurgence in the larger social context, but focussed largely on internal factors instead.[1]

After briefly reviewing the less politically-significant Tabligh and Arqam movements, we shall discuss the origins, roles and political impact of ABIM and PAS.

Tabligh

Jamaat Tabligh—or Tabligh, as it is commonly known—is a missionary movement which originated in India and has since spread throughout the world. Set up in the 1920s, it began growing in Malaysia in the 1950s as a result of the efforts of Indian missionaries. In Malaysia, the Jamaat Tabligh built or took over and operated from mosques (a feature it shared with other movements among Malaysian Indian Muslims). Initially Tabligh

---

[1] Similarly, while there have also been many writings and analyses by the protagonists, as well as other participant observers, especially in the Malay language, we do not propose to review this literature here. A list of English-language references is provided in the bibliography. Moreover while there are undoubtedly international forces involved in the current Islamic resurgence, the following review will emphasise those aspects of the current state of Islam which are unique to Malaysia.

This point needs particular emphasis because of the widespread tendency, especially among Western journalists, to draw misleading parallels because of superficial similarities in form or rhetoric.

gained support in towns with large Indian Muslim communities, such as Penang, Kuala Lumpur and Singapore. More recently, with the resurgence of Islamic missionary activity, Tabligh has succeeded in penetrating the Malay community, even in the villages.

In Malaysia, Jamaat Tabligh is an informal, unregistered missionary movement. Like other Islamic movements, Tabligh's teachings claim that its practices are in accordance with the Prophet's example. Tabligh's methods are basically simple ones. An interested individual merely needs to attend talks by visiting Tabligh missionaries at nearby mosques. The themes of these talks are fairly predictable—the superiority of Islam, the reasons why the Prophet's deeds should be emulated, the proper conduct of prayers, the individual's responsibility to perform missionary work (*dakwah*). The Traditions (*Sunnah*) emphasised in Tabligh teachings are those which relate to daily life: the Prophet's style of eating, dressing, and socialising, as well as his habits, speech, prayer and missionary activities. Few explicitly political or economic issues are dealt with, nor is any profound social criticism either encouraged or undertaken by Tabligh members. According to Tabligh sources, as individuals become good Muslims, social problems like corruption and exploitation will automatically disappear from society.

The simple and inoffensive approach adopted by the Tabligh movement has particularly attracted unmarried men, since only males are allowed to participate in their travelling missionary groups. Tabligh has, moreover, also attracted participants from among the unemployed and alienated village youth. At the same time, there are also highly educated professionals in the movement.

Because of its apolitical stance, Tabligh is rarely viewed with suspicion by the Malaysian authorities. But its presence may and has generated unease in local communities, either because of its Indian association or because it is seen as being in competition with other Islamic groups for followers. Critics have argued that Tabligh's stance favours the status quo, and, hence the government of the day. For example, it is widely believed that Tabligh has been encouraged by the government of Thailand since it provides an alternative to the more militant Malay secessionist movements. Tabligh has also been criticised by members of other Muslim movements for not providing a sufficiently deep understanding of Islam for its followers, though the organisation has organised camps and other gatherings attended by thousands of followers.

Darul Arqam

Darul Arqam was founded in 1968 by twelve Muslims under the leadership of Ustaz (Religious Teacher) Ashaari Muhammad, previously a religious teacher in a government school in Selangor and a PAS activist.

Darul Arqam means 'Abode of Arqam', Arqam being the companion of the Prophet in Mecca when his followers gathered clandestinely before the flight to Medina. The number of founders, twelve, also has a special significance in Islam since Moses—acknowledged as a prophet by Muslims—was accompanied by twelve tribal leaders when leaving Egypt. It is also believed that prior to the Prophet's migration from Mecca to Medina, the basis for the spread of Islam had already been laid in Medina by twelve believers, the first in Medina to accept Islamic teachings.

Thus, followers of Arqam believe that any life based on genuine Islam must involve migration (*hijrah*), as practised by the Prophet. Arqam's most important migration took place in 1972, when many Arqam followers moved to a settlement on the outskirts of Kuala Lumpur, the village of Sungei Penchala. Here, the followers of Ustaz Ashaari cleared eight acres of land, and set up homes, a mosque and a school for the use of the Arqam community.

Ustaz Ashaari has been a vocal critic of other Islamic movements, which—according to him—merely theorise, shout slogans and conduct seminars on the struggle to establish an Islamic state—a critical allusion to PAS and ABIM. According to him, to establish an Islamic state, it is imperative that an Islamic society be first established, by creating a community of families and individuals who practice true Islam. Hence, the Islamic settlement in Sungei Penchala was developed into a model Islamic community, in a communal mode. It contains Arqam families leading their daily lives according to Islamic teachings, and trying to emulate the Prophet and his disciples. Arqam has expanded in part by setting up similar communities and centres elsewhere in Peninsular Malaysia, especially in Pahang.

From the outset, Darul Arqam has reflected the ideas of Ustaz Ashaari himself, whom Arqam claims to be their most learned, charismatic and pious leader. In the initial stages of the development of the Sungei Penchala settlement, Darul Arqam succeeded in attracting many Malay youths, particularly students from private upper secondary schools and institutions of higher learning, to participate in their activities such as talks and courses. In these courses, Arqam leaders claim that Islamic practices in Malaysia are vastly different from true Islamic practice. For this, they blame the secular system of government which separates politics from religion, allegedly due to Jewish and Christian influence. Hence, according to Arqam, Malaysia is not truly Islamic. Upholding true Islam must start with renunciation of the Jewish-influenced way of life. Judaism and Christianity are equated with the West. Hence, according to Arqam, the existing Western-based political and economic systems must be replaced by Islamic systems.

Similarly, individuals must renounce Western styles of dress and behaviour, including free association with the opposite sex, music, etc. Arqam members are encouraged to dress in Arabic garb, with turbans and *jubbah* (robes) for men and *purdah* (veils) for women, since such clothes were also worn or approved of by the Prophet. They are also encouraged to eat from a common tray, and to observe other eating customs ostensibly practised by Prophet Muhammad. Arqam has attempted to produce *halal* (religiously acceptable) food as an alternative to food produced by non-Muslims, such as soya sauce and noodles. Arqam members are expected to participate in communal prayer five times day, hold supplementary devotional sessions and attend religious lectures. They are discouraged from watching television or other entertainment as these are said to distract them from religious devotion and to expose them to dangerous Western influences.

Arqam maintains that the existing official education system is un-Islamic, and runs its own schools as alternatives for Muslims who do not wish to send their children to government schools. Special clinics have been set up for Muslims who do not wish to be treated in government clinics, which are also said to be un-Islamic, e.g. because women patients are treated by male doctors, and medicines may contain non-halal material.

The period between 1972 and 1978 witnessed Arqam's fastest development. They succeeded in attracting tens of thousands of followers by offering a new approach to Islam in Malaysia and maintaining that the struggle to uphold an Islamic state must be preceded by creating an Islamic society, such as that pioneered by the Arqam settlement in Sungei Penchala. Arqam's initial approach—popularly viewed as anti-establishment 'in its own way'—succeeded in attracting many educated youths, including those educated in Islam.

Arqam's rapid growth in the mid-seventies coincided with the period when PAS was in the National Front ruling coalition (see below). The void left by PAS's co-optation provided opportunities for other Islamic movements, especially those considered anti-establishment. Arqam leaders portrayed PAS as weak because it did not sufficiently emphasise genuine Islamic education, causing PAS members and supporters to be spiritually weak. Thus, according to Arqam, it was not surprising that PAS was unable to establish a truly Islamic state while it ran the government in Kelantan state (1959–77), and eventually joined non-Islamic parties in the National Front in 1973.

Almost from the outset, Arqam's closest rival has been ABIM (see below), mainly because the main target of their missionary work has been fairly similar, namely young anti-establishment students. Not surprisingly therefore, apart from the government and PAS, ABIM was the object of much of Arqam's criticisms. ABIM was said by Arqam to have failed for not employing Arqam's missionary methods, which were supposed to be those of the Prophet. ABIM's emphasis on organisation—including membership and meetings for discussion—was portrayed as being Western, and not a method practiced by the Prophet. ABIM's activities often took the form of seminars and working papers, which Arqam denounced as frivolous, noting that in ABIM, only papers—not people—were working (a pun on the 'working papers' presented at ABIM functions). According to Arqam, seminars and conferences were a waste of time and energy, and ineffective in strengthening one's faith in Islam. Arqam emphasised that without faith, Islamic movements would weaken and fail. Arqam leaders held similar views on Islamic movements abroad. The failures of Jamaat Islami in Pakistan and Ikhwan-ul-Muslimin in the Middle East were all attributed to weak faith and failure to emulate the Prophet.

The end of the 1970s witnessed the first major challenges to Arqam's growth. Though Arqam still had substantial influence around Kuala Lumpur, it began losing many of its original followers. In 1977 a number of leaders left the movement after disagreement with the leadership's decision to encourage polygamy. In 1979, several senior Arqam members deserted Sungei Penchala over Ustaz Ashaari's unorthodox beliefs and teachings about Sufi orders.

By the late 1970s, Arqam had begun to change its strategy by reducing its attacks on the government and UMNO's leadership. They concentrated instead on developing internal programmes and projects, and conducting talks and seminars with little criticism of the government. Nevertheless, the criticisms of other Islamic movements, such as PAS and ABIM continued. This was especially the case in the late 1970s and early 1980s, when both PAS and ABIM were greatly influenced by the Iranian Islamic Revolution—dismissed by Arqam as merely a Shiah uprising. Arqam also initiated several dialogue sessions and meetings with government leaders, such as Dr Mahathir Mohamad (then Deputy Prime Minister) and state-level religious leaders. Such friendly ties eased pressure on Arqam from government efforts to control the Islamic resurgence. At one point, when one of its schools caught fire in 1980, Arqam even received financial aid from the Social Welfare Department. In 1981, Dr Mahathir publicly lauded Arqam as a genuinely Islamic movement, and in so doing cast doubt on the legitimacy of movements such as ABIM, Tabligh and PAS. Meanwhile, Arqam's new approach undermined its earlier role as Islamic critic, particularly for those seeking Islamic alternatives to the status quo. This enabled ABIM and PAS to capture the Islamic opposition, particularly after the virtual expulsion of PAS from the Barisan Nasional government in 1977.

Thus, while Arqam is still very much in existence, numerous crises have left Ustaz Ashaari as the sole remaining founder of the original twelve still identified with Arqam. Caught up in theological controversy, Arqam has made even more compromises with the powers-that-be to ensure survival. Meanwhile, however, its activities are increasingly confined to spiritual and family affairs, thus further reducing its already minimal political impact.

In 1986, new charges of heresy emerged against the Arqam leadership over Ashaari's belief that a certain local Muslim personage (Suhaimi) would soon return as the Imam Mahdi to save the Muslim ummah on the eve of Doomsday (*Hari Kiamat*). Those who stayed with Ashaari sought to protect their position by publicly supporting Mahathir's political leadership and increasingly attacking PAS on ostensibly Islamic grounds. By late 1988, it became clear that this respite was only temporary as one state religious department after another banned Ashaari's latest publications on the subject. While a ban on Arqam is unlikely, it also seems increasingly unnecessary given its willingness to help the regime undermine PAS's Islamic legitimacy. Yet, by 1990, it seems unlikely that Arqam would be able, let alone allowed to grow to its previous strength, despite its willingness to serve the political ends of the regime.

ABIM

Angkatan Belia Islam Malaysia (ABIM), or the Malaysian Islamic Youth Movement, was formed in 1971 by several alumni of the National Association of Malaysian Islamic Students (PKPIM). Since its formation, ABIM has received its strongest support from Muslim youth in institutions of higher learning. ABIM leaders include those with either secular or religious education, usually at the tertiary level, both from local universities and abroad. This combination has enabled ABIM to influence a wide cross-section of people. Between 1974 and 1982, ABIM was led by the charismatic Anwar Ibrahim. Prior to becoming president of ABIM in 1974, Anwar Ibrahim had been head of ABIM's communications bureau, and had also been president of both the University of Malaya's Malay Language Society and PKPIM. He is credited with considerable skills, especially in oratory and public relations. Despite his parents' close association with UMNO (his father was a government MP) and the fact that he had a secular education, Anwar succeeded in developing a formidable religious reputation.

ABIM grew increasingly influential after 1973 for a number of reasons. As we have pointed out, PAS's admission into the Barisan Nasional ruling coalition created a void which was partly filled by anti-establishment Islamic elements. ABIM's non-partisan political stance and more moderate (compared to Arqam) religious approach enabled ABIM to penetrate schools, the government bureaucracy and communities not already under PAS influence, e.g. in Perak, Selangor and Negri Sembilan. It was, furthermore, able to make inroads among PAS supporters disappointed by PAS's apparent opportunism by joining the ruling coalition.

ABIM's version of Islam has claimed ideological and even organisational affinity with established Islamic movements abroad, especially Maulana Maududi's Jamaat Islami in Pakistan and the Ikhwan-ul-Muslimin (Muslim Brotherhood), both of which have argued for the establishment of Islamic states, while opposing secularism and nationalism (as un-Islamic). Not surprisingly then, ABIM criticised the government under UMNO leadership, arguing that existing policies served to perpetuate un-Islamic colonial traditions and secular practices which separated religion from political, social and economic issues. ABIM leaders argued that Islam's status as the nation's official religion was insufficient; the Constitution should instead clearly declare Malaysia an Islamic state, with the laws of the country based on the *syariah*, the economy interest-free, and with a *zakat* (tithe) system replacing the existing taxation system. Moreover, together with the PKPIM, ABIM proposed the formation of an Islamic bank and an Islamic university as alternatives to the existing banking and university systems. ABIM also criticised UMNO for having the Malay race, and not Islam, as the basis of its struggle.

ABIM's demands seemed more precise and pristine compared to PAS's then nebulous notion of an Islamic state—a notion fused with Malay nationalistic sentiments. In the mid-seventies, ABIM was critical of PAS for compromising with government which ABIM considered un-Islamic. In states where PAS exercised a degree of power, such as Kelantan and Kedah, ABIM activities were either hindered by the state government, or prohibited outright by PAS officials in important state positions during the period when PAS was in the ruling Barisan Nasional coalition.

Even more than Arqam, ABIM emphasises the importance of education, and has tried to upgrade the quality of Islamic training for its members. Several private schools have been set up by ABIM activists. These schools use the government school curriculum, and are attended by drop-out students who wish to retake government examinations. Apart from this, an additional subject—Islamic principles—is taught, emphasising aspects of Islam, including culture, politics and economics. These schools have also provided bases for ABIM recruitment, activities and mobilisation. Many such students have eventually succeeded in gaining admission to institutions of higher learning and become student activists under the leadership of PKPIM, the ABIM wing on the campuses. ABIM has also set up Islamic kindergartens, and then private Islamic primary schools, with the ageing of its membership.

ABIM also launched a two-prong strategy to explain the basis of its struggle by organising talks, forums and seminars, and publishing pamphlets, magazines and books. ABIM has also conducted study groups at branch, state and national levels for its members. In these study groups, a systematic programme is implemented, beginning with the recitation of Quranic verses. This is usually followed by commentary on its meaning—ranging from classical to contemporary interpretations, usually by Ikhwan's Syed Qutb or Jamaat's Maududi. Then come readings and interpretations of *hadith*, and then of selected Islamic texts, usually from Ikhwan and Jamaat sources. The programme normally ends with a discussion of current national and local issues, and with reports on ABIM activities at various levels. These study groups or *usrah* form the core of ABIM activity as they ensure constant contact between leaders and members, besides deepening members' understanding of and commitment to ABIM's struggle and current concerns. The *usrah* is also the yardstick for measuring the success of ABIM activity, and is an important instrument of control in ABIM's hierarchical organisation.

ABIM's overt involvement in the political arena is usually dated from 1977, with the political crisis in Kelantan, then a PAS-dominated state. As a result of the crisis, PAS withdrew from the ruling National Front coalition, and state-level elections were held. ABIM supported PAS in the crisis, arguing that in comparison to UMNO and other political parties, PAS, though not without its own weaknesses, was far more Islamic. ABIM's stand was that, as an Islamic association, it should safeguard the dignity of Islam from being undermined by UMNO. ABIM mobilised virtually its entire leadership to campaign for PAS in Kelantan, and recruited numerous tertiary-level students to campaign in Kelantan. Despite the PAS defeat in the elections, this was an important turning point in ABIM's development. With newfound PAS support, it began to spread its influence in rural areas. Strong links between ABIM and PAS were forged, and the government became nervous about the potential threat of the new alliance.

In the 1978 general elections, ABIM's support for PAS was even more evident. Besides launching a nationwide campaign to support PAS, three of ABIM's top leaders contested the general elections on the PAS ticket. They were Ustaz Fadhil Noor (ABIM Deputy President), Ustaz Nakhaie Ahmad and Syed Ibrahim, all leading members of the ABIM central leadership. Numerous state ABIM leaders also participated, including Haji Abdul Hadi Awang, the ABIM head in Trengganu, who also contested on a PAS ticket. With the exception of Ustaz Nakhaie Ahmad, PAS and the ABIM leaders were defeated in the elections. But ABIM was encouraged by the election results since most of its leaders lost by narrow margins. ABIM's success was recognised by PAS leaders who, as a consequence, were increasingly confident in allowing ABIM leaders to assume positions of leadership in PAS. Thus, Ustaz Nakhaie Ahmad became secretary general of PAS, Fadhil Noor its vice president, and Syed Ibrahim treasurer. ABIM was also entrusted with conducting PAS cadre training camps, and organising PAS candidates to work in them. ABIM's membership and programmes in rural areas were increasingly synonymous with those of PAS. ABIM thus became closely associated with PAS, and many viewed ABIM as a transition for individuals interested in subsequent involvement with PAS for election purposes.

Apart from ABIM's role in assisting in the PAS challenge to UMNO on government policy and administrative matters considered un-Islamic, ABIM also tried to gain non-Malay support for its other policies. Its leaders began to maintain that the major problems faced by contemporary Malaysian society were due to UMNO's narrow ethnic policies, including the New Economic Policy (NEP). According to ABIM leaders, the solution was to be found in an Islamic state, which would not merely benefit a particular race or ethnic group. To achieve this end, ABIM declared 'Islam as the panacea to the problems of a plural society' as the theme of its annual convention in 1979, viewed by many as its most successful ever. ABIM went on to promote this theme as the basis of its short-lived campaign against 'narrow nationalism' and ethnic chauvinism (*assabiyah*). Most people saw this as an attack on UMNO. At this stage, Anwar even accepted an invitation to address the leadership of the Chinese based opposition Democratic Action Party. Meanwhile, on university campuses, Islamic student associations under PKPIM's leadership were mobilised to oppose student groups linked to the Federation of Peninsular Malay Students (GPMS), which has been controlled by UMNO since the 1970s.

Between 1979 and 1981, ABIM reached the pinnacle of its popularity. In rural areas, ABIM was received as the champion of the *ummah*, addressing itself to social as well as religious issues. In urban areas, ABIM worked primarily through student movements. ABIM was becoming so successful that the government took steps to curtail its influence. On campuses, student-sponsored programmes were brought under the control of university Student Affairs Departments (HEP), specifically to curb ABIM influence. Similarly, ABIM supporters in government offices were penalised, e.g. by being transferred to remote areas. In the villages, the government placed tight conditions on individuals wishing to give speeches or religious talks in mosques, where they were required to obtain prior authorisation from state religious departments, which normally only approved individuals acceptable to the government. In some states, the government set up state religious foundations to provide alternatives to ABIM programmes by organising their own talks, seminars and religious courses. They even set up their own private schools, charging far lower fees than those charged by ABIM schools, while remunerating teachers more handsomely.

In 1981, the Societies Act Amendment Bill was tabled. This bill created a new category of political associations to be severely curtailed. Though never explicitly stated, it is generally believed that the amendments were primarily targeted at ABIM—among others—because of its open support for PAS, and its foreign financing from international Islamic bodies such as WAMY (World Assembly of Muslim Youth) and IIFSO (International Islamic Federation of Student Organisations), which are in turn supported by Saudi Arabia, Kuwait and other conservative Arab states.

Opposition to these amendments was headed by ABIM, which thus gained a new opportunity to lead other similarly affected public interest societies, and to project its own organisation and leadership, particularly Anwar Ibrahim. The campaign to oppose the amendments took the form of forums, talks and a mass signature campaign all over the country. As a consequence, Anwar succeeded in achieving a breakthrough in constituencies previously considered closed to ABIM and other Islamic movements. Even though the campaign was not completely successful in dissuading the government from proceeding with the amendments, it nevertheless succeeded in getting various organisations in the country to come together to voice their opposition to the government. Meanwhile, in contrast to PAS and Arqam, ABIM achieved considerable success by widening its influence beyond the Islamic movement.

In mid-1981, UMNO underwent a change of leadership. Hussein Onn resigned as party president and Prime Minister for reasons of health. He was succeeded by then UMNO Deputy President and Deputy Prime

Minister, Mahathir Mohamad, who was confirmed as party president at the 32nd annual UMNO General Assembly that year. Education Minister Musa Hitam was appointed Deputy Prime Minister, after successfully being elected Deputy President against Finance Minister, Tengku Razaleigh Hamzah. The new Mahathir-Musa leadership—promoted by the press as the 2M leadership—was hailed as marking the beginning of a new era. Both leaders had gone to university locally and came from commoner families, unlike the previous prime ministers, who came from aristocratic or royal families, and had had their tertiary education abroad. The new leadership released many political detainees held under the Internal Security Act (ISA) by previous administrations. Several new policies and changes were introduced, such as the 'punch card' system, the use of name tags by civil servants, a common time zone for Peninsular Malaysia, Sabah and Sarawak, and most importantly, the 'clean, efficient and trustworthy' slogan for the administration, giving the impression that the 2M leadership was serious about eradicating corruption and other abuses, besides improving the efficiency and accountability of the Malaysian administration.

Several months after the leadership change, the government introduced two major new policies, namely the Look East policy and the policy of assimilation of Islamic values. Coupled with its 'Buy British Last' policy, these were interpreted by some as reflecting a decision to no longer emulate the West, and to accept a policy of Islamisation. Meanwhile, Dr Mahathir also announced plans to set up the International Islamic University and an Islamic Bank, while prohibiting Muslims from entering the Genting Highlands casino and serving alcohol at official functions. ABIM began to voice cautious support for these proposals, particularly Mahathir's Islamisation policy.

Several months before early general elections expected in 1982, another remarkable turnaround occurred. ABIM declared that it would not actively support any political party, including PAS. In his meetings with student leaders associated with PKPIM, Anwar Ibrahim explained that ABIM did not want to be equated with PAS, but instead desired to retrieve its image as a non-partisan association. This decision probably also reflected several developments in the PAS-ABIM relationship, with some ABIM leaders feeling that their close relationship had benefited PAS far more than ABIM. ABIM leaders also felt that increased government pressure due to the link with PAS had frustrated ABIM's own development.

The Iranian Islamic revolution, initially extolled by ABIM, subsequently influenced PAS more than ABIM. For example, PAS accepted the concept of ulamak leadership. The takeover of PAS by more radical younger leaders led to the resignation of the old PAS leadership (under Asri) under pressure from the younger generation (mainly from ABIM), who supported the notion of ulamak leadership. Some older leaders (headed by Asri) eventually returned to the UMNO fold through a shell organisation, Hamim (Hizbul Muslimin), which they justified by referring to Mahathir's Islamisation programme. The celebration of the Iranian revolution by the younger generation in PAS alienated their erstwhile colleagues among the ABIM leadership. This occurred when ABIM leaders were beginning to express unease over developments in Iran, where non-ulamak Muslim groups were being increasingly marginalised, if not eliminated. ABIM's ties with Islamic movements based in Saudi Arabia and Kuwait, such as WAMY and IIFSO, also influenced the views of the ABIM leadership on international issues involving Iran.

As PAS-ABIM relations began to sour, at the height of the popularity of the 2M leadership, Dr Mahathir invited Anwar Ibrahim to join UMNO. On 29 March 1982, just before the nomination of candidates for the April 1982 general elections, Anwar announced his decision to resign as ABIM president and to join UMNO. He would stand against the incumbent PAS Member of Parliament in Permatang Pauh, his birthplace, and where his father had been an UMNO MP earlier in the sixties. To justify his eligibility for candidacy, Anwar claimed that his mother had been paying his UMNO membership dues for years without his knowledge—a claim which smacked of subterfuge.

The reaction of ABIM leaders—who generally seemed to condone Anwar's decision, although rumours of a split spread—further undermined the ABIM-PAS relationship, and led to confusion among followers on both sides. Several attempts to bridge these differences failed. ABIM tacitly supported Anwar, claiming that Anwar was not 'selling out', but was instead 'infiltrating' UMNO—albeit under Mahathir's auspices—to transform and thus Islamise it, and eventually, the state and the nation. PAS, on the other hand, insisted that UMNO was based on an anti-Islamic ideology of ethnic chauvinism (*assabiyah*), and hence a transition to genuine Islam under its auspices was out of the question. Moreover, Anwar was heading the UMNO campaign against PAS, an Islamic party, and not by taking on un-Islamic opposition parties such as the DAP. The subsequent landslide victory for the National Front ruling coalition in the April 1982 general elections was largely credited to Mahathir, including his success in bringing Anwar into UMNO.

Those in ABIM who supported Anwar's decision referred to contemporary developments in Pakistan and Sudan as parallels, which had influenced Anwar, although others used these same events to criticise Anwar. Nor did other circumstances help Anwar and his supporters justify his decision. Anwar and ABIM were known to have disapproved of former UMNO secretary general, Sanusi Junid's switch from ABIM to UMNO in 1974; observers rhetorically asked what had changed in the interim to make Anwar's switch less opportunistic than Sanusi's had been. After all, Anwar had been detained without trial for 22 months from the end of 1974 for his alleged role in student demonstrations in support of peasant protests in and near Baling (in Kedah) in November. Mahathir—then Education Minister—was held responsible for the harsh repression that followed, and for the draconian 1975 amendments to the Universities and University Colleges Act (UUCA), while Sanusi—then Deputy Home Affairs

Minister—was responsible for those very 1981 amendments to the Societies Act, which Anwar had actively opposed. Indeed, during the earlier period of co-operation with PAS, Anwar had dismissed the possibility of his joining UMNO—still on people's mind because of the late Tun Razak's well-known invitation to him in the early seventies—by comparing UMNO to a septic tank, i.e. not something to be cleaned from within.

Yet, for those with longer memories, the Mahathir-Anwar rapprochement was surprising only for its timing, not for the partnership involved. Anwar had first distinguished himself in University of Malaya campus politics in the late sixties as the ardent Malay-nationalist president of the Malay Language Society (PBMUM). During the events of May 1969, he was associated with those—like Mahathir, from within UMNO—who were agitating for the replacement of Tunku Abdul Rahman as prime minister because of his allegedly soft and compromising stand on ethnic, linguistic and cultural issues. Anwar did not then reject the Tunku for his 'pro-capitalist, neo-colonialist' policies, a critique advanced at that time by the, then, left-led University of Malaya Student Union (UMSU). Not unlike Mahathir, who attended a Kissinger seminar at Harvard in 1966 on a fellowship from the Asia Foundation (then recently exposed as a CIA front), Anwar would later be active—as president of the Malaysian Youth Council (MYC)—in the CIA-backed World Assembly of Youth (WAY). Yet, to be fair, both probably see themselves as genuine Third World nationalists, wary of the West and its intentions. Whatever their (varying) commitments to Islam, both are essentially modernist (Mahathir perhaps more so), and privately suspicious of the ulamak. Both have Indian-Muslim ancestry, and hence, perhaps are all the more committed to their versions of the "Malay cause". They were probably both quite aware of the limitations of the narrow Malay ideology to which they are publicly obliged to subscribe. Hence, while both may invoke Islam to strengthen Malay identity, they also hope that a modernist Islam can help circumvent the cul-de-sacs of narrow Malay nationalism. The late Temple University Professor Ismail Faruqi—who is often credited with bringing the two men together again in the early eighties—was certainly one who saw such potential in a modernist approach to Islam.

These developments had lasting repercussions for ABIM. In the villages, much support was lost as members deserted ABIM for PAS as a result of Anwar's 'defection'. Some of ABIM's private schools came under PAS control, while many state-level ABIM leaders joined PAS or ceased to be active in either Islamic movement. In the campuses, ABIM's influence rapidly declined. PKPIM lost credibility as the leader of the Islamic movement on the campuses, only retaining support among the few remaining ABIM loyalists. Several attempts to challenge the ABIM leadership from within have been unsuccessful, largely due to the nature of a constitution which greatly favours incumbents. With support diminishing, most ABIM leaders felt they had little choice but to follow Anwar in furthering Islamisation within UMNO and the government. To achieve this, some ABIM leaders channelled much energy into ensuring the success of Islamic institutions such as the International Islamic University, the Islamic Bank, an Islamic insurance scheme and other projects for which Anwar had either been responsible or with which he had been associated.

With Mahathir's support Anwar was able quickly to entrench himself politically. Soon after the 1982 general elections, Anwar was appointed Deputy Minister in the Prime Minister's Department. Remarkably, later that same year, he was elected UMNO Youth President, and not long afterwards, appointed Minister of Culture, Youth and Sports, followed by a stint as Agriculture Minister, before he was appointed Education Minister, a senior ministerial post, in 1986. At the April 1987 UMNO General Assembly, which saw the UMNO leadership split into two camps of almost equal strengths (see Crouch and Khoo in this volume), Anwar was elected one of the party's vice presidents.

In a short space of time, Anwar succeeded in ascending the political ladder to become Mahathir's heir apparent, while spreading his influence in UMNO and the government. In view of Anwar's political successes within UMNO and the government, ABIM leaders have apparently grown more confident in their 1982 decision regarding Anwar. The organisation has since become less hesitant to show selective support for government policies, and has correspondingly restrained itself from openly criticising government policies and actions. Through this policy of critical support for the Mahathir administration, especially for its Islamisation policy, ABIM has developed into an officially acceptable pressure group, presumed to reflect Anwar's personal preferences, which might occasionally be at variance with official policy. Several of the top ABIM leaders closest to Anwar have become increasingly active in UMNO, benefiting from Anwar's sponsorship, and in turn strengthening Anwar's own position in the party and the government. Within ABIM too, those most closely identified with Anwar have continued to dominate ABIM's secretariat.

Since Anwar's crossover to UMNO in early 1982, ABIM's public posture has changed considerably. ABIM's virtual silence on a whole range of public interest issues has been very conspicuous. For example, it failed to take public stands on the 1983 murder of Jalil Ibrahim and the related revelations about losses of 2.5 billion ringgit by Bumiputra Malaysia Finance (BMF), the government-owned Bank Bumiputra Malaysia subsidiary in Hong Kong; the subsequent improprieties involving Maminco and Makuwasa; the November 1985 killings of Memali local PAS leader Ibrahim 'Libya' and his followers; the detention without trial of PAS leaders, including several former ABIM activists; the November 1986 visit of Israeli president, Chaim Herzog to neighbouring Singapore, which triggered off a series of unusually well publicised protests; the draconian December 1986 amendments to the Official Secrets Act; and the campaign against abuses in the privatisation of the North-South Highway to an UMNO-owned company without any relevant construction experience in late 1987.

The last two issues both generated opposition coalitions comparable to the one which opposed the 1981 Societies Act amendments. ABIM leaders closest to Anwar now assert that this is the time for consolidation, not demonstration; for preparation, not protest. Perhaps unfairly, the popular impression by the mid-eighties was that ABIM's new profile was dictated by its support for Anwar's UMNO strategy—encouraging cynics to redefine the organisation's acronym ABIM as the Anwar Bin Ibrahim Movement.

Since 1982, then, the political standing of ABIM has changed considerably. It is no longer thought of as an independent pressure group, particularly for voicing issues relating to abuses and injustices in society. This mantle has increasingly been taken over by PAS in matters concerning Islam (as well as other issues), although in this role, PAS is perhaps less sophisticated and competent than ABIM was. This has left the field open to other pressure groups, although they seem unlikely to capture ABIM's old legitimacy and constituency. ABIM's social and political role has been very much reduced, both in terms of membership and popular political support. It is increasingly clear that ABIM's political strength was crucially dependent on Anwar's skills, its student constituency and its alliance with PAS, without which ABIM has had its wings severely clipped.

PAS

The Pan-Malaysia Islamic Party, PAS (Parti Islam SeMalaysia) was set up in 1951 in Butterworth, Penang. Many of its founders were members of UMNO's religious bureau, who defected and formed their own party as a result of differences of opinion about the nature of the state to be established after independence from the British. Some former members of the Hisbul Muslimin—the by then defunct Islamic organisation aligned in the forties with the leftist Malay Nationalist Party (PKMM) and the Centre for Popular Forces (Pusat Tenaga Rakyat or Putera)—were also involved in setting up PAS. For PAS supporters, the new state had to be Islamic, implementing Islam in all spheres of life, including law, the economy, etc. This contrasted with UMNO's vision of a secular state. According to PAS, religion was not to be confined to one bureau in an Islamic political party, but should encompass all aspects of life, including politics (see Kessler, below, for further discussion of these ideas). In the initial stages, PAS was led by those with a traditional religious training in the 'pondok' schools, which had their roots among the Malay peasantry, particularly the rice farmers of Trengganu, Kelantan, Perak, Perlis and Kedah. It is not therefore surprising that PAS has had a tremendous influence in these states, even forming the state governments of Kelantan and Trengganu after the first general elections in 1959. After several years under a lack-lustre leadership, PAS had invited Dr Burhanuddin Al-Helmy—the religiously-trained homeopath and radical nationalist leader who had led the Malay Nationalist Party (PKMM) and the leftist-led PUTERA-AMCJA coalition in the mid-forties—to assume the party leadership. Although he nominally remained at the party helm until his death in 1969, his influence was undermined by his detention without trial from the mid-sixties.

At the outset, PAS's ideology combined the visions of Malay nationalists with those struggling to establish an Islamic state. It was generally considered a Malay chauvinist party for its constant criticism of UMNO's co-operation with non-Muslim/non-Malay political parties. Even PAS's entry into the ruling National Front coalition during 1973–77 was justified in terms of PAS's responsibility to the Malays after the racial riots of 1969, and the need to make a success of the pro-Malay New Economic Policy (NEP) introduced by then Prime Minister, Tun Abdul Razak.

While in opposition, PAS has been under constant pressure from UMNO, the dominant party in the ruling coalition. For example, in 1961, the federal government succeeded in bringing about the downfall of the PAS state government in Trengganu. Several PAS leaders, including Dr Burhanuddin, were later detained, allegedly for having supported Sukarno during the Indonesian Confrontation against Malaysia. As a result of Burhanuddin's detention, his health deteriorated. He died in 1969 shortly after release. In 1968, several PAS members of the Kelantan state Legislative Assembly were allegedly abducted, brought to Kuala Lumpur, and forced to make public declarations on television under oath, swearing that they would leave PAS and support UMNO. However, they returned to PAS after being allowed to return to Kelantan.

UMNO launched a massive campaign to recapture Kelantan in 1969. A special manifesto was produced, promising government expenditure in Kelantan exceeding $500 million if PAS was defeated. In this period, UMNO also formed a youth corps called the "Pemuda Tahan Lasak" (the Rough and Ready Youth) to subvert PAS's campaign activities. Eventually, UMNO succeeded in gaining two additional seats in the May 1969 elections. The death of Burhanuddin that year and the changed political circumstances after the elections and racial riots of May 1969 enabled the PAS leader, Asri, to bring his party into the expanded ruling coalition in the early seventies.

In 1977, PAS was faced with a new political crisis when the UMNO leadership in Kelantan supported anti-Asri PAS elements in a bid for power. As a result, a new breakaway party from PAS, Berjasa, emerged. PAS was left with little choice but to leave the Barisan Nasional coalition.

At the same time, the central government declared a State of Emergency in Kelantan. The elected state government was suspended, and direct administrative control was assumed by the central government through a Director of Operations, Hashim Aman, who was later appointed Chief Secretary (KSN) to the government. Under this Emergency administration, UMNO launched a massive smear campaign against PAS, and then called snap state elections. For the first time in Malaysian elections history, public rallies—the most important platform for PAS and other opposition parties—were banned. Only public talks in enclosed areas were allowed.

UMNO's campaign machinery, on the other hand, included the press, radio and television. It gained further publicity by officiating at the opening of mosques and government schools. The official excuse for the ban was that, at the time of the elections, the Communist Party of Malaya (CPM) would be celebrating an anniversary, and might therefore cause public disorder. However, on discovering the usefulness of the ban in weakening the opposition, the government has since maintained the ban on public rallies in subsequent elections, despite the elimination of the communist threat in the eighties.

Without effective means to respond to UMNO propaganda under Emergency rule and the split in the PAS leadership, PAS lost control of the state government of Kelantan. PAS won only two of the seats contested, Berjasa 11 and UMNO 28. For the first time, UMNO was able to form the Kelantan state government, which it did in coalition with Berjasa. PAS's position was further undermined in the national elections held later in 1978, although it did recover much of its 'normal' share of the vote (see Crouch, Lee & Ong, 1980). Even in Trengganu, once a PAS stronghold, the party lost all the seats contested. Berjasa's position within the ruling Barisan Nasional coalition has since declined with each subsequent general election (1982 and 1986), and after the UMNO split in 1987–88, its leadership has been identified with the dissident UMNO faction led by Tengku Razaleigh, a Kelantan prince, though many of its supporters have drifted to PAS and UMNO.

The erosion in PAS support in 1978 undermined the leadership of Asri and his old guard. The entry of ABIM leaders into PAS from 1978 had initially been welcomed by Asri, resulting in the appointment of Nakhaie Ahmad and Fadhil Noor—both prominent former ABIM leaders—as Secretary General and Vice President respectively. In Trengganu, former ABIM state chief, Haji Abdul Hadi Awang was appointed state liaison chief. By 1980, however, attitudes towards ABIM had cooled as a new generation exerted pressure on the PAS leadership. The ex-ABIM elements demanded changes in the party to abandon its policy of combining Islam with Malay nationalism, to rid the party of Malay nationalistic elements, and to pursue a more purely Islamic vision. The new guard also urged PAS leaders to sustain their political work between elections. PAS leaders, they argued, should conduct themselves as true Muslims as exemplified by Prophet Muhammad, including the observance of daily prayers and other obligatory rituals. The PAS leadership was also urged to abandon Western lifestyles, and to improve party organisation, strengthen cadre training and increase its activities. Within a short time, PAS activities came under the control of the new guard.

Asri felt increasingly isolated. In the PAS elections of 1980, the post of Deputy President—held by Asri loyalist, Abu Bakar Omar—was contested by Yusof Rawa, former Malaysian Ambassador to the Shah's Iran and the man who defeated Mahathir in the 1969 general elections. Yusof Rawa won with the support of ex-ABIM members and in the face of

Asri's open support for the incumbent. Asri used his powers to appoint Abu Bakar Omar to the post of PAS secretary-general, ousting Nakhaie Ahmad from that post. He appointed other loyalists as state liaison chiefs (except in Trengganu, where the entire party leadership was now under the control of the new guard identified with Abdul Hadi Awang).

Under the symbolic leadership of Hadi, an influential and charismatic religious teacher, Trengganu became the centre of PAS new guard activity, as PAS began to recover from its crushing 1978 debacle. Hadi had received his early education in local religious schools, and furthered his studies in Medina University, later completing a Masters degree at Al-Azhar. He returned to Trengganu in the mid-1970s to work with the Trengganu Islamic Foundation. This gave him the opportunity to speak at mosques and other state-controlled premises and functions. At the same time, he continued his father's tradition of making the Rusila Mosque his centre of teaching every Friday, and became state ABIM chief. Thus far, his activities had not been veiwed with concern by the authorities.

Hadi became more active in PAS after contesting the 1978 general elections as the PAS candidate for Marang (which includes Rusila). Hadi lost by a mere 68 votes, although PAS did not win a single seat in Trengganu. Meanwhile, his oratorical abilities and fluency in Arabic had already started attracting thousands to his weekly Friday lectures at Rusila. His simple village lifestyle endeared him to his following. His talks were filled with quotations from the Quran, and stories of the prophets, often used as metaphors for current social problems. As with other ABIM and PAS leaders, he emphasised the need to set up an Islamic state. To achieve this, Muslims had to rise and struggle against the un-Islamic and colonial practices of UMNO. He also emphasised that if one died in the sacred struggle to uphold genuine Islam, such a death would constitute martyrdom. The Islamic Revolution in Iran encouraged some of his followers to compare him to Iran's 'clerical' leaders. Hadi was touted as PAS's answer to Anwar after the latter defected to UMNO. However, despite his superior religious knowledge, fluency in Arabic and considerable rhetorical abilities, Hadi lacks Anwar's political pragmatism, tactical and organisational skills, as well as the public relations adeptness, which have been so crucial to Anwar's broad popular appeal.

1982 witnessed the culmination of the leadership crisis between the old and new guards in PAS. Asri's authoritarian conduct in unilaterally choosing the candidates for the April 1982 general elections was construed as intended to isolate the ulamak, particularly in Kelantan. This forged an alliance between the ulamak and the new guard, which successfully undermined Asri's leadership at the PAS assembly after the 1982 elections. Recognising their isolation, Asri and his followers resigned en bloc, surrendering the party to the young guard and the ulamak, but taking away four of the five incumbent PAS MPs and a number of State Assemblymen to later form Hamim, the latest PAS splinter party. For all intents and purposes, Asri has since supported Mahathir and Anwar, and in late 1988,

Hamim was formally dissolved, with members free to join any party of their own choice. With Asri in UMNO, some former Hamim members have returned to the PAS fold, while what is left of the party has joined the Berjasa, PAS and the UMNO dissidents led by Tengku Razaleigh, to form an Islamic Unity Movement (Angkatan Perpaduan Ummah).

The years since the ascendancy of the new PAS leadership in 1982 have seen a curious mix of greater ideological consistency combined with strategic incoherence. Acutely aware of the Malay nationalist underpinnings of the party's espousal of Islam under Asri, the new leaders have tried to articulate a more pristine version of Islam, inadvertently surrendering Asri's turf to Mahathir, Sanusi and Anwar's 'born-again Muslim' UMNO. In a sense the new UMNO has isolated the new PAS ideologically, compelling the PAS leadership to constantly seek new issues. Constrained by their ideology as much as their strategic grasp of the limited range of issues available, they have been very much on the defensive in the face of Mahathir's on-off Islamisation campaign, and have, sometimes, even unwittingly played into the hands of the UMNO leadership.

Having declared its own Islamisation policy under Mahathir, UMNO has been on the offensive. From the mid-seventies, faced with the Islamic resurgence, the UMNO-dominated coalition government had been making an increasing number of largely symbolic concessions to Muslims, such as increasing the profile, role and activities of the various government-controlled Islamic organisations. Meanwhile, the authorities also tried to control and curb other Islamic activities and teachings, by legal means and by condemning them as 'misleading', 'deviant' or 'heretical'. Unlike the essentially defensive concessions made to the Islamic resurgence in the seventies, under Mahathir in the eighties, UMNO began to meet the PAS challenge head on by trying to outflank and isolate PAS, while co-opting Arqam and ABIM. In particular, Mahathir, Sanusi, and others, and later Anwar as well, have tried to improve UMNO's Islamic image. Sansusi has even gone to the extent of (falsely) claiming that it is Malaysia's oldest and the world's third largest Islamic political party (Mauzy & Milne 1984: 644). Tensions among Muslims became increasingly polarized along partisan lines, involving media-exaggerated—'kafir-mengkafir' (mutual denunciations as non-believers) and the 'two imam' (separate communal prayers)—phenomena.

In 1982 the new PAS leadership was initially preoccupied largely with trying to get itself better organised; repairing the damage caused by Asri's resignation and the break with ABIM following Anwar's 'defection'; and responding to the new policy initiatives of the Mahathir administration. Apart from internal preoccupations, the new PAS leadership was finding it difficult to deal with Mahathir's Islamisation policies, as they argued simultaneously that UMNO was not sincere and that the policy did not go far enough. Caught up in UMNO's clever response, PAS could only claim ideological purity and pedigree, not fully appreciating that it was conceding a significant portion of its old constituency in the process.

In late 1983, however, a new Mahathir initiative offered a political opportunity, which PAS grabbed desperately, despite its awkward political and ideological implications. Anticipating the ascension to the Malaysian throne of a reputedly maverick sultan, Mahathir sought to amend the Federation Constitution to limit the ruler's discretionary prerogatives. Some argue that the entire exercise was quite unnecessary and inspired by poor advice, while others maintain that the effort was part of a concerted effort to concentrate power in the hands of the executive. In any case, the matter soon developed into a confrontation between the new commoner leadership of UMNO and the nine royal houses of the land. Elements in the new PAS leadership seized this opportunity to oppose the Mahathir administration and align itself with the royal houses (especially on the East Coast). In so doing, it tried to portray itself as the true champion of the Malay community by identifying with the hereditary rulers' constitutional claim to be protectors of the Malay race and Islamic religion since colonial times. There was a risk, however, of eroding the PAS heritage of representing peasant Islam, rather than official, and hence royal Islam. Besides gaining the goodwill of some of the royal houses, then, it is unlikely that PAS made much headway as the episode soon ended in an awkward stalemate.

Unlike its opportunitistic response to the constitutional crisis, PAS's next two initiatives were much more consistent with the new Islamic ideology it was espousing. In 1984 and 1985, PAS put considerable effort into identifying itself as representing the *mustadhafin* (the meek) as opposed to the *mustakbirin* (the arrogant); fighting for the *adil* (just) against the *zulm* or *zalim* (wicked). While these moral categories have strong religious connotations in Islam, they have also considerable social significance, especially in recent times as a consequence of the influence of Dr Ali Shariati, the leading ideologue of Iran's Islamic Revolution. Although PAS did not go as far as Shariati in developing universal moral class categories, nevertheless this important new PAS initiative—independent of ABIM influence—was a significant breakthrough, providing the theological legitimacy for more socially oriented interpretations of the contemporary relevance of Islam for Malaysian society.

1985 also saw the beginnings of PAS's own campaign against *assabiyah*, which, in the Malaysian context, generally refers to ethnic chauvinism. Not unlike ABIM earlier, PAS denounced ethnic chauvisnim in relation to its advocacy of Islam as the solution to the problems of Malaysia's plural society. However, breaking significantly with the ABIM heritage, and going well beyond Anwar's ambiguous—some even claim opportunistic—formulations, PAS leaders, notably Hadi, went on to reject ethnic discrimination and privileges, including the NEP and Bumiputraism, as inimical to the spirit of Islam.

Carried away by the warm reception for its anti-*assabiyah* position among the Chinese community, PAS pushed on to organise an auxiliary organisation, the Chinese Consultative Committee (CCC), to mobilize Chinese political support for PAS, and its advocacy of an Islamic state. While PAS did succeed in regaining a degree of credibility among the Chinese, the CCC failed to really take off. The prospect of an Islamic state continues to be perceived as a threat by non-Muslims, and even many Muslims.

Meanwhile, the mood of rising militancy among ardent PAS members and supporters, encouraged by the Iranian revolution of 1979 and strengthened by the leadership change of 1982, led to greater harassment from the state. In 1984, several activists from the PAS youth wing were detained under the Internal Security Act. Government permits, which are required for all public functions, and the use of public premises and facilities, were increasingly denied to PAS. Attendance at the few functions allowed inevitably soared, while audiotapes and even videotapes of PAS speeches, especially those by Hadi, became increasingly popular. In early 1985, in the run-up to a by-election, a group of UMNO supporters (allegedly including paid thugs) harassed and attacked people attending a PAS election meeting in Lubok Merbau, killing a PAS supporter. A PAS leader, who produced a pamphlet about the incident soon afterwards, was subsequently detained without trial and later subjected to restricted residence away from his hometown. In November 1985, the police attacked Memali—a village in the Baling district of Kedah, where Ustaz Ibrahim 'Libya' led a community of militant PAS supporters—killing 14 villagers (four policemen died) and arresting many more. The unexpected and unprecedented (as far as PAS was concerned) harshness of the repression of 1985, especially the Memali incident, shocked PAS militants into recognising the repressive character and potential of the state. Indications since then would suggest that most PAS members, including the national leadership, have chosen to back off. Despite much PAS rhetoric about the martyrdom (a fate exalted in Islam) of the victims of Lubok Merbau and Memali, the PAS leadership probably recognised that PAS was hardly prepared mentally, let alone physically and organisationally, for violent struggle. Cynical observers have commented that UMNO called PAS's bluff, and won. It is also remarkable how Mahathir's and Anwar's Islamic credentials came through virtually unscathed. For example, when UMNO deputy president Musa Hitam resigned as Deputy Prime Minister and Minister for Home Affairs in early 1986, anti-Musa elements in UMNO and many PAS people placed responsibility for the Memali incident exclusively on Musa's shoulders, even though Musa has alleged that Mahathir and other Kedah-based UMNO leaders were involved.

In mid-1986, PAS finally agreed to initiate efforts for co-operation among the various opposition parties. These efforts eventually culminated in a joint declaration, as well as a hastily arranged and poorly enforced electoral understanding. However, this was rejected by the strongest opposition party, the predominantly Chinese Democratic Action Party (DAP).

The electoral pact may have been a failure, but the joint declaration—originally drafted in the name of the *Harakah Keadilan* (Justice Movement) or HAK, which also means truth or right—identified broad areas of consensus covering a wide range of political, social and economic issues, while explicitly acknowledging fundamental ideological differences, e.g. on the nature of the desired state. Equally significantly, a PAS spokesman had earlier publicly conceded that an Islamic state could not be established immediately even if PAS were to come to power, especially without the agreement of most of the population. The joint declaration clearly demonstrated the potential for a broad coalition, involving, if not led by, PAS, which could offer a viable popular alternative to the UMNO-dominated status quo. Not surprisingly then, in the election campaign that followed, the ruling BN coalition took great pains to discredit the coalition and ensure its electoral defeat, thus consolidating the DAP's role as the main opposition party. Shocked by their failure at the polls, especially after overestimating their own strength in the first electoral test for the new PAS leadership, some PAS leaders from the overwhelming Malay East Coast blamed the joint declaration as well as the anti-*assabiyah* campaign and the CCC initiative for PAS's failure to secure greater Malay support. Not surprisingly then, with little support from within and outside the party, these important initiatives have since been shelved by the party leadership. However, earlier tensions between PAS and the small leftwing Malay based People's Party (*Partai Rakyat*) were reduced in the process, leaving the door open for further co-operation in the future.

In early 1987, there was renewed talk of an UMNO-PAS dialogue, ostensibly in the interest of Muslim unity. Talks did not take place, however, since there was little real interest on the part of UMNO, which had just handed PAS its worst ever electoral defeat in terms of parliamentary seats won. While bolstering Anwar's image as a Muslim statesman, this suggestion undermined the credibility of PAS leaders implicated in the planned talks.

In 1987 also, PAS completed building its national training centre (*pusat tarbiyah*), and began publishing a weekly newspaper, *Harakah* (Movement), which replaced the glossier thematic magazine-format publication begun in late 1986. These activities were made possible by the fact that PAS enjoys considerable financial support from its committed supporters, many of whom expect divine rewards for their worldly sacrifices.

In the 1986 annual PAS *muktamar*, held soon after the August general elections, an engineer reputed to be a leader of the semi-clandestine IRC (Islamic Representative Council) was appointed deputy head of PAS Youth. He was expected to eventually succeed the aging incumbent Youth head. The IRC was originally established in Britain in the mid-seventies, and spread to Malaysia, North America and elsewhere soon after. By the mid-eighties, it dominated many Malaysian Muslim student organisations abroad, and is believed to have considerable influence in Malaysia as well, especially on university campuses. The IRC also claims to be linked to Ikhwan, although it has been frustrated by Ikhwan's seeming approval for ABIM, which has been the IRC's main rival since the late seventies. At the PAS *muktamar* in April 1987, however, after a spate of adverse publicity about the IRC (which IRC members, probably correctly, suspect to have been ABIM-inspired), the IRC man barely kept his seat on the Youth executive committee, and was promptly replaced as deputy head. Meanwhile, another IRC leader was replaced as deputy (to Hadi) of the PAS training (*tarbiyah*) committee. This eclipse of the IRC within PAS resulted in well-publicised attacks by those associated with the IRC and others on PAS's allegedly Shiah orientation. These typically pointed to PAS support for the Iranian regime, and Hadi's public support for it after a visit to Iran. The latter was particularly embarrassing for the IRC because Hadi had previously been touted by the IRC as Ikhwan-endorsed, and hence, acceptable to the IRC. Hadi himself appears to have been quite oblivious to much of this, thus only confirming his reputation as being more theological than political.

Although some IRC supporters continue to be prominent within PAS, the IRC leadership may have decided to move on to greener pastures. In view of its historic rivalry with and animosity towards ABIM, it is unlikely that an easy rapprochement with ABIM can be achieved despite similarities in their ideological orientations. However, citing the willingness of Ikhwan in Sudan and elsewhere in the Arab world to collaborate with autocratic forces as long as they proclaim receptivity to Islamisation, it appears that the IRC leadership has come to some kind of compromise with the Mahathir regime, citing its espousal of Islamisation.

Meanwhile, the new PAS has become more vociferous in its opposition to Mahathir's UMNO, which it still denounces as un-Islamic and hypocritical. But UMNO has improved its Islamic credentials, thus isolating PAS as extremist, and capturing the political middle ground of Malay nationalism combined with Islam, voluntarily conceded by the new PAS leadership from the mid-1980s. Ironically, some of the ABIM leaders originally responsible for denouncing Malay chauvinism and *assabiyah* in UMNO have had to make an ideological about-turn, either to make headway within UMNO themselves, or to legitimise the current stance of their colleagues trying to do so. Needless to say, this has strengthened the religious element in the inter-ethnic divide, exacerbating tensions which continue to wrack Malaysian society in its fourth decade of independence.

Until the UMNO split from early 1987, tensions continued to run high between PAS and UMNO supporters at the grassroots level, especially with the continued growth of UMNO political patronage and 'money politics'. There has been discrimination against PAS members in access to government services, facilities and subsidies, particularly in the villages, causing growing animosity between PAS and UMNO followers. In several villages in Kelantan and Trengganu, separate mosques were constructed in the same village for followers of the two parties, while separate prayer sessions have been conducted in some mosques according to party affiliation. Official reports on this situation invariably cast PAS as the villain of the piece. Ironically, while PAS's apparently greater ideological consistency— at the expense of major political-strategic advances—may have deepened but not broadened its base, its electoral support—as the leading Muslim-Malay opposition party—grew in reaction to mounting popular frustration, disillusionment and even disgust at the growing abuses of those in power.

Since the UMNO split in early 1987, there have been profound shifts in Malay politics (see Crouch, above). Not to be left out, since mid-1988, Malay political leaders outside UMNO have responded to Tengku Razaleigh's call for Muslim and Malay unity. From late 1988, political co-operation between PAS and the UMNO dissidents began to develop. This could well become the key link for an alternative multi-ethnic coalition capable of capturing power in fair elections. PAS's ability to steer itself through this fast changing situation was slightly undermined by Vice President Nakhaie's surprise resignation in September 1988 from all party posts—citing the party's poor management, organisation and decisiveness—and subsequent defection to UMNO in April 1989, soon after PAS's annual *muktamar*. More than anyone else in the party's top leadership, Nakhaie had been primarily responsible for the party's improved organisational capacity and some bold new initiatives in the mid-eighties. While Nakhaie initially claimed that he had resigned in frustration at the party leadership's failure to appreciate, follow through and support such initiatives, his subsequent conduct eroded much of the support and respect he once enjoyed in PAS. The new leadership around Fadzil Noor, confirmed at the March 1989 muktamar, could still enhance PAS's ability to develop such initiatives, which will be crucial for mounting an effective all-round challenge to the ruling BN coalition.

Concluding Remarks

From this review of the development and changing character of the main Islamic movements in Malaysia, it should be clear that they have rather diverse political characteristics, implications and visions. Tabligh's contribution to the current Islamic revival in Malaysia can hardly be said to be politically threatening. And while Arqam may have posed a challenge in the past, by offering alternative economic and social institutions ostensibly modelled on the Prophet's example, it has been severely crippled and compromised in recent years by the theological controversies in which its leader has become embroiled. Both Tabligh and Arqam continue to encourage alternative spiritual lifestyles, which emphasise other worldliness. But neither emphasises the establishment of an Islamic state, nor poses any direct threat to the political status quo.

ABIM has, for some time, advocated a modernist and reformist interpretation of the political positions and strategies advocated by Ikhwan in the Arab world and Jamaat in Pakistan. It demonstrated an early, though unsustained enthusiasm for the Iranian Revolution. Through such eclecticism, it has managed to retain links with, and derive moral and material support from a broad range of Muslim tendencies, while rhetorically promoting Islam as an alternative to both capitalism and socialism. ABIM's eclecticism has also allowed it to avoid addressing important questions, especially if they happen to be politically awkward or embarrassing, and to adopt a broad range of inconsistent positions. Such pragmatism has made it possible to justify both the alliance with PAS in the past and to rationalise support for Mahathir's policies since then. In fact, ABIM can look with considerable satisfaction at the new Islamic institution building and other initiatives associated with Mahathir's Islamisation, since many of them represent the fruition of previous ABIM demands. But the pace and the outcome of the reforms may still embarrass ABIM and its tacit support for the regime, while ambitious ABIM leaders would prefer to be more heavily involved in planning, implementation and control. To be sure, ABIM and ex-ABIM leaders are already occupying strategic positions in most of the new projects, although tensions between long-serving Muslim government officials and the new crop of ABIM-supplied 'Muslim professionals' are unlikely to disappear. Further Islamisation may still come about, especially in the educational field. Anwar retained the powerful Education Ministry after the May 1987 cabinet reshuffle. Recognising that the fate of the Islamisation programme, as well as Anwar's (and hence their own) ascendance rests very much on Mahathir's patronage, ABIM leaders are now in an awkward position. They must support Mahathir, who, Islamisation notwithstanding, was also responsible for the 1975 amendments to the UUCA (which they vociferously condemned in the past), various other unpopular laws and policies, as well as recent abuses and the growing concentration of power.

Though not overly preoccupied with the matter now, some of the more far-sighted ABIM leaders recognise the limitations of Islamisation in the Malaysian context. They are probably also not certain how far Mahathir will go within these limits. While insisting that the government's Islamisation projects are more than merely symbolic concessions to Islam, many are also sceptical about how far Islamisation will have to go to be acceptable to the PAS leadership. Many believe that continued Islamisation would succeed in co-opting more Islamic dissident (including PAS) leaders, especially those considered—by some ABIM leaders—to be more reasonable and moderate. (While some insist that the ulamak will never be satisfied with anything less than the complete displacement of the 'secular political elite', there is little evidence for such an 'all or nothing' view in the contemporary Malaysian context.) Such a 'power sharing' arrangement is not an easy thing to achieve, and is unlikely to be sought by Mahathir (though not necessarily by Anwar) in more favourable or compelling circumstances. Even if the PAS leadership, or at least a sizeable section of it, were to be 'won over', the roots of Muslim-Malay dissent will nevertheless remain in the absence of more fundamental egalitarian reforms of broader scope. Such reforms, although firmly rooted in the spirit of Islamic justice, are not currently envisaged by UMNO, ABIM or even PAS.

In the area of economics, for instance, the Islamic alternative is conceived by both ABIM and PAS in rather simplistic formal-legal terms, i.e.

the elimination, or disguise, of interest (rather than usury), the collection and distribution of *zakat* and *sadagah*, and the establishment of a *baitulmal*—rather than in terms of more holistic socio-economic structures and relations, whether capitalist or otherwise. Yet, the simple elimination (or disguise) of interest, or the literal substitution of *zakat* for more progressive taxation and public expenditure systems, without other reforms, are bound to exacerbate, rather than reduce inequality (Naqvi 1981). Hence, unless PAS develops its Islamic critique of the Malaysian status quo along more progressive lines (see, for example, Engineer 1987; Irfani, 1985; Shariati, 1979; Taleghani, 1983), it will not be able to offer a meaningful, viable and popularly acceptable alternative to the Malaysian people, Muslims and non-Muslims. It will instead remain isolated in the corner UMNO has cleverly driven it into.

Acceptability to non-Muslims is crucial here, and not just because they make up almost half the population of Malaysia. Over a third of the population of Peninsular Malaysia is Chinese, and over a tenth Indian, while non-Muslims are in the majority in both Sabah and Sarawak. While essentially mute spectators to the rapidly unfolding drama of Islamic resurgence as far as Muslims are concerned, most non-Muslims have felt ignored, if not threatened by what they see as increasingly powerful, assertive and intolerant Muslims and Islamic movements. While some non-Muslims in the ruling coalition may reluctantly accept the government's Islamisation campaign as necessary to deal with the supposed threat posed by PAS in particular and the Islamic resurgence in general, most others view it as yet another confirmation of the secondary status of the non-Malay, non-Muslim allies of UMNO in the coalition. Non-Muslim fears are fuelled by ignorance and a growing sense of alienation, bordering on helplessness. It is unlikely that such apprehension about the Islamic resurgence and its consequences will recede unless a viable alternative, Islamic or otherwise, addresses the sources of their frustration and disenchantment. Only a progressive Islamic approach would enable PAS to make such a breakthrough.

Finally, there is another silent constituency which tends to be overlooked. In Malaysia, Malays are, by definition Muslims, at least nominally. However, it would be a serious mistake to dismiss, as it is quite common to do in Malaysia, those Malays who do not approve of the Islamic resurgence or the government's Islamisation programme as not being genuine Muslims. While nominal Muslims are understandably alienated from these currents, there are also many 'genuine' Muslims who remain sceptical of the resurgence, or at least of its rhetoric and political consequences, including Mahathir's Islamic posturing. Precisely because they are Muslims, they feel even more constrained to express concern or dissent about various Islamic political trends. It is difficult to estimate their numbers, let alone their strength, considering the constraints they feel. Although largely unorganised and sharing few other common concerns or bases for unity, they are nonetheless a force to be reckoned with, especially if 'pushed to the wall' or caught in circumstances of flux and change.

In conclusion, however, the likelihood of PAS developing a progressive Islamic position is not very great, though not impossible, as often presumed. Instead, the rapprochement between PAS and the UMNO dissidents since late 1988, with the formation of a broad Muslim-Malay opposition coalition, probably is a prelude to a multi-ethnic opposition coalition including the DAP. If such a major realignment does not occur and if Anwar eventually succeeds in heading the government, Islamisation may develop even further, eventually isolating and eroding the Islamic opposition, but also, in the process, exposing the limitations of the Islamic alternative as conceived by UMNO, ABIM and perhaps even much of PAS as well.

Bibliography

Syed Muhammad Naguib Al-Attas, 1978. *Islam and Secularism*, Kuala Lumpur: ABIM.

Aliran (ed), 1979. *The Universalism of Islam*, Penang: Aliran.

Ashgar Ali Engineer, 1987. *Islam and Its Relevance to Our Age*, Kuala Lumpur: Ikraq.

Crouch, Harold, 1980. Lee Kam Hing & Michael Ong (eds), *Malaysian Politics And The 1978 Election*, Kuala Lumpur: Oxford University Press.

Funston, J. N., 1980. *Malay Politics in Malaysia: A Study of PAS and UMNO*, Kuala Lumpur: Heinemann.

Gale, B. (ed), 1986. *Readings in Malaysian Politics*, Kuala Lumpur: Pelanduk.

Hussein Mutalib, 1981. Islamic Revivalism in Malaysia—The Middle East and Indonesian Connection. Malaysian Society Third Colloquium paper, University of Adelaide, August 1981.

Irfani, Suroosh, 1985. The Progressive Islamic Movement. In Ashgar Khan (ed), *Islam, Politics and the Senate*, London: Zed Press.

Jomo, K. S., 1986. *A Question of Class: Capital, the State and Uneven Development in Malaya*, Singapore: Oxford University Press.

Kessler, C. S., 1978. *Islam and Politics in a Malay State: Kelantan 1838–1969*, Ithaca: Cornell University Press.

Kessler, C. S., 1979. Islam, Society and Political Behaviour: Some Implications of the Malay Case. *British Journal of Sociology*, 23, pp. 33–50.

Kessler, C. S., 1980. Malaysia: Islamic Revivalism and Political Disaffection in a Divided Society. *South East Asian Chronicle*, 75, pp. 3–11.

Lyons, M. L., 1979. Dakwah Movement in Malaysia. *Review of Indonesian and Malaysian Affairs*, 13, pp. 34–45.

Mauzy, D. K. and Milne, R. S., 1983/84. The Mahathir Administration: Discipline through Islam. *Pacific Affairs*, 56, 4, pp. 617–648.

von der Mehden, Fred R., 1980 Islamic Resurgence in Malaysia. In J. L. Esposito (ed). *Islam and Development.*

Mohamed Abu Bakar, 1981. Islamic Revivalism and the Political Process in Malaysia. *Asian Survey*, 21, pp. 1040–1059.

Muzaffar, Chandra, 1987. *Islamic Resurgence in Malaysia*, Petaling Jaya: Penerbit Fajar Bakti.

Nagata, J., 1984. *The Reflowering of Malaysian Islam: Modern Religious Redicals and Their Roots*, Vancouver: University of British Columbia Press.

Syed Nawab Haider Naqvi, 1981. *Ethics and Economics—An Islamic Synthesis*, Leicester: Islamic Foundation.

Shamsul, A. B., 1983. A Revival in the Study of Islam in Malaysia. *Man*, 18, pp. 399–404.

Shariati, Ali, 1979. *The Sociology of Islam*, Berkeley: Mizan Press.

Taleghani, Sayyid Mahmud, 1983. *Society and Economics in Islam*, Berkeley: Mizan Press.

Taufik Abdullah & Sharon Siddique (eds), 1985. *Islam and Society in Southeast Asia*, Singapore: Institute of Southeast Asian Studies.

Zainah Anwar, 1987. *Islamic Revivalism in Malaysia: Dakwah Among The Students*, Petaling Jaya: Pelanduk.

5

Peasants, Proletarianisation and the State: FELDA Settlers in Pahang

Halim Salleh

This paper will highlight the politics of Felda production. It will be shown that settlers had been openly as well as covertly retaliating against Felda since the beginning of Felda land schemes. These were carried out by individual settlers as well as by organised groups of settlers and in some cases, via political parties. The question here is why settlers retaliate against a state agency which is supposedly working to promote their well being?

Based partly on fieldwork conducted in central Pahang in 1984,[1] this paper suggests that Felda production essentially depends on the state's ability to control peasant labour force for large scale production. This is clearly shown in the fundamental Felda-settler relationships relating to land ownership, finance and labour control which separate the settlers from the control over the means of production and the products. Essentially, this turns the settlers into proletarians but for obvious political and economic reasons, they are not transformed into pure wage workers. They are instead considered by the state as if they were independent if not privileged citizens who are enjoying the benefits of a major government sponsored rural (land) development project. Consequently, the protests and everyday forms of resistance that the settlers engage in are characterised by a desire to deproletarianise themselves and to assert their standing as individuals. This article seeks to explain the nature of the settlers struggle.

---

[1] The fieldwork centred mainly on a rubber and an oil palm scheme which I have renamed Pahang Tengah 1 (PT1) and Pahang Tengah 2 (PT2) respectively.

Felda Land Schemes in Malaysia

Felda is a state authority which combines state and foreign capital with largely land-poor Malay peasants (the settlers) to produce cash crops, mainly rubber and oil palm, in land schemes for the world market.[2] A typical Felda land scheme normally consists of 1,600–2,000 hectares of plantation modelled on the organisation of a private estate where settlers and cash crop cultivation are blended together in a settlement (Mahesan 1984). Settlers are grouped together in a central residential complex around the local management office complex. They are provided with basic facilities such as a mosque, a maternity clinic, a food credit shop (operated by Felda Trading Corporation) and additional shops for extra provisions as well as a school and a recreation field. Some established schemes are also provided with water supply and electricity.

Operationally, a land scheme is controlled by a manager who is responsible to his immediate regional controller (controlling about 15–30 schemes) who in turn answers to senior officials at Felda headquarters in Kuala Lumpur. A manager is normally assisted by an assistant manager, one social development assistant for religious affairs (SDA-R), one social development assistant for women's affairs (SDA-W), several field supervisors each of whom, similar to conductors on private estates, control and supervise the work of about 50–70 settlers. These officials are also assisted by a team of clerical and general workers consisting of clerks, typists and drivers.

Indisputably, Felda land schemes have been very successful. From a modest beginning of a few land schemes in 1958, they expanded in the 1970s and 1980s (under the New Economic Policy) into a major programme for poverty eradication surpassing all other types of land schemes conducted by Rubber Industry Smallholders Development Authority (RISDA), Federal Land Consolidation and Rehabilitation Authority (FELCRA), Regional Development Authorities (RDAs) and the state governments (Malaysia 1986: 306). Today Felda has a total of 422 land schemes (comprising 715,205 hectares of plantation) with 289 land schemes operated by 106,510 settler households and the rest by contract workers (Felda Annual Report, 1987: 10–12). It has also expanded to Sabah and Sarawak. By 1984, Felda controlled 23.22 per cent rubber and oil palm plantation in peninsular Malaysia and produced 8.33 per cent rubber and 26.22 per cent oil palm for the country (Malaysia 1984: 117–120). This is comparable to the operation of any one of the major plantation agencies in the country (Barlow 1978: 446). In fact, it has been claimed that Felda is now one of the biggest modern plantation agencies in the world (Graham and Floering 1984).

---

[2] The types of crops planted in Felda land schemes include oil palm (498,499 hectares), rubber (190,559 hectares), cocoa (20,278 hectares), sugar (5,118 hectares) and coffee (751 hectares) (Felda Annual Report, 1987: 9).

The economics of production demonstrates Felda's success further. Land schemes are not only cost effective and profitable investments (Singh 1965; Hussain Wafa 1972: 182) but they are also regarded as beneficial to the settlers. In the 1970s for instance, the settlers obtained an average monthly income ranging between $205.50–$599.59 which was several times higher than that received by their fellow peasants in traditional villages who averaged about $100.20 per month (Khera 1976: 29; Lim Sow Ching 1976: 233). This pattern was repeated in the 1980s although the settlers in oil palm schemes generally registered better average monthly income than those in rubber schemes.[3] This justifies the claim that the income of poor peasants improves tremendously once they join Felda land schemes.

Settlers Protests

It will be shown below that the income question is not unproblematic but most writers on Felda land schemes (eg. Lim Sow Ching 1976; Khera 1976; McAndrews 1977; Shamsul Bahrin 1971; Shamsul Bahrin and Perera 1977; Chan and Ritcher 1982) seem to accept Felda's achievements as a matter of course. They neither problematise Felda land schemes nor take into account the fact that Felda's operation is contradicted by settlers' protests, retaliations and resistance. Given the centrality of this contradiction to the present concern, it is necessary that we now discuss the nature of the settlers' struggle against Felda in detail.

Assault on Felda Officials

One way settlers expressed their resentment against Felda was to demand speedy implementation of the block system.[4] This is because the system

---

[3] The distribution of average monthly income of Felda settlers may be summarised as follows.

Year	Oil palm settlers ($)	Rubber settlers ($)
1982	624	402
1983	765	484
1984	1,231	505
1985	889	421
1986	376	405
1987	522	530

(*Source*: Felda Annual Reports 1983: 16; 1985: 20 and 1987: 21).

[4] This is the work system adopted by an oil palm scheme after it reaches break-even point. Under the system settlers are divided into several work gangs (called blocks) consisting of about 20-25 settlers with each settler assigned to a working plot of about ten acres or 550 tree stands. Felda appoints one settler in each work gang as a block leader to coordinate production work. Each work gang (block) is required to sell the produce to Felda-owned processing mills at the price determined by the latter and

provides them with an actual income as opposed to the preceding work systems such as *kong* work[5] and temporary block system[6] where settlers are paid a cash advance which counts as a debt to Felda. When the demand was not met, settlers normally overpowered the land scheme officials and locked them up in their offices or in meeting halls. Subsequently, settlers would stage a demonstration until senior Felda officials agreed to settle their demands. This was the pattern that occurred in one of the most publicised cases at Bukit Kuantan Felda scheme in Pahang in December 1976.

Following the original Felda plan, settlers in 15 blocks demanded the implementation of the block system in January 1977, that is, one year after the scheme broke even. The manager, however, calculated that if this was done, Felda would not be able to collect as much loan repayment as would be possible if the system was implemented in July 1977. Presumably under instructions from Felda headquarters in Kuala Lumpur, he turned down the demand and extended the date to July 1977. As settlers were tired of their low cash advances under the then temporary block system while their working plots were already productive, some 300 of them overpowered the manager, his assistant and 19 members of the *Jawatan Kuasa Kemajuan Rancangan or JKKR* (Land Scheme Development Committee)[7] who were at a meeting in the local community hall on 27 December 1976 and locked them up by barricading all exits to the building. They provided their "prisoners' with food, drinks, cigarettes and blankets until the next day when the police was summoned and the director-general of Felda arrived from Kuala Lumpur to negotiate a settlement.

In the end Felda agreed to the settlers' demand but it imposed stricter conditions on the latter: settlers were to be charged (higher) loan repayment at $144 per month instead of $120 per month had they agreed to the implementation of the block system in July 1977. In addition, the settlers were also threatened with the withdrawal of a financial loan system called the "guaranteed minimum income" which could mean that under periods of low production, they might not receive any financial advance at all. As a result, 13 out of the 15 blocks agreed to postpone the implementation of the block system

---

proceeds from the sales are computed as a block income. Deductions are made for loans and other personal financial obligations to Felda (such as cash advance, food credits and other debts) before the "balance", which is actual cash-in-hand, is distributed equally among block members.

[5] This work system is used during the pre-productive stage of a land scheme. Basically, it allocates each settler to specific daily tasks which Felda management considers appropriate for an eight hours stint of work.

[6] This is similar to the block system except that settlers are given cash advances instead of a real income.

[7] Hereafter referred to as JKKR. This is a committee of block leaders which assists the local scheme management. It has representation in the higher level settlers committee at the regional level called the *Gabungan Jawatan Kuasa Kemajuan*

until July 1977. (NST, 30 Dec 1976; UM, 29 Dec 1976; BH, 30 Dec 1976, 3 Jan 1977 and 13 Jan 1977).

The extent of this form of protest is difficult to ascertain. Felda officials claim that it was common in the 1960s but press reports noted only twelve cases of major strikes and detention of officials in the period 1964–1983.[8] Following the pattern at the Bukit Kuantan land scheme, however, settlers did not succeed in their demands because they had no bargaining power. In cases where settlers were persistent, the police were mobilised to free the "imprisoned" officials (UM, 27 July 1978). The Minister of Land and Regional Development, in 1978, charged that detention and other assaults on Felda officials were "criminal acts; the offence is no less severe than extortion or kidnapping" (NST, 11 August 1978). Thus, he condemned the settlers involved in such protests as ungrateful "kidnappers and gangsters" and promised to charge them in the court of law before expelling them from land schemes (*ibid.*). However, this does not seem to have deterred the settlers because they have continued to detain Felda officials to express their demands until today (S, 6 May 1989).

Attack on Individual Officials

The settlers' anger might also be directed at individual Felda officials. However, similar to the patterns of retaliation among Malay estate workers (Zawawi Ibrahim 1983) and within the general framework of what Scott (1976) called the "moral economy" of social relations among the peasantry, the relationship between officials and settlers seems to be mediated by some degree of moral consideration. My fieldwork in Pahang indicates that officials who were considerate (*timbang rasa*), as shown by their reluctance to impose fines and penalties on settlers, were treated with courtesy if not respect. In contrast, officials who were strict and inconsiderate were treated with scorn, challenged to fist fights and threatened with physical violence. In 1984, for instance, an official at PT2 Felda shop was slapped in the face by a settler because the former refused to give him extra food credit.[9] Similarly, a settler in a nearby scheme slapped the

---

Rancangan or the Regional JKKR which again sends a representative to the national settlers committee called the *Jawatan Kuasa Perunding Peneroka* or the *JKPP*. The three committees constitute what is known as the JKKR system.

[8] These were reported in various ways by the following daily papers: MM, 21 October 1964; UM, 15 December 1973; SE, 23 November 1974; NST, 23 November 1974; UM, 29 December 1976; NST, 30 December 1976; BH, 30 December 1976; SE, 3 January 1977; BH, 3 January 1977; S, 3 January 1977; UM, 12 January 1977; BH, 13 January 1977; NST, 1 August 1978, 11 August 1978 and 28 October 1978; UM, 3 August 1978; NST, 14 June 1980; UM, 26 June 1982; SS, 1 May 1983; NST, 17 July 1983 and 20 January 1984.

[9] In the context of Malay society and culture, slapping someone in the face is not

face of his land scheme manager in a quarrel on the implementation of the block system. Felda records also noted three serious cases of attack on individual officials in the period between 2 July 1983 and 26 May 1984. Apparently, physical threats on individual Felda officials are quite common.

Independent Sale of the Produce

Settlers also retaliated against Felda in non-violent ways. One major form was to defy Felda's rules. Instead of selling the produce only to Felda Mills Corporation (Felmill) as stipulated by the Settlers' Agreement (see below), some settlers reportedly organised themselves and collectively sold their produce to the highest bidder. This was carried out either openly or in clandestine manner (BH, 9 July 1976; UM, 11 June 1976). The immediate cause of such action was usually a protest against low and non-negotiable prices determined by Felmill. For instance, reports suggest that Felmill paid as low as 50 per cent below the price offered by independent buyers for both rubber and palm oil fresh fruit bunches (FFB) on certain occasions (BH, 27 March 1978; UM, 23 June 1975). In some cases, the decision to sell to private buyers also arose as a form of protest against alleged short-weighing and under-grading by Felmill officials.[10] In any case, it was advantageous for settlers to sell their produce independently because they could sell it at the prevailing market price and avoid various deductions on their income (see below).

As Felda lost quite substantially from such acts of defiance (BH, 9 May 1976), it responded in 1973, first, by mobilising the police and local rubber licensing authority to curb the sales. Second, it launched campaigns to correct the so-called "wrong attitude" by arguing that the practice is disadvantageous because it would only delay collection of loans and thus the final ownership of land by settlers (ST, 13 June 1973). Also, it warned the settlers that it was against the Settlers' Agreement and denounced the practice as illegal (UM, 12 February 1975). Thus, depending on the quantity involved, it promised either to confiscate the produce or expel the settlers involved. To this end, Felda introduced its own policing system in 1976 in the form of the Felda Security Corporation (Felsco) whose workers now carry out twenty-four hour surveillance at all entry and exit points of land scheme complexes. In addition, Felda also established a special task force at its headquarters in Kuala Lumpur to investigate particular land schemes involved. However, in spite of all this, a discussion with Felda officials in

---

only an act of physical violence but also a derogatory act to express extreme disrespect.

[10] In one reported case, it was claimed that each settler in the land scheme lost as much as $50 per month because of short-weighing by Felmill officials (UM, 3 January 1974).

1984 indicated that "illegal" sales continue, though on a somewhat smaller scale. In any case, it would appear awkward if not politically unfeasible to take action such as expelling settlers in large numbers, particularly when their grievances were real.

Strikes

Another form of non-violent retaliation is the strike. Reported cases show that this consisted of mass refusal to work in the *kong* system, refusal to harvest the crops and refusal to accept their monthly balance (NST, 14 June 1980; UM, 15 December 1973). Apart from the strike launched against insufficient supply of food under the *kong* system (BH, 4 December 1974 and 24 December 1974), the immediate cause of such strikes revolved essentially around the settlers' demand to control their labour and the produce. For instance, the first reported strike launched in 1964 by settlers at Chalok rubber scheme in Trengganu was in protest against the change in work allocation based upon the household to one organised on a collective basis (MM, 20 October 1964). The settlers feared that, under the proposed collective work system, the more hardworking among them would lose the proceeds from their labour to others. The same was true in the strike staged by rubber settlers at Palong Empat scheme in Negri Sembilan who protested against the implementation of the block system: the settlers sought to protect the control over their (household) labour by refusing to tap their trees when the block system was imposed on them. While on strike, they also petitioned local politicians, the Minister of Land and Regional Development and the Prime Minister to intervene. This finally forced Felda to withdraw the block system in rubber production (UM, 26 August 1982).

Other immediate causes of strikes included protests against unreasonable deduction on income and a reduction in the price paid by Felmill. This was the case in the strike mounted by the settlers at Taib Andak land scheme in Johor in 1980.

The local Felmill suddenly reduced the price for their FFB from $174 per metric tonne to $143 per metric tonne whereas the market price for oil palm remained steady. At the same time Felda was also deducting excessively at about $700–$800 per month on their income whereas Felda had previously agreed to do so at a lower rate. To express their resentment to such high handed dealings by Felda, the settlers simply refused to accept their cash income altogether (NST, 14 June 1980). Subsequently, they sent petitions to their local UMNO chief as well as to the Prime Minister to inform them of their plight. The settlers refused to deal with Felda officials and the Minister of Land and Regional Development had to intervene to bring the two parties together. After three hours of talk, the Minister managed to strike a deal by getting Felda to raise the price by $19 per metric tonne (UM, 25 March 1978; BH, 27 March 1978).

According to the Settlers' Agreement, Felda has the legal right to punish striking settlers but it has not taken such action so far. Somewhat similar to the case of independent sale of the produce, it seems that punishing the settlers in large numbers including the whole population of a land scheme would be politically unfeasible if not explosive. Also, this is because non-violent protests are generally double edged: settlers not only confronted and demanded changes from Felda directly but they also sought refuge under their UMNO political masters or at least by making their complaints known to them. Why do they rely on this political party? Let us now consider the rise of UMNO in land schemes and see how it affects settlers' protests.

Political Protests and Political Control

It must be noted that settlers do not have access to formal channels of protests because the latter simply do not exist. Unlike the protection given to land by the Group Settlement Act 1960 (see below), there is absolutely no legal provision whatsoever to protect the interests of settlers. Instead, they only enjoy the rights and privileges of normal citizens. In stark contrast to the completeness of Felda rules and regulations governing production, collection of loans and income deductions, there is no formal procedure to handle protests and resistance from settlers. Any protest arising from their status as settlers, therefore, are out of order, if not illegal.

UMNO in Felda Land Schemes

However, it may be suggested that settlers in Felda land schemes are among the most politicised groups of people in the country. In the 1960s and 1970s, support for political parties in the government, particularly UMNO was one of the important undeclared criteria for entry into Felda land schemes. Today, membership in UMNO is declared as a major prerequisite making entry into a land scheme a major reward for supporting UMNO candidates in political elections (see discussion below). Hence, settlers are familiar with both UMNO as a political organisation as well as the formal political process even before they settle in land schemes.

In this context, it may be expected that every settled Felda land scheme today has an UMNO branch and this is linked, through the UMNO hierarchy, to the local and the state party chiefs and finally to government ministers and the Prime Minister. Given the political background of settlers, it may also be expected that UMNO commands a major following in land schemes. According to the UMNO Division of Jerantut, Pahang, for instance, 60 per cent of the settlers (including women and youth) in Felda land schemes in the District were registered members of UMNO in the early 1980s (UMNO, 1983). To this extent, it may be argued that UMNO forms a major political channel through which settlers can express their interests. This is especially so since they do not have any formal channel to protest against Felda itself.

Political Protests Through UMNO

It is a well known fact among settlers that it was local UMNO branches in land schemes that organised such protests as selling the produce to independent buyers and strikes. The work of the local UMNO branch at the PTI rubber scheme is a case in point.

In 1972 Felda collected the latex from settlers at the scheme to sell it to a private company in Kuala Lumpur because the Felda Marketing Corporation was yet to be formed. By the end of the year some 42,000 gallons of latex at the cost of about $10,000 could not be accounted for. The local UMNO branch formed an action committee and called a strike. Settlers at the scheme either stopped tapping altogether or sold their latex to independent buyers. They also sought assistance from the local member of Parliament from UMNO to negotiate with Felda. After two months, Felda heeded their demands and reimbursed the payment for their 42,000 gallons of latex.

This is also true of selling the produce to independent buyers. For instance, due to the low price paid by Felmill, the UMNO branch in Felda Lasah 2 land scheme in Perak protested in 1975 by making a press declaration that they were selling their produce independently until Felmill rectified the situation (UM, 23 June 1975). This clearly challenged one of the fundamental clauses in the Settler's Agreement. However, the fact that it was carried out by a local UMNO branch gave credibility to the settlers' protests as being part of the wider UMNO struggle to protect the interest of the Malays.

On the same basis, settlers' grievances and demands are expressed through their local UMNO branches which submit them directly to their Chief Ministers and the Minister of Land and Regional Development. For instance, the UMNO Division of Jerantut, Pahang submitted a memorandum in early 1983 to the Minister of Land and Regional Development asking the latter to provide appropriate basic amenities, a sufficient amount of cash advances to new settlers, individual accounting of work for the block system and an increase in the prices of FFB and rubber similar to that paid by private processing mills (UMNO, 1983). It argued that this was necessary because such issues had been used by opposition political parties to win over the votes of settlers in the 1982 general election.

Undoubtedly, such demands put the sense of commitment and responsibility of UMNO leaders to the test. To protect their political interests, UMNO leaders responded either directly in favour of settlers or promised to look into the matter. So far none of the Jerantut UMNO demands have been entertained, but it is known that several cases of expulsion from

Pahang land schemes were reversed by the Minister of Land and Regional Development in the early 1980s. This caused some embarrassment to the managers of the land schemes concerned while officials at Felda headquarters in Kuala Lumpur suggested that such political interference had also created difficulties to Felda management. To this extent, UMNO may be considered a champion of the settlers and constituting a major challenge to Felda management. It is not immediately known to what extent the recent (1988) UMNO crisis has affected the political party as a vehicle of settlers' protests, but it may be expected that dissenting settlers would find the so-called UMNO team B—now legally constituted as *Semangat 46*—attractive.[11]

The Challenge from PAS

PAS and other opposition political parties also provide formal channels for settlers' protest. MacAndrews (1979) for instance, noted that disenchanted settlers in the Bilut Valley scheme in North Pahang, supported the *Parti Sosialis Rakyat Malaysia* (PSRM) to express their resentment against Felda in the 1970s. In the 1980s, the main opposition political party that settlers have identified with is PAS.[12] Basically, the party advocates establishment of an Islamic way of life within an Islamic state of Malaysia. As UMNO had turned the country away from this path, PAS leaders denounce UMNO, its members and its policies for capitalist development as un-Islamic.[13] Such opinions are echoed by PAS supporters in land schemes as well. For instance, they argue that they are forced into the forbidden system of usury (*riba*) as shown by payment of interest on their loan repayment by virtue of being in land schemes. Likewise, they argue that the block system provides them with a forbidden (*haram*) income because Islam forbids a follower to deprive others of their labour which is possible under the block system.[14] Thus far this has not caused any serious difficulty in the operation of the block system but the underlying implication of the argument is that the operation of Felda land schemes is un-Islamic.

It is difficult to determine the number of PAS supporters in land schemes today. But we do know that the growth of the political party has been suppressed by Felda officials. As observed in central Pahang land schemes,

---

[11] The split in UMNO and subsequent rise of *Semangat 46* as an alternative Malay political party is discussed in greater detail by Crouch as well as Khoo Khay Jin in the present volume.

[12] Developments in 1987 indicated that another opposition political party, the Democratic Action Party (DAP) began to gain support in Felda land schemes.

[13] This generated a heated debate between PAS and UMNO in the 1980s (Chandra Muzaffar 1987: 85ff).

[14] As noted earlier, the block system provides equal income to members of a block though they do not necessarily contribute their labour equally.

PAS exists clandestinely amongst small groups of settlers who carry out their political meetings in small-group religious gatherings. But the threat of settlers' protests through Islam seems quite real because the fundamentalist protest ideology seems compatible with their materialist demands. The latter was expressed by a PAS lawyer in two booklets which accuse Felda of turning settlers into workers similar to coolies in colonial estates because it deprived them of their basic legal protection and welfare provisions. The booklets also criticise Felda for deducting settlers' income excessively, not providing them with secure land tenure and holding them on constant threat of expulsion. On this basis, the lawyer challenged Felda and the state to recognize the contribution of settlers to the economy and on behalf of the latter, demanded a fairer deal (Suhaimi Said 1984a and 1984b).

To curb the development of such protest, Felda in 1983, ordered its officials, particularly social development officials in land schemes to control all religious talks and gatherings in land schemes particularly those conducted or organised by suspected supporters of PAS-Muslim fundamentalist groups. If necessary, they are to liaise with their local State Religious Affairs Department and the police to stop such gathering (Felda, Circular Letter, 23 August 1983). Working together with members of JKKRs and UMNO, Felda officials therefore suppressed PAS political meetings. According to PAS supporters, Felda officials in land schemes in the Jengka Region in Pahang had, in several instances, stopped PAS guest speakers from entering land schemes, disrupted religious meetings while they were in session and threatened to take disciplinary action, including expulsion of the settlers who had organised such meetings.[15] As PAS cannot so far establish a strong base in land schemes and it is being opposed by both UMNO and Felda, much of the protests by PAS settlers remain covert and largely controlled.[16]

The Settlers' Association

The cases of settler retaliations and protests sketched so far indicate that settlers are simply dissatisfied with the operation of land schemes conducted by Felda because they wanted more from a land scheme than simply temporary access to land. This is clearly expressed by the demands

---

[15] Suhaimi Said (1984a: 53–54) for instance, cited eight cases where PAS meetings were either prohibited or disrupted in land schemes in the Jengka and central Pahang regions in 1984.

[16] It is interesting to note, in this context, that the Temerloh PAS lawyer, Haji Suhaimi Said, was arrested in 1985 under the Internal Security Act, a legal provision for the state to detain anyone without trial, but was later released with restrictions to his movement. He was again detained in 1987 and released in 1988.

of the Johor Settlers Association.[17] The major objective of the association, according to the president of the association, is to "fight for land, for rights and for freedom to control" their own lives like any other citizen in the country though the immediate concern, according to the secretary of the association, is to secure the return of some $300 million in superfluous deduction Felda had carried out on settlers' income thus far. To these ends, the association sent a memorandum to the Minister of Land and Regional Development in early 1983 asking for recognition as well as sanction from the Minister to expand the association to other states in the country. In particular, the association proposed the formation of a joint consultative body consisting of members from Felda and the association to replace the JKPP because the present structure of decision-making process in Felda land schemes, in the words of the president of the association, is "a guided democracy". Alternatively, the association demanded self-determination and self-reliance.[18]

As may be expected, the response from Felda was hostile. It refused to recognise the association and avoided dealings with it altogether. The Minister also dismissed the need for the association as irrelevant because he believed that the JKKR system as well as UMNO branches in land schemes were already sufficient to cater for settlers' welfare (BH, 8 May 1983). Accordingly, Felda took immediate steps to suppress the association from spreading to land schemes outside Johor by threatening to expel the settlers involved. The president of the association was likewise disciplined for creating disharmony among settlers as well as for instigating settlers to protest against Felda. He was also accused of fostering alliances with opposition political parties such as PAS and the Democratic Action Party (DAP), even though he is a local UMNO leader. The president of the association, however, contested the charges through the legal process. For the first time, therefore, Felda was taken to court by a settler.

In the final analysis, it may be argued that Felda tried to control if not

---

[17] The association was registered in 1981. Unless stated, the information on the association was provided by the president and secretary of the Johor Settlers Association in an interview I conducted at Felda Taib Andak land scheme in Kulai, Johor, in December 1985.

[18] Their demands include, among other things, the following;

    a. replacement of the JKKR with a Village Development and Security Committee.

    b. land rights similar to those possessed by other citizens in the country.

    c. independence for settlers' cooperatives and opportunities to take up Felda contracts and organise production.

    d. clarification on the role of Felmill (either as a buyer of the produce or an agent which processes the produce for a fee).

    e. that the Felda shop not compete with settler-operated shops.

    f. self-management in loan free schemes and reduction in Felda management control after the implementation of the block system (Johor Settlers Association, 1983).

abolish all formal channels of protest by settlers. To ensure that future settlers would be fully controlled, new recruits from 1984 would not only be required to sign the Settler's Agreement binding them to Felda but also to sign an oath of loyalty to Felda and the state before they are allowed to settle in a land scheme (Minister of Land and Regional Development, 1984). They are also to be chosen only from *bona fide* UMNO members so as to make Felda land schemes a reservoir of UMNO supporters (Chief Minister of Pahang, 3 November 1984; MM, 3 March 1985). The main reason seems to be the threat to the political and economic hegemony of the state posed by settlers' protests. For instance, while the Chief Minister of Pahang denounced protesting settlers as ungrateful (UM, 6 October 1984), the Prime Minister cautioned that settlers should not "bite the hand that feeds them" (quoted in NST, 2 March 1985). To solve the problem once and for all, however, the Deputy Prime Minister (in 1985) simply ordered settlers who resent Felda rules and regulations to quit the land schemes (NST, 24 February 1985). His reason was similar to that expressed by the Minister of Land and Regional Development in 1978, namely that, "Felda is not afraid of losing its settlers because when one goes, one thousand others are waiting" (quoted in BH, 11 August 1978). Obviously, the dominance of Felda and the state in land schemes is facilitated by the problem of landlessness and a surplus population in the country as well.

Everyday Resistance

How else do settlers protest against Felda? Considering that formal channels of protest are either controlled or denied by Felda, settlers are faced with two other possible options: either they opt out of land schemes altogether or they resist Felda on an individual basis and in the ways they know best.

Felda makes it very clear to all settlers that the doors of land schemes are always open for them to get out. Most settlers, however, find the option rather unfeasible. In the first place, they would not only lose that proportion of the loan they have already repaid since there will not be reimbursements from Felda, but they would also lose out on the income for the latest month since Felda does not pay the settlers until about five weeks later. In the second place, most settlers do not own land nor do they have any alternative employment opportunities. As a result, most of them continue to stay in land schemes and resort to the second option, that is, to rely on private strategies to gain as much immediate returns as possible and to deny Felda control over their individual lives. Following after Scott (1985), we may call this form of protest everyday settler resistance.[19] Some of the major ways they opt to do so include individual smuggling of the produce, non-cooperation, non-compliance and embezzling JKKR funds.

Smuggling the produce out and selling it to independent buyers outside land schemes is one of the most common forms of everyday resistance. This is particularly prevalent in rubber schemes because rubber is easily sold to independent rubber dealers in small quantities. It is also easily concealed for transportation because it cannot be distinguished from any peasant produced rubber and it may be transported through jungle tracks instead of the main roads. In contrast, FFB cannot be sold independently by individuals. While harvesting work requires collective labour, the FFB can be sold only to processing mills in large quantities. However, settlers who smuggle out the produce bear the risk of being caught by Felsco officers and punished (UM, 31 August 1978).

Non-cooperation with Felda management, particularly on voluntary work, constitutes another common way through which settlers resist Felda. For instance, settlers in a scheme in central Pahang reported in 1984 that they refused to clear and beautify their settlement area as well as decorate the land scheme office to prepare for a visit by a government minister. This was to express their resentment against a politician who, they believed, was coming to accuse them of being ungrateful to the government.[20] Obviously, such non-cooperation also expresses the individual settler's resistance against the state.

Similarly, non-compliance to Felda rules and regulations is another clear form of individual resistance against Felda. This is particularly expressed by the settlers who, in direct defiance to the Settler's Agreement, either work full-time in wage employment outside their land schemes or work as well as live outside their land schemes.[21]

Finally, it is quite common for individual settlers to embezzle JKKR funds. This is possible because JKKR normally gives out small loans for activities such as vegetable growing or minor house repairs. Generally speaking book-keeping by members of a JKKR is far from systematic. This provides room for settlers to deny having borrowed money from the JKKR when the latter cannot produce evidence for the loans. In this way, settlers gain a little from the JKKR. To control such embezzlement therefore, Felda instructed in October 1984 that all JKKR accounts be sent to their respective regional controllers' offices for auditing.

---

[19] J. C. Scott (1985: 290) for instance, argues that individual acts should be considered as resistance because "As a first approximation, I might claim that class resistance includes *any* act(s) by member(s) of a subordinate class that is or are *intended* either to mitigate or deny claims (for example, rents, taxes, prestige) made on that class by superordinate classes (for example, landlords, large farmers, the state) or to advance its own claims (for example, work, land, charity, respect) vis-a-vis those superordinate classes".

[20] This would have qualified as a boycott had it been organised (Scott 1985: 250).

[21] A survey by Felda officials indicated that as many as 27 per cent of settlers in a particular land scheme were involved in full-time employment elsewhere (Mohd Fadzil Yunus 1975: 160–172).

I believe it would be difficult if not ambitious to recount here, as Scott would suggest,[22] all the acts settlers carried out with the *intention* of protecting or claiming their interests. What is noted here is simply an indication that there are, in land schemes, forms of resistance which are individualised and highly dependent on individual stratagems, degree of consciousness and above all, plain guts. In terms of consequences, this is no less important than the open and direct as well as collective protests discussed earlier. While the settlers involved actually gain economically, the acts also invited defensive as well as punitive measures from Felda similar to its reactions to other forms of protests. To this extent, these individual acts also qualify as "real resistance" (White 1986).

Relations of Felda Production

Notwithstanding the differences in the forms of settlers' protests and resistance against Felda, the preceding discussion implies that a project of the UMNO government to return the favour and improve the livelihood of the poor people who voted for UMNO in political elections is being resisted by the people themselves. Why is this so? A similar question may be posed about the poor in general: why do they retaliate against a major New Economic Policy project to improve their well-being? To conceptualise the settlers' struggle in its proper perspective, it is necessary that we now examine the position of the settlers in Felda land schemes. Who are the settlers and how do they relate to Felda? To what extent do fundamental areas of Felda-settler relations suggest deep seated contradictions and antagonisms between settlers and Felda? A brief note on landownership, control over settlers' finance and management control in Felda land schemes is in order.

Land Ownership

Land in Malaysia is convertible into individual property through registration and grant of title by the state. An individual who has a title to land therefore has the "power to sell it, borrow on it and transmit after death with the minimum legal formality and expense" (Jarret 1951: 9). Thus, following Harnecker (1976: 30), an individual in Malaysia who owns land is not only a legal owner in the sense of having legal title to it but also a real owner of land because he/she has the rights to "use, enjoy and dispose of" the land attached to the title (cf. Hegedus 1981: 110–124). In the sense of relation of production defined by Bettelheim (1976), land in

---

[22] One aspect of J. C. Scott's (1985: 290) definition of resistance for instance, "focuses on intentions rather than consequences".

Malaysia thus became private property.[23]

In contrast, land designated as Felda land schemes is not private property. It is governed by a special land legislation known as the Group Settlement Act introduced in 1960.[24] The objective was to prevent the land in land schemes from being subdivided for whatever purpose (sale, mortgage or inheritance), a phenomenon common to the Malay population. For this reason a major part of the GSA-1960 deals with questions of ownership, rights of control and use of the land. This may be noted as follows.

First, the GSA-1960 provides sufficient powers to Felda to decide on the organisation and use of the land (Section 7(1) of the GSA-1960). Likewise Felda is given the power to cultivate the land by permitting, on behalf of a state authority, land-poor citizens to work on it as settlers who, after the land scheme begins production, are to be registered as "occupiers in expectation of title" (Sections 10(1), 19(1) and 19(2) of the GSA-1960). To ensure that Felda has sufficient power to control the settlers, the Act provides that the holdings "be brought fully under cultivation with the appropriate crops by the date specified by the Manager and shall thereafter at all times be maintained and cultivated according to the rules of good husbandry" (Section 17(a) of the GSA-1960).

Second, settlers mobilised into land schemes "in expectation of title" are given legal title to the land either on individual basis (Section 14 of the GSA-1960) or as a group (Section 34(3b) of the GSA-1960) subject to the provision of sections 20 and 34(3d) of the Act which require that settlers must first complete their payments for CAC[25] as well as any money (including loans and interest), services, materials and equipment given to them (Section 20(2) of the GSA-1960). Until such time, settlers are permitted to work only as occupiers "in expectation of title" similar to any agricultural worker who has no claim to land. For this reason, all settlers in Felda land schemes are required to sign a Settler's Agreement which lays down Felda rules and regulations including the conditions for expulsion from a land scheme before they are allowed to settle down in a land scheme.

Up to 1988, only 1,053 settlers have been granted legal titles to land because they have repaid their loans (S, 3 November 1988). But the provision of section 15 and 16 of GSA-1960 prevented the land from being private property similar to land outside "group settlement areas". Section 15 for instance prevented the land from being subdivided or leased. Similarly, the land may be transferred or transmitted upon the death of a

---

[23] "Private property" in the sense of "relation of production" (or an economic relation) corresponds to the power of a category of agents to allocate particular means of production for a given use, and to dispose of the products obtained from this utilization." (Bettelheim 1976: 73).

[24] Hereafter referred to as GSA-1960.

[25] CAC or Consolidated Annual Charges consist mainly of the costs for land premium, quit rent and survey fees.

settler but due to the provision of section 16, a holding must be transferred as a whole. In any case, the express condition on the land titles gives Felda the right to manage the land.

One important provision of the GSA-1960 must be noted at this point. The GSA-1960 was constructed as an integrated document. In this instance, the provision of section 11(3) stands out above the rest. It states that,

> Express conditions imposed under, and conditions and obligations implied by virtue of the provisions of, this Act *shall run with the land* (emphasis added) and shall bind the holder thereof and shall commence to run from the date of occupation in expectation of title authorised by entry in the register of holdings or from the date of alienation, whichever is the earlier.

There are two major points here. First, the GSA-1960 binds land schemes with both express and implied conditions on titles to land.[26] While express conditions are clearly stated on the title to land (such as the types of crops to be grown and management of the land to be vested in Felda), the implied condition is that settlers are bound by all other provisions though they may not be written on land titles (Section 11(4) of the GSA-1960).

Second, and most binding on settlers, is that the provisions of the GSA-1960 "shall run with the land". This means that until a land scheme is declared dissolved by the Minister of Land and Regional Development, the rules of the GSA-1960 continue to bind settlers whether or not they are granted legal (ownership) titles to land. In other words, as long as a land scheme exists the GSA-1960 provides Felda with the power to control the land as well as the settlers. Effectively settlers are separated from their means of production.

It is doubtful whether settlers really understand the legal implications of the GSA-1960 but a nightly prayer group (averaging 15–20 settlers) at the PT1 mosque I associated with during the fieldwork in 1984 was quite definite on the matter. They knew they would get their title like their fellow rubber settlers at Kg. Awah land scheme some thirty miles away,[27] but they also knew, through reports in the local Malay daily, that their counterparts in Chalok rubber scheme in Trengganu had no power to replant their land with rubber because Felda had decided in favour of oil palm (UM, 28 April 1984). Likewise they were aware, from cases of

---

[26] This is quite different from other land legislations which rely only on express conditions on land titles.

[27] I was not present at the land title presentation ceremony at Kg. Awah land scheme. However, one of the senior officials involved in the ceremony later reported that settlers refused to cooperate in the preparation for the Chief Minister's visit to officiate the ceremony because they could not believe that they would be granted their land titles. The official described that, after being presented with the titles, some of them held their land title in the air in joyous disbelief.

deaths and divorces in the land scheme, that dealings on their working plots are restricted. They knew that they could not own their working plots as private property, though they have been repaying their loans and consolidated annual charges on it as if they owned the land. They are allowed on the other hand to buy land outside the land scheme and own it as their private property. Since this is difficult because income from their working plots is insufficient, they felt cheated and resented Felda. Putting all these in the context of formal Felda requirements for work and production, and more important, the lack of alternative forms of employment open to them, some of them considered their position as merely renting (*sewa*) land from Felda while some others saw themselves as tagging along (*tumpang*) Felda. However, somewhat exaggerating their similarity to estate workers, one of them stated that, "this [land scheme] is Tun Razak's estate", signifying, of course, that they did not own it.[28]

If anything, the land question in Felda land schemes simply reinforces the bourgeois ideology of landownership because the concept of landownership does not provide settlers with real control over their land. Coupled with their desire to protect their immediate interests, they therefore protest against Felda to reverse the situation and make land a private property. This is most obvious in the case of the Johor Settlers Association which demanded that they be given full control over their land and their lives.[29] In other words, the settlers protest against Felda because they resent being proletarianised.

Settlers' Finance

Felda obtains state grants and loans[30] as well as borrows from international money lenders[31] to finance the land schemes. Therefore, to maintain the financial viability of the land schemes, it controls settlers' finance through a complex system of income deductions.

Following the Settlers' Agreement, settlers are bound to sell all their

---

[28] Tun Abdul Razak was the Minister of Rural and National Development in the 1960s when Felda land schemes were first launched as a major project for rural development.

[29] Another case is worthy of note. Settlers in Ulu Jempul land scheme in Pahang who have completed repayment on their land defied Felda regulations in 1988 and opted to sell their produce to the highest bidder because they believed that they now own the land. This has generated a legal battle between Felda and the settlers (personal communication).

[30] For instance, in 1984, loans from the Federal government constituted about 60 per cent of all loan capital to Felda. The rest consisted of state grants and loans from foreign money lenders (Felda Finance Division, 1984).

[31] This includes the World Bank, the Asian Development Bank, Saudi Fund for Development, Kuwait Fund for Arab Economic Development and the Japanese Fund for Overseas Economic Cooperation (Felda Annual Report, 1987: 18).

produce to Felda Marketing Corporation or Felma. The latter pays the amount realised on each market day directly to the Settlers' Accounts Department in the Finance Division, Felda headquarters in Kuala Lumpur. At this point, the monthly gross income of each land scheme is recorded and deductions for major financial obligations borne by settlers such as loan repayment[32], operating costs[33] and food credit[34] are made before the balance is sent to land schemes for managers to deduct for expenses such as cash loans and education charges on children incurred by settlers at the scheme level. However, the final balance (cash income) is paid out to settlers only after further deductions have been made for debts and fines incurred at the block level. Normally settlers receive their income (called balance) about five weeks after they send their produce to Felda mills.[35]

However, as a method of operation, Felda deducts settlers income for operating costs regardless of their gross income and carries out other deductions only when the remaining settlers' income exceeds $350 and $250 for oil palm and rubber settlers respectively. The income level represents what Felda calls the "guaranteed minimum income". In times when settlers' income, after deductions for operating costs have been made, fall below this level, Felda stops collecting loan repayment, CAC and other deductions for Felda[36] and tops up the income to the minimum level with cash advances. The latter is considered as a debt to Felda. This is to allow settlers to pay for their food and other charges at the scheme level so that the land scheme continues to operate even under adverse price or production conditions. As a result, settlers face serious cash crisis in meeting their daily non-food requirements as well as accumulate debts to Felda for arrears in loan repayment, CAC and other charges when price or production or both are not favourable. In such circumstance, they resort to taking extra food credit to resell it for cash thus increasing their debts to Felda. Conversely, the amount of their income above the minimum level is taken

---

[32] This is calculated at 6.25 per cent compound interest on the principal (about $50,000 per settler) and broken down into 180 equal monthly instalments with any outstanding amount being charged 6.25 per cent simple interest.

[33] In the case of oil palm schemes, this consisted of transportation costs, the costs of fertilizer, crop insurance, maintenance of agricultural roads and deduction for the Settlers' Development Fund (at $0.60 per tonne of FFB). For rubber schemes, the items in this category consisted only of the cost for marketing services (at 0.0088184 cents per kilogramme) and deductions for the Settlers' Development Fund (at 0.0063 cents per kilogramme).

[34] Depending on the productivity of a land scheme, settler households are provided with an automatic food credit up to about $350 per month by the Felda Trading Corporation (Felda shop).

[35] There is a slight difference for rubber schemes. Due to the danger of rubber being sold clandestinely by settlers, a special arrangement is made to pay rubber settlers about 75 per cent of their gross income every three days.

[36] This includes deductions for a replanting fund and repayment of cash advances.

to settle their debts and arrears when their gross income improves. Thus, it is only under very favourable conditions that settlers would be able to enjoy reasonable cash income.

Considering that price as well as production in Felda schemes fluctuate regularly[37], it may be stated that the income deduction system creates a permanent system of seasonal cash crisis among the settlers. To examine its long term impact, it is necessary to observe the income pattern of a land scheme in greater detail.

The PT2 oil palm scheme began production in 1980. The average total income per settler in 1980–84 period was $1020.54. Out of this amount, 21.84 per cent was deducted for costs of operation, 45.29 per cent for charges on loan repayment, CAC, replanting fund and food credit, and 4.74 per cent was deducted to pay for activities and fines at the scheme level. This left an average cash balance of $289.36 or 28.13 per cent of the total gross income per settler. At the same time, however, records showed that the settlers owed an average of $387.02 to Felda for arrears in food credits and loan repayments. This meant that though settlers were being paid a cash balance, they were still indebted to Felda at the average of $97.66 per settler.

It must be recognised that expenses for operating costs and food as well as personal loans had to be borne by settlers as any independent producer would. Likewise, it may be recognised that charges made at the land scheme level were also necessary to organise production on such a scale. However, the point is that no settler at PT2 land scheme had ever earned any real income up to the end of 1984. Though the land scheme produced a significant amount of total income, the fact that the settlers are financially controlled and regulated by Felda to repay loan capital at a pre-determined monthly rate pushed them into a state of perpetual indebtedness. Such is the exploitative power of interest-bearing capital. By the time they complete repaying their loans, which normally takes about twenty-five years, settlers would have out-lived their productive years and their tree crops would also be due for replanting.

In contrast to the burden borne by settlers, Felda extracts sufficient surplus not only to service and repay the loan capital which is largely acquired from the state but also to create a reserve fund to protect and expand Felda operations. Up to the end of 1983 for instance, Felda has accumulated $646.7 million in reserve and this is expected to increase to $944.6 million in 1989 (Felda Finance Division, 1984). Though a large proportion of the fund was invested in fixed deposits and used to buy

---

[37] Rubber production is affected by periods of wintering and rainfall while oil palm production fluctuates according to rainy season. Apparently, palm oil fruit production increases after a rainy season.

interests in banking, trading, plantations and manufacturing, a substantial amount (43.24 per cent) was used to expand Felda operations by forming new subsidiaries and joint-venture companies with private capital (Felda Annual Report, 1983: 19). Operating on commercial basis, these companies expanded rapidly.[38] For instance, from eight companies with a total paid-up capital of $110.11 million in 1984 (Nasir Yusuf 1984: 10) the subsidiaries expanded to twelve companies in 1987 with a total paid-up capital of $172.05 million (Felda Annual Report 1987: 25). The number of joint-venture companies remained the same in the 1984–1987 period, but their total paid-up capital increased from $57.4 million to $105.5 million (Alladin Hashim 1984: 9: Felda Annual Report 1987: 30). Consequently, Felda today operates as a group of companies with Felda controlling the settlers to produce cash crops and the subsidiaries performing particular tasks in crop handling and processing for sale. In this way, Felda circulates the surplus extracted from the settlers within its own group of companies and expands as a major (state) corporation in agriculture. The settlers, of course, have the opportunity to stake a claim in Felda subsidiaries by buying shares in the *Koperasi Pelaburan Felda* (Felda Investment Corporation), a Felda company which mobilises savings from settlers and other Felda personnel for investment in profitable companies, including Felda subsidiaries,[39] but this is restricted by the amount of their expendable income which, as shown above, is quite limited.

What is then the economic benefit of land schemes to settlers? A settler at PT2 land scheme once put it, "we get only the loose fruit (of palm oil bunches), the main bunches belong to Felda". This was quite moderate. The more critical of his friends likened their position to that of Felda contract workers. In other words, Felda's control over settlers' finance brings forth its nature as (state) capital which extracts and accumulates the surplus from the settlers. For this reason the settlers resent Felda and they express this in whatever ways most convenient, either as a group or on individual basis. However, the fact that Felda does not turn them into pure wage workers affects the nature of their protests. Quite different from the proletarian ideology which generates class struggle amongst agricultural wage workers in general (Paige 1975), the settlers are struggling against Felda to prevent the process of proletarianisation.

---

[38] Up to the end of 1983 for instance, Felda subsidiaries accumulated a total profit of $122.43 million (Nasir Yusuf, 1984: 15 and 17). In 1987, the subsidiaries obtained a net profit of $70.97 million while joint-venture companies registered a net profit of $31.94 million (Felda Annual Report 1987: 26 and 30).
[39] Felda Investment Corporation owns a total of 26.4 per cent shares in Felda subsidiaries (Felda Annual Report, 1987: 25).

Management and Social Control of Labour

Since the GSA-1960 excludes Felda land schemes from the jurisdiction
of district administration (Beaglehole 1976), a manager carries out his
work as a local administrator, planter, trainer of his subordinates and
community leader for settlers in his land scheme (Felda, Management
Services Unit, 1971). This means that besides controlling settlers for
productive work, he also liaises with relevant government departments to
secure the provision of physical infrastructure, social amenities, schools,
a health centre and a mosque as well as maintain the general well-being
of the population settled on the land scheme.

Of course the primary task of a manager is to operate the land scheme
as a unit of production. To do so, he mobilises his assistant and field
supervisors to carry out administrative and supervisory work on the plantation.[40] This requires each field supervisor to supervise daily work of
roughly 50 to 75 settlers respectively. To do so, each field supervisor
organises all tasks in the plantation in a time-table following a regular
annual cycle giving each settler the details of the tasks, the time period in
which they are to be carried out and dates for inspection. To facilitate
closer working relationships, each field supervisor also holds monthly block
meetings and regular social gatherings such as holding feasts among settlers under his supervision.

Felda realises that it cannot simply organise settlers to work without
some form of social control. This is clearly shown in social development
work carried out by social development officers in charge of religious and
women's affairs, that is the SDA-R and SDA-W respectively. Apart from
minor administrative duties[41], the former is heavily biased towards Islamic
religious work which includes supervising religious activities at the mosque
and the religious school, holding religious classes, meetings and courses
for both men and women, and liaison with religious bodies outside the
land scheme. In this way the SDA-R monopolises the teaching of religion in the land scheme. But why is social development promoted mostly
in the form of religious work? One obvious reason seems to be the con-
viction among Felda policy makers that settlers can be transformed into
a viable labour force through the inculcation of Islamic values.

The work of SDA-W is simply to control women so that they become
useful adjuncts to men. This is expressed by Felda as creating "happy
families" (*kesejahteraan keluarga*) wherein the wives are expected to be

---

[40] Their administrative duties include supervision of i) settlers' non-farm economic
activities, ii) settlers' cooperative, iii) activities for youth and iv), operating a death
benefit fund.
[41] This involves counselling the so-called "problematic" or disobedient settlers,
organising a reading room in the land scheme, distributing leaflets and a Felda
news bulletin called the *Majalah Peneroka*, and giving out loans to needy settlers'
children.

submissive and loyal to their husbands, look after the cleanliness of their homes and carry out other domestic chores, plan their families and raise the young and when necessary, supplement their household incomes by cultivating vegetable crops. This requires a SDA-W in a land scheme to organise and supervise the activities of women both at home and outside it, counsel them whenever necessary and generally work towards creating a stable home life in a land scheme.

What if the settlers and their women fail to cooperate? The manager may simply mobilise casual labour to clean up untidy house compounds with the costs charged to the settler households concerned but obstinate settlers are dealt with much more systematically. The Settlers' Agreement allows a manager to punish obstinate settlers and, depending on the severity of the offences, this ranges from simple warning letters to withdrawal of food credit and finally to expulsion from land schemes. Up to April 1984, one per cent of Felda settlers have been expelled for a variety of offences (NST, 10 March 1988).[42] To make sure that productive work is carried out according to plans, Felda also gives power to field supervisors and block leaders to impose fines and penalties on uncooperative, obstinate and lazy settlers. To legitimise all these, Felda rules and regulations including the details of penalties imposed on settlers are endorsed by the Felda controlled JKKR system.

In contrast to the independence which they previously enjoyed in their original villages therefore, their lives in land schemes are somewhat restricted. While the deputy director of Felda Social Services in Kuala Lumpur, in 1984, considered such social and economic regimentation as inevitable requirements of what he called a modern agricultural system, settlers at PT1 land scheme saw themselves as being "trapped" (*terperangkap*) within the Felda enclosure. Given the insecurity of their position as shown by the constant threat from Felda to expel them as well as their uncertain income, it seems inevitable that settlers find ways and means to resist and retaliate against Felda. In the context of the other inherent resentments against Felda discussed earlier, it seems that the strict

---

[42] Following the Settlers' Agreement, Felda considers the following to be punishable offences.

i. *Criminal Offences*: a) Physical assault as well as verbal abuse on Felda personnel. b) Obstructing Felda personnel from carrying out their duties. c) Fighting and using physical violence against fellow settlers and outsiders. d) Robbery, stealing, cheating and misuse of fertiliser, produce and property belonging to Felda or fellow settlers. e) Rape.

ii. *Offences related to Religious Affairs Department*: a) Committing adultery. b) Being in close proximity. c) Cheating on spouse. d) Spreading deviant Islamic teachings.

iii. *Other offences*: a) Failure to work in the plantation. b) Failure to harvest/tap the produce. c) Failure to comply with directives issued by local management.

iv. *Leaving a land scheme without prior permission from the manager*.

management and social control imposed by Felda makes settlers protests and retaliations in Felda land schemes inevitable.

Conclusion

It may be concluded that there is an inherent antagonism in the relationship between Felda and settlers in Felda land schemes. Although resettlement on land schemes promises land ownership and a better life, the organisation of Felda land schemes effectively denies the settlers full control over their land, finance and their labour. The settlers, therefore, feel that they are dominated and controlled by Felda and its officials as if they were wage workers. They therefore fight to gain control over the means of production and control over their own lives. Clearly, they see this is justifiable because, as poor citizens, they should be allowed to own the promised land and as land owners, they should be allowed to decide on the running of their own economic and social lives.

Apparently, their protests gained considerable political significance. For in November 1988, and following the recent (1988) crisis of Malay politics, the state has tried to ease the tension by announcing changes in the system of land ownership in Felda land schemes; changes which promise the settlers individual land titles. Will this reduce the settlers' demands to control their land, labour and produce?

I do not believe so. Instead, it may be reiterated that the settlers' struggle in an integral part of Felda production because it lies in the inherent contradiction within the form of production itself. Felda's control over the use of land, settlers' finance and settlers' social lives is essential to protect the viability of land schemes as units of commodity production and thus the basis for state (and foreign) capital accumulation in agriculture. This would have been less problematic had the settlers been turned into pure wage workers. However, such a move would not only contradict the present ideology of (peasant) development but more important, it would also threaten the political basis of state power because the Malaysian state is an elected one. It is also important to note that such protests and resistance continue in spite of various control mechanisms imposed by Felda. Therefore, unless and until there are changes in the organisation of production, including favourable changes in the GSA-1960 to combine state, capital and settlers' interests in some agreeable form, I believe the particular pattern of settlers' protests and control noted above will continue.

Bibliography

Alladin Hashim, 1984. "Penyertaan peneroka dalam pembangunan Felda", Kertas Kerja No. 2. Persidangan Pegawai Felda.

Barlow, C, 1978. *The Natural Rubber Industry*, Kuala Lumpur: Oxford University Press.

Beaglehole, J. H., 1978. *The District: A Study in Decentralisation in Malaysia*, Great Britain: Oxford University Press.

Bettelheim, C., 1976. *Economic Calculation and Forms of Property*, London: Routledge and Kegan Paul.

Chan, P. and Richter, H., 1982. "Land Settlement, Income and Population Redistribution in Peninsular Malaysia", in G. W. Jones and H. V. Richter (eds), *Population Resettlement Programs in Southeast Asia*, Development Studies Centre Monograph No. 30, Australian National University, Canberra, pp. 73–92.

Chandra Muzaffar, 1987. *Islamic Resurgence in Malaysia*, Petaling Jaya: Penerbit Fajar Bakti Sdn. Bhd.

Chief Minister of Pahang, 1984. Text of speech on the occasion of granting land title to settlers at Kampung Awah land scheme in Pahang on 3 November.

Felda Annual Report, 1983, 1985 and 1987.

Felda, Management Services Unit, 1971. "The Role of the Manager". Paper presented at Felda Managers Seminar.

Felda, Circular Letter, Operations, Administration No. 22, dated 23 August 1983.

Felda Finance Division, 1984. Felda Headquarters Kuala Lumpur.

Graham, E. and Floering, I., 1984. *The Modern Plantation in the Third World*, London: Croom Helm.

Group Settlement Act, 1960. Federation of Malaya, Act of Parliament No. 13 of 1960.

Harnecker, M., 1976. *Basic Concepts of Historical Materialism*, Draft Translation by W. Sadler and W. Sutching, Department of General Philosophy, University of Sydney, Australia.

Hegedus, A., 1981. "Towards a Sociological Analysis of Property Relations" in T. Bottomore (ed), *Modern Interpretations of Marx*, Oxford: Basil Blackwell, pp. 110–124.

Hussain Wafa, S, 1972. "Land Development Strategies in Malaysia: An Empirical Study", Unpublished PhD Thesis, Stanford University.

Jarret, N. R., 1951. "Land Tenure in Malaya", *Eastern World*, vol. 5, Nos. 3 & 4 (March-April), pp. 9–10.

Johor Settlers Association, 1983. "Memorandum kepada Datuk Rais Yatim, Menteri Tanah dan Pembangunan Wilayah".

Khera, H. S., 1976. *The Oil Palm Industry of Malaysia: An Economic Study*, Kuala Lumpur: Penerbit Universiti Malaya.

Lim Sow Ching, 1976. *Land Development Schemes in Peninsular Malaysia*, Kuala Lumpur: Rubber Research Institute.

MacAndrews, C., 1977. *Mobility and Modernisation: The Federal Land Development Authority and its Role in Modernising the Rural Malays*, Jogjakarta: Gadjah Mada University Press.

——, 1979. "The Felda Land Development Scheme in Malaysia" in J. Wong (ed),

Group Farming in Asia, Singapore: Singapore University Press, pp. 140–152.

Mahesan, T., 1984. "Felda Settlement Planning - A Preliminary Reappraisal", Paper presented to a training course on Land Administration, Felda Institute of Land Development, Trolak, Perak, 6–11 August.

Malaysia, 1984 (Ministry of Finance). *Economic Report 1984/5,* Kuala Lumpur: Government Printing Department.

Malaysia, 1986. *Fifth Malaysia Plan 1986–1990,* Kuala Lumpur: Government Printing Department.

Minister of Land and Regional Development, 1984. Text of the Minister's Speech at the Opening of Vice-Chairpersons and Felda Managers Conference, February.

Mohd Fadzil Yunus, 1975. "Peserta-peserta yang tidak bekerja di ladang" in Bahagian Penyelidikan dan Penilaian, Jabatan Khidmat Pembangunan Sosial Felda, *Kajian-kajian Kegiatan Pembangunan Sosial Felda,* December, pp. 160–172.

Nasir Yusof (Haji), 1984. "Perbadanan Felda dan Peranan Ketua-Ketua Peneroka Sebagai Ahli Lembaga", Working Paper No. 4, Vice-Chairpersons and Felda Managers Seminar.

Paige, J. M., 1975. *Agrarian Revolution: Social Movements and Export Agriculture in the Underdeveloped World,* London/New York: The Free Press.

Scott, J. C., 1976. *The Moral Economy of the Peasant,* New Haven/London: Yale University Press.

——, 1985. *Weapons of the Weak: Everyday Forms of Peasant Resistance,* New Haven/London: Yale University Press.

Shamsul Bahrin, T., 1971. "Policies on Land-Settlement in Insular Southeast Asia: A Comparative Study", *Modern Asian Studies,* vol. 5, No. 1, pp. 21–34.

Shamsul Bahrin, T. and Perera, 1977. *Felda: 21 Years of Land Development,* Kuala Lumpur: Felda.

Singh, S., 1965. "Economic aspects of three land development schemes organised by the Federal Land Development Authority in the Federation of Malaya", Unpublished PhD Thesis, Australian National University.

Suhaimi Said (Haji), 1984a. *Saya Seorang Peneroka,* Temerloh: Penerbitan Ujud Baitul Fath.

——, 1984b. *Masalah Politik Peneroka Felda,* Temerloh: Penerbitan Ujud Baitul Fath.

UMNO, 1983. "Kajian Kemasyarakatan Felda Di Daerah Jerantut" (Social Survey of Felda Schemes in the District of Jerantut) by Chairperson, Bureau for Social Life in Felda Schemes, UMNO Division of Jerantut, Pahang.

White, C. P., 1986. "Everyday Resistance, Socialist Revolution and Rural Development: The Vietnamese Case", *Journal of Peasant Studies,* vol. 13, No. 2 (January).

Zawawi Ibrahim, 1983. "Perspectives Towards Investigating Malay Peasant Ideology and the Bases of its Production in Contemporary Malaysia", *Journal of Contemporary Asia,* vol. 13, No. 2, pp. 198–209.

Newspapers & Periodicals

Berita Harian (BH)
Malay Mail (MM)   *Sunday Star* (SS)
New Straits Times (NST)   *Utusan Malaysia* (UM)
The Star (S)
Straits Echo (SE)

6

Archaism and Modernity: Contemporary Malay Political Culture

Clive S Kessler

[This] is a study not of tradition as an aspect of historical continuity, but of traditionalism: the manipulation, invention, and recombination of cultural patterns, symbols, and motifs so as to legitimate contemporary social realities by imbuing them with a patina of venerable historicity . . . Apparent [cultural] continuities . . . are the results of processes of traditionalism—the interpretation, creation, or manipulation of contemporary ideas about the past to bestow an aura of venerability on contemporary social relations. Traditionalism is a common . . . cultural device for managing or responding to social change . . . [People] invoke tradition to legitimate the present by reference to an idealized, ahistorical past . . . The seeming continuities [that] this process stresses (and creates) all too often strike observers more forcefully than the changes and transformations that at once set the stage for the manipulation of tradition and are cloaked by its success.

— Bestor (1989: 2, 4, 10 & 11).

I

The social sciences, especially in their studies of the non-European world, may still be said to be haunted by the spectre of "modernization". As modernization proceeds, a covertly still influential approach contends, it does so unevenly. Those areas or domains of social life that undergo this process of transformation become, wholly or in part, "modernized"; what remains unaffected, by contrast, becomes known as "traditional". In this sense "tradition" is residual: it is the residue of the past, that part which survives undisturbed and is accordingly, at least for the moment, preserved.[1]

---

[1] There is no need to cite the vast literature on "modernization" theory, expository and critical. It suffices merely to recall the title and tenor of Daniel Lerner's landmark study (1958): *The Passing of Traditional Society: Modernising the Middle East.*

The approach adopted in this discussion of some aspects of contemporary Malay political culture rests upon a different, even contrasting, understanding. Its starting point is the recognition, announced by the political scientists Lloyd and Susanne Rudolph (1967), of "the modernity of tradition". In this view tradition is not simply the surviving residue left undisturbed by advancing yet incomplete modernization. Rather, it is essentially new, modern, contemporary—a recent construct. The recognition of and an attachment to the "pastness" of certain cultural materials (what we come to call "traditions") is itself, in this view, a product of modernity.

How can this possibly be? In what we might want to call "traditional" societies, there is no conscious, ideologized attachment to the legacy of the past. In them, instead, the past lives on unproblematically, thereby continuing to shape the present. Such societies experience and justify themselves in terms of the purportedly still unfolding rule of the "eternal yesterday".[2] Only when this eternal yesterday ceases to exert its pervasive guidance of social life is the claim consciously advanced, generally with some strategic or persuasive intent, that some parts of the socially constructed "life-world" derive not from new circumstances but from the past, and are accordingly to be prized, revered, and cherished by virtue of their "pastness".

They are to be valued, it is now contended, because, in a world of rapid change that threatens massive dislocation, these more familiar, ancient, and deeply rooted cultural elements may—indeed, should—provide some reliable grounding of personal authenticity and for collective, often national, identity. It is only when its continuity is rendered problematic that the past itself becomes recognizable. No longer just pervasively yet invisibly "there", it now becomes visible and also "thinkable": an object of attachment to which one may—even should—be loyal, and something which can therefore also justify loyalty to other things. In other words, it has the power to confer legitimacy.

The past, in this view, is not an "unchanged residue". It is not that which we see left behind us when, occasionally looking back over our shoulders, we move forward beyond it. Instead—as a recent study of Riau Malay culture (Wee 1985) suggests—the past is like the image that we see in the rear-vision mirror of a rapidly moving car. As we move forward, we see an image of what we have been through and experienced. But this view of the past is shaped by our direction into the future; indirect and refracted, it is formed on shifting ground in an ever-moving present. Left behind and lost from direct view, the past is ground on which we can no longer stand. It therefore becomes something to be recaptured, revisited, defended—because it now seems suddenly susceptible to loss, abandonment, and attack.

---

[2] See Max Weber's typification of "Traditional Authority" (Weber 1978, I: 226–231).

The very dislocation of modernity, the rapidity of culturally ungoverned advance, creates a disorder whose remedy, it is now claimed, is some re-affirmation of a past which alone can provide authentic moorings for identity and some secure groundings for appropriate action. Within this reflex there is a strange and little recognized paradox. The unacknowledged product of disjunctive modernity rather than of unfolding cultural continuity, a view of the "traditional" past is invoked to serve as an alternative to disruptive modernization; it is unwittingly proffered as the remedy for a condition of which it is itself an unrecognized symptom. Conscious traditionalism—the assiduous cultivation of archaism—is therefore like standing upon a ladder while seeking to extend it downwards to some secure place on solid ground below.

Yet this "idea of the past"—of the inherent authenticity and legitimizing power of what is seen to have survived from our predecessors—becomes a resource now capable of being consciously used to fashion and legitimate a form of life that exists only in a problematic and contingent present. For this reason, going beyond Rudolph and Rudolph, we may speak not merely of the inherent "modernity" of tradition but, as Hobsbawm and Ranger (1983) do, of "the invention of tradition".

II

Consistent with the central theme of the essays in *The Invention of Tradition*, this account is concerned (even if the authors of those essays do not themselves use the term) with "political culture". Every society has its own cultural understandings of power and politics. Power and politics do not pre-exist culture. On the contrary, they are culturally constructed, as Clifford Geertz (1980 & 1983; cf. also Anderson 1972) persistently reminds us. Power must first be imagined, he notes, if it is to exist at all— if people are to invoke or respond to it. The fundamental question therefore is not the mechanics but the symbolics of power, not so much how it works but how its workings are imagined.

It is in culture that people fashion power as well as acceptance of it. Legitimation is inevitably a cultural process since it is concerned with the moral grounds upon which people consider rule in general or some particular command as binding and valid. If power and its transmutation through a process of legitimation into authority is intrinsically a cultural phenomenon, then culture itself, and all particular cultures, are inherently political. Every culture therefore includes an at least implicit "political culture", a cultural construction and management of politics. In most societies that political culture is explicit, recognized, conscious, and often even "ideologized", as both legitimate and legitimating, on grounds of "tradition": of the continuing integrity and morally binding authenticity of its "pastness". Most societies, and certainly contemporary Malay society within Malaysia and beyond its territorial boundaries, have in this sense a distinctive political culture.

But while this is true of virtually all modern societies, in the Malay case there is much more to the question of political culture. For Malay society does not merely "have", as do so many societies, a distinctive cultural process of political life. Malay culture, furthermore, is distinctively and centrally political in character. Many other cultures turn upon, or locate their central values and preoccupations in, a variety of other concerns: in salvation (e.g., Buddhism), cleanliness and pollution (e.g., Indian and caste-type societies), honour and shame (e.g., Mediterranean societies), the harmony and congruence of the natural and social worlds (e.g., totemic societies), sacrifice, renunciation, ecstasy and mystical transcendence, or whatever. Malay culture, however—certainly not uniquely but most significantly—centres upon an identity which is political; is grounded in a specific historical experience, that of Melaka and what was modelled upon it, which is political; and is focused upon certain social institutions (those of the sultan and sultanate) that are political—as Milner (1982) has argued, making explicit what many others have taken for granted, in his study of *Kerajaan*.

Malay society and culture, as they conceive of themselves, rest centrally upon a political condition: upon people having and being subjects of a *raja*, a ruler. The polity, a *kerajaan*, is not only a ruler's domain but his subjects' sociocultural condition, that of having a *raja*. Not any supposed functional imperatives of social order nor any alleged material determination of economic process but the cultural presuppositions of a political order itself are the fundamental basis of Malay social existence. That social order is basically a political order and social existence is a political condition, one of being involved in the reciprocal relationship between ruler and ruled. A Malay might step, physically or socially, beyond the reach of such relations—but only at the price of attenuating his full social identity as a Malay. Aboriginal or "tribal" peoples, pirates, and slaves were problematically in the Malay cultural world but, because of their only indirect or mediated involvement to it, they were not of it. They had not autonomously contracted into the culturally paradigmatic relationship between ruler and the ruled.

Not only, then, is there a "Malay political culture". Nor is it merely the case that Malay culture is inherently political, revolving substantially around relations between ruler and ruled. While social existence itself—a real or complete social existence as a Malay—came to consist of an essentially political condition of involvement in rule, in a realm, these political relationships between Malays as subjects and their leaders who endowed them with a full or completed Malay identity were on the whole relationships that were nothing but cultural. These central political relations were not derivately economic (within some system of Oriental despotism, for example), nor were they essentially legal-political (since the ruler's powers of command and domination were often far from absolute), nor were they even primarily religious (though that was an important aspect of them). Rather, in origin and content they were entirely cultural. It was the symbolic recognition exchanged between the two parties that made the ruler a ruler and the subject, by virtue of his recognition of political relationship to a Malay ruler, a Malay. This process, this transaction of identity-bestowing and polity-creating recognitions, was nothing other than a cultural process. Malay culture may accordingly be characterized as an inherently political culture. Hence the central importance, the almost exclusive significance, of political elements both within historical Malay culture and also within that modern but purportedly "traditional" construction of the past that constitutes the cultural basis of contemporary Malay identity. For the historical period and also with their consciously reworked significance in the modern, we must note here the importance of the genres and conventions of classical Malay literature, especially the *Sejarah Melayu* and *Hikayat Hang Tuah*.[3] Similarly, we might recall not merely the political but the broadly cultural significance of the *daulat* belief complex, beliefs in the magical or supernatural character of legitimacy; the traditional and also the modern system of royally awarded titles (*gelaran*), ranks (*pangkat*), and honours (*pingat*) and their role in defining the Malay sociocultural order; the significance and the emotionally mobilizing power of the motifs of royalty and sovereignty in the symbolic processes of Kelantanese Malay *main peteri* healing seances[4]; and the highly ceremonialized form, with all its attendant and derivately courtly etiquette (which is to say centrally cultural character) of all those political occasions in which adherence to certain "traditional" forms of Malay dress, manners, speech, and even bodily comportment is mandatory. An UMNO party assembly, for example, or the opening of a congress of Malay intellectuals must therefore be properly "clothed", both in material and manner, and it is adherence to this cultural order that appropriately forms or reconfirms Malay social identity and order. Their cultural propriety invests with political legitimacy these various gatherings, together with their occasions and purposes, and the notion of Malay identity and sociability as inherently political in character is thereby reaffirmed. Thus a *main peteri* healing seance and a wedding ceremony alike are majlis, a meeting or audience governed by the solemn rules and forms of political occasions with their deliberative, even diplomatic, seriousness—their blend of elegant formality and finely edged strategy.

Such an itemization could be pursued much further, but need not. Simply to call such instances to mind is amply to underline the quite extraordinarily political character of Malay culture; of the ideal Malay identity grounded in it; and of the powerfully and fundamentally cultural (which is to say symbolic and expressive as opposed to instrumental and coercive) character of Malay political processes. Just as Bruce Kapferer (1988) argues of Sinhalese culture, it was through the symbolic construction and sustaining of a social order capable of encompassing others that Malay political order was historically established; this is why, in the present as in the past,

---

[3] A notable recent commentary is that by Helen Musa (1989).
[4] I refer here to my own analysis, Kessler (1977).

attempts by non-Malay minority groups to repudiate, contest, or redefine the presuppositions of their cultural encompassment are experienced as threats to the integrity not only of the political order but to the majority's paradigmatic cultural identity as well.[5]

III

Such reference to the events of 1969, to their deep-seated cultural dimensions, and to the total redefinition since 1970 of the foundations of the postcolonial Malaysian political order that they prompted, leads into the heart of the matter. There are circumstances in which a political order whose coherence and integrity are largely grounded in symbolic process can easily be inclusive. In a world of broad, expansive, and even overlapping cultural and subcultural areas—such as Nusantara once historically was—regimes of this kind can readily encompass minority populations within the normative presuppositions of a majority or paradigmatic population's existence. In these circumstances cultural order may often spill over political boundaries—inasmuch as definitive boundaries exist at all under such conditions. But the modern world—that wrought historically by the experience of colonial domination and its aftermath—is a world parcelled out between exclusive, often competing, territorially organized polities, generally nation-states. The coherence and integrity of these new forms of political society rest upon political control, no longer upon their capacity to encompass culturally what cannot be directly controlled.

Yet these new regimes based upon an ability to manage rather than to incorporate a diverse population must nevertheless authenticate themselves, and generally do so on what are seen as historical grounds: grounds of the validating sanction, even sanctity, of uninterrupted, unfolding tradition. Cultural order—an order grounded in the presuppositions of the dominant, paradigmatic community's existence and the historical authenticity of its political identity—no longer provides an alternative to a more tightly structured political-administrative order but serves as its indispensable justification and legitimation. Culture, cultural existence, cultural identity, and the strategic institutions of cultural reproduction (in Malaysia both the national and the non-Malay school systems are notable instances) are filled with political meaning and relevance: not so much politicized from within (which they may also be) as inevitably made, because of their location in a field of political forces, a focus of political contestation. Questioning of

---

[5] Kapferer's analysis of a political culture of symbolic inclusion, and of the implications of efforts by non-ascendant groups to repudiate or redefine the terms of their encompassment, may provide some insight into the character of the events of May 1969, as well as into more recent controversies in the 1980s over the question of who is an "immigrant" and over the status of Chinese and Indian studies at Universiti Malaya and of Chinese education and culture generally.

the dominant cultural order, and the attempts by those it encompasses to redefine the terms of their inclusion within it, become politically threatening. They now threaten not negotiable cultural order but the authenticating presuppositions of a political order dependent upon cultural legitimation of some seemingly "traditional" or "historic" character. In this situation, the refusal or withholding of assent to incorporation on given terms becomes a form of rebellion.

In Malaysia these historically created problems of legitimation have a multiple, overdetermined nature. It is not merely the disjunctions of modernization within the indigenous Malay cultural and political order itself that must be bridged. Further, colonialist "modernization" did not so much modernize Malay society as "traditionalize" or freeze it, while introducing substantial non-Malay population elements whose emergent communities became, generally at the expense of Malay exclusion, the focal domains of modernizing social transformation. Malayan society, or the immigrant enclaves added to it, underwent modernization, but not Malay society which was peripheralized, rigidified, and ossified.

Under colonial auspices a "plural" society was created, one marked by the insulation of the indigenous Malay cultural sector from modernizing forces. Since 1963, moreover, the inclusion of Sarawak and Sabah within an expanded peninsula-based federation has further complicated the articulation of the political-administrative order and the paradigmatic cultural order historically authenticating it. The paradigmatic or definitive group within the Malaysian polity is Malay, autochthonous (*bumiputera*), and Islamic: Islam, through the restrictions it places on intermarriage and other ritual mechanisms preserving social distance, helps preserve the integrity of the boundaries of Malay society, as well as its dignity; and this Islamically-fortified Malay ascendancy is justified on the grounds that Malays are the indigenous people and therefore entitled to make theirs the nation's definitive, paradigmatic cultural identity.

Hence the definition of the national community as one based upon, and giving effect to, Malay ascendancy (*ketuanan Melayu*). This, in contemporary Malaysian politics, is axiomatic—but there is much that goes beyond the axiomatic. In various parts of Malaysia there are now population elements that, in relation to this axiomatic paradigm, are anomalous: there are Muslims who are neither Malays nor *bumiputera* (Indians, Arabs, Chinese, Burmese, etc.); Muslim Malays who are not *bumiputera* (Acehnese immigrants, for example); Malay *bumiputera* who are not Muslims (including certain *asli* groups, and at least one recent convert from Islam to Christianity); *bumiputera* Muslims who are not Malays (such as the Melanau and similar peoples in the east Malaysian states); *bumiputera* who are neither Malays nor Muslims (which includes both ethnic Thais and also various *asli* groups on the peninsula as well as some tribal populations in the eastern states); and Malays who are neither *bumiputera* nor Muslims (including various Javanese and Batak Christian immigrants). What, for example, is the status of a (probably illegal) Bugis immigrant in

Sabah? A Muslim, but a Malay and *bumiputera*? The situation is by no means simple.

All these overlaps and residues complicate the process of cultural legitimation of the political order. For the more blurred are these ideally clear-cut cultural categorical boundaries, the more problematic the legitimacy of the political order becomes. Yet the more complicated and untidy the reality, the more urgent and indispensable is the politically authenticating process in which the logic and character of this political order are unambiguously fused, at the ideal or normative level, with the cultural identity and unfolding common destiny of the paradigmatic, definitive, culturally ascendant group. Hence, in the face of these legitimation gaps, the critical political importance within the nation of the Malay majority's historic traditions—not as a matter of cultural inertia or continuity but for the articulation of state and society: the definition of a modern national community and the stabilization of a modern political regime.

Not simply a survival from the past or an outcome of its continuing unfolding, tradition is something inherently modern. Fashioned from largely customary or antique elements, it is a new construct—an artifice or device needed when the severing of historic continuity, of major links with the past, first made the present problematic and the distinctiveness of the past recognizable. In Malaysia this occurred during the colonial period. The formalization, the elaboration, the codification of Malay courtly cultural order took place as an effect of a system of indirect rule that reserved Malay religion and custom to the noble and aristocratic classes of the old sultanates who were now encapsulated within the colonial social order. Both they and their British protectors were provided in this system with an incentive to participate in this elaboration of ceremonial and status, the "invention of tradition": the Malay courtly classes because it provided some new, less directly political basis, following their political displacement, for their ascendancy over the *rakyat* classes; and the British because it helped consolidate their rule, buttressing their own position by amplifying the deference-commanding eminence of those through whom they governed. It fashioned for both parties a mutually gratifying link grounded in the complementary claims of Malay aristocrats and British officials to some authoritative social superiority.[6]

While the elements drawn into this process of formalization were generally Malay in their cultural origins, the process was not what it appeared and is still generally taken to be: a mere extension or internal elaboration of tradition. Rather, the sources, the impetus, and the model were external and distinctively modern. While in some cases (e.g., Kelantan) the model of Thai administrative culture, dress, and etiquette

---

[6] The definitive account of the peculiar (and at times quite ambivalent) Anglo-Malay symbiosis that British paternalism engendered between the old Malay ruling families of the former sultanates and their colonial protectors is Roff (1967).

may occasionally have played a subsidiary role, it was the experiences and practices of the colonial power itself, Britain, which overwhelmingly provided the principal pattern and push for this traditionalizing process, for the modern reconstruction or "invention" of Malay "tradition".

As two of the essays in *The Invention of Tradition* make clear, this external British model or impetus had a double source. First, as David Carradine demonstrates (1983), what are now seen as the most ancient of Britain's great royal ceremonials and traditions are the product of two quite circumscribed and recent periods or processes of efflorescence: one preindustrial in the sixteenth and seventeenth centuries; the other and more pronounced phase—in the face of advancing modernity—of "invented ceremonial splendour . . . centred on royal power" (ibid: 161) in the late nineteenth and early twentieth centuries. This newly "traditionalized" British monarchial system quickly became the model for the conscious "traditionalization" of the "Malay monarchies" now subservient to it; and the Malay rulers, themselves adept in political assimilation to British ways, entered eagerly into the process of symbolic and ceremonial status emulation.

Second, as Bernard S. Cohn (1983) shows in a companion analysis, in nineteenth century India an iconic "tradition" was produced via a succession of imperial "assemblages" and durbars, consciously devised and elaborately, even opulently, staged practices and spectacles. These public ceremonializations of hierarchy and precedence, of status and moral authority, enacted what Cohn terms the operational or implicit "colonial sociology"—the articulation of the various components and elements of Indian society within or beneath the structures of imperial governance. Anyone tempted to doubt the influence of the British India model in providing impressive representation of authority in the peninsular states— that of "traditional" Muslim Malay monarchy under British protection and tutelage—need only consider the character and persuasive purposes of the old "Mughal" style Selangor secretariat building complex in Kuala Lumpur: a gracious view even today of Malay tradition appearing on numerous tourist brouchures and posters, and a vista which in 1989 immediately confronted all who attended the Commonwealth Heads of Government Meeting in Kuala Lumpur—a modern, international, postcolonial durbar par excellence!

Despite great differences of scale, the parallels are striking between the Indian and the similarly fragmented Malay case: the various sultanate states with their own mutual rivalries, their distinctive courtly traditions, practices, and complex systems of honour and precedence. No less significant is the time at which these two persuasively replicable British-created processes for modern political consolidation in the name of an apparently venerable past occurred. These politically legitimating and authority-consolidating traditions were devised and elaborated both in Britain itself and by the British in India in the period from 1870 to 1914: that is, during the very same period in which, following the Treaty of Pangkor, British rule, in the name of political "protection" and cultural preservation, was imposed upon the peninsular Malay states; and in which something entirely new, to be known in its heyday as "British Malaya", was created upon the strategic fiction of precisely what British domination had overturned and undermined—the precolonial, culturally organised Malay *kerajaan* polity. That elements from that precolonial cultural-political order were appropriated by the British in their construction of a cultural legitimation in no way entails that that legitimation itself, and still less the problems and purposes that it addressed, were in any way (as they are so routinely seen and claimed) "traditional".

As Hobsbawm argues (1983: 1) in outlining the "invention of tradition" thesis, like the seemingly ancient pageantry and public ceremonial of the British monarchy, many so-called traditions which "appear or claim to be old are often quite recent in origin." Moreover, they are "sometimes invented"—and with a purpose. "Normally governed by overtly or tacitly accepted rules . . . of a ritual or symbolic nature", the practices on which invented traditions are built "seek to inculcate certain values and norms of behaviour by repetition, which automatically implies continuity with the past . . . with a suitable historic past."

> However [Hobsbawm continues] insofar as there is such reference to a historic past, the peculiarity of "invented" traditions is that the continuity with it is largely fictitious. In short [invented traditions] are responses to novel situations which take the form of reference to old situations, or which establish their own past by quasi-obligatory repetition. It is the contrast between the constant change and innovation of the modern world and the attempt to structure at least some parts of social life within it as unchanging and invariant, that makes the "invention of tradition" so interesting for historians of the past two centuries (ibid: 2).

Tradition in this sense must be clearly distinguished from the kinds of custom that dominate so-called "traditional" societies. For Hobsbawm, tradition is not merely modern and inescapably so. It is also manufactured, strategically crafted, by those suddenly in need of a serviceable past or needing urgently to refurbish a past that has become somehow (the irony is a nice one!) out of date: by communities coming into being or undergoing fundamental transformation and reconstruction and, specifically, by those exercising or contending for ascendancy within them. Inventing traditions for Hobsbawm "is essentially a process of formalisation and ritualisation, characterised by reference to the past, if only by imposing repetition" (ibid: 4).

> There is probably no time and place with which historians are concerned which has not seen the "invention" of tradition in this sense. However, we should expect it to occur more frequently when a rapid transformation of society weakens or destroys the social patterns for which "old" traditions had been designed, producing new ones to which they were not applicable, or when such old traditions and their institutional carriers and promulgators no longer prove

sufficiently adaptable and flexible, or are otherwise eliminated: in short when there are sufficiently large and rapid changes . . . Adaptation took place for old uses in new conditions and by using old models for new purposes . . . In all such cases novelty is no less novel for being able to dress up easily as antiquity. More interesting . . . is the use of ancient materials to construct invented traditions of a novel type for quite novel purposes (ibid: 4–6).

Strategic recourse to elements from a purportedly ancient and venerable past characterizes many societies. Typically, "a large store of such materials is accumulated in the past of any society, and an elaborate language of symbolic practice and communication is always available." At times new traditions were "readily grafted on old ones, sometimes they could be devised by borrowing from the well-supplied warehouse of official ritual, symbolism and moral exhortation—religion and princely pomp, folklore" (ibid: 6).

Modern nations, then, are what Benedict Anderson (1983) calls "imagined communities", created initially as ideas through the invention of tradition before they find political expression and embodiment in the institutional apparatus of a state. There is, accordingly, a curious paradox:

> modern nations and all their impedimenta generally claim to be the opposite of novel, namely rooted in the remotest antiquity, and the opposite of constructed, namely human communities so "natural" as to require no definition other than self-assertion. [Yet] whatever the historic or other continuities . . . which nobody would seek to deny . . . much of what subjectively makes up the modern "nation" consists of such constructs . . . The national phenomenon cannot be adequately investigated without careful attention to the "invention of tradition" (Hobsbawm 1983: 14).

IV

The "invention of tradition" argument, as Hobsbawm makes clear, does not apply solely to the colonial period, even though that period of disjunctive, legitimacy-eroding modernization was also one of decisive efflorescence of "traditions". It applies also to the postcolonial period—or even, we could say of the Malaysian case, to both phases of the postcolonial period.

The first, from 1957 to 1970, witnessed the establishment *inter alia*, as the symbolic and ceremonial apex of the new political order, of a unique system of elective constitutional monarchy. As, arguably, is insufficiently recognized, under this uniquely Malaysian arrangement the powers of the monarch or *agung* are not simply (as in some more familiar systems of "constitutional monarchy") the embodiment of the power of the constitution itself and thus also indirectly of popular sovereignty, nor are the ruler's powers simply those that are granted, delimited, and institutionalized by the constitution. Rather, the constitution in effect recognizes that the *agung*, and behind him the sultans from whose ranks the *agung* is temporarily drawn, enjoy powers that are not simply created by or based within but exist prior to and outside of constitutional authority and the constitution itself. What the crisis of 1983 turned upon, and seems to have left less than fully resolved, is a contention that the constitution allows the rulers powers whose sources, being based in cultural and religious tradition, are not grounded within the constitution nor altogether circumscribed by it.[7]

Around this formal constitutional focus were developed, in the period immediately preceding and following independence, the rituals and ceremonials of the new monarchy and the new national system of titles and honours (including those of Tun and Tan Sri). Together, these innovations added further levels of involuted complexity to the modern but historically based Malay system of status and rank—and thus also, in quasi-traditional form, a newly elaborated complexity to the Malay social order, social etiquette, and sociability generally.

At the same time, as part of this process of the elaboration and consolidation of tradition, the new institution of a national monarchy—because of its five-year rotational character—came also to enhance and strengthen the position of the sultans in their own states: not simply because the national monarchy provides, in significantly expanded and central form, a model of what "Malay monarchy" can now be and aspire to in the modern world. Every sultan, moreover, as a prospective or potential *agung* is now further ennobled and amplified, both culturally and politically, by the ascendant *agung*ship, for which he is ever in principle eligible.

Indeed, this is a position to which the sultans are also connected, and by which they are now magnified, not simply as possible incumbents on some occasion but continually, as electors at every instance of selection and succession. This power is, indeed, not occasional but continuing since,

---

[7] During 1983, in anticipation of the first election of an *agung* in the period since his own accession to the prime ministership—and in the midst of a populist democratic upsurge with which, in the public mind, he and his then Deputy Prime Minister Datuk Musa Hitam were closely identified—Dr. Mahathir attempted to specify somewhat more precisely the relationship between the prime minister, as head of the elected government, and the *agung* as head of state. This attempt took the form of a campaign, which was to prove quite divisive and last until early 1984, to amend the federal constitution so as to remove the *agung*'s right to refuse assent to legislation passed by parliament and also to transfer from the *agung* to the prime minister the right to declare a state of emergency (suspending the operation of ordinary legal and political conditions). These proposals also had implications for the similar, if lesser, powers of the individual sultans in their own states. Ultimately, the outcome of the struggle—the meaning of the final compromise that was reached—remains somewhat unclear though it does seem that Dr. Mahathir's victory, if it be seen as one, was rather Pyrrhic: limitations to royal prerogatives were set, but only via measures that seemed in themselves to concede, or confirm, that the rulers did enjoy those powers, which they had graciously consented to modify or redefine, in the first place—and, by further implication, that those powers, though now reconciled within the constitution, derived from sources that the

as seemed to be demonstrated during the 1983 crisis, the *agung* in some sense remains answerable to his brother sultans who elected him foremost among them. An *agung*, it thus seems—a particular incumbent that is— might hypothetically wish or be tempted to make concessions, for example, that his royal peers will not permit him to make. The *agung*ship's answerability to an implicit royal fraternal consensus or potential veto thus adds an extra dimension to the power and position of every sultan: the ruler in his own state becomes the beneficiary of his own entitlements as a member of the federal Council of Rulers, as well as of his royal brothers' exercise of those same powers—the power not so much to be a king but to create one who is ultimately accountable to his eight brother electors.

In the precolonial *kerajaan* system, the ruler's position derived from the reciprocal but asymmetrical recognition of his subjects; in the colonial period, this position was buttressed by British power, the power either to support the ruler or else to find some more acceptable claimant; in the postcolonial period, yet another dimension or basis of royal power—of the power of individual sultans in their own states—has been created by their involvement as both potential incumbents and continuing electors of the kingship, the *agung*ship at the federal or national level.

Focused politically on the *agung*ship, the first phase of postcolonial traditionalization from 1957 to 1970 was concerned largely with the formal institutions of national governance through the heads of the old ruling families. The second since 1970 has been far more widely directed, but also with enormously significant political implications, towards the character, identity, and social placement of the rapidly expanding Malay middle class that has emerged as a result of the New Economic Policy. This process has recently been noted by Joel Kahn, who begins his brief

---

constitution itself now recognized were of extra-constitutional origins. For an excellent discussion of the constitutional crisis see Lee (1986). Most apposite also is the magisterial comment by Hickling (1987: 55–57): "Clearly, in the eyes of an orthodox constitutional law lawyer, a constitutional Ruler is one who rules in accordance with a constitution; and a constitutional Ruler is, under a democratic parliamentary system, a Ruler who does as he is told by the elected representative of the people. [Yet] sovereignty is not always where it seems to be . . . It was perhaps too much to expect that at the stroke of midnight on the eve of independence in 1957 the Rulers could immediately alter their outlook, their way of life, their accustomed attitudes . . . As for the position of [*agung*], the office itself was created in 1957. Some jurists argue, with great force, that in consequence the powers of the Supreme Head of the Federation—that sum total of federal sovereignty—are limited by the Federal Constitution. Others affirm that the office is to be understood only in historical, evolutionary perspective; the powers of the Supreme Head flowing from the disposition of existing powers made at the time of independence. The issue is important in academic eyes: does the Supreme Head of the Federation have prerogative powers outside the Constitution? . . . The self-declared supremacy of [the] Constitution, of its own bid for supremacy, is not as yet fully accepted."

commentary by observing that Malaysia seems "currently awash with the symbolism of 'traditional Malay culture'" (1988/89: 6). Centrally involved in this process of traditionalization—as targets and consumers rather than creators—have been the members of the new Malay middle class: various groups closely and multiply identified with the national government as the products of its affirmative action policies, as its dominant party's primary basis of power, and very often also as the personnel of its bureaucratic apparatus. As the former ("traditional") Malay peasant cultural order declines or is eroded, the Malay middle class becomes increasingly involved in and committed to what is now seen as "traditional Malay culture": a simulacrum, a hyper-realization even, of Malay tradition that, since it goes far beyond whatever existed in the past, is nothing if not modern. It is, says Kahn, "Malay neo-traditionalism": the sincerely held, honestly sustained world-view and basis of identity commitment of many members of

> a new Malay middle class. Members of this group are inclined to romanticise the culture of the village with which they maintain only tenuous links. Overwhelmingly members of a salariat, rather than a class of entrepreneurs, they are less inclined than the latter to give unreserved support to unfettered economic modernisation. In fact many are quite openly fearful of the consequences of rampant commercialism. "Ethnically blind" market pressure might well challenge the political basis of their current advantages — the New Economic Policy . . . This is far from the whole story. Malay neo-traditionalism is not the only possible critique of modernity . . . But a concern to reconstruct Malay identity through the symbols of a traditional, village-based, feudalistic and patriarchal Malay culture makes a lot of sense for a large segment of Malaysia's new Malay middle class (ibid: 8).

V

Just as this Malay neo-traditionalism and the ethnic identity grounded in it are, as Kahn notes, not "fixed for all time . . . an immutable given of that society" (ibid), so too the political culture from which they stem is also not fixed but malleable, contestable, and divergently interpretable.

If Malay culture is an insistently political culture, then it derives from and finds its "traditional" or historical model in the Melaka sultanate. Its charter is to be found in how that paradigmatic historical epoch or experience is known: through classical Malay literature, especially the *hikayat* literature, notably the *Sejarah Melayu* and the *Hikayat Hang Tuah*. Yet this is a problematic, contestable heritage. Without going into the kind of complex literary, historiographic, textual, and partisan polemics that P. E. de Josselin de Jong (1965) analysed a quarter-century ago in "The Rise and Decline of a National Hero" (and which have continued and multiplied ever since), one can simply note that three quite distinct political "messages" are frequently read in the definitive yet ambiguous Melaka experience and three divergent injunctions inferred from it: a quiescence-encouraging, conservative-authoritarian (some call it "feudal" or "patriarchal") view that "Malays do and shall not rebel against their rulers"; the solidary nationalist or survivalist *défi* that "Malays and their culture shall not disappear from this world"; and the view—which can variously be read in liberal popular sovereignty or social contract terms, as a cry of populist insurgency, or within an Islamic discourse of moral and legal legitimacy—that "Malays shall remain loyal to their rulers so long as their rulers rule over them with justice".

Malay culture is an insistently political culture, but what its politics are, especially under modern competitive conditions, is multivocal and open-ended, not definitively specified or foreclosed by the past from which they are held to stem. Tradition and traditionalism have no single, necessary political import or direction once the presuppositions of domination have been relativized by the fracturing of historical continuity. Rather, their meaning is reached, and always reached anew, through interpretation: not so much discovered, as something already immanently "there", via "hermeneutic" interpretation but actually constructed in a constitutive process in which people interrogate and, with the accents and emphases of the present, create or invent an appropriately serviceable past.

For all the repeated claims—now a truism—that Malay political culture, focusing upon the Melaka period and therefore upon the sultanate as an institution, is one that emphasizes, values, and cultivates a regard for leaders, especially rulers, we might instead recall a different and often forgotten sociological truism: that leaders do not exist of themselves, simply awaiting the gathering around them of followers. Rather, it is followers, through the recognition and support that they bestow, who make leaders. Like leaders, too, leadership itself is an emergent, secondary, contingent reality, the product of a process that leaders may elicit but do not control.

We might therefore suggest that, in their important and challenging works, Chandra Muzaffar (1980 [?]) and Shaharuddin Maaruf (1984) have somehow indirectly highlighted what is fundamental: not the problem of leadership but that of followership.[8] All the conventional concern (in Malay literary, cultural, and sociological studies) with leaders, protectors, and heroes in this view may well be a displaced or disguised recognition of what is uneasily central to Malay politics and culture: not leadership, which is not conceptually or socially problematic, but followership, which is. If this is so, then our efforts are misdirected, too, when—in critical rather than approving spirit—we characterize Malay political culture, historical or contemporary, as a culture of absolutism or domination. For

---

[8] My reproach of Chandra Muzaffar and his remarkable book may be less than fully justified inasmuch as his focus, as his subtitle spells out, is upon relationships between leaders and followers (especially their cultural definition and values), not upon leaders as autonomous actors and initiators, as the core of leadership itself.

our focus, like the social and political processes themselves, should centre not upon the leader or ruler but upon the situation, the existential predicament even, of those who attain a fully Malay identity by acknowledging him. From the point of view of such a follower, Malay political culture is not a "culture of silence" nor a culture of blind obedience but a culture of deference—a culture, if one is to survive, of necessary, often ambivalent, and at times even dissimulating deference.

That there seems to be no adequate word, no available concept, to express something that is so pervasive and fundamental is indicative of how problematic followership is in Malay society. What seems to receive far more attention and cultural elaboration, and to become a focus of explicit concern, is the obligation that followership entails and the form in which deference is both represented and justified: *hormat* (generally rendered as "respect" or "honour"). *Hormat* is not so much the honour that some distinction of mind or moral character merits and thus earns, but the deference that is owed to a social position. It is deference—the recognition and acceptance of followership—operationalized, we might say.

No mere sociological conundrum, this cultural fact has immediate political significance. The trauma and transformation of Malay politics since April 1987—the consequences of the irreconcilable conflict for leadership of the UMNO and through it of the Malay people and Malaysian nation—need to be approached not as coffee-house talk and "instant" journalistic accounts do—in terms of rival leaders, their personalities, and the rival "teams" that they thereby managed to assemble. Instead, we need to look at the other side of the coin: to consider what has happened in terms of the inescapability, the inherent dilemmas, the fatefulness of choice (especially wrong choice!) of "followership" as an obligatory but risky condition of Malay political life and social existence. Alike, the wrenching tale of the relationship of Hang Tuah and Hang Jebat and, no less forcefully, the dilemma of contending UMNO politicians wishing to be loyal to a party somehow suddenly and unacceptably divided into two "teams" both tell us about something central to Malay society and political culture: not the sanctity and legitimacy of rulers and leaders but the agonies of a risk-fraught, choice-complicated obligation of followership. It is these realities of intelligent strategic and moral choice, within a society that requires demonstrations of deference, which lurk behind mere invocations of the follower's solemn obligation of comprehensive but unspecified "loyalty".

Yet perilous as it might be, there was no legitimate alternative to followership. Independence—standing outside of relations between ruler and ruled—was not a permissible option. A popular etymology that is sometimes offered equates as cognate the words *merdeka* (or *merdaheka*) [personal freedom, national independence] and *menderhaka* [to rebel, commit treason]. To *menderhaka* [from *derhaka* or sometimes *durhaka*], it is accordingly suggested, is nothing other than to seek personal *merdeka* or to attempt what in a later era came to be termed *berdikari*: to stand in this world on one's own feet—free, autonomous, masterless, unbound by ties of dependence, subservience, or "followership". Whether the etymology provided is genuine or spurious matters little. Even if erroneous, the fact that this purported derivation is sometimes offered powerfully makes its point: that, akin to rebellion, independence or the refusal of followership is, somewhere in Malay popular consciousness, impermissible.[9] Fully to be a Malay, this understanding again emphasizes, one must have a ruler, be ruled as a follower.

VI

Traditionalism—the obligatory, authenticity-assuring character of historically formed political culture—is a paradoxical thing. Nothing, in conclusion, might more incisively illustrate the point than an ironical development in recent Malay politics. After three predecessors each stamped by his origins within established (and "traditionalizing") Malay sultanate circles, Dr. Mahathir Mohamed succeeded to Malaysia's prime ministership: the first non-royal or non-aristocratic incumbent of the position, the first non-lawyer (and apparently the first non-golfer). As prime minister he was at first something of an outsider, a "man in a hurry", an impatient modernizer: a man with a clear vision of doing, achieving, realizing, not merely preserving and maintaining. Although not, at least outwardly, the same kind of uncompromising secularist, he seemed somehow to be in many ways a latter-day Malaysian Ataturk.[10]

Yet as his prime ministership unfolded, and as into 1987 and beyond his grasp of his party was eroded (paradoxically, by the modern, non-deferential opposition of a rival, Tengku Razaleigh Hamzah of Kelantan, enjoying a most elevated "traditional" status), he was confronted with challenge and crisis—and with various "legitimacy deficits" that had to be made good. To ensure his position and secure his continuing political grasp, this quite untraditional and even anti-traditionalistic leader had his lieutenants devise for him a new campaign with its own song, a regime-stabilizing anthem: *Lagu Setia* ["The Loyalty Song"].

---

[9] Although in their original Sanskrit the two terms are semantically distinct, this (Prof. Amin Sweeney advises me: personal communication) does not preclude their being identified with each other in local folk etymologies. Meanwhile, from a modern literary reanalysis of the relationship of Hang Tuah and Hang Jebat to their sultan (and of the meanings of treachery and rebellion in a sociopolitical context of hierarchy and deference), Ulrich Kratz (1989) also identifies the inherently ambivalent character of obligatory loyalty in Malay political culture.

[10] Since drafting this sentence I have come across another writer struck by the same parallel: Ozay Mehmet (1989).

"SETIA"

Demi negara yang tercinta
Dicurahkan bakti penuh setia
Demi raja yang disanjung tinggi
Kesetiaan tak berbelah bagi
Kepada pemimpin kepada rakyat
Khidmat diberi penuh taat
Sama berkerja sama berusaha
Setia berkhidmat untuk semua
Rela berkorban apa saja
Amanah bangsa tetap dijaga
Kami berikrar penuh setia
Untuk agama bangsa dan negara
"SETIA"

"LOYALTY"

For our beloved nation
A devoted outpouring of loyal service;
For our much lauded sultans
Allegiance is undivided:
To our leaders and to the people
Service is rendered in obedient loyalty.
Working together, striving together
In faithful service to all,
Ready to sacrifice anything, everything
To maintain and secure the people's trust;
We vow our absolute allegiance
To our faith, people, and nation.
"LOYALTY"

With remarkable rapidity, the presence of *Lagu Setia* became pervasive, not only through the media but also less formally. The fact that ordinary people in the street could everywhere be heard humming it soon showed that it was somehow finding a place in their hearts. If the sources of its evocative power, enduring popularity, and undoubted political efficacy are to be identified, *Lagu Setia* must be analysed at the several levels on which it operates, including the semantic, the iconographic, and the musical. Its semantic power stems from the tensed polarity that it establishes and the connections that it then makes between a set of attitudes or sentiments and their appropriate objects. The former consist of *bakti* (devoted, loyal, or faithful service), *setia* or *kesetiaan* (loyalty, obedience, allegiance), *khidmat* (service), *taat* (obedient loyalty, often conveyed in the portmanteau expression *taat setia*), *korban* (sacrifice, readiness to sacrifice or subordinate oneself to a cause), and *amanah* (trust, charge, security).

While these attitudes and their behavioural expression cluster closely around several overlapping and conventional notions of loyalty, the range of items yoked together in the song as the objects or beneficiaries of this categorical allegiance is more varied: the beloved homeland (*negara yang tercinta*) or modern nation-state; the leaders (*pemimpin*) meaning primarily its modern political leaders; the traditional royalty, the customary Malay state rulers or sultans (*raja*); religion (*agama*, meaning in fact the Islamic religion); and the people (*bangsa*, meaning race, nation, or people generally but with some implication of the primacy of the Malay people). Also included among the objects of these expressions of loyalty are the *rakyat* (common folk, primarily the Malay peasantry and commoners but including the common people generally) and, less equivocally *semua* (all, everybody)—with, however, the seemingly implied proviso that the citizenry as a whole will be the beneficiaries of this general outpouring of loyalty if their own primary loyalty to the nation and its various leaders, traditional and modern, remains unwavering.

As for the political diction and rhetoric employed, a noteworthy feature of this list of appropriate varieties and objects of allegiance is the enhanced formality, the special honorific or ceremonial dignity, with which most of them are endowed by their resonant, recognizably Arabic and Sanskritic derivation. While the foreign origins, in Sanskrit, of *negara*, *raja*, and *bangsa* and, in Arabic, of *rakyat* and *khidmat* are perhaps by now largely forgotten (these words seeming to many ordinary Malays to be, like *pemimpin* and *semua*, of purely Malay rather than derived origins), the overall impact of this collection of impressive loan words—the solemnity that their condensation of traditional notions of prestige and legitimacy effects—is in political terms powerful.

The dignifying halo effect conveyed by this condensed collection of prestigious terms is intensified by another feature of *Lagu Setia*'s lyrics. As with poetic expression in general, but markedly in Malay whose strength, as Anthony Burgess notes (1987: 371), lies in its valuing of semantic subtleties, not syntactic complexities, *Lagu Setia* defies any simple or exact translation. (Only an approximate interpretation, one of advisedly "telegraphic" incompleteness to capture something of the diffusely beguiling quality of the original, is offered above.) What its words, like its visual aspect, present is a sequence of images that somehow are understood to "go together"—though, significantly, what their relationship to one another actually is, both within the song and in the sociopolitical world which its addresses, remains unclear and largely implied. Yet this vagueness is the basis of its evocative power. Through a series of images, verbal and visual, *Lagu Setia* conjures up a succession of mood pictures. The power of these images, like that of much of the lyrics and imagery of contemporary Malay popular music, lies in their evocative vagueness, their open-endedness and multivocality, even ambiguity. The words, particularly in association with their accompanying images, connote far more than can be simply or directly expressed in any linear explication. Indeed, something of their irresistible power seems to reside precisely in the inexhaustible and therefore irrefutable plenitude of what they diffusely suggest.

Analysing the visual imagery of *Lagu Setia* as it appeared on television presents certain problems, since its immediate success and popularity eventually led to the production of a succession of renditions and versions, each with its own sequence of visual images. But while the later realizations became more adventurous, both in content and style (increasingly drawing upon images from the everyday working life of ordinary folk), the earlier, more definitive versions projected their meaning through the exclusive use of more conventional political imagery.

In one early version featuring a variety of scenes from the national day parade and celebrations in Kuala Lumpur, the sequence of images accompanying the words of *Lagu Setia*—from the introductory bars and display of the *Setia* logo, through the succeeding twelve lines of lyrics, to the final return of the same logo—was as follows:

[Introductory music]	*Setia* logo (crossed hands)
	View from high above of citizens carrying a large Malaysian flag
	Uniformed armed forces parading through Kuala Lumpur on national independence day.
	Malaysian flag fluttering in breeze.
1 Beloved homeland	View of Kuala Lumpur on national day.
	View of modern parliament house buildings.
2 Overflowing loyalty	Parade of uniformed groups: nurses, fire brigade, police.
3 Praised sultans	*Agung* in informal dress and mood surrounded by members of cabinet, also in informal mood and wearing *Semarak* uniform (see below).
	Agung walking, accompanied by aide-de-camp formally bearing brandished sword.
4 Undivided loyalty	Parading naval personnel and infantry.
5 Leaders and people	*Agung* and cabinet members, the latter again in *Semarak* uniform, on platform at parade

	Citizens of various races observing national day parade.
6 Loyal service	Uniformed police on parade
7 Striving together	Armoured cars and tanks, fire engines, police vehicles, and ambulances driving past.
8 Serving all	Government servants marching past.
	Private sector workers from major national companies, airlines, hotels etc. marching.
	Paramilitary police in marching salute.
9 Sacrifice	Infantry and armoured troops.
10 Trust and security	UMNO politicians led by veteran leaders, some in wheelchairs, parading past.
11 Swear loyalty	A group of students raising national flag and swearing an oath of national loyalty.
	Agung and cabinet ministers.
12 Religion, people, & homeland	Symbol of mosque.
	Crowds of bystanders and spectators of all races.
	Representation of Malaysian flag made by large numbers of placard-bearing citizens seen from afar.
	Setia logo.

Clearly, the verbal and visual elements or levels of *Lagu Setia* work in tandem. While in general the two work together, leading in the one direction, on occasion their combination—rather than condensing or focusing their common meaning—seems somehow to compound the appealing vagueness or play into the beguiling ambiguity of the lyrics. While loyalty in the abstract is emphasized throughout, it is not always clear from whom or to whom that loyalty is really meant to flow: those mentioned in the words? those depicted in the visual images? those singing the song? those in its audience to whom the song is directed (when, for example, the words suggest that "service is to be rendered in complete and loyal devotion", there is a certain ambiguity whether those depicted are to be seen as rendering loyal service or whether "we", those singing or listening to the song, are being urged to sustain such loyalty and devotion to those who are depicted.) The overall effect, then, is to create a diffuse mood holding together under the aegis of a pervasive and obligatory sense of loyalty all the elements invoked and depicted in *Lagu Setia*. In turn, all those elements—the objects and icons of appropriate loyalty in this corporatist vision of the Malaysian state—are drawn together by the visually central symbol of the *agung*, generally portrayed in full traditional regalia and receiving ceremonial deference and homage but also occasionally depicted, like the ministers in his government, in relaxed and informal mood, and even, in the original and perhaps most memorable television versions of *Lagu Setia*, saluting the admiring citizenry while riding by on his much loved high-powered motor cycle.

Lagu Setia and the campaign for its promotion were the pivotal and symbolically focusing activity within a wider campaign known as *Semarak*, a condensation of *Setia Bersama Rakyat* ("Loyalty With the People"). Devised by the Minister for Information (who held overall responsibility for the national radio and television channels and who also served as the general secretary of the governing UMNO political party), *Lagu Setia* and *Semarak* were projected through a closely coordinated and, as it was to become, long-lasting campaign. In its broader dimension, *Semarak* involved a series of popular rallies, held throughout the country and attended by the Prime Minister (accompanied by various cabinet ministers, all of them wearing a special *Semarak* campaign uniform— neat, informal, and quite sporting, but suggesting a modern, team-oriented, business-like approach). Meanwhile, *Lagu Setia* was soon to be heard everywhere, but most notably several times daily before major news bulletins on national television. In addition, for some weeks after the campaign's inception, a principal item in those news bulletins was a succession of stories featuring groups of public servants (drawn each day from a different government department or public agency) lining up outside their offices—rather like schoolchildren at morning assembly—for a ceremonial singing, led by their minister or administrative director, of *Lagu Setia*. Scenes of these occasions, in turn, were soon to figure prominently in some of the regularly repeated versions of *Lagu Setia* shown during station breaks and at other key times during normal daily transmission.

In addition to its verbal and visual impact, the musical character and appeals of *Lagu Setia* also warrant some brief mention. In no way a conventional patriotic song of some quasi-military kind, the tune of *Lagu Setia* is consistent with its soft-edged, multivocal meanings. When the earlier versions, recorded by the national radio choir, were replaced with others sung by and even visually featuring one of the nation's most popular and likeable young female vocalists, its unconventional character became even more pronounced—and what was in Malaysia a patriotic song was soon to be widely heard on the lips of citizens of neighbouring Singapore who, with their own loyalties and caring little for its political meaning and purposes, nevertheless allowed themselves to fall in love with its mood. Patriotism and loyalty, as pop singer Fran Peters projected them with her most pleasing voice and personality, were indeed a kind of falling in love, a voluptuous yearning, a chaste seduction. Born of a devastating political conflict and inspired by a basic crisis of legitimacy, *Lagu Setia* was itself inspired and inspiring, a master stroke of political genius. It reimagined and reinvented loyalty as something modern, subtle, low-key; it made the unfashionable attractive. It modernized the traditional and archaized the modern.

Yet, for all its political brilliance—even, in fact, underlying its political acuity—*Lagu Setia* remains a puzzling and paradoxical creation. That most "traditionalistic" or archaic of Malay political values—the notion of obligatory followership in loyalty essentially to the principle of loyalty itself—was mobilized to help assure the political survival and ascendancy of an altogether untraditionalistic leader devoted to a vision based upon anything but a reverence for the obligatoriness of tradition. But, even as the song was sung invoking a tradition of loyalty, its visual accompaniments on television were largely images of modernity, of modern nationhood and the appurtenances of the nation-state. These, however, were fused and framed by images of the quintessence of traditional Malay legitimacy: that of Malay monarchy itself, but here quite unarchaically represented by an apparently populist father-of-his-people on a motorcycle! If we could fully fathom this symbolism, its power and efficacy— if we could only analyse in all its intricacy the complex strategic resourcefulness of *Lagu Setia* with its subtle combination of verbal and visual imagery—we might be better able to put into words an appreciation of the paradoxical modernity of a politically persuasive contemporary Malay cultural traditionalism. To attempt that task is to begin to take seriously the study of contemporary Malay political culture.

Bibliography

Anderson, B. R. O'G. (1972) "The Idea of Power in Javanese Culture" in C. Holt, B. R. O'G. Anderson, & J. T. Siegel (eds.), *Culture and Politics in Indonesia*, Ithaca: Cornell U.P., pp. 1–69.

Anderson, B. R. O'G. (1983) *Imagined Communities: Reflections on the Origin and Spread of Nationalism*, London: Verso/NLB.

Bestor, T. C. (1989) *Neighborhood Tokyo*, Stanford: Stanford U.P.

Burgess, A. (1987) *Little Wilson and Big God*, London: Heinemann.

Carradine, D. (1983) "The Context, Performance and Meaning of Ritual: The British Monarchy and the 'Invention of Tradition', *c*. 1820–1977", chapter 4 in Hobsbawm & Ranger (eds.), *The Invention of Tradition*, pp. 101–164.

Chandra Muzaffar (1980 [?]) *Protector? An Analysis of the Concept and Practice of Loyalty in Leader-Led Relationships within Malay Society*, Penang: Aliran Publications.

Cohn, B. S. (1983) "Representing Authority in Victorian India", chapter 5 in Hobsbawm & Ranger (eds.), *The Invention of Tradition*, pp. 165–209.

de Josselin de Jong, P. E. (1965) "The Rise and Decline of a National Hero", *Journal of the Malaysian Branch of the Royal Asiatic Society* 38, ii: 140–155.

Geertz, C. (1980) *Negara: The Theater State in Nineteenth-Century Bali*, Princeton: Princeton U.P.

Geertz, C. (1983) "Centers, Kings, and Charisma: Reflections on the Symbolics of Power", chapter 6 in Geertz, *Local Knowledge: Further Essays in Interpretive Anthropology*, New York: Basic Books, pp. 121–146.

Hickling R. A. (1987) *Malaysian Law*, Kuala Lumpur: Professional Law Book Publishers.

Hobsbawm, E. (1983) "Introduction: Inventing Traditions", chapter 1 in Hobsbawm & Ranger (eds.), *The Invention of Tradition*, pp. 1–14.

Hobsbawm, E. & T. O. Ranger (eds.) (1983) *The Invention of Tradition*, Cambridge: Cambridge U.P.

Kahn, J. S. (1988/89) "Constructing Malaysian Identity: A View from Australia", *Ilmu Masyarakat* 14: 6–8.

Kapferer, B. (1988) *Legends of People, Myths of State: Violence, Intolerance, and Political Culture in Sri Lanka and Australia*, Washington D.C.: Smithsonian Institute Press.

Kessler, C. S. (1977) "Conflict and Sovereignty in Kelantanese Malay Spirit Seances" in V. Crapanzano & V. Garrison (eds.), *Case Studies in Spirit Possession*, New York: John Wiley, pp. 295–331.

Kratz, U. (1989) "Durhaka" (paper presented to the International Conference on Malay Studies, University of Malaya, August 1989).

Lee, H. P. (1986) "Postscript: The Malaysian Constitutional Crisis: King, Rulers and Royal Assent" in F. A. Trindade & H. P. Lee (eds.), *The Constitution of Malaysia: Further Perspectives and Development—Essays in Honour of Tun Mohamed Suffian*, Petaling Jaya: Penerbit Fajar Bakti, pp. 237–262.

Lerner, D. (1958) *The Passing of Traditional Society: Modernising the Middle East*, Glencoe, Ill & New York: Free Press & Crowell-Collier-Macmillan.

Milner, A. C. (1982) *Kerajaan: Malay Political Culture on the Eve of Colonial Rule*, Tucson: University of Arizona Press (Association for Asian Studies Monographs 40).

Musa, H. (1989) "Hang Jebat Visits Kuala Lumpur: Malay Villain as Hero in Contemporary Malaysian Drama" (paper presented to the Sixth Colloquium, Malaysia Society, Australian Association for Asian Studies, Sydney, June 1989).

Ozay Mehmet (1989) "Mahathir, Ataturk, and Development", chapter 3 in V. Kanapathy et al., *The Mahathir Era: Contributions to National Economic Development*, Subang Jaya: International Investment Consultants, pp. 36–48.

Roff, W. R. (1967) *The Origins of Malay Nationalism*, New Haven: Yale U.P.

Rudolph, L. I. & S. H. Rudolph (1967) *The Modernity of Tradition: Political Development in India*, Chicago: University of Chicago Press.

Shaharuddin bin Maaruf (1984) *Concept of a Hero in Malay Society*, Singapore & Kuala Lumpur: Eastern Universities Press.

Weber, M. (1978) *Economy and Society: An Outline of Interpretive Sociology*, 2 vols (eds. G. Roth & C. Wittich), Berkeley: University of California Press.

Wee, V. (1985) "Melayu: Hierarchies of Being in Riau" (Ph.D. thesis, Anthropology, Australian National University, Canberra).

7

Class, Ethnicity and Diversity: Some Remarks on Malay Culture in Malaysia

Joel S Kahn

The dominant images we have of Malaysian society—whether they are conveyed to us in the sociological literature, the speeches of politicians, the brochures of the tourist industry, or the everyday discourse of ordinary Malaysians—are images of diversity. This image of a society composed of a diversity of groups is so strong that it overrides otherwise strong political, ethical and/or theoretical disagreements about the nature and future of Malaysia. Malaysian politics, for example, is shot through with presumptions of 'communalism'. Political parties are almost all communally based. And even those who profess dissatisfaction with this state of affairs inevitably confess themselves resigned to it on account of the diversity of their constituencies. Academic theorists may disagree about how to characterise Malaysian society—is it a plural society, an ethnically-divided society or a class society? And they may as a consequence differ in the ways in which they interpret diversity—for some it is taken to be a fundamental aspect of social structure, while for others it amounts to false consciousness or cultural lag and hence a survival, albeit a particularly tenacious

[1] The materials in this paper are derived largely from the preliminary stages of a research project being conducted in Malaysia by myself and Dr Maila Stivens on the emergence of a new Malay middle class. The research was funded by a pilot grant from the Australian Research Council and grants from the Monash Special Research Funds, which I gratefully acknowledge here. The 1987/88 visit was sponsored by SERU and the Department of Anthropology and Sociology at the Universiti Kebangsaan Malaysia. I am especially thankful to Dr Yussof Ismail, Dr Shamsul A. B. and Wendy Smith for all their assistance.

I received comments and criticisms on earlier drafts of this paper from Wendy Smith, Shamsul A. B. and K. S. Jomo, for which many thanks. I would particularly like to thank Francis Loh and Khoo Kay Jin who gave me detailed comments and criticisms, some of which I have incorporated here. Although I may not have accepted all their criticisms, the paper would have been much poorer without their helpful comments.

survival, from a traditional past. And there are significant differences in views of the desirability of such a state of affairs. Should Malaysians accept and learn to live with multiculturalism, even make it the *sine qua non* of national identity, in ways being pursued for example by Australia's Labor Government? Or should national identity in Malaysia instead be constructed around the culture of just one of Malaysia's groups, the so-called indigenous Malays?

This paper has a limited objective, that is to examine critically the contention that Malaysian society is in fact best characterised as diverse, or rather that it should be seen as any more diverse than any other modern society. And if we conclude as I do that the presumption of diversity is in many ways a misleading one, it becomes important to ask two questions. First, since diversity has a phenomenological reality in the lives of contemporary Malaysians and observers alike, why should this be so? Second, are there not real dangers inherent in us perpetuating this image of diversity?

I shall attempt to deal with these issues by examining one way in which the diversity of Malaysia's people is and has been constructed, i.e. by means of a notion of culture. Here I shall focus on the example of Malay culture in particular.

Conceptualising Diversity in Malaysia: Race, Culture, Ethnicity

One term frequently used to define Malaysian social diversity is "ethnic", as in the expression "Malaysian society is made up of a number of different ethnic groups—the Malays, the Chinese, the Indians, the Orang Asli, etc." At least in modern social scientific jargon the term ethnic refers to two separable phenomena: the existence of more or less objective markers of human difference on the one hand, and the social recognition of these markers on the other. In the words of Anthony Smith, who has probably more than any other put the 20th century "ethnic revival" into theoretical and historical perspective: "an 'ethnic group' as a type of community requires both a common culture and a coextensive 'sense of community' . . ." (1981: 203n). Ethnicity is in this view perceived as a two-level phenomenon. It is, at least for Smith, "based on" culture, but it also requires a self-conscious recognition of the distinctiveness of the culture upon which it is based. Only when both cultural differentiation and group identification coincide can we speak of ethnic identification. Without a 'sense of community', the "set of symbols and values" which might be used to mark ethnic distinctiveness merge with a whole series of other potential ethnic markers, none of which have effective social meaning. Without cultural differentiation, argues Smith, ethnic identity lapses. "An ethnic group cannot shed all its cultural dimensions or 'signs' and retain this sense of identity intact." (*ibid*: 66)

The significance of this is that while for Smith ethnicity exists at the level of consciousness or subjectivity, it is at the same time apparently "based on" existing, objective characteristics of human diversity. For Smith these existing characteristics are conceived of as cultural. In Malaysia they are sometimes thought of as racial, sometimes cultural, and sometimes both together. To say that Malaysian society is ethnically diverse, therefore, is the same thing as saying that it is thought to be made up of different cultural/racial groups which are socially recognised. But of course this observation, being itself another manifestation of that recognition, is a mere tautology. Evaluating the claim means instead assessing the view that the ethnic characterisation is a 'correct' one even in its own terms, that is whether the perception of ethnicity, on the part of observer and observed, does indeed reflect a pre-existing diversity, whether racial or cultural.

Assessing the Claim of Diversity

Is contemporary Malaysian society made up of a set of cultural and/or racial groups, namely the Malays, the Chinese, etc.? Is there a problem with this? To see that there is, it is useful to look briefly at the intertwining histories of the concepts of culture and race. As it came to be used by anthropologists, particularly through the pioneering works of Franz Boas and his students in America, the meaning of the word "culture" underwent significant changes in the 1920s and 1930s, and these meanings are with us today. While in the Anglo Saxon world prior to that time 'culture' was used interchangeably with 'civilisation' to refer to what we now sometimes call 'high culture' (a usage which is partially retained in the world of 'cultural studies'), for American anthropologists after Boas culture came to be seen as something possessed by all. While for nineteenth century writers 'we' were always thought to have more culture than 'them', for Boas and his followers 'they' if anything had more culture than 'us'. Put succinctly by Stocking, the noted historian of anthropology, culture in the nineteenth century could only be conceived in the singular; in the twentieth, under Boas's influence, we think now only of cultures, in the plural (see Stocking 1968).

In this classical formulation culture came to encompass two related meanings. On the one hand it referred to a universal human attribute, to that aspect of our existence not organised by biology; to the way humans, as opposed to other animals, adapt to their environment. Culture was thus described as 'superorganic' or 'extrasomatic', and thus as that part of our heritage which could only be handed down from one generation to another by human symbolic communication. On the other hand was the assumption that while the capacity for culture was a human universal, cultures were themselves highly variable. While we humans are all more or less the same biologically, we differ in the ways in which we organise even the most basic aspects of our existence. In this sense 'culture' was thought of as a counterweight to 'race'. Indeed for Boas and many of his students, establishing the cultural rather than the physiological bases of human variation amounted to a mission.

But how useful are both race and culture in characterising Malaysian society? Let us look first at race. Human biologists and physical anthropologists have long since abandoned the notion of race, focussing instead on genetics in their search for the biological bases of human behaviour and the diversity of human populations. There are a number of reasons for the demise of race, but they boil down to the fact that the view that humanity can be divided up into a set of discrete and unchanging groups on the basis of a relatively small number of phenotypic or observable physiological characteristics has proved unworkable. No such set of characteristics has permitted us to classifying all of humanity unambiguously into individual racial groups. Even if it were possible to carve up humanity in this way, it would be impossible to conclude anything from the exercise. There are simply no good reasons to suppose that the observable characteristics on which racial classifications are based in themselves have any other meaning. Although race has unfortunately lived on in the popular imagination, then, it has lost its hold in biology. What this shows, of course, is that races are, and have always been, ideological entities with a presumed (indeed falsely presumed) biological foundation.

If racial categories are not what they seem, it seems natural to conclude, with the early anthropologists, that Malaysian ethnicity is based not on race but on culture, a solution suggested in Smith's formulation mentioned above. There are, however, two major difficulties with the concept of culture as it was conceived by these early anthropologists, and as it is used today in analysing ethnicity. The first is that it is impossible, particularly in the modern world, to define discrete cultures except in a totally arbitrary way. In other words there are no more other cultures than there are other races. The second and related problem is that a culture is an intellectual construct. It exists, in other words, only in the mind of the observer. Since the observer is, more often than not, an anthropologist or some other member of the intelligentsia, we have the paradoxical situation that a concept designed to capture the lifeways of the masses continues to be the property of the elite. The idea of cultural diversity, then, becomes just another way in which elites choose to construct people as different, and this continued nineteenth century focus on human difference, whether perceived in racial or cultural terms, can have some very disturbing effects as we shall see.

The idea of culture, then, suffers from the same logical faults as the concept of race. For just as it is impossible to define discrete and unchanging human groups on the basis of a handful of observable physiological characteristics, so it is impossible to define individual cultures on the basis of single cultural characteristics. "Culture" is therefore as much a construction as is race.

There is, for example, no such thing as Chinese, Malay, etc. culture, objectively demarcated out there in the world. It is constructed as part of ethnic discourse. This does not seem to me to be particularly heretical claim in the light of recent developments in social theory. But because I have found some resistance to it, let me briefly spell out what I mean by turning to the example of the Malays.

What is a Malay? The Malays, Malaysia's politically-dominant ethnic group, constitute some 57% of the population of peninsular Malaysia. The fact that such statistics are available suggest that the definition of a Malay is straight-forward. But, there is no Malay race, in the sense that there is no set of physiological or genetic markers that could define a discrete and unchanging biologically-defined category. Just as for "Chinese-ness" or "Indian-ness", there must be a continuum of both phenotypes and geno-types that overlap with others. The absolute boundaries drawn by census-takers are bound to be biologically arbitrary.

What about cultural characteristics—language, dress, world view, dom-estic architecture, handicrafts, leisure pursuits or religion? In theory these might be, and indeed are, used to identify specific ethnic groups. But in fact, as we have seen, the view that ethnic categories arise on the basis of objective cultural differentiation is no less misguided than the notion that racial categories arise from real, biologically-defined markers. The social category "Malay" does not coincide with the linguistic category of Malay-speakers. For one thing it would have to include Indonesian-speakers, and exclude at least some Malaysians regarded as Malay who speak a different first language, like Javanese or even English. And to further complicate the issue there have certainly been times, for example, when some of the best A-level results in the Malay-based national language have been achieved by students who would be categorised by most Malaysians as Chinese.

And while we are no doubt treading on sensitive ground, what is Malay religion? Malays, we are usually told, are Muslims. But so are the majority of Indonesians and of course a large number of ethnically-diverse peoples throughout the world. If a Malaysian Chinese converts to Islam, does he or she become a Malay? Not in the eyes of many Malays. In any case, what precisely is a Muslim? The differences in content of the everyday practices and of ordinary religious beliefs are not always so objectively different that it would be possible to assign every Malaysian unambigu-ously to one religion or another. The definition of a Muslim, Christian, Buddhist, Hindu, or animist in Malaysia must be made somewhat arbi-trarily (for example by referring to indigenous self-categorisations).

Finally, of course, there is the problem of the subjective relativity of cultural boundaries. So-called Malays may identify themselves differently in different contexts, just as the average Australian may use an ultimately all-inclusive, but clearly arbitrary notion of "Asian", under which he or she subsumes all Malaysians regardless of ethnic affiliation. The point is that in Malaysia, just as in Australia, people are neither objectively similar nor dissimilar. It is all a question of whether one is committed to con-structing humanity as a universal category or a set of diverging ones. And, if the latter, which out of the maze of criteria used for defining diversity will be adopted.

Cultures, as conceived by early anthropologists and now by Malaysians and observers of Malaysia alike, do not exist out there in the world, defining neat and sharp boundaries between isolable human groups. And this brings us to the crux of the matter. The idea of *a* culture is an ideological construct, it is the creation first of anthropologists and now, increasingly, of non-anthropologists. To take it as axiomatic that Malaysian society is somehow made up of discrete and highly different groups, whether these are defined in racial or cultural terms, instead of a group of human beings who in all essential characteristics are the same is, therefore, more problematic than first appears.

Once we recognise, however, that cultures are just as much constructions as are ethnic groups, important questions about the processes of cultural constitution in the modern world are raised. Two of particular relevance to the contemporary Malaysian situation are the following:

1 How is culture being constructed (and reconstructed) in the current situation?
2 Why is culture being defined in the ways that it is?

Answers to these questions should take us some way towards an understanding and evaluation of the fragmentation of culture that is a central theme of this volume.

Constituting Malay Culture in the 1980s

An example of the way culture is constituted in contemporary Malaysia is found in the current attempts to constitute 'traditional Malay culture' in the discourse of members of the new Malay middle class, the topic of a research project which is currently in its early stages. My discussion of this phenomenon here is, therefore, highly provisional.

Malaysia is currently awash with the symbolism of "traditional Malay culture". Outside the Western-oriented tourist industry, pockets of this symbolism can be found in the domestic tourist and leisure markets, the contemporary arts and architecture, the government-sponsored handicraft industry, popular magazines and newspapers, advertising copy, museum layout, the publications of Malay academics and, of course, in the speeches of civil servants and politicians. It must not be assumed that any of the areas of public life are totally permeated by Malay traditionalist discourse.

Not only have the symbols of Malay culture entered all these areas of public life, but the cultural arena has itself become intensely politicised. There has been widespread argument, for example, over the national language policy, particularly among educationalists. And the National Cultural Policy, introduced to promote 'nation building', has been the subject of intense debate since its proclamation in 1971. And in these cultural arenas, the values of a national culture and a national language based on the 'traditional' language and culture of the Malays have been a powerful force.

This "Malay culture industry" is, on its own, not an entirely new phenomenon. But apart from its pervasiveness, four other features of the symbolism are quite specific.

First, there is its social context. The makers of these images, as well as the consumers, are overwhelmingly part of a growing Malay middle class of civil servants, educators and professionals. This group ranges from relatively low paid clerks in government offices, teachers and middle level civil servants, academics, employees of the media, employees of state-owned enterprises and a smaller number of white collar workers and business people in the private sector. Its membership has been swelled by the government's pro-Malay New Economic Policy, introduced after the Kuala Lumpur communalist riots of 1969. They live in the new housing estates which have mushroomed on the edges of Malaysia's main urban centres, having had preferential access to home finance. While urban-based, many of them maintain links with the Malay villages from which they came, and to which they return on occasion to visit their, usually elderly, kin.

Ironically, the revived interest in a traditional, rurally-based Malay culture is taking place in a social setting characterised by a massive decline in what is considered to be the traditional Malay peasant community. This produces some fascinating paradoxes. The images generated by this culture industry in travel brochures, museums, newspapers, magazines, books and films depict Malay villagers as philosophical players of Malay games and fliers of kites, who like nothing better than watching dance dramas depicting the life of the Malay court. In my time in a Malay village in the mid 1970s I never once saw anyone flying a kite or playing *congkak* (a game resembling backgammon currently being revived by a Kuala Lumpur firm). And the villagers I knew had little interest in the performances of "traditional" Malay dance drama currently being staged in luxury hotels in Kuala Lumpur, preferring instead to watch *Dallas* and *The Professionals* on television. Traditional Malay wedding gear, a favoured display at local cultural centres was rejected by village brides who favoured platform shoes and blue taffeta.

A second feature of this culture industry concerns the nature of the images themselves. While many purport to symbolise the culture of Malaysia as a whole, a number refer explicitly and exclusively to the culture of just one of Malaysia's ethnic groups—the Malays.

Thirdly, many of these images (but not all—there are significant exceptions) represent Malay culture in a feudal and patriarchal manner. Dance dramas abound with reference to the "traditional" life of the Malay court and aristocracy. In a fascinating set of videos produced by the government's Handicraft Development Corporation to publicise the life and work of "traditional" artisans, the artisans are largely males. The commentary draws attention both to the role of the craftsman in the traditional royal entourage, and depicts the crafts*man* as the centre of the domestic and economic unit.

Finally, like the anthropological images of Malay culture which these so closely resemble, these portray Malay culture as the very antithesis of modern society. Where the latter is urban, impersonal and rushed, the former is rural, personalised and contemplative. The peaceful rural setting of the activities of the artisan is contrasted explicitly with the noise and bustle of Kuala Lumpur. The social and ecological adaptiveness of the traditional Malay house stands in sharp contrast to the hot and noisy urban high rise.

The growth of a Malay culture industry seems to demonstrate the way in which Malay culture is being constructed in contemporary Malaysia. But this statement needs to be carefully qualified in two main ways. First, I am discussing a discourse in which the emphasis is placed on cultural rather than religious identity, and in doing so I have not discussed the doubtless still very significant role played by Islam in definitions of Malayness. In so doing I do not intend to suggest that Islam is insignificant in current Malay political culture, only that many other studies have been devoted to this religious dimension (see, for example, paper by Jomo and Shabery, this volume), while relatively little attention has been paid to what is in my view a significant discourse on Malayness in which Islam plays a relatively minor role. Second, it is misleading to speak of this development in the singular since, as we shall see, there are significant differences among the different visions of Malayness which are emerging.

Before attempting to analyse these aspects of contemporary Malaysia neo-traditionalism, let us examine the flavour of the cultural revival. Difficult, as it is, to document in a rigorous fashion, the contours of the phenomenon can be drawn only impressionistically. Take, for example, the following extracts from my field notebook written on only the second day of a visit to Malaysia in 1987:

Kuala Lumpur, 7 December 1987

—Visited the Central Market, previously a decaying colonial construction in downtown KL. The Market has now been completely renovated, and contains within a three storey complex, shops, restaurants and, on the roof, foodstalls.

The shops and stalls sell handicrafts (Malay and *Orang Asli* [Malaysia's Aboriginal people]), *dodol* and other traditional Malay sweetmeats, kites, batek as well as some Western consumer goods. The atmosphere differs radically from KL's larger shopping centres both in architectural style (colonial building painted postmodern pink) and the balance of shopping and eating in favour of "traditional Malaya" instead of westernised consumerism. Brochure advertises a program of cultural performances in the evening at the Market.

—On television tonight watched part of a broadcast of the world *silat* championships [*silat* is the traditional Malay-Indonesian art of self-defence] with participants from all over the world. The overall

winner of the competition was the Indonesian team, with Malaysia coming in second (Holland and Spain did surprisingly well).
—Today sees the beginning of a State of Perak cultural week, sponsored by the government of the State of Perak and organised by the University of Malaya. Events are to include performances of traditional Malay dance, drama and music and a number of cultural exhibitions.
—Is this all part of a revival of Malay culture by and for the middle classes?

The following stories, taken from Malaysia's main government controlled English-language newspaper, *The New Straits Times*, are further testimony to the rediscovery of Malay tradition (inverted commas around tradition are implied throughout):

Evidence of the renewed importance of traditional forms of government:

Backing for Adat Supreme Council
Seremban: Wed—The Adat Chiefs of Negeri Sembilan today pledged support for the formation of an Adat Supreme Council to solve the crisis over the appointment of the 10th Datuk Kelana of Sungai Ujong . . . (NST, 24 December 1987)

Increased attention to traditional medicine:

State Museum to grow, list traditional herbs
Kuala Terenggqanu, Wed—The State Museum has embarked on a plan to grow and catalogue plants that are being used by *bomohs* [Malay healers] for traditional medicine . . . (NST 7 January 1988)

Using traditional Malay medicine for AIDS
Kuala Lumpur, Tues.—Traditional Malay medicine can be used to treat AIDS victims, Malaysian Association of Traditional Malay Medical Practitioners president Haji Radin Supathan said today.

He added that AIDS was not a modern disease as it afflicted mankind even as early as the time of Sodom and Gommorah . . . (NST 27 January 1988)

National Interest in Malacca's traditional mode of transport:

Float carves a niche for local tourism
Malacca, Wed.—Malaysia carved a niche in tourism when it won the prize for the best float outside the United States in the international category at the recent Rose Bowl Parade in Pasadena, California . . .

The winning Malaysian entry was the bullock-cart, a symbol synonymous with Old Malacca . . .

It is not surprising then that the huge bullock-cart decked with flowers, songket material and *waus* and drawn by two mechanical bulls, was designed by Malacca businessman Abu Samah Ismail.

Encik Abu Samah, 38, has a deep love for this ancient mode of transport. He offered his expertise to MAS [Malaysian Airlines System] and the TDC [Tourist Development Corporation] in designing a float as close as possible to the authentic bullock carts which plied Malacca at the turn of the century . . . (NST 7 January 1988)

Reviving traditional Malay games:

Local firm's twist to old games
Kuala Lumpur: Who would have thought that Malaysian children would be playing age-old traditional games or *sukan rakyat* with modern, mass-produced equipment!

A Malaysian company, Warisan Niaga, is doing just that to ensure that traditional games don't die out.

It will also be selling equipment to play the games as part of a promotion drive held in conjunction with the KL Weekly Fest.

The public can buy these traditional game sets at Sulaiman Court, which will become a lively Fest celebration centre every Sunday (NST, 6 January 1988)

Traditional Malay Dance stirs interest

Citirasa
Ramli Ibrahim is out to capture the essence of dance with *Citirasa . . . Citirasa*, a Malay dance drama produced by *Yayasan Seni*, is currently being staged at the City Hall Auditorium in Kuala Lumpur . . .

In it, Ramli concentrates on dance forms derived from traditional Malay court dances . . . (NST, Sundate, 17 January 1988)

Dance drama to be staged on March 19
Kuala Lumpur, Fri.—A dance drama depicting the glorious days of 17th century Kelantan under the reign of its famous monarch, Che Siti Wan Kembang, will be staged at a hotel here on March 19 to raise funds for the Kelantan State Muzium Trust Fund.

Aptly titled "Che Siti Wan Kembang", it is jointly sponsored by the Malaysian Airline System (MAS) Edaran Otomobil Nasional (EON) [the distributors of the "Malaysian Car", the Proton Saga] with the co-operation of the Culture and Tourism Ministry and the Kelantan State government.

In conjunction with the staging of the $80,000 dance drama, a dinner would be held at the hotel. Each table would cost between $1,000 and $5,000 . . .

Choreographed by a veteran court dance, Encik Ismail Bakti, the dance drama will be performed by 70 members of the Kumpulun Penari-Penari Istana Kelantan Darul Naim.

Tengku Sharifah Azwan, daughter of the Rajah of Perils, will be dancing in the lead role of Che Siti Wan Kembang.
(NST, 23 January 1988)

Traditional Themes in Television Drama:

New Drama in Store over RTM [sic]
RTM's Drama Division has . . . come up with dramas to fill the *Drama Minggu Ini* slot for next month or so . . . the titles of the drama in the

DMI slot . . . include *Kemuing Kenanga*—a fictional period drama about an old Malay Kingdom in which the loyalty of its ministers and citizens is being questioned. (NST 27 January 1988)

The same story describes the success of the ongoing weekly comedy series *Jenaka-Hang Setia* which pokes gentle fun at Malay rural dwellers presented less as peasants than as bearers of real Malay culture.

But we don't need television dramas to depict traditional Malay heroes. A series of stories appearing in the NST in January reported on purported sightings by villagers in Perak and Pahang of Datuk Sagor who according to historical records was hanged in 1877 for leading a revolt against the British. The sightings generated considerable interest, and their possibility was "not denied" by official sources, as the following report shows:

Sagor—no serious research by Museums Department

Kuala Lumpur, Fri.—the Museums Department does not propose to carry out any serious research into claims that 19th century Malay warrior Datuk Sagor is still alive in the absence of convincing evidence.

But the Department was following developments about Datuk Sagor through press statements made by certain quarters and the legendary fighter's descendants, Antiquities Director Kamarul Bahrin Buyong said today.

He said that going by historical accounts, Datuk Sagor, whose real name was Ngah Kamaddin, was hanged by the British in 1877 for leading a revolt together with Datuk Maharalela in Pasir Salak, which resulted in the death of the first British Resident in Perak, J. W. W. Birch, in 1875.

Enak Kamarul Bahrin said the reason for the Department not conducting any research was not because it did not believe the evidence received by certain quarters about Datuk Sagor being still alive, but because such evidence was inconclusive . . .

A Pahang cultural expert, Haji Zakaria Hitam or "Pak Zek", has claimed Datuk Sagor is still alive and is now 130 years old. (NST 23 January 1988)

The above constitutes a far from exhaustive series of cuttings mostly from a brief (2 week) period in January, 1988. The impression derived from the first few days in Kuala Lumpur and reading the local papers that some sort of revival of traditional Malay culture was in process was strengthened as the research visit went on.

After moving to the "research site", a middle class housing development in Seremban (capital of the state of Negeri Sembilan) we were urged by neighbours to visit *Mini Malaysia* in Ayer Keroh (half an hour away by car in the neighbouring state of Malacca). Mini Malaysia was planned and built several years ago by Malacca's State Tourist and Progress Boards, largely for the cultural edification of Malaysian tourists. Located then at the end of the new toll highway, it is well placed for day trippers from Kuala Lumpur and points south. Situated in Ayer Keroh, a new holiday resort with reasonable rates pegged to attract the Malaysian middle classes, it also attracts the domestic tourist trade.

The day we visited, Mini Malaysia and the Malay outdoor restaurants which surround the entrance, were busy. There were over 100 cars in the car park, and around 10 chartered buses. Admission fees were modest indeed ($1.00 for adults, 50c. for children). Expecting a tasteless Malaysian Disneyland, we were surprised to find an elegant layout of traditional Malay houses, one for each state of peninsular Malaysia, and two from East Malaysia (Sabah and Sarawak). Each house differs slightly according to regional architectural tradition. And each house stands as a small museum for appropriately selected elements of state (Malay) culture.

Thus there are traditional kitchen implements; life-size mannequins set out as for a wedding ceremony in regional dress; and old-fashioned music boxes with small dancing figures which, when a coin is inserted, play the traditional music associated with the region; a few agricultural implements and items of fishing equipment.

Apart from the houses, there is a small open air theatre where pop groups and traditional Malay ensembles play concerts, a "games hall" where there are exhibitions of top spinning and traditional Malay games; and a souvenir shop selling mostly Malay handicrafts being marketed by the national Handicraft Development Board (see below).

Two characteristics of the large numbers of people visiting are worth noting—first, the ratios were overwhelmingly Malay as opposed to western, Chinese and Indian (not surprisingly in view of the Malayness of the cultural exhibition). Second, as far as one can tell these things, visitors were mostly middle class urban dwelling Malays. They come in cars, in small family groups, mostly in Malay/westernised dress etc.

One scene I observed in the Negeri Sembilan house illustrates the paradoxes of the whole operation beautifully. A young family (husband, wife, wife's mother, and two young children) wandered through the house. When they came to the kitchen they turned to the wife's mother to explain the uses of the traditional kitchen implements. Most Negeri Sembilan village women would know these things. But urban middle class Malay housewives increasingly use western utensils and gadgets. The young women had, it seems, not come into contact with bamboo water containers and the serrated coconut graters on display.

While Malacca's state government may be more active than most in this new Malay culture industry, the state government of Negeri Sembilan has also put a good deal of effort into tasteful (and expensive) packaging of the culture of the Negeri Sembilan Malays, said to be a mixture of the culture of Minangkabau migrants from Sumatra in the 15th and 16th centuries, and that of indigenous Malays. Just outside Seremban towards the toll road the government has commissioned a beautiful new wooden museum, and also re-erected on the site two old Negeri buildings—a *Balai*

Adat (council hall) and a very old Negeri house. Although on my visits considerably less crowded than Mini Malaysia, the Negeri Sembilan cultural centre is also clearly designed for domestic Malay consumption as well as for the occasional, but rare, western tourist. It has featured prominently, however, during 1990's "Visit Malaysia Year".

One could go on with this, to list further examples of this Malay cultural revival in the speeches of politicians and bureaucrats and publications of all major political parties when taking up the issue of national cultural policy. For example one major UMNO figure who has occasionally expressed dissatisfaction with the direction taken by the dominant faction, has drawn on a remarkably similar stock of images to contrast the present with the past when, he claims, UMNO was in touch with, indeed built up from its grass roots in the traditional Malay villages while today it is being run from the centre by bureaucrats and technocrats.

But I have said enough both to indicate the scope of the phenomenon and to sketch in some of the basic characteristics of the images of "traditional Malay culture" currently being constituted. In all this it is important to bear in mind that the processes whereby Malay culture is being constructed in the late 1980s are new processes. While they may incorporate both elements from Malaysian culture history and notions about a timeless "tradition", we are not here dealing with a simple recognition in ethnic discourse of a pre-existing set of cultural traits and markers. Malay culture itself is what is being constructed.

Explaining Ethnicity?: Class, Culture and the Inadequacies of Reductionism

Why is Malay culture being constructed today in the ways discussed above, if it could just as well be constructed differently? Why should at least some Malays be choosing to define themselves as members of a culturally distinctive group at all, given that it is equally possible to construct all Malaysians as more or less the same? And why should Malaysians in general be committed to a discourse of diversity?

At least in much of the academic literature on Malaysian society such questions are linked to the problem of ethnicity. Typically such analyses pose the problem in the following terms: if ethnicity is the social recognition of existing cultural differences, then why and under what circumstances do these cultural differences achieve saliency? And there have typically been three somewhat different answers to the question when phrased in this way.

First there are those who would argue that individuals experience their own cultures in a primordial way, and that such primordial sentiments exercise a much stronger pull on individuals' identification than any more recent calls for identification with the nation.[2] Second, there are those who would argue that ethnic identification is the consequence of individual strategies for the maximisation of wealth, power and/or prestige. Here individuals will assume a particular ethnic identity, and call for others to follow, in order to maximise a political following, or access to basic resources.[3] Finally there are those who prefer an explanation in class terms. Class theorists have argued that ethnicity is, in fact, a form of false consciousness imposed on the masses by an elite seeking to 'divide and rule'.[4] Others have instead tried to make sense of Malaysian ethnicity by looking at the coincidence between ethnic group and class formation which has resulted from Malaysia's mode of insertion into a capitalist world economy.[5]

While each of these approaches has its own merits, it remains that the construction of Malay culture in particular, and the Malaysian discourse on diversity in general, is especially intractable to "ethnic explanation" in any of the above senses.

While doubtless the ability to mobilise blocs by calling on ethnic loyalties presents individual brokers with distinct advantages in the competition for power and resources, on its own this can only partially explain the motivations of followers, many of whom may well not personally gain from the power and/or wealth of ethnic leaders. And assuming that at least some members of these blocs do not share in this power/wealth, then the strategic explanation is inadequate. Its advocates will still need to call on ethnicity itself as a residual explanation.

Similarly, to interpret the current reworking of "Malayness" as the ideological dimension of class hegemony in Malaysia is problematic, not so much because the ability of hegemonic groups to privilege their own cultural vision is difficult to understand (it is clearly easier in Malaysia than in the West to ensure the hegemony of official discourses), but because it is not at all clear why, given the constellation of class interests, anyone should have a particular stake in promoting all these varied visions of 'traditional Malay culture'. Indeed the current Prime Minister of Malaysia has gone on record as believing, and the evidence is that he continues to believe, that 'Malay tradition' is a far from desirable phenomenon, and that it would be far better if it were to disappear altogether (see Mahathir 1970; Khoo, this volume). And even were we to suggest that images of

---

[2] The best known analysis of primordialism, at least in the Southeast Asian context, is provided by Clifford Geertz (see Geertz, 1963).
[3] Probably the best example of such an analysis of Malaysian ethnicity is provided by Nagata (1979).
[4] See, for example, Kassim Ahmad (1968), Abdul Rahman Embong (1974), and Cham (1975).
[5] Among these more sophisticated class analyses of Malaysia, influenced by the work of structural Marxists and world systems theorists are: Zawawi 1983; Hing 1984; Hua 1984; Jesudason 1988; Husin Ali 1984 and, of course, probably the best-known work on class in Malaysia, Jomo 1986.

Malay tradition are cynically generated by those in power simply to dupe the Malay masses, we would be a long way from understanding why it is that the Malay masses ever bother to believe in them.

Equally difficult to swallow would be any simple equation of 'Malay cultural values' with the interests of the masses seeking to challenge the currently hegemonic class, for at least in the examples given here, Malay culture is neither inevitably oppositional in content, nor is it exclusively, or even largely, a creation of the peasantry or the working class. The production, dissemination and consumption of its central images has been largely an activity of those I have loosely termed "middle class".

This is not to say that the current discourse on Malay culture has nothing to do with class. It is instead to argue that any class analysis of it will need to be both fine-grained, taking into account the complex and competing ways in which often the same images are used by very different forces in economic and political conflict and, at the same time, that a class perspective will also leave a residue of the phenomenon completely beyond explanation.[6]

Explanations of ethnicity, whether phrased in terms of individual "strategies" or class "interests", therefore, must ultimately rely upon primordialist assumptions to explain what I have termed the ethnic residue, i.e. the attachment to blocs and/or social movements of individuals who do not share in the strategies of their leaders or the interests of the class in question. And both kinds of approach are equally unable to explain the use of cultural symbolism even by the central actors, much less produce any understanding of the meaning of that symbolism. Culture and identification must here be treated in a way which reduces them to the role of cloak, hiding the "real" intentions of those who profess the believe in them.

Must we then fall back upon variants of the theory of primordialism? At least for the case at hand, this approach is equally unsatisfactory. Firstly, explaining the rise of cultural particularism in contemporary Malaysia by reference to the continued strength of primordial ties fails to account for the non-unilineal trajectory of ethnic attachment. The fact is that well-springs of primordial attachment must lie in the past. And however strong, tradition can by definition at best only remain in a steady state or be gradually eroded in the onward march of modernity. What primordialist theory cannot really adequately explain is the apparent *increase* in the strength of ethnic identification and conflict from within the very process of modernisation itself.

A second, and related difficulty with the use of primordialist explanations should already be evident in the above discussion. For at least some existing notions of Malayness are constructions, and not mere

---

[6] See Kahn, 1981, for a discussion of the ways in which Marxist theories of ethnicity, in which an attempt is made to reduce it to class, must still take ethnic attachment as a given.

reflections of a Malay culture which has always existed out there in the world as assumed by theories of primordialism.

And this in my view is the central difficulty with each of the 'ethnic explanations' discussed above. They all in one way or another operate with Smith's distinction between ethnicity, conceived of as the appropriation in subjectivity of objective cultural differentiation, and proceed from there to their different explanations. The problem is, as we have seen, with the assumption that cultural differentiation is itself an objective phenomenon, rather than itself being constructed out of ethnic discourse.

We must surely question this way of theorising the relationship between occupationally disparate individuals, the social movements in which they participate, and the imaginations which link them together. Ethnic movements are frequently judged to be non-class movements because their membership is apparently disparate according to the (observer's) principles of class analysis. In this, however, ethnic movements are no different from any other, including supposedly "purer" class movements. The latter inevitably involve what for want of a better term might be called intellectuals, and a closer look at what many of them mean by class consciousness reveals that it is they who turn out to be the main articulators of class consciousness[7]. Both for methodological and for ethical reasons, it is perhaps better if these intellectuals would cease claiming to "speak for the other" as it were, and instead subject their own discourse to the kinds of critical, sociological analysis to which they inevitably subject the ideologies of others. This judgement holds both for avowed Marxists, and also for the new generation of subalternists, moral economists, and "historians from below".

Let me be clear about what I am saying. I am not suggesting that, because we are intellectuals and not peasants/workers or whatever, we can never validly claim to be part of a movement which involves these 'others'. What I am suggesting is that an account of class consciousness, ethnicity or whatever will never be complete until we can account for our own espousal of one or other of these discourses. It is for these reasons that the contention that the class analyst or the strategic analyst can in some way stand outside, holding to an 'explanation' which is somehow epistemologically superior to that of the participants, that needs to be challenged.

This brings us back to the perception of cultural variation in contemporary Malaysia. There is reason to suppose that the construction of cultures in this sense in an activity of the elites and the middles classes in general, an anthropological enterprise which is no longer restricted to the practitioners of the academic discipline, but one which involves academics and non-academics alike. That non-western intellectuals, politicians,

---

[7] A more extreme conclusion, namely that Marxism is the consciousness of intellectuals, has been reached by Gouldner (see Gouldner 1985).

publicists and the like similarly engage in culture construction in no way contradicts this statement. There must be forms of analysis available to us which include us rather than exclude us from the process.

Culture and the Critique of Modernity: Re-orienting the Debate

As far as the particular issue at hand is concerned, as outsiders we can clearly perceive the extent to which current notions of Malay cultural uniqueness are constructions, rather than merely reflections in thought of a pre-existing Malay culture. But to provide a purportedly "scientific" explanation for them which reduces them to something else (political or economic motivation, the search for identity, etc.) is not just ethically, but theoretically dodgy.

By reducing Malay culture to a search for convenient markers of identity, casting it in the mould of a shallow invented tradition designed to dupe the masses, or discovering in it some kind of hidden protest—all these approaches, while offering insights, ultimately reduce Malaysians themselves to mere shadows, unable to recognise that their culture is not real at all. So long as we assume that Malaysian society cannot be analysed except from the perspectives of either class or individual strategies, this will be the inevitable consequence.

Of course identifying the problem is not the same thing as solving it. I certainly do not mean to offer the facile anthropological solution, which invites us simply to step outside our own intellectual traditions into the world of the other. Such a procedure is seriously flawed on methodological grounds in any case (see Kahn 1989). In any case the simplistic assumption of a yawning chasm between the world of social science and the world of Malaysian culture(s) is itself seriously open to question. It seems to me better to assume that most contemporary Malaysians, and not just Malaysian academics, are perfectly capable of developing a dialogue with those wider cultural assumptions which also inform the discourse of Western social science, and hence to develop in this case Malay culture in a discursive arena to which social scientists also have access. After all, social theory itself, which might be described as constituting the cultural perspective of social scientists, has emerged precisely in the context of a dialogue with outsider national traditions. And in much the same way, contemporary Malay culture is being created in the context of a debate with "the west" on the one hand and notions of modernity on the other.

To see that the working and reworking of contemporary Malay culture represents in some basic sense a creative dialogue with modernity, I shall conclude this paper with a brief critical discussion of what is in many ways a very interesting text. In selecting this one text I do not wish to suggest either that it is typical of the project of constructing Malay culture as a whole, nor that it is necessarily either definitive or desirable. I want only to try to show how it focuses our attention on the potentially distinctiveness and creativity of at least some of the current debate over Malay culture, and its relation to a developing national culture.

The text, published in late 1987, is entitled *The Malay House: Rediscovering Malaysia's Indigenous Shelter System* (Lim 1987). The author is a young Chinese researcher, Lim Jee Yuan, who studied architecture at the Universiti Sains Malaysia. Lim now works in Penang. At the time I met him in 1988 he was working for the Consumers' Association of Penang (CAP), a non-governmental organisation concerned with the rights of consumers, broadly conceived.

Research for the book was started in the late 1970s and continued into the early 1980s. But at least in its writing up, the book reflects the kind of populist ideas about appropriate technology, small is beautiful, the critique of science and valuation of 'indigenous' knowledge systems particularly associated with CAP itself.

The book is, like many of the more official (state-produced) products of the current cultural revival, handsomely produced, with line drawings and colour photographs. It seems destined for the coffee tables of at least the more 'progressive' members of Malaysia's new middle class. The audience, I have been told, consists largely of members of the English-educated professional middle class currently creating new ideas about tastefulness, distinctiveness and the like.

The Malay House manifests many of the features of other products of the current Malay cultural revival. It focuses on features of Malay, as opposed to Chinese or Indian, culture (even though the author himself is of course not so-categorised); not surprisingly, given the author, it dwells very little on what for some is the essence of Malayness, i.e. adherence to Islam; it portrays Malay life as largely rurally-based; it draws our attention to cultural (in this case architectural) regionalism, conceived as a state based diversity; it stresses the intimate ahd harmonious relation between Malay culture and the physical and geographical environment within which it is situated; it draws attention to the developed aesthetic sense of the Malay; it emphasises a Malay sense of community as opposed to individualism—communal norms shape the layout of domestic space, as well as the organisation of labour in housebuilding; and it focuses on the importance of spiritual values in the lives of traditional Malay villagers.

The book is, in short, an aesthetically pleasing attempt to constitute Malays as peaceful, rurally based, community oriented people by means of modern techniques of research, photographic reproduction and publication.

The images in *The Malay House* build up a picture of Malay culture which is, without doubt, both selective and constitutive. But it is more than this. Lim does not pretend that he can simply recapture a bygone age. We are in this text being asked to "learn from" traditional architecture certain things which can be made relevant to the modern scene, characterised as it is by high rates of urbanisation, the domination of often unsuitable "modern" (i.e. western) architectural forms, highly developed markets in land and housing, land shortages, Government and international low cost housing schemes and the like. Emerging out of a debate with and critique of existing architectural design and housing policies, the text in fact stresses the importance of adapting existing housing expertise to the demands of a world which is already modern. At one level architecturally anti-modern, the argument in the text is paradoxically modernist.

Lim Jee Yuan's text is, therefore, in part a vehicle for social criticism. But it would be unfair to argue that it is an empty vehicle, an arbitrary cover for a political dissatisfaction which is located somewhere else. Genuinely committed to a creative and very modern reconstitution of Malayness under new circumstances, it presents us with architectural styles and cultural values which are only apparently premodern. In fact what is being offered is a cultural critique of modernity, or better an argument for making existing modernity more modern. And the focus on domestic architecture is no less, or more, "material" than any narrowly political or economic critique would be. Indeed at one level one can think of no more material aspect of our existence than our domestic space.

The *Malay House* is not difficult to understand in its own terms. We do not, for example, need to have recourse either to primordial sentiments (the author would by definition not have such attachments to Malay culture in any case), or to hidden economic, political or strategic agendas to make sense of the symbolism and discourse of the text. In this sense the text reads itself. But this does not mean we cannot evaluate it. How might this be done?

Perhaps the first academic reaction is that the text is "inaccurate" or misleading, i.e. that it is an incomplete account of Malay domestic architecture, to say nothing of "Malay culture". Most of the images in *The Malay House* are of houses of the better-off, the well-to-do. And even here the selection is largely of houses of descendants of the minor nobility. Similarly there is a clear attempt to find a single architectural type as emblematic of the style of domestic architecture for each state. The stress is then not just on the similarities in all Malay houses, but on the creation of distinctive regional styles (this is evident also at mini-Malaysia). Of course actually occurring styles in each state vary tremendously. Similarly there is a element of androcentrism in the presentation of houses as places for living but not for working, and hence an underplaying of women's use of houses as places of production and labour.

But to treat the text on these grounds as though it was inventing tradition, thus excluding the critic from exactly the same accusation, would be unsatisfactory. We might quibble with certain aspects of the author's own procedures of selection, but we should not forget than an alternative which focussed on the houses of the poor and/or which was less androcentric would be equally selective. Here it is less selectivity that is the problem than the principles being used for selection. The argument that other principles should have been employed is a valid one, but it must be stressed this a political and/or ethical not a scientific argument. Does this leave us with no other procedures of verification? Are all forms of culturalist discourse therefore equally valid, to be distinguished only on political and ethical grounds? While this might be the conclusion of the postmodernist, I would suggest here that this would be premature. If we take a text such as *The Malay House*, one which presents a culturalist critique of modernity, it contains in fact two somewhat different projects, one of which is defensible and one of which is not on largely academic grounds.

On the one hand *The Malay House* is part of a project to construct Malay culture as a discrete and unchanging body of norms and values. This project, as I have argued, is unworkable. The reason why we can attack it for its selectivity stems not from the fact that another angle would be any less selective, but that the construction of cultural otherness in this sense must always be selective. We cannot and should not talk as though Malaysia, or any other society for that matter, were made up of isolable cultures. On these grounds *The Malay House* is open to intellectual critique, according to principles of rational argument which most people would share.

On the other hand *The Malay House* is doing something rather different. It is criticising a particular kind of discourse, a variant of architectural modernism, by undermining its claims to universalistic validity. Such critical uses to which concepts of cultural variation have been put are often laudable. It is, for example, highly worthwhile to use cultural diversity as a means of criticising those who would dominate by means of their own culturally-specific ideologies posing as universal truths. In this sense, for example, the idea of cultural variation becomes a valuable corrective to those assertions about national identity in Malaysia which are so clearly the product of particular cultural traditions (this is precisely the context of the earliest ideas about culture developed in nineteenth century Germany in opposition to British and French cultural imperialism). Although in important ways different, this kind of critique of dominating patriarchal discourse has been made by feminists.

The tremendous value of culturalist critiques, such as that articulated in *The Malay House*, then, is that they warn us against false universalism, not that they necessarily challenge the *possibility* of universalism. It is only when they begin constructing unchanging and discrete other cultures that they do the latter, and this, as we have seen, is ultimately impossible.

Bibliography

Abdul Rahman Hj Embong, 1974. "A Comment on the State of the Sociology of Race Relations and Political Sociology in Malaysia". *Jernal Antropologi san Sosiologi*, 3, pp. 63–8.

Cham, B. N., 1975. "Class and Communal Conflict in Malaysia". *Journal of Contemporary Asia*, 5 (4), pp. 446–61.

Geertz, C., 1963. 'The Integrative Revolution'. In C. Geertz (ed.), *Old Societies and New States*, New York: Free Press, pp. 105–57.

Gouldner, A., 1985. *Against Fragmentation: the origins of Marxism and the sociology of intellectuals*, New York: Oxford University Press.

Hing Ai Yun, 1984. "Capitalist Development, Class and Race". In S. Husin Ali (ed) 1984, pp. 296–328.

Hua Wu Yin, 1983. *Class and Communalism in Malaysia*, London: Zed Books.

Husin Ali, S. (ed), 1984. *Ethnicity, Class and Development: Malaysia*, Kuala Lumpur, Persatuan Sains Sosial Malaysia.

Jesudason, J., 1988. *Ethnicity and the Economy: The State, Chinese Business and Multinationals in Malaysia*, Singapore: Oxford University Press.

Jomo, K. S., 1986. *A Question of Class: Capital, the State and Uneven Development in Malaya*, Singapore: Oxford University Press.

Kahn, J. S., 1981. "Explaining Ethnicity: A Review Articles". *"Critique of Anthropology*, 4 (1), pp. 43–52.

——, 1989. "Culture: Demise or Resurrection?". *Critique of Anthropology*, 9(2), pp. 5–26.

Kassim Ahmad, 1968. "Communalism and National Unity". *Intisari*, 3 (2).

Mahathir Mohamed, 1970. *The Malay Dilemma*, Singapore: Donald Moore Press.

Nagata, J., 1979. *Malaysian Mosaic*, Vancouver: University of British Columbia Press.

Smith, A., 1981. *The Ethnic Revival*, New York: Cambridge University Press.

Stocking, G., 1968. *Race, Culture and Evolution*, Chicago: Chicago University Press.

Zawawi Ibrahim, Wan, 1983. "Theories on Race Relations: A Critical Review". Paper presented in the 'Modernization and National-Cultural Identity' conference, Persatuan Sains Sosial Malaysia, 10–12 January 1983.

III

Domination, Resistance and
Cultural Fragmentation

8

Dongjiaozong and the Challenge to Cultural Hegemony 1951–1987

Tan Liok Ee

Dongjiaozong is the term always used in Chinese when speaking of two organizations which have worked closely together in articulating and mobilizing Chinese opinions in Malaysia[2] on education as well as a wide range of other issues. Better known in English as the United Chinese Schools Committees' Association (UCSCA) and the United Chinese Schools Teachers' Association (UCSTA)[3], both organizations are national groupings of state or district level organizations. The UCSTA is a federation of Chinese School Teachers' Associations (CSTA) and the UCSCA of Chinese School Committees' Associations (CSCA).[4]

[1] A first draft of this paper was written while attached as Visiting Fellow to the Department of Pacific and Southeast Asian History, Research School of Pacific Studies, Australian National University during sabbatical leave from Universiti Sains Malaysia. The hospitality of ANU during my sabbatical is gratefully acknowledged. In revising the paper for this publication, I have benefitted especially from comments by Khoo Kay Jin and F. Loh Kok Wah.
[2] The Federation of Malaysia, incorporating the 11 states the Federation of Malaya (a political unit first constituted in 1948 and which obtained independence from the British in 1957), Sabah and Sarawak, as well as Singapore was formed in 1963. To avoid inaccuracy and confusion, the terms Federation of Malaya or Malaya are used for the pre-1963 period while Malaysia is used for the post-1963 period as well as in general statements. *Dongjiaozong* leaders have in the past few years tried to liase with, and extend their influence to, Chinese schools in Sabah and Sarawak. This paper, however, focusses mainly on their activities on the peninsula. Singapore, though briefly a component of Malaysia, is excluded from the discussion.
[3] In Chinese the UCSCA is commonly referred to as *Dongzong* and the UCSTA as *Jiaozong* (both abbreviations for their full Chinese titles) and the two together as *Dongjiaozong*.
[4] See Jiaozong 1987: 685–739 for list of CSTAs and their histories and Dongzong 1987: Vol. I for details on CSCAs.

Studies of Malaysian politics which have assumed either a consociational paradigm or that nation-building requires the submersion of linguistic and cultural differences in order to create a single identity have presented these two organizations, and especially the Chinese school teachers, as chauvinists or extremists insensitive to and intolerant of the demands of living within a plural society.[5] To characterize them as pressure groups[6] whose main role is to voice Chinese aspirations still suggests that they are polarities impinging upon the inter-ethnic compromises being negotiated by a core of moderate elite.

This paper suggests that the central aspect of *Dongjiaozong's* role lies in its challenge to ruling group policies on culture and education. The unitary (*danyuan*) approach to nation-building based on one language, one education system and one culture is rejected as hegemonic and inimical to the rights of ethnic minorities. From their alternative vision of a multiethnic nation, what is required is a pluralistic (*duoyuan*) approach to all aspects of cultural policy.[7]

The main phases in *Dongjiaozong's* chequered history interface with major turning points in Malaysian politics. Initially, from 1951 to 1957, *Dongjiaozong* leaders pitched themselves against British policies which were seen as directed towards Anglo-Malay hegemony. At the same time they also attempted to negotiate with a political elite that was leading calls for early Independence. By 1959, however, these negotiations had broken down and *Dongjiaozong* moved into open opposition against state policies. There was a period of comparative lack of direction between 1962 and 1972 before *Dongjiaozong* reemerged in 1973 under a new group of leaders to again challenge government policies on education and culture. Before discussing these phases in detail, we should first understand something about the socio-economic background of the Chinese school teachers and managers.

The Location of *Dongjiaozong* Within Chinese Society

In 1951 when the UCSTA was formed there were, in the Federation of Malaya, 6,369 Chinese school teachers serving in 1,171 schools with a total of just over 200,000 students.[8] Teachers in Chinese schools in the immediate post-war years were poorly paid and had no job security at all.

---

[5] For example, Enloe (1967: 324) places the ethnic teachers' associations at "the extreme right of the integrationist spectrum" and Means (1976: 217) classifies Chinese teachers as "militant Chinese communalists".

[6] As, for example, in Tan Puay Ching 1980.

[7] For a fuller discussion on conflicting concepts of the nation in Malaya see Tan Liok Ee 1988a.

[8] Figures calculated from Federation of Malaya, Annual Report on Education, Kuala Lumpur, 1951.

Salaries of trained teachers in 1946, for example, ranged from $65 to $120 a month when their counterparts in English schools were being paid between $240 to $400.[9] Teachers were employed on yearly contracts and found their livelihood dependent entirely on the pleasures of the managers of their respective schools. The 1952 Annual Report on Education (p. 9) had the following description of their plight:

> The teachers in Chinese schools have always been insecure as wage-earners in this country, with the inevitable shifts and straits and lack of professional dignity and social status which have made them poor itinerants, packing bag and baggage for the annual mass migration to other jobs in other schools . . . . .

The teachers described themselves as being worse off than experienced domestic servants (Jiaozong, 1987: 12–13).

However, teachers as an educated intelligentsia were held in great respect by an immigrant society which placed a high value on education. On their part, the teachers saw themselves as the moral conscience of society because of their education and their position as intellectuals. The majority of the Chinese school teachers in the pre-war and immediate post-war years were born and grew up in China.[10] The tradition in which they were educated taught that "learning was for this world and that it had a moral and social purpose" (Wang 1983: 2). Within this basically Confucian tradition, it was a moral and social duty for the educated to propound and uphold what was right. The highest admiration was always reserved for

> . . . . those who were fearless in their pursuit of principles and who followed their ideals no matter what the obstacles and, most of all, were brilliant in their ability to articulate these ideals, whether in poetry or in prose (*ibid*: 3–4).

The first generation UCSTA leaders, several of whom wrote poetry and were skilled calligraphers, saw their social and political role as intellectuals within such a tradition. The UCSTA's struggle on behalf of Chinese education was usually described as a moral duty (*yiwu*).

Moral duties apart, practical problems such as poor pay and insecure tenure also called for attention. Improvements in conditions of work was one of the three immediate objectives the UCSTA set itself in its Inaugural Manifesto.[11] The government, on its part, recognized that such improvements were enticing carrots to draw the teachers and the Chinese schools

---

[9] Figures obtained from Malayan Union, Annual Report on Education, 1946, pp. 26 and 89 and enclosure on salary scales of teachers in Director of Education File No. 101/47, Arkib Negara, Kuala Lumpur.

[10] See biodata of UCSTA leaders in Dongzong 1987: Vol. III, 820–823.

[11] The other two were to uphold Chinese culture and education and to cooperate with the government in improving Chinese education. See full text of Inaugural Manifesto in Jiaozong 1987: 12–13.

within its control. A New Salary Aid Scheme instituted in 1953 improved working conditions for teachers and increased direct state control over Chinese primary schools.[12] The incorporation of Chinese primary schools into the national system in 1956 and those Chinese secondary schools which chose to enter the national system in 1961 furthered this process as teachers within the national system came under various common salary schemes.[13]

By 1962 there were more than 13,000 teachers in Chinese schools absorbed within the national system. In contrast there were just over 1,000 teachers employed in independent or private Chinese secondary schools. With another revision in salary schemes in the early seventies, all teachers in national schools became employees of the state, subject to the same restrictions on political activities as other civil servants. Against this background, it is understandable why the dominant role within *Dongjiaozong* passed from the UCSTA to the UCSCA in the seventies and eighties.

The government could, in any case, also wield the stick against teachers in private schools. This was emphasized in 1961 when UCSTA president Lim Lian Geok was deregistered as a teacher and asked to show cause why he should not also be deprived of his citizenship. Lim is exalted as a hero and martyr in recognition of a sacrifice that few others would make. UCSTA leaders always had to strike a balance between their principles and more general utilitarian considerations. Most parents expected an education to lead to better opportunities for success. The Chinese schools, to survive, had to meet such expectations.

Turning to the Chinese school managers, we find that their leadership status was based not on respect for their learning or scholarship but on wealth and the philanthropic deployment of wealth. The management committee of a school usually came from its biggest financial contributors. The men who headed the state level Chinese School Committee Associations (CSCA), always located in the capital city of each state, would be amongst the richest and most influential businessmen holding leadership positions in several Chinese *shetuan* (social organizations).[14]

As the focal points of what Skinner has called "leader interlock clusters" (1961: 209)[15], they could mobilize the *shetuan* in support of the *Dongjiaozong* position. In the early 1950s, the *shetuan* were mobilized as citizens' organizations (*minjian tuanti*) to oppose colonial policies decided without elected representatives of the people. After Independence, the same

---

[12] For details see Enclosures in Education (Chinese) Kelantan File No 15/52, Arkib Negara Kuala Lumpur and discussion in Tan Liok Ee 1985: 104–107.
[13] The 1956 changes were the result of the Razak Report recommendations and the 1961 were due to the Talib Report. Both reports are discussed later in the paper.
[14] On *shetuan* organization and leadership in Malaya see Wan Ming Sing 1967 and Wong Nyuk Nyen 1981.
[15] This is illustrated in Tan Liok Ee 1985: Tables 3.1, 3.2, 3.3 for CSCA leaders in Perak, Selangor and Penang.

strategy was used to counter or undermine the ruling coalition's claim that its policies were a consensus acceptable to all ethnic groups. The UCSCA leaders of the 1950s, mainly wealthy businessmen, were unlikely to challenge seriously the socio-economic or political order. They were also more likely to view education in utilitarian terms. Increased government aid meant a decrease in their financial obligations to the schools while absorption within the national system meant better prospects for students. Such arguments were frequently effective in swinging the school managers round to the official position.[16]

Not unexpectedly therefore the UCSCA was throughout the 1950s the quiet and more vulnerable partner in the *Dongjiaozong* partnership. However, in the 1970s when the UCSTA was weakened by the majority of its members becoming state employees, the UCSCA was conversely reinvigorated by a new breed of leaders. This included for the first time professionals, in particular lawyers, many of whom were educated in Chinese schools in the 1950s and 1960s. Businessmen, of course, remained an important group within the UCSCA but these came not from amongst the biggest and richest but rather from what might be considered middle-level businessmen, a group more threatened by post-1969 changes in government policies. The most active came from managers of independent Chinese secondary schools in Selangor, the Federal Territory and Perak.

The teachers and managers thus come from different socio-economic backgrounds. They have in the past stood, and in the independent Chinese schools they still stand, in an employee/employer relationship. The close alliance between them within the rubric of *Dongjiaozong* has often muted conflicts over pay and working conditions. What binds them together is a common vision of a nation in which the Chinese language, Chinese schools and Chinese culture have a legitimate status.

1951–1957: Fighting for Legitimacy Within

The post-war years saw rapid political changes on the peninsula. In the face of vehement Malay opposition to the Malayan Union, the British moved quickly to reach agreement on an alternative constitutional framework with the Malay rulers and the conservative Malay elite, comprising leaders of the United Malays National Organization (UMNO)[17]. The declaration of a State of Emergency in June 1948 outlawed not only the Malayan Communist Party (MCP) but also other radical nationalist groups

---

[16] As, for example, when the Chung Ling High School in Penang was offered full government assistance in 1955 to entice other schools to follow its policy of using English as the main medium of instruction. See Tan Liok Ee 1989.

[17] See Allen 1967; Mohammed Noordin Sopiee 1976; Stockwell 1979.

which wanted an immediate end to British rule.[18] The Malayan Chinese Association (MCA) was formed, with British encouragement, in February 1949 to provide an acceptable alternative for rallying the Chinese politically.[19] At this stage the majority of the Chinese were still uncertain and confused by their future political role and the issues of citizenship and a new nationality.[20]

The colonial government's attempt to revamp education policy in the context of decolonization[21] alerted Chinese school teachers to impending changes in the related areas of language, education and culture. The release of two reports on education, within a month of each other in 1951, sparked off a heated controversy. The Barnes Report proposed a national system of schools which taught in both English and Malay at the primary level and in English at the secondary level. The Report claimed that a new social unity was possible only if the Chinese and Indians accepted that their languages and schools could have no place in the future national system. A totally different approach was recommended by the Fenn-Wu Committee, appointed to look into the future of Chinese education in Malaya.[22]

To many Chinese the Barnes Report revealed that the colonial government's intention was to use education policy to impose an Anglo-Malay cultural hegemony. The renunciation of their own cultural identities was the price Chinese and Indians must pay for admission into the national polity. The Chinese school teachers responded by organizing themselves to oppose such a policy. The inaugural meeting of the UCSTA was held in December 1951. Its declared objective was to fight for a legitimate place for the Chinese language and the Chinese schools, together with their Malay, Indian and English counterparts, *within* the national system.[23]

The UCSTA had to tread a careful path in opposing British policies. With the Emergency still at its height, the Chinese school teachers, with their history of radical political involvement, were already targets of close surveillance. Any taint of links with the MCP or hint of radicalism would have led to the organization's closure. On the other hand, the assassination of David Chen, a well-known Guomindang stalwart, almost immediately after he became the first president of the UCSTA indicated that the MCP could also cripple the organization if it so wished.[24] Under the circumstances, UCSTA leaders kept carefully within the bounds of legal dissent

---

[18] See Stenson 1969; Short 1975; Cheah Boon Kheng 1979.
[19] See Chan Heng Chee 1965; Heng Pek Koon 1988.
[20] See Cheah Boon Kheng 1978; Seah Soo Lin 1988.
[21] On post-war British education policy see Tan Liok Ee 1990.
[22] For more details on the two committees and their reports see Tan Liok Ee 1985 and Fennel 1968.
[23] See Jiaozong 1987: 297–304.
[24] See Tan Liok Ee 1985: 144–146.

while mounting a high profile campaign through frequent press releases, pamphlets and speeches.

The UCSTA position was that the large majority of the Chinese had relinquished their political ties with China and now thought of themselves as Malayans. This should not, however, mean they must forsake their language and culture. In multi-ethnic societies, diverse cultural traditions must have the right to exist and the freedom to grow. British education policy was denounced as colonialistic and undemocratic, imposed by a nominated and therefore unrepresentative Council despite loud protests from *Dongjiaozong* and major Chinese *shetuan*.[25]

Early UCSTA statements frequently evinced great pride in Chinese culture as "one of the most refined (cultures) in the world". At times this pride was expressed in more supercilious terms, as, for example, in the claim that:

> Malaya has, as yet, no culture of its own. Its present culture is a mix of Eastern and Western cultures. And of that Eastern half, a large part comes from Chinese culture.[26]

After Lim Lian Geok became UCSTA president in December 1953, UCSTA statements changed in emphasis and tone, showing greater sophistication and awareness of the need for sensitivity in a multi-ethnic society. More than any other UCSTA leader, Lim addressed the issue of a new political identity and loyalty. In a speech in 1955, for example, Lim said,

> . . . . We, the Chinese, who are born and bred here, already look on Malaya as our home; we must of course be concerned about Malaya's future, even more must we be concerned about the welfare of all Malayans . . . . .[27]

In an attempt to communicate with Malay society, Lim wrote a Hari Raya Puasa message in 1956 for *Utusan Melayu*, a leading Malay daily, in which he called on Malays and non-Malays alike to work towards greater inter-ethnic understanding through a change in psychological outlook. The migrant peoples, he said,

> . . . . must cultivate the outlook that Malaya is our first homeland. You must know that even if you have another ancestral country, your descendants are the sons and daughters of Malaya. For them Malaya is their ancestral country, Malaya is their permanent homeland.[28]

---

[25] Major speeches, memoranda, press statements are reproduced in Jiaozong 1987.
[26] The first quote is from UCSTA statement to the Select Committee on Education, 1952, and the second from Chen's speech at the inaugural meeting of the UCSTA on 25 December 1951 (Jiaozong 1987: 312–313 and 177 respectively).
[27] Reproduced in Lin Lian Yu 1986: 52.
[28] *Ibid.*, preface.

In a speech to Chinese school teachers in Negri Sembilan in 1957, he called on them to

> .... teach the children to be loyal to Malaya. Yes, our ancestors and even some of us came from other places. But we must understand that in the process of living, the link between man and land becomes inextricable, stronger even than that between him and his ancestors (Jiaozong, 1987: 391–392).

The UCSTA position was strengthened after November 1952, when UCSTA, UCSCA and MCA leaders agreed to work together on the Chinese education issue. The first meeting of UCSTA, UCSCA and MCA leaders was hailed in the Chinese dailies as the coming together of the 'Big Three' (*sanda*) organizations of Chinese society.[29] Thus began a working relationship with the MCA which lasted till 1959. Through the MCA, UCSTA leaders were subsequently drawn into the inter-ethnic bargaining that preceded the first general elections scheduled for July 1955.[30]

The UCSTA issued a pamphlet on 25 October 1954 to explain its position to the Chinese public. It protested the injustice of giving the right to vote to only 8 per cent of the more than two million Chinese residents of the Federation but welcomed the elections as a first step towards a representative democratic system. The UCSTA was prepared to support the Alliance, comprising UMNO, MCA and the Malayan Indian Congress[31] because all Malayans wanted an end to colonial rule. However, the UCSTA remained firm in its commitment to fight for Chinese to be an official language and for the Chinese schools to enjoy an equal position with other schools (Jiaozong, 1987: 350–351).

On 12 January 1955 a historic meeting took place in Malacca between UMNO, MCA and *Dongjiaozong* leaders. In the bargain negotiated, *Dongjiaozong* leaders agreed that "the question of Chinese becoming one of the official languages would not be brought up again until after the Federal elections" while UMNO leaders pledged that "if the Alliance were returned to power, it would see to it that the Chinese were given a chance to preserve their schools, language and culture".[32] This was written into the Alliance's election manifesto which pledged "to allow the vernacular schools their normal expansion", "to encourage rather than destroy the

---

[29] See, for example, Sin Chew Jit Poh 10 November 1952. For the common stand of the three organizations on language and education see Tan Cheng Lock 1954.
[30] By late 1954, the British had agreed to hold the first federal elections in 1955. See Means 1976: Chapter 10.
[31] What began as an UMNO-MCA electoral pact at the local level in 1952 had by 1954 been formalized, with the inclusion of the MIC, into the Alliance. On the early years of the Alliance, see Clarke 1964; Heng Pek Koon 1988.
[32] In "Minutes of a meeting on 12th January 1955 at the Residence of Dato Sir Cheng Lock Tan in Malacca", Document IX/155, Tan Cheng Lock Papers, Institute of Southeast Asian Studies, Singapore. See also amendments and comments in Jiaozong 1987: 361–64.

schools, language, or culture of any race living in the country" and "to accord equal treatment to all aided schools".[33] The terms of reference of the Razak Committee, appointed immediately after the Alliance victory to rewrite education policy, also carried echoes of this agreement.[34]

It appeared then to *Dongjiaozong* leaders that their negotiations in Malacca might bear fruit. Indeed, *Dongjiaozong* leaders were able to maintain comparatively cordial communications with Dato Razak Hussein as Minister of Education through MCA leaders during the crucial period in which the Razak Committee was drafting a new education policy and new legislation to effect that policy. They were pleased when the Razak Committee recommended that all four existing streams of primary schools, Malay, Chinese, Tamil and English, be accepted into the national system.[35] With this, the UCSTA won half the battle for legitimacy that had been their objective. Also, through an agreement reached with Razak, the new Education Ordinance of 1957 did not explicitly state that the ultimate objective of policy was to institute Malay as the main medium of instruction in all schools. This had been one of the major points of contention in the Razak Report.[36]

The Razak Report's recommendation that the Chinese secondary schools be allowed to continue teaching in Chinese proved to be an empty concession. The Report's introduction of two public examinations, to mark the completion of lower and upper secondary education, provided the instrument by which a change in language of instruction could be effected. This became apparent when the government revealed that the examinations were to be conducted in the official languages of the country, that is either English or Malay.[37]

In the final analysis, therefore, the UCSTA's agreement to temporarily shelf the official language issue proved to be a costly concession. UMNO leaders regarded the issue as thenceforth closed and UCSTA leaders never again found themselves in a comparable position of strength to press the issue. During the period of discussions over the Merdeka Constitution, the MCA found itself wedged between the demands of the *shetuan* and UMNO leaders' reluctance to consider them.[38] The UCSTA, still entangled in negotiations with UMNO and MCA leaders on the medium

---

[33] "Merdeka Within Four Years", The Alliance Election Manifesto for the 1955 elections, copy courtesy of Too Joon Hing.

[34] See Federation of Malaya 1956: 1.

[35] *Ibid.*, Paragraph 54.

[36] See *ibid.*, Paragraph 12. On *Dongjiaozong* negotiations with Razak over this point, see Chinese press reports of 5 July 1956 reproduced in Jiaozong 1987: 375. See also Lim Lian Geok's account in *ibid*: 456–457.

[37] See Tan Liok Ee 1985: Chapter 5.

[38] The *shetuan* demands were that citizenship for non-Malays should be based on *jus soli*, all citizens should have equal rights and Chinese should be an official language. See Wong Yoke Nyen 1981: Chapter 7 and Heng Pek Koon 1988: Chapter 8.

of examinations as well as other details of the Razak Report and the new Education Ordinance, was torn between supporting the *shetuan* position and sustaining their negotiations with the Alliance.[39]

These negotiations would have collapsed if UCSTA leaders had joined *shetuan* leaders in their bid to block final agreement between Alliance leaders and the British on the Constitution. Apart from this, UCSTA leaders also recognized weaknesses in *shetuan* leadership as well as the extent to which popular sentiment favoured a quick transition to Independence.[40] As Lim Lian Geok explained to UCSTA members, disappointment on the issue of education had to be contained because:

> At this point, the most important principle we must hold on to is the attainment of Independence. Absolutely everything must be decided on the basis that it does not harm Independence. This means that if some things we are fighting for may disadvantage the Independence struggle, then we must cope with it in the spirit of tolerance.[41]

UCSTA leaders soon found their tolerance limits tested.

1957–1961: Conflict and Confrontation

After Independence, UMNO leaders were more adamant that public examinations could only be conducted in the official languages. A change of leadership in the MCA in 1958 revived the working relationship between the 'Big Three' and raised hopes that, with general elections due soon, the issue might be settled in another pre-election bargain. During this brief, and for the MCA fatal, period of a few months the MCA leadership gave its support to two massive gatherings of Chinese social organizations organized by *Dongjiaozong*. At the second of these meetings, held in April 1959, 1,200 representatives from 747 organizations accepted a statement entitled "The General Demands of the Malayan Chinese community on Chinese Education".[42]

This exercise, followed soon after by the MCA's demand for an allocation of at least a third of the seats to be contested by the Alliance in the 1959 general elections, proved too much for UMNO leaders who were already under severe pressure from within their own ranks. The result was a political crisis the resolution of which established clearly that UMNO was the dominant party within the Alliance. The MCA was

---

[39] See Tan Liok Ee 1985: Chapter 5.
[40] Interview, Lim Lian Geok, Selayang Selangor, 2 April 1982. See also Wong Yoke Nyen 1982. The *shetuan* leadership had been discredited by revelations of their links with the Guomindang.
[41] In his speech at UCSTA Annual General Meeting, 12 December 1956, reprinted in Jiaozong 1987: 181–182.
[42] See full text in Tan Liok Ee 1985: Appendix F.

decimated after the crisis when many of its leaders left the party.[43] For the *Dongjiaozong*, it was the beginning of open confrontation against not only UMNO but also the MCA.

From a letter which Tunku Abdul Rahman wrote to Lim Lian Geok just before the UMNO-MCA crisis, it was already clear that the actions of the UCSTA were viewed as a deliberate and direct challenge to the Alliance. The Tunku described Chinese education as "an issue that has caused confusion and suspicion in the minds of the Chinese masses against the Alliance". He then went to say:

> It is hard to escape the impression that the motive for bringing up this issue just before the forthcoming parliamentary election is tantamount to pointing a pistol at the Alliance, with a threat that unless we give in to the demands of the teachers, the teachers will strive to turn the Chinese masses against the Alliance.[44]

After winning the 1959 elections, the Alliance got back to the education issue. The Talib Committee was appointed to review education policy. Unlike the period when the Razak Committee worked on its report, *Dongjiaozong* was now completely cut off from the MCA and any behind the scenes meetings with the Talib Committee.

Where the Razak Report had tried to marry divergent linguistic and cultural commitments with the objectives of a national policy, the Talib Report stated unequivocally that the "legitimate aspirations" of the various communities were simply "incompatible" with the creation of a national consciousness and the position of Malay as a national language. It thus recommended that all national secondary schools must teach only in the official languages of the country, that is either in English or Malay. This meant that Chinese secondary schools must either change their medium of instruction to be accepted as national schools or forego all government aid to become self-financing private schools.[45] Students of Chinese primary schools, which still remained within the national system, would benefit from the introduction of free primary education recommended by the Report. Their long term existence, however, was uncertain as Clause 21(b) of the Education Act of 1961 gave the Minister of Education the power to change the language of instruction in primary schools from English, Mandarin or Tamil to Malay.

For exactly a year after the release of the Talib Report, the Alliance government mounted an all-out campaign, backed by an organized state machinery which mobilized state level education department staff and the influence of local and national MCA leaders, to win the Chinese secondary schools over to accepting its terms. The benefits of lower fees, better employment and job prospects for students, better pay and stability

---

[43] On the 1959 crisis see Moore 1960 and Haas 1967.
[44] See full text in Jiaozong 1987: 84.
[45] Federation of Malaya 1960: Paragraphs 17–20.

of employment for teachers, an end to constant worry over recurrent expenditure for managers were repeatedly stated in meetings organized to persuade the managers of schools as well as in pamphlets and speeches.

Against these pragmatic and utilitarian appeals, Lim Lian Geok led the UCSTA's counter-campaign which centred, in contrast, on a purely moral appeal that an unjust policy must be resisted. The managers of secondary schools were urged to reject government aid and uphold education in the mother-tongue through self-reliance (zili gengsheng). The confrontation was open and intense, erupting in frequent sharp exchanges between MCA and UCSTA leaders in the Chinese press.[46]

Though even Lim Lian Geok himself thought he was fighting a losing battle, yet the government found the UCSTA campaign a sufficient threat to require coercive action against Lim. In August 1961 Lim's registration as a teacher was withdrawn. He was also asked to show cause why his citizenship should not be revoked. A government statement alleged that he had "deliberately misrepresentated government education policy in a manner calculated to excite disaffection" and made "emotional appeals of an extreme communal nature calculated to promote feelings of ill-will and hostility between different races in the Federation in a manner likely to cause violence".[47] With Lim silenced, the open confrontation between the government and *Dongjiaozong* stopped. Soon after, newspaper reports of schools deciding to convert began appearing. In the final account, 54 schools joined the national system while 16 others chose to reject the government's terms and became independent schools.[48] While the government could claim that its policy was accepted by the majority of the schools the fact that several very large and well-known schools[49] remained outside its fold partially vindicated the *Dongjiaozong* position.

1973–1987: The Challenge Renewed

For a decade after the conflict over the conversion of the Chinese secondary schools, both the UCSTA and UCSCA lost their fervour and dynamism. With the formation of Malaysia, the clash of alternative visions of the nation was centered on the conflict between the UMNO-led

---

[46] The Chinese press gave prominent coverage from August 1960 till the end of 1961. For excerpts see Jiaozong 1987: 436–468.

[47] Straits Times, 12 August 1961. After a long legal battle, Lim finally lost his citizenship in November 1964.

[48] See lists in Jiaozong 1987: 469 & 932. Of the 54 which converted 20 established private or independent branches to absorb students who were rejected from the national schools because they were over-aged or due to poor performance in the primary school leaving examinations which sifted out the top 30% for the national secondary schools.

[49] Amongst them were Foon Yew in Johore Baru, Kuen Cheng in Kuala Lumpur, Pay Fong in Malacca and Han Chiang in Penang.

Alliance and the Malaysian Malaysia campaign, led by Singapore's Peoples' Action Party, a discussion of which lies beyond the scope of this paper. There was a brief episode of excitement just before the National Language Act was enacted in 1967 when Sim Mow Yu, then UCSTA president as well as Vice-Chairman of the MCA Youth Section, tried to resurrect the issue of Chinese as an official language. This ended with Sim being sacked from the MCA, a move clearly intended to emphasize that the MCA did not want to be in any way implicated in the UCSTA campaign.[50]

Through the 1960s, enrolments in Chinese primary schools dropped steadily as Chinese parents were increasingly won over by the brighter prospects offered by an English education. As more national secondary schools were established, the private or independent Chinese secondary schools (ICS) also faced declining enrolments with a few schools closing down and several barely surviving.[51] The ICS found a fresh lease of life when, as pointed out earlier, new blood was infused into the UCSCA leadership.

In 1973, the new UCSCA leadership established a committee to look into the problems facing the ICS. This committee proposed that the ICS, instead of being adjuncts of the national system, should function as a system of alternative schools practising the educational principles espoused by *Dongjiaozong*. The committee proposed a common curriculum, a complete range of new textbooks in Chinese, and, two common examinations paralelling the public examinations for secondary school students (Dongjong, 1987: Vol. II, 522–525). The administration of this 'system' required an expansion of full-time UCSCA staff from 2 in 1974 to 40 in 1986.[52] Regular seminars and meetings of administrative personnel from ICS all over the country were organized to draw them into *Dongjiaozong's* programme.[53]

UCSCA arguments for the ICS appeal to an interesting mix of educational principles and pragmatic considerations. It is claimed that the ICS offer a better education because teaching in the mother-tongue is widely recognized to be most effective pedagogically. It is also claimed that the ICS, unlike the National schools, maintain the Chinese tradition of emphasizing moral and social education as an integral part of schooling. Thus

---

[50] On the 1967 episode see Roff 1967 and Tan Puay Ching 1985.

[51] Total enrolment in the ICS dropped from 34,400 in 1962 to 18,500 in 1972 (Tan Liok Ee 1988b: 63) while the percentage of Chinese students entering the first year of secondary education in the ICS in comparison to those leaving Chinese primary schools dropped from 51.9 percent in 1958 to 8.3 percent in 1970 (Jiaozong 1987: 902).

[52] From 1976, textbooks for the whole range of subjects taught at secondary level in Malaysian schools were produced. The first Unified Examinations for ICS were held in 1975 with 6,000 entrants. This increased to more than 12,000 in 1986. See reports in Dongzong 1984.

[53] Reports on them are available in Dongzong 1987: Vol 3.

they preserve Chinese cultural values as well as produce better members of society. Some *Dongjiaozong* leaders also claim that as private establishments the ICS can be less elite or examination-orientated and thus more student or education-orientated.[54]

The UCSCA, realizing the importance of access to tertiary education in the eyes of most parents, has obtained recognition for the ICS examinations as the bases of entry into the National University of Singapore, several universities in Taiwan and even universities in western countries. Some ICS also conduct journalism, computer and commercial classes to boost the job opportunities of their graduates. As a result of all these efforts enrolment in the ICS has increased steadily from around 27,000 in 1973 to 50,000 in 1986.[55]

Quite apart from the UCSCA leaders' more dynamic approach, increased enrolment in the ICS from the late 1970s into the 1980s is due also to the effects of major policy changes following the 1969 racial riots. In 1970, the Minister of Education, invoking the power vested in him by Clause 21 (b) of the 1961 Education Act, announced that beginning from 1971 all English primary schools would use Malay as their medium of instruction. Six years later the conversion process began in the national secondary schools and by 1983 tertiary institutions followed suit. With this, the objective of the national language as the only medium of instruction was attained, leaving only the Chinese and Tamil primary schools as obtrusive anomalies. Parents who previously looked to English schools as the gateway to socio-economic mobility had to reassess the situation.

The New Economic Policy, initiated in 1971, brought major changes to the social, economic and political life of the country. The implementation of its second prong, which calls for social restructuring to eradicate identification of race with economic function, has led to protests of racial discrimination, increased frustrations amongst non-Malays and greater ethnic polarisation.[56] More specifically in education, admission to tertiary institutions is adjusted to an ethnic quota. Finally, the replacement of the Alliance by a larger coalition, the Barisan Nasional, has further strengthened UMNO's position within the ruling coalition, thereby exacerbating non-Malay fears of Malay political power while the declared National Culture Policy is perceived as furthering Malay cultural hegemony.[57]

In such a context, the *Dongjiaozong* stance of resisting political and cultural hegemony has won extensive support. Statements such as the following by Lim Fong Seng, UCSCA president since 1973, struck responsive chords amongst many Chinese:

---

[54] See various speeches on the ICS reproduced in Dongzong, 1987: Vols. II and III.

[55] For a general discussion on the ICS see Tan Liok Ee 1988b.

[56] See various articles in Syed Husin Ali (ed) 1984.

[57] On the government's attempts to impose a policy on national culture, see Tan Sooi Beng's article in this book.

To say that minority communities must succumb to the political strength of the dominant community is to subscribe to an extremist racist ideology which goes against the principles of democracy and human rights.[58]

Similarly the *Dongjiaozong* vision of a society which is "fair and just" (*gongping heli*) to all has appeal even to those who are not educated in Chinese.

On their part, the new generation of UCSCA leaders had in fact also tried to expand *Dongjiaozong's* base of support within Chinese society by involving a wide range of social and cultural organizations in raising the working funds needed for the ICS projects outlined above. Rather than obtaining big donations from individuals as in the past, money was raised through high-profile fund-raising campaigns involving all levels of society, including working-class organizations. This trend was started in Perak in 1973 when in a dramatic manifestation of community support, barbers, taxi-drivers, hawkers, shopkeepers, and many other groups, donated a days' takings to the ICS fund. This snowballed into other states arousing in the process greater interest in the ICS. The result was increased enrolments and expansion programs for many Perak ICS.[59]

In the same way, *Dongjiaozong* has financed its legal battle with the government over the establishment of the Merdeka University by raising funds all over the country through what it dubbed the 'A dollar A person' (*yiren yiyuan*) campaign.[60] The Merdeka University, first mooted by the UCSTA in 1967 and revived by the new UCSCA leadership in the seventies, was an issue which brought *Dongjiaozong* once more into a direct conflict with the MCA.[61] To the MCA the attempt to establish a university teaching in Chinese was both unpolitic and impractical. But to *Dongjiaozong* leaders, and their supporters, the Merdeka University symbolized a basic constitutional right. The government's refusal to permit a Chinese university was contested in court as denying a right enshrined in the constitution.[62] In the event, the government's position was upheld by the Supreme Court bringing the saga to an end in 1983.[63]

By the early 1980s, *Dongjiaozong* leaders had begun to broaden their concerns beyond language, education and culture.[64] *Dongjiaozong* joined

---

[58] From Lim's preface in Dongzong 1987.
[59] See Pili Huaxiao Dongshihui Lianhehui 1976.
[60] Campaigns in each location usually started off with a public gathering in which the proposal for the Merdeka University and *Dongjiaozong's* objectives in pursuing it were explained.
[61] See Lu Tingyu (ed), 1968 and Jiaozong 1987: 555–566.
[62] For different perspectives on the Merdeka University issue see Duli Daxue youxian gongsi 1978a, 1978b, 1979; Yahaya Ismail 1978 and Aliran 1979.
[63] For a discussion of implications of this decision see Visu Sinnadurai (Dato') 1986.
[64] These remain, of course, issues in which Dongjiaozong continues to play a

many other non-communally based citizens' organizations in criticizing government policies or opposing new legislation to restrict the scope for dissent from organizations in civil society. Opposition to the 1981 Societies (Amendment) Act is one example, support for the Papan citizens' protest against the location of a dump for radio-active waste another.[65]

As for the formal political process itself, *Dongjiaozong* leaders have been far less certain of its role. The close working relationship with the MCA of the 1950s has never been reestablished. Rather there have been spates of extreme antagonism. Just before the 1982 general elections, there was a dramatic announcement of an agreement between *Dongjiaozong* leaders and the Gerakan Rakyat Malaysia, a component party within the Barisan Nasional. Two "Chinese educationists" who ran as Gerakan candidates were openly backed by the *Dongjiaozong* during the election campaign. After the elections, however, Lim Fong Seng hastened to explain that *Dongjiaozong* did not intend to be embroiled in party politics.[66] In the 1986 elections *Dongjiaozong* leaders no longer campaigned openly for Gerakan candidates. Instead, in the few months before the elections, its leaders were reported to have met with Parti Islam se Malaysia (PAS), an Islamic opposition party which had embarked on the new strategy of trying to win over non-Malay votes. No concrete agreements materialized but much discussion was generated in Chinese newspapers on the likelihood of Chinese organizations supporting a Malay opposition party in order to bring about a 'two-party' system in Malaysia.

The high profile of *Dongjiaozong* leaders was maintained in 1987 when a controversy erupted over the appointment of persons who were not literate in Mandarin to key administrative posts in Chinese primary schools and ex-Chinese secondary schools which had joined the National system. Protest meetings called by *Dongjiaozong* saw its leaders sitting together on stage with MCA, Gerakan and Democratic Action Party[67] leaders. While this was hailed in the Chinese press as an unprecedented show of Chinese unity, it was viewed by UMNO leaders as a betrayal by their colleagues from the Barisan Nasional.

The furor over this issue contributed to the general heat of a political situation charged with an atmosphere of crisis ever since the UMNO elections in April 1987. In October 1987 the presidents of the UCSTA and UCSCA, a vice-president of the UCSTA as well as two other persons who have been closely associated with *Dongjiaozong* activities, were amongst 107 persons detained by the government in a massive sweep against several

---

leading role in Chinese society as, for example, in 1983 when it led 15 major Chinese organizations in submitting a joint memorandum on national culture. See Memorandun Kebudayaan Kebangsaan: Keluaran Khas 1983.

[65] A convenient source for more recent developments, apart from Malaysian newspapers, is the Far Eastern Economic Review.

[66] See Lim's press statement 6 May 1982, reprinted in Dongzong: Vol. 2, 430–431.

[67] The DAP is the leading non-Malay opposition party.

groups.[68] It remains to be seen whether 1987 will mark yet another milestone in the history of *Dongjiaozong*.

Conclusion

This paper has argued that Dongjiaozong emerged to play a prominent role in Malaysian politics because its leaders in the early fifties persuasively articulated an alternative vision of a democratic multi-ethnic nation in which there could be space for minority languages and cultures. From this alternative vision, Dongjiaozong leaders have challenged the legitimacy of state policies on language, education and culture because these conflict with the ideals of a fair and just society. Through its history we can see two major limitations in *Dongjiaozong's* challenge to the state's attempts to exert cultural hegemony.

First, *Dongjiaozong* has remained entrapped within the prevailing parameters of a political discourse which casts all its actors in ethnic terms. In the crucial pre-Independence years, *Dongjiaozong* was drawn into the inter-ethnic bargaining that structured the pattern of Malaysian politics for subsequent decades. In doing so, it legitimated the formula of elite representation of communal interests. Though their alternative vision of the nation centres on the concept of plurality, *Dongjiaozong* leaders have failed to translate this into practical terms. Few attempts have been made to actively include other minorities in its campaign for an alternative approach to nation-building in a multi-ethnic society. The legitimacy of a pluralistic vision of the nation could have become more compelling and persuasive after Malaysia, with its more numerous and complex ethnic groups, replaced the Federation of Malaya.

Second, *Dongjiaozong* has had to contend with the state's power to determine and effect policy within a society in which the dominant ideology defines the value of education in terms of socio-economic mobility. By determining the most effective channels of this mobility through, for example, prescribing specific examinations at particular stages of schooling or controlling access to tertiary institutions, the government bolstered the hegemony of dominant values as well as support for its policies. *Dongjiaozong* leaders, on the other hand, could not challenge the legitimacy of government policy as well as the hegemony of dominant value

---

[68] They were Lim Fong Seng, president of the UCSCA; Sim Mow Yu, president of the UCSTA; Ong Tin Kim, a prominent *Dongjiaozong* leader in the seventies and a Gerakan Member of Parliament and Permanent Secretary in the Ministry of Communications at the time of his arrest; Twang Pik King, a Vice-president of the UCSTA and headmaster of an ICS in Selangor; and Kua Kia Soong who had worked for the UCSCA for several years in the early eighties. Ong was released after questioning but the others were served with two-year detention orders. They have since been released, in batches together with other detainees.

orientations. The problems encountered in seeking a balance reveal a more fundamental limitation in *Dongjiaozong's* challenge to cultural hegemony.

Political realism dictated that *Dongjiaozong* should negotiate with Alliance leaders for the Chinese schools to be incorporated within the national system. To the extent that they were successful, as for example in 1956 with the primary schools, they directly enhanced the legitimacy not only of the ruling elite but, ironically, also of the national system thereby established. When they failed, as in 1961, this was due not just to a more assimilative state policy but also because MCA leaders and the majority of the secondary schools recognized the sheer pragmatism of falling in line with the government. Fragmentation within Chinese society was obvious, so also was the fact that *Dongjiaozong* spoke for a fraction and not the whole of Chinese society. It is significant that in this context Lim Lian Geok stated the *Dongjiaozong* position in essentially moral terms while the government reinforced pragmatism by exerting its coercive powers.

Pragmatism, however, has also accounted for the resilience of the Chinese schools, thereby strengthening *Dongjiaozong's* position. Without discounting the appeal of the argument that education in the mother-tongue is a basic right, it is questionable whether the Chinese schools could have continued to attract large numbers if a knowledge of Chinese had no social or economic value whatsoever. The same considerations, of course, also dictate that the national language as well as English be acquired, in some circumstances and for some parents at the cost of knowing the Chinese language. Fluctuating enrolment trends in the Chinese schools show that their survival depended, and depends, to a large extent on the perceived value of a Chinese education in the eyes of parents.

Increased enrolments in, and Chinese support for, the ICS in the last two decades, indicate some success in *Dongjiaozong's* more recent attempts to show that its principles can be translated into practice without sacrificing utilitarian considerations. However, to the extent that the national system can still provide a significant channel for socio-economic mobility, it is doubtful whether the ICS can in the foreseeable future attract a majority of Chinese students away from the national secondary schools. It is even less likely that more significant numbers of other Malaysians can be attracted to the ICS. Until and unless an alternative ideology redefining the value of schooling can also be persuasively articulated, any challenge to the national system must remain confined within terms which offer more effective channels to mobility within the existing socio-economic structure.

Bibliography

Aliran, 1979. *The Real Issues: Merdeka University*, Penang: Aliran.

Allen, James de V., *The Malayan Union*, New Haven: Yale University Southeast Asia Studies Monograph Series No. 10.

Chan Heng Chee, 1965. "The Malayan Chinese Association". M.A. Thesis, University of Singapore.

Cheah Boon Kheng, 1978. "Malayan Chinese and the Citizenship Issue, 1945–1948". *Review of Indonesian and Malaysian Association*, Vol. 12 No. 2, pp. 95–122.

———, 1979. *The Masked Comrades: A Study of the Communist United Front in Malaya, 1945–1948*, Singapore: Times Books International.

Clarke, Margaret, 1964. "The Malayan Alliance and its Accommodation of Communal Pressures, 1952–1962". M.A. Thesis, University of Malaya.

Dongzong chuban xiaozu (Dongzong). 1984. *Disan jie quanguo Huawen duli zhongxue xingzheng renyuan yantaohui ziliao ji* (Select Papers for the Third National Seminar for Administrative Staff in Chinese Independent Schools). Kuala Lumpur: UCSCA.

———, 1987. *Dongzong sanshi nian* (The UCSCA these 30 years). In 3 volumes. Kuala Lumpur: UCSCA.

Enloe, Cynthia, 1967. "Multi-ethnic Politics: the Case of Malaysia". Ph.D. Dissertation, University of California (Berkeley).

Federation of Malaya, 1951a. Report of the Committee on Malay Education (Barnes Report).

———, 1951b. *Report of a Mission invited by the Federation Government to Study the Problem of the Education of the Chinese in Malaya: Chinese Schools and the Education of Chinese Malayans* (Fenn-Wu Report).

———, 1952. *Education Ordinance*.

———, 1956. *Report of the Education Committee* (Razak Report).

———, 1957. *Education Ordinance*.

———, 1960. *Report of the Education Review Committee* (Talib Report).

———, 1961. *Education Act*.

Fennel, Thomas Rixon, 1968. "Commitment to Change: A History of Malayan Education Policy, 1945–1957". Ph.D. Dissertation, University of Hawaii.

Haas, Roy, 1967, "The MCA 1958–1959: An Analysis of Different Conceptions of the Malayan Chinese Role in Independent Malaya". M.A. Thesis, Northern Illinois University.

Heng Pek Koon, 1988. *Chinese Politics in Malaysia: A History of the Malayan Chinese Association*, Singapore: Oxford University Press.

Jiaozong jiaoyu yanjiu zhongxin (Jiaozong). 1987. *Malaixiya Huaoxiao Jiaoshihui Zonghui qingzhu sanshisan zhounian jinian dekan* (Commemorative Publication on the 33rd Anniversary of the UCSTA). Kuala Lumpur: UCSTA.

Lin Lianyu, 1986. *Huawen Jiaoyu Huyu Lu* (Appeals for Chinese Education), Kuala Lumpur: Lim Lian Geok Foundation Committee. (Posthumous Collection)

Lu Tingyu (ed), 1968. *Jiaoshi Zhazhi Duli Daxue Zhuanhao* (Teachers' Journal: Special Issue on the Merdeka University). Kuala Lumpur: UCSTA.

Means, Gordon, 1970. *Malaysian Politics*, London: Hodder and Stoughton, 2nd edition.

Memorandum Kebudayaan Kebangsaan: Keluaran Khas (Memorandum on National Culture: Special Publication). 1983. Kuala Lumpur: 15 Leading Chinese organizations in Malaysia.

Mohammed Noordin Sopiee, 1976. *From Malayan Union to Singapore Separation, 1945–1964*, Kuala Lumpur: University of Malaya Press.

Moore, Daniel Eldridge, 1960. "The UMNO and the 1959 elections". Ph.D. dissertation, University of California.

Pili Huaxiao Dongshihui Lianhehui (ed), 1976. *Pilizhou Huanwen Duzhong fuxing shi* (History of the Renaissance of the Independent Chinese Schools in Perak). Ipoh: Pili Huaxiao Dongshihui Lianhehui.

Roff, Margaret, 1967. "The Politics of Language in Malaya" in *Asian Survey*, 7 (5), pp. 316–28.

Seah Soo Lin, 1988. "Kerakyatan dan Kaum Cina di Tanah Melayu, 1945–1948" (Citizenship and the Chinese in Malaya, 1945–48), B.A. Academic Exercise, Universiti Sains Malaysia.

Short, Anthony, 1975. *The Communist Insurrection in Malaya, 1948–1960*, London: Frederick Muller.

Skinner, G. W., 1961. *Leadership and Power in the Chinese Community of Thailand*, Ithaca: Cornell University Press.

Stenson, Michael, 1969. *Repression and Revolt: the Origins of the 1948 Communist Rebellion*, Athens: Ohio University Press.

Stockwell, A. J., 1979. *British Policy and Malay Politics during the Malayan Union Experiment, 1942–1948*, Kuala Lumpur: Malaysian Branch of the Royal Asiatic Society Monograph No. 8.

Syed Husin Ali (ed), 1984. *Ethnicity, Class and Development in Malaysia*, Kuala Lumpur: Persatuan Sains Sosial Malaysia.

Tan Cheng Lock, 1954. *Memorandum on Chinese Education in the Federation of Malaya*, Kuala Lumpur: Art Printers.

Tan Liok Ee, 1985. "Politics of Chinese Education in Malaya, 1945–1961". Ph.D. Dissertation, University of Malaya.

——, 1988a. *The Rhetoric of* bangsa *and* minzu*: Community and Nation in Tension on the Malayan Peninsula, 1945–1957*, Melbourne: Monash University Centre for Southeast Asian Studies, Working Paper No. 52.

——, 1988b. "Varying Responses to Changing Demands: Chinese Independent Schools in West Malaysia" in *Changing Identities of the Southeast Asian Chinese Since World War II*, edited by Jennifer Cushman and Wang Gungwu. Hongkong: Hongkong University Press.

——, 1989. "Whither Chinese Education in Malaya: the Controversy over Chung Ling High School, 1955–1957" in *Journal of the South Seas Society*, Vol. 44, pp. 67–90.

——, 1990. "Dasar Pendidikan dalam konteks Dekolononisasi: Semenanjung Tanah Melayu, 1945–1955" (Education Policy in the Context of Decolonization: the Malay Peninsula, 1945–1955) in *Kolonialisme dan Imperialisme: Satu Tinjauan Sejarah* (Colonialism and Imperialism: An Historical Survey) edited by Cheah Boon Kheng and Abu Talib Ahmad. Petaling Jaya: Fajar Bakti.

Tan Puay Ching, 1989. "The Role of the UCSTA in the Struggle for Chinese Education and Language Status, 1960–1969". B.A. Academic Exercise, Nanyang University. Subsequently published with the same title in *Southeast Asian Journal of Educational Studies*, Vol. 21/22 (1984/85), pp. 1–78.

Asian Journal of Educational Studies, Vol. 21/22 (1984/85), pp. 1–78.

Visu Sinnadurai (Dato'), 1986. "Rights in Respect of Education Under the Malaysian Constitution" in *The Constitution of Malaysia: Further Perspectives and Development* (essays in honour of Tun Mohammed Suffian), edited by F. Trindade and H. P. Lee. Petaling Jaya: Fajar Bakti.

Wan Ming Sing, 1967. "The History of the Organizations of the Chinese Community in Selangor with Particular Reference to Problems of Leadership, 1857–1962". M.A. Thesis, University of Malaya.

Wang Gungwu, 1983. *The Chinese Intellectual: Past and Present*, Singapore: National University of Singapore Faculty of Arts and Social Science Lecture No. 2.

Wong Yoke Nyen, 1981. "The Role of Chinese Organizations in Malayan Politics (1945–1957): Special Reference to Citizenship and Education". M.A. Thesis, University of Malaya.

Yahaya Ismail, 1978. *Politik Universiti Merdeka* (Politics of the Merdeka University), Petaling Jaya: Dinamika Kreatif.

9

Perspectives on Gender: Problems in Writing About Women in Malaysia

Maila K Stivens

My central concern in this paper is to look at what I see as a continuing problem for any study of Malaysian society, the problem posed by feminist challenges to the prevailing paradigms of social science. This problem is part of a larger set of difficulties posed by taking gender as the object of analysis in Third World contexts, or perhaps, better, post-colonial contexts—Malaysia would probably fail to qualify for Third World status any more on a number of counts. I shall argue that much writing on Malaysian women has not embraced western feminist agendas in any very wholehearted way, and that that unwillingness to do so is far from surprising.

Post-colonial Society and the Gendering of Knowledge

One of the major achievements of feminism in the west has been its challenge to the dominant paradigms of western social science. We shall set aside the political level challenges, where feminists and others would no doubt argue about the degree of success. Within the realm of knowledge-making, feminism has achieved varying acceptance of its deconstructive enterprise: for example, literary theory has more or less fallen to the women warriors, while most areas of economics have continued to completely ignore feminist arguments.

Clearly there has been a massive neglect of gender in most social science discussions of Malaysian society. Thus I and others have on many occasions berated male colleagues for 'ignoring women'. Yet it was clear that prior to the 1970s gender was only one of a number of absences in scholarly work on Malaysia, the other notable absence being class.

As I shall argue in this chapter, redressing these sins of omission is a far more complex task than it might appear. At issue are a number of problems that arise when foreign, in this case second-wave feminist, discourses, are imported into post-colonial contexts. Malaysian scholars today find themselves confronting not only their own history of domination by colonial and post-colonial thought, but a contemporary crisis in the latter. The centres of transatlantic knowledge production beat their breasts about the fragmentation of post-modernity, asserting that intellectual life has passed through and beyond all the guiding principles inherited from the Enlightenment. We now have no faith in science, in Reason, in all the projects of modernity. All is fragmented and arbitrary.

Western feminism of various varieties has been party to and itself transformed within these developments. Of course, there are many varieties of feminism, roughly polarising into the woman-centred radical and cultural feminist versions originating in such writers as Millett, Dinnerstein and others in the early 1970s and the socialist feminists struggling to fit an analysis of gender into the categories of thought inherited from political economy. In some ways the radical and cultural feminists have faced less difficulties than the socialists. If one argues for an essential fixed core woman as the object of analysis and sees a universal patriarchy which should be overthrown, one clearly has fewer problems than the socialist feminist who suggests that we should not have woman as a universal category as our object, but gender, and gender placed in historical context. She (and occasionally he) has to go on and argue that gender and class, the central object of historical materialism, can be brought into some theoretical marriage that will explain why some societies are more patriarchal than others. It is not surprising that socialist feminists have had to harp upon this unhappy marriage between political economy and feminism. Western feminist social science, as the inheritor of these traditions, shares similar difficulties in sustaining some of its projects in such a climate.

Of course, we might well argue that for the Third World (or however we want to characterise it), such fragmentation is nothing new. Western intellectual woes about the collapse of their paradigms into fragments of post-modernity take little account of the difficulties colonial and post-colonial societies have had in relating as the orientalised Other to the 'modern' paradigms in the first place. How, asks Marnea Lazreg, in a recent piece about the perils of writing as a woman about women in Algeria (1988), 'can an Algerian woman write about women in Algeria, when her space has been defined, her subjects objectified, her language chosen for her?' As Fox-Genovese suggests, however, the retreat from the 'modern, the proclamation of the death of the author, also looks very suspicious, coming at a point when the white, male cultural elite was beginning to have to share its status with the women and peoples of other races and classes (1986: 134)'. A similar point is made by Mascia-Lees et al (1989: 15), who caution against the de-politicisation inherent in so-called post-modernism.

But we should beware of assuming that contemporary encounters between First World feminism and post-colonial society form the first expression of feminism in such contexts. Feminist struggles, of course, were prominent in some nationalist anti-colonial struggles (see Jayawardena 1986), including those in colonial Malaya (a point we can deduce from Manderson 1981).

One of the difficulties for would-be Third World feminists lies in the fact that western feminist challenges to the dominant modern paradigms have themselves been one of the major forces leading to collapsing paradigmitis, even while some feminists counsel distance from post-modernist concerns. Indeed, some thinkers have claimed feminism as a post-modern philosophy, (for example Flax 1987).[1] I find that claim depressing, however, as it undercuts many of the political projects that feminist anthropology has tried to sustain over the last fifteen or twenty years. But such conclusions were one predictable outcome of the feminist deconstruction of all in its path, including the categories of science itself.

Recent years have seen a number of highly influential books on gender and science which have challenged the bases of supposedly scientific thinking. Keller (1985) and Harding (1986a, 1986b, 1987), among others, have argued that the basic models of scientific thinking have been gendered in themselves. The very models of scientific thinking have been hopelessly deformed by layer upon layer of gendered assumptions built into the so-called scientific model. The feminist critique of this androcentrism has added a whole new dimension to debates about the social construction of knowledge.

Thus, we have a Eurocentric feminist discourse turning in on itself, challenging and deconstructing its own inherited categories, categories from which it has only partly escaped. Given such problems, what should the response of feminist social science be to the challenge posed by Third World women and women of colour to eurocentric feminism and its location, in spite sometimes of its best efforts, within the dominant paradigms of western social science?

Anthropology and Eurocentric Feminism

Much of the writing on gender in Malaysia that I am looking at here has been produced by anthropologists, both local and expatriate. These scholars share the intellectual difficulties of both feminism and anthropology: both practices are seen as being in crisis or at least in some sort of impasse, having inherited some of the contemporary disarray in social thought, the abdication from totalising theories and, especially, the difficulty of having an object outside the terms of 'normal' western discourse. At the same time, feminist anthropologists share other feminists' concern with redeveloping theory.

---

[1] See Flax (1987), Fraser and Nicholson (1988) and Benhabib and Cornell (1987) for discussion of these points.

As Marcus and Fischer (1986) point out, the debate over gender difference stimulated by feminism replicates some of anthropology's earlier cultural critiques. Anthropology has acted as a continuing critique of domestic concerns in the west, as a critique of western culture:

> The domain of the exotic has been displaced by other descriptive domains for posing important differences within and alternatives to mainstream American life. Unlike the evocation of far-off cultural worlds to teach us lessons about ourselves, these other domains already exist within our own social worlds. Feminism falls into the same rhetorical strategies that were once used for playing off the dissatisfactions of civilised society against the virtues of the primitive. Men are acquisitive, (capitalist), women are nurturant (reciprocity-oriented) (1986: 135).

Marcus and Fischer do not develop the point, although it would be worth exploring this analogy between the critical roles of feminism and anthropology within western culture. Yet the potentially doubly critical role of feminist anthropology has failed to develop within feminist scholarship. Indeed, as Strathern points out, anthropology's comparative perspective poses problems for some forms of feminism in its challenge to universals, which undermines political claims to a single sisterhood (1985, 1987; Moore 1988).[2] These problems are perhaps reasons for feminism's having clearly turned away from the comparative perspectives provided by anthropology.

Anthropology also poses problems for its feminist practitioners, continuing to fail, in my view and that of others (Moore 1988), to engage with the critique they provide of its modes of representing gender. Anthropology has always faced difficulties in the area of the relationship between doing research and theory building, and such difficulties are acute for feminist anthropologists.[3] They are especially acute for such scholars based

---

[2] Delmar puts it very well when she says, "Women in a sense are feminism's greatest problem. The assumption of a potential identity between women, rather than solving the problem, became a condition of increasing tensions. Of these tensions, not the least important is the intellectual tension generated by a crisis of the concept 'woman' within feminist thought. As a concept 'woman' is too fragile to bear the weight of all the contents and meanings ascribed to it. The end of much research by feminists has been to show the tremendous diversity of the meaning of womanhood across cultures and over time (1986: 28)". Delmar's discussion of what she sees as a real crisis within feminism, sees the appropriation of psychoanalysis and critical theory as very problematic—in an attempt to understand the sexed subject, we have seen a movement from the unsatisfactory terms 'man' and 'woman' to the differently unsatisfactory terms 'masculinity' and 'femininity'.

[3] See Strathern (1985, 1987), Moore (1988) for discussion. A discussion of these issues formed the core of an international conference at the University of Amsterdam in December 1988.

in peripheral countries, who find themselves operating a peculiarly western discourse that has operated to provide a critique of the 'West'. Trying to deconstruct much of the analytical framework inherited from western intellectual traditions in order to proceed, they find it awkward and problematic to attempt the process of reconstruction. 'Western' feminists have a difficult task in reclaiming gender from the vast edifice of concepts that implicitly include it, but exclude any real consideration of its workings. Peripheral feminists find this process of reconstruction doubly awkward. The aim of all feminist scholarship is to situate itself within political endeavour (Mascia-Lees et al 1989), but feminist anthropologists in postcolonial societies render the unified political projects of 'western' feminists problematic by challenging their universality. At the same time, they may challenge visiting expatriate scholars, sometimes characterising them as theorists bearing a hegemonic, colonising 'western' intellectual tradition. But their defining themselves as 'authentic' 'political' representers of their local voices, as against an essentialised 'West' (Said 1986), is itself highly problematic.

It is, then, not surprising that pessimistic feminist anthropologists east and west feel marginalised both within the discipline, and within feminist movements. The most pessimistic feel that feminism is decreasingly interested in feminist anthropological contributions, after a period in the early 1970s when it engaged with questions of pan-cultural universals of gender. This marginality, both institutional and theoretical, seems to be becoming acute within some recent feminist theorising: in spite of feminist rejections of the limiting categories of its inherited western thought, much of the latter has failed to move beyond its own intellectual and geographical boundaries, taking an increasingly eurocentric path of post-structuralist theory making.[4] But the celebration of difference seems to have relegated many kinds of difference among women out of the picture, especially difference outside the centres of knowledge production.[5]

---

[4] Discussions of the problems posed by the Eurocentrism of western feminism feature in Mohanty (1988), Lazreg (1988) and Moore (1988), Fraser and Nicholson (1988), Ramazanoglu (1989), Fox-Genovese (1986), Spivak (1987), Hooks (1984) and Trinh (1989).

[5] For example, this ethnocentric inheritance has structured the way in which the (western) feminist critique of 'family' has proceeded: The patriarchal elementary family of feminist writing has probably been more present in ideology than concretely. Feminism seems to have accepted the reified family of western popular discourse, rather than trying to deal with the range of difference existing outside the North-American and European centres of knowledge production. There seems to have been comparatively little serious attention paid to the discourse and practice of family life outside the first world in some central feminist texts (as for example in Barrett and McIntosh's Anti-Social Family 1982).

The 'Perils' of Research on 'Women' in Malaysia

Thus, there are clearly sizeable theoretical difficulties standing in the way of anyone trying to write on women in Malaysia. But these 'perils' (cf Lazreg 1988) have a history. Second-wave feminism in the 1970s put a great deal of effort into berating men for gross androcentrism. These sometimes churlish complaints were entirely justified, just as much in Malaysia as elsewhere; androcentrism has greatly impoverished Malaysian social science, I would argue. But these accusations did not in themselves provide any solution about how to write and do research about Malaysian women. Those problems emerged, as I have suggested, as altogether more intractable.

Malaysian women, like the Algerian women of Lazreg's piece, would have good reasons for not embracing feminist versions of themselves as the oriental and sometimes victimised Other and the whole intellectual baggage that comes with some feminist interpretations. Up to now, however, such concerns have not surfaced in Malaysian scholarly writing about gender in any coherent way, although they are clearly there in some of the hostility to 'expatriate' scholars that has found expression in some instances.

Some attempts to rectify the androcentrism of Malaysian social science have emerged as part of the recent flowering of Malaysian scholarship. A generation of younger (if no longer absolutely young) scholars there and in neighbouring countries has effected some kind of an epistemological break in the predominantly empiricist and positivist traditions of most Southeast Asian scholarship. Studies of agrarian transformation, class and power proceed apace.[6] No doubt strongly influenced by their western post-graduate studies, a generation of female scholars has responded with various degrees of vigour to the western feminist movement, producing a growing mass of material about 'women in Malaysia' and other countries in the region.[7]

The Challenge of Androcentrism

It is the character of this latter body of work that is my central concern here. It would, I think, be fair to suggest in a general way that much of this work, although often extremely rigorous, well-researched and innovative, has also frequently been very empirical in character, a catalogue of

---

[6] See Robison and Higgott (1985) for a critique of the dominance of empiricist discourses in Southeast Asia. See Jomo (1986) for a full discussion and bibliography of these new trends in Malaysian studies. See also Shamsul (1986), Shahril Talib (1984), Scott (1985) and Ong (1987).

[7] For a bibliography covering a considerable volume of this work see Hing Ai Yun et al (1984). See also Hong (1983), and Fan Kok Sim (1982).

attempts to put women back into a social science that has been cast in paradigmatic terms that exclude gender as a category. I shall suggest a number of reasons why a lot of this work should have remained generally so solidly within the dominant terms of debate. The radicals' attempts to apply dependency and other theories of uneven development to Malaysian society have, of course, not been without their problems. But I shall suggest here that the 'women's' literature has faced greater problems in breaking out of this epistemological mould and that there are a number of reasons for this.

I have already suggested that feminist scholars face considerable difficulties in having to deconstruct much of the analytical equipment previous analyses of a given society worked with. I can illustrate these difficulties by some reference to my own work in the Malaysian state of Negeri Sembilan from the mid-1970s to the present. Like all others doing such research, I inherited a large number of concepts from previous scholars, including 'matriliny', the 'Malay peasantry' and 'gender'. In each case, I have found myself involved in a measure of feminist deconstruction. Concepts such as 'family', 'kinship', 'household', 'village', 'tradition', *adat perpatih* (loosely translated as 'matrilineal customary law'), and 'peasant;' have all required some pretty savage demolition work.

Take the concept 'peasant': in the literature on agrarian society world-wide, this term almost always denotes or is read as a male. Peasants work, (read men work), peasants do or do not resist, (read men resist, form classes), peasants drag their collective feet (read men . . .), peasants are the object of state action, peasants (men) are heads of household and so on. Studies of the Malay peasantry until very recently have given ill-defined and inexact accounts of the relative situation of the sexes in terms of labour inputs, land-holding and control over agricultural production. Central to this are assumptions about the 'black box' of the peasant household as a residential or productive unit. Gender difference within the household is almost totally ignored. One can do the same exercise with the term 'the Malay farmer', who inhabits a particular discourse in writings on development of an ultra-empiricist character.

It is astonishing that until recently hardly any published accounts of Malaysian rural society, including some of the most widely quoted like Michael Swift's (1965), actually counted the number of male and female owners of land. Gender never appears because it is hidden within concepts that implicitly include it, but exclude any real consideration of its workings within the social order. I have argued in relation to my own work on Negeri Sembilan that this failure to even count heads in an empirical fashion is a highly significant one. The social scientist does not count male and female property because he (and much less likely a she) assumes the household forms a unity, because he is mesmerised by all the sociological models that do not consider gender differentiation in the household. Thus the role of inheritance practices has been almost totally ignored in many of the central discussions of peasant differentiation in Malaysia and elsewhere until recently. But I would suggest that we cannot begin to understand agrarian change in Malaysia without looking at the dynamics of inheritance and the relationship between male and female landholding in a given system. Yet most of those scholars that look explicitly at inheritance (mainly anthropologists and customary law experts)[8] do not analyse gender relations or agrarian political economy sociologically. And those that have looked at agrarian transformation do not look at gender or inheritance.

For example, the 'classic' anthropological studies of the Malay peasantry, Raymond Firth (1966), Swift (1965) and Syed Husin Ali (1975) were all sensitive to the need to understand the political economy of agrarian society, although they did not address gender relations. A notable exception, addressed below, was Rosemary Firth's work on Kelantan (1966). Later prominent works, however, such as Scott (1985) Jomo (1986) and Shamsul (1986), similarly do not address the relationship between male and female landholding in the evolution of agrarian society, even though they give sophisticated analyses. Other social scientists such as Banks (1983), Fujimoto (1983) and Kuchiba et al (1979) betray little awareness of the possible importance of gender difference in peasant social forms. Almost no works within a large body of literature address the issue of female landholding, apart from Gibbons et al (1981), Peletz (1988) and a number of writers influenced by feminism, including Fett (1983), Strange (1981), Ng (1984) and my own work. The importance of women's landowning among Malays is directly addressed in Stivens, Ng and Jomo (n.d.).

In particular, I have argued that most previous attempts to characterise the linkages between non-capitalist enclaves and the dominant capitalist sector have been blind to the significance of gender differentiation within so-called peasant sectors. A cornerstone of my argument has been the need to deconstruct the peasant household and to explore the political significance of female land ownership. The largest land holders in Rembau, Negeri Sembilan,[9] where I carried out my first fieldwork, were in fact women, a

---

[8] See Hooker (1972). I found that not only were the majority of rice land titles in the study villages in female hands, but also over half the rubber titles (Stivens 1985a).

[9] The research reported in my Ph.D. Thesis ("Women, Kinship and Economy in Rembau, Negeri Sembilan, Malaysia," London University) was carried out initially in three adjacent villages in Rembau district, Negeri Sembilan, from 1975 to 1976 funded by a studentship in the Department of Anthropology, London School of Economics, from the then SSRC (UK). Further visits were made in 1982 (funded by the Hayter Fund), 1984, 1985, 1986, and 1987–8 (funded by the Australian Research Grant Scheme). The focus of the original research was on gender and transformation of the agrarian economy. Later research visits have centred more on macro-level change. The 1987–8 research has involved an investigation of work and family in the 'new' Malay middle class, research to be further developed with an ARC grant from 1990–1992).

question not considered in the differentiation debates.[10] Nor was tenancy there straightforward, but tied up in complicated family arrangements over time, a cycle obscured by the categories employed in the debates such as 'landless', 'tenant' and 'landlord'. Apparent landlessness may be a feature of the earlier part of the household demographic cycle, and 'tenancy' and 'landlordism' may be extremely difficult terms to use, individual households often being owner cultivators, tenants and landlords simultaneously. For example, an elderly couple in Rembau may cultivate a small bit of rubber land one of them owns, share crop a fellow villager's rice land, and rent out the wife's own rice land because it is now too distant for them to comfortably work.

It is not really surprising, therefore, that the dominant discourses that have arisen dealing with the peasantry in Malaysia have been able to marginalise gender. Even the growing body of writing on 'women and development' has mainly been confined to the compensatory mode of analysis, adding women to the existing paradigms. It has not on the whole taken the more demanding path of theorising gender as part of the social forces constructing and transforming the society. In this, it of course resembles much western feminist inspired writing elsewhere that has had similar difficulties in moving to see gender as a central analytical concept for history (cf Scott 1986). Rather, there has been a dominant feminist discourse of 'effects on women of . . .'

---

[10] The complexities of Negeri Sembilan land tenure are described at considerable length in both the thesis arising from the original research and in Stivens (1985a). 'Adat differentiated two kinds of landed property, ancestral land and acquired land. Usufruct rights were transferred from mother to daughter in the colonial period (mainly rice land and orchards). Ancestral land was not alienable and was not a commodity. The rules about acquired land were more problematic. A holder of acquired land could in theory dispose of it while alive, but had no power to make testamentary disposition. On the death of the owner, it should devolve according to matrilineal rules, but there has been much debate about how many times it had to descend before it was counted as ancestral property' (Stivens 1985a: 8). With the rubber booms, the category of acquired land into which rubber land appears to have fallen took on new significance, and produced considerable complications in land administration, with Islamic law making claims to determine its inheritance.

Almost none of the enormous literature on Negeri Sembilan and its famous 'matrilineal' system addresses the issues in gender relations on feminist agendas, 'western' or 'eastern'. Matrilineal customary law in Negeri Sembilan alerted a number of writers to the 'problem' of gender, but even that visibility of women's land owning did not seem to enforce any changes in conceptual apparatuses in most work on the peasantry of the state, with the notable exception of Azizah binti Kassim (1969). Other writers on Rembau, who address land tenure in varying degrees include Norhalim (1976), Nordin bin Selat (1976) and Peletz (1981, 1988). In the other Negeri Sembilan districts the extent of female landowning is discussed in Fett (1983), Azizah binti Kassim (1969) and McAllister (1987).

For example, Strange's very useful and comprehensive account of economic factors affecting rural women's participation does not deal with the debates about peasant differentiation and the possible role of female landowning in this, although she does count male and female owners of land in her fieldwork area of Rusila (1981). Contributors to Hing Ai Yun's pathbreaking collection (1984) similarly provide very useful detailed discussions, but perhaps find the 'women and development' framework limits more ambitious explorations of gender and social transformation. Similarly, the proliferating and again often excellent collections dealing with women and development in Asia, with Malaysian contributions, also often eschew the higher grounds of theory sought by some western feminists concerned with gender in social transformation.[11] Even Cecilia Ng's excellent account of rural gender relations (1984) is nonetheless not explicitly concerned with the intervention of gender relations in history. Again, Aihwa Ong's ambitious account of the impact of modernising discourses on kampung dwellers providing wage labour to factories in Central Malaysia, an account of 'how ordinary men and women live and refashion their own images and culture' (1987: 195) does not actually place gender relations as part of the transformative process, but rather recounts women's experiences of capitalist transformation. Of course, to locate gender relations as part of such transformations is a demanding project: it is one thing to prescribe it, but quite another to successfully execute it.

As I shall argue below, it is not enough to tack a feminist demand or question onto other previously defined concerns, whether analytical or more overtly political. It has become clear in many areas of social analysis that, to quote Harding, the very act of feminist intervention can transform discourse, stretching the intended domains of theories and reinterpreting their central claims (1986a: 646). In the process, and this must especially be the case in peripheral societies, feminist concerns can also become distorted by the encounter.

We could point the finger of androcentrism at other areas, including work on the state and other political processes. Feminism and analyses of the state have also failed to connect in any very significant fashion in Malaysian social science. The competing strands of positivist political science and radical discussions deriving their terms of debate from African debates about the over-developed colonial and bureaucratic states have both more or less completely avoided gender. Not for them the admittedly

---

[11] See Heyzer (1985; 1987), Hing Ai Yun and Rokiah Talib (n.d.). Other works include Maznah Mohamad (1990). Papers from conferences such as Kanita (1983) and one on Women Workers in Malaysia in 1985 also mainly express the dominant women in development discourse discussed above. While belonging to this 'school', the numerous graduation exercises in the Departments of Anthropology and Sociology at the University of Malaya and the National University also often contain useful material on women's lives from the students' own milieux.

problematic feminist conception of the patriarchal state (one that I would resist, but that is not the issue here—see Dahlerup 1987). There have, however been some feminist analyses of women and politics and the effects of state policies on women.[12]

Second-wave western feminism, of course, has always argued for an expanded notion of politics that takes it outside the received ideas of political science. This is especially necessary in Southeast Asia, where political science has often been totally ensconced within empiricist, positivist traditions. (Cf Robison and Higgott, 1985, Stivens, 1991).

Finally, in this churlish recital of the failings of male-stream enquiry in Malaysia, I would point to the rather strange case of 'matriliny' and its relationship to anthropology. Anthropology's response to Malay matriliny has been a curious one, even on occasion pretending that all is really 'normal'. This reaches an extreme in Michael Swift's work, where he suggests that he will treat land as if it is owned by men (without specifying what ownership means, 1965: 36)!

Certain observers of Negeri Sembilan *adat perpatih* in the colonial period were only too aware that we had to consider gender in trying to analyse the nature of Negeri Sembilan society. Because it was seen to have an exotic form of social structure in which gender could not be obscured within the received categories, gender had to be considered. It is noteworthy that British colonial ideology, at least up to the 1930s, dealt with issues in a way that feminism would relate to, whereas later anthropologists were firmly located within the androcentrism of mid-twentieth-century empiricist anthropology.

Work on Women in Malaysia

Most would probably agree that the study of women's place in Malaysia began with the earlier 'classic' studies by the visiting scholars Rosemary Firth (1966, her research carried out just before World War Two) and Judith Djamour's (1965, dating from the early 1950s). Both pioneering works have had tremendous authority, setting the terms of subsequent debates about 'woman's place', and not just in Malaysia. Both of their research projects were conceived of as complementary to some degree to their anthropologist spouses' work. Looking at the 'woman's side' which was not necessarily accessible to the male researcher, produced a position radical for the time, in which *women* became the object.

---

[12] Lenore Manderson's book exploring the relationship between the Kaum Ibu, the women's arm of the United Malay National Organisation, and the main political organisation (1980) is a notable exception here, whose contents are closely tracked in Dancz's later volume (1987). Noraini Abdullah's thesis on women and politics also deals with aspects of women's political participation (1984). Shamsul Amri Baharuddin (n.d.) explores the state's endorsement and enforcement of an ideology that subordinates women, as do Jomo and Tan (n.d.).

Gender as an object in contemporary Malaysian writing has emerged out of a complex intellectual history that has not simply been the imposition of western (sometimes) feminist models imported by overseas scholars. First, there is the significant power of the colonial legacy and its complex inter-relation with the constant reinvention of woman within the local society. Elsewhere, some western feminists have oversimplified this relationship, suggesting that colonial officers' misogyny worldwide was a major factor in directly producing female subordination.[13] The same writers argue for a loss of women's status in colonial Malaya. I have discussed this claim elsewhere (1985a) but will briefly look at it here. Rogers (1980: 127–8, 140) quotes Ester Boserup (1970: 61) quoting Michael Swift (1963) to suggest that women in Negeri Sembilan were robbed of their land by misogynistic colonial officers who were antagonistic to 'matriliny'. I would argue, however, that Malayan colonial attitudes towards "matriliny' and the questions of gender order thrown up by the very category seem to have been far from straightforwardly masculinist. Officers like Taylor (1929, 1948) and de Moubray (1931) are on record in the 1920s and 30s as suggesting that *adat perpatih* worked better as a system of indirect rule than the non-matrilineal systems operating in other Malayan states. In this, they were echoing earlier Annual Reports (eg Negeri Sembilan Annual Report 1892) voicing similar opinions. De Moubray waxed eulogistically about how *adat perpatih* protected women and they were not likely to be found starving on the streets as were the women of London's East End (1931: 217). There is clearly scope for a further exploration of the place of these colonial ideologies in constructing the concepts of the Malay Woman.

Firth and Djamour did not wholly invent Kelantan and Singapore Woman. Second-wave feminist scholarship in Malaysia has inherited a complex, continuously evolving set of ideas about gender in the country, what some would call a discursive formation—formed not simply locally but also through the important interventions of colonial ideologies and practices, and anthropological and other social science discourses. But we need to emphasise the power of outside scholars to set agendas, especially in a colonial situation, and even when those agendas are later strongly contested. Firth and Djamour's work entered and drew upon a pre-existing set of ideas about women in the society. There is, however, clearly a direct line from their writings to that of other expatriates such as Diane Lewis

---

[13] It is probably invidious to single out works here, but Barbara Rogers' otherwise useful (1980) book which made a very positive intervention in a then overwhelmingly androcentric 'development' discourse fails in my view to deal with the complexities of the interactions between gender relations and imperial and colonial power. She sees many of the ills of contemporary women in the underdeveloped world as deriving from the effects of colonial misogynist ideology, rather than from structural causes lying in the relationship between uneven capitalist development processes and gender relations.

(1962) whose work predates the expansion of home-grown Malaysian scholarship and on to the later work of Heather Strange (1981, based on work done in 1965 and a later return field trip) and many others. That picture, of a relatively autonomous rural or city-dwelling Malay woman, enmeshed in matrifocal kinship, subject to religious ideologies but able to find support of various kinds in the social order, is continuously echoed in later work.

This picture is greatly modified in some of the last decade or so's literature on Malaysian factory women, who begin to be pictured at home as heavily controlled by fathers and brothers, prey to patriarchal ideologies both there and at work. The latter work alleges that such patriarchal structures and practices had always existed but had been obscured within androcentric scholarship. The first to make such arguments were Grossman (1979) and Lim (1978), who brought Malaysian women factory workers onto the world scholarly and activist stages. They were followed by the think-piece of Pearson and Elson (1984), and Ong's theoretically sophisticated culturalist account of women factory workers' responses to capitalist disciplines (1987). Other contributors to the literature on female factory workers with a range of viewpoints include Ackerman (1980, 1984), Jane Cardoso and Khoo Kay Jin (n.d.), Jamilah Ariffin (1980, 1982 and others), Raymond Lee, (1979), Fatimah Daud (1985), numerous papers by Wendy Smith, Jamilah Ariffin and Smith (eds, n.d.) Khadijah binti Hj Muhamed (1978) and Stivens (n.d.).[14]

These studies have produced a mass of empirical material and some sophisticated analyses of the relationship between gender and class action within the new international division of labour in the region. The by now substantial body of work on factory women represents in varying degrees a successful alliance between the radical writings on class in Malaysia and feminist concerns. Some of this writing, however, could also be seen as a prime example of the appropriation of Other women's experiences; papers on women factory workers began to appear on the itinerary of most women and development conferences, to the resentment of some local Malaysian scholars, who felt that their work and objects had been appropriated and put into frameworks they did not recognise or want to recognise. The local empiricism was sometimes upset at international socialist feminism making off with Malaysian women for their theorising, theorising often taken out of historical and geographical context.[15]

---

[14] There has been a large project on women factory workers for a number of years at the University of Malaya and a number of conferences, all involving sizeable numbers of contributors. Also see the work of O'Brien (1979 and others) contextualising women's work within political economy.

[15] An example of such writing was Pearson and Elson's influential 1984 article, written by two authors who then had no first-hand experience of research in Malaysia.

While there has been other work on critiques of state action, family planning and women's health, until recently little work has addressed other central areas of concern to western feminism, including family, mothering, domesticity male violence and sexuality.[16] There are clearly many reasons for this, not simply the priorities of 'development' dominating much Malaysian academic work. A presentation of an earlier version of this paper at the University of Malaya in 1988 produced some tension by even mentioning the issues of sexuality and Islam in feminist writing. Given such difficulties, it is hardly surprising that local academics are loth to address such difficult topics. By contrast, expatriate scholars have much greater freedom to deal with such areas, although as I suggested, the simple imposition of western feminist frameworks is highly intellectually hazardous. Lately, however, there are signs of a fast-growing interest in such agendas, with activists within NGOs raising some of these issues. There have also been conferences addressing such issues as women and Islamic law, marriage, divorce and childcare. It remains to be seen how such interventions will negotiate some of the difficulties facing them both theoretically and politically nonetheless.

Gender and Ethnicity

It will be readily apparent from the accompanying bibliography that work on Malay women has far outweighed work on women from other Malaysian ethnic groups. This is again a sensitive political issue, but there are probably a number of reasons for this situation. First, what some might see as a degree of Malay cultural hegemony has played a very large part, particularly in the last decade or so where non-Malays are under-represented numerically among social science academics. People naturally find it easier to research the group from which they originate. I have already noted the pressures operating on some more radical scholars, although it is equally clear that some of the perspectives brought by political economy have themselves contributed to creating the economistic discourse dominating studies of women. In addition, the political, economic and scholarly agendas set by the implementation of the New Economic Policy and other state initiatives set in train by this policy have meant that a lot of research has been slanted towards Malay women.[17]

---

[16] See the numerous works of Manderson, arising out of her research on the history of health services, looking at issues of women's health from a western feminist anthropological perspective. Expatriate importations include Massard (1983) and Couillard (1987).

[17] The minute body of work on non-Malay women includes Susan Oorjitham's work on Indian women factory workers (n.d.) and Rohana binti Ariffin's work on trade unions (1987) and Lebra and Paulson (1980) on Chinese women. *Orang asli* gender relations are discussed in Howell (1983, 1984) and Couillard (1980), Gomes (1986) and Dentan (1979). See also Lai Ah Eng (1986).

Feminism and Post-colonial Society

It is easy to see, then, that recent work on 'women' in Malaysia has been heavily focussed on economic participation, somewhat selectively concentrated on working class women and 'women in development'. This work, much of it in the best traditions of British empiricism moving to an alliance with some more materialist analysis, certainly avoids the perils of some other work on post-colonial women in other parts of the world, which is overwhelmingly orientalist. In the Middle East, for example, there has been an absolute obsession with the symbolism of the veil, the 'Muslim Woman' figuring as a highly reductionist category in that body of writing (Lazreg 1988). In Malaysia, she also exists, but often as a peripheral part of collections discussing a number of Islamic societies worldwide.

It is hardly surprising that much writing on Malaysian women has been very cautious about embracing western feminist agendas. I have been pointing to a number of reasons inherent in the conditions of production of knowledge in post-colonial situations in general and in Malaysia in particular that complicate such writing to an enormous extent. In her parallel discussion of Algeria, Lazreg notes how the interest of US feminists in women there:

> has spurred a growing literature that is notable for its relative lack of theoretical import. With a few exceptions, women who write about North African and Middle Eastern women do not identify themselves as feminist, yet their work finds its legitimacy in academic feminism's need for information about their subject matter (1988: 82) . . . 'Eastern' feminists have simply adjusted their enquiry to fill the blanks in the geographical distribution made available to them by US feminist liberalism (1988: 83).

She contrasts this with the radical approach of US minority women who consistently challenge the academic feminist project, pointing out problem areas. Her main point is that this is no accident of the intellectual history of one region. Rather, 'the Algerian and Middle Eastern feminist project unfolds within an external frame of reference and according to equally external standards' (1988: 81). In her view, the feminist project in these circumstances is warped and lacks the potential for personal liberation that it does in the US or Europe.

There are many exact parallels in the relationship which Malaysian writings have with feminism. Liberal feminism provides some gaps to be filled with suitable data on women: consultants and academics are happy to oblige. We should not underestimate the role that the consulting process can have in setting intellectual agendas in contemporary post-colonial situations. In Malaysia, an active industry produces a large number of reports in response to national priorities set by various external agencies and the internal political process. Naturally, to even get 'women' in their liberal feminist guise onto these agendas has often involved substantial feminist struggle. Pressure has been brought, for example, by a sizeable number of 'women and development' conferences over the last decade or more. The fees from such consultancies are, however, an important condition of the production of knowledge, setting much work firmly in the economic mould, and excluding less 'relevant' issues.

Studies of Malay women differ in a significant way from some of the Middle Eastern studies. For example, even expatriate scholars have not joined the feminist critique of Islam found in some feminist writings on the Middle East. There, the religious paradigm that gives religion a privileged explanatory power is all powerful and therefore also assumes a central place in critical writing. The volumes on 'Muslim Women' and their obverse, the denunciations of Islam in particular at international conferences, are both classically orientalist. Perhaps we could argue that the absence of such orientalism from a lot of writing on Malaysian women is as much due to a degree of Malay hegemony as to resistance to colonial intellectual heritages. In 1985, for example, some local female scholars admitted in private conversation that they avoided taking critical positions—for example suggesting some discussion of marriage law—because to do so would bring them under intolerable political pressure from certain elements, which they felt unable to withstand. Ironically, this avoidance presumably keeps them from suffering some of the intellectual subsumption under religion that has beset their Middle Eastern sisters.

Perhaps somewhat perversely, I feel that it is a pity that some of the admittedly highly problematic concerns of orientalist western feminism have until now been mostly absent from Malaysian discourse about gender. The use of the Malay female body veiled and obscured within political symbolisation in the last fifteen years or so calls for a spot of transatlantic feminist post-structuralist analysis of the link between the state, nationalism and sexuality.[18] Of course, that would be a classic example of transposing first world concerns onto post-colonial contexts.

Naturally, there are other pressing reasons for writing on women in Malaysia's having avoided such difficult terrain: radical critiques in the country face a parlous political situation and some academics may feel that it is safer to write about women within frameworks that do not challenge the dominant ways of knowing. Empiricist accounts of 'women' do not have to disturb either hegemonic powers or paradigms: 'women' can be slotted in, but kept marginalised, and gender relations as an object do not emerge. These constraints may work to exclude the more radical critiques of the economic and political orders and the gender relations within them and to exclude the more adventurous from the rewards of the local academy.

---

[18] The dangers of the highly orientalist 'woman-as-victim' approach are readily apparent in writings such as those of Mary Daly. Such appropriation of Third World women's experiences is also however, readily apparent in socialist feminist and other 'women and development' writings (e.g. Rogers 1980).

In spite of such difficulties, however, as noted there have in fact been a number of recent feminist conferences addressing women's movement issues, some with the explicit aim of effecting changes in women's situation. Whether such action can overcome the problems inherent in post-colonial political practice of what some might see as imported western feminism remains to be seen. One way out of such impasses might be to suggest that such feminism is most definitely not simply an import but a product of the contradictions thrown up by Malaysian modernity and its gender relations. To reconcile such a position with the unease produced by the appropriation of Other feminisms may, however, require some exercise of what Spivak has called strategic positivist essentialism in a highly visible politics (1987).

A further question arises. Do the women who are our objects share any of our vision of them? The issue as to whether imposing western feminism denies agency to such women in its analysis of victimhood is a very real problem.[19] I am probably not well placed to answer this question in the Malaysian case, as Rembau women's rhetoric often took on the unsettling air of a feminist consciousness-raising group, with multiple complaints against men. And of course, to argue that if our informants do not recognise themselves, then somehow the project is invalid, brings us up against many of the core issues of consciousness in social theory.

Such arguments, do however, return us to the issue of what exactly the feminist project can, or should be in peripheral societies. These perils and problems are not confined to Malaysian social science work on women. As I have suggested, feminist anthropology in general, practised either in post-colonial or in the core countries, has similar problems.

Conclusion

There are thus many sources of unease involved in writing as a woman on Malaysian women. Many of the dominant conceptualisations of gender inherited from social science have proved highly problematic and in fact their testing in feminist waters has highlighted their conceptual failings.[20] But while western scholars face enormous difficulties in deconstructing all their conceptual tools, as suggested, these problems pale before the challenges posed to those who seek to apply the concepts struggling forward from Eurocentric feminism to objects in the Third World. One solution to this impasse would be the course advocated by some black feminists in the

---

[19] But since this piece went to press Ong (1990) has appeared attempting to do just this.
[20] A prime example of this would be the flurry of writings on the household in feminist history, sociology and anthropology. Endless reconstructions and deconstructions of the concept have led in the end to increasing assertions that the concept has really limited use (cf Sanjek 1982).

US suggesting that they must produce new discourses in which to describe and prescribe their own condition. Such a proposal, however, ignores some of the contradictions posed by class: elite women academics are perhaps no 'closer' to their objects/subjects than the expatriate scholar with her western intellectual baggage. Another solution might be the strategic positivist essentialism of Spivak already mentioned. The challenge for local Malaysian scholars is to construct new forms of discourse that escape from the present strictures.

Bibliography

Abdullah, N., 1984. "Gender, Ideology and the Public Lives of Malay Women in Peninsular Malaysia". Ph.D. Thesis, University of Washington.

Ackermann, S., 1980. "Cultural Processes in Malay Industrialisation: A Case Study of Malay Factory Workers". Unpublished Ph.D. Thesis, University of California.

——, 1984. "The Impact of Industrialisation on the Social Role of Rural Malay Women" in Hing Ai Yun et al (eds), *Women in Malaysia*, Kuala Lumpur: Pelanduk, pp. 40–60.

Azizah binti Kassim, 1969. "Kedudukan Wanita Di-Dalam Masharakat Melayu Beradat Perpatih Di-Negeri Sembilan". (Women's Situation in Malay Adat Perpatih Society in Negeri Sembilan). Unpublished MA Thesis, Universiti Malaya.

Bailey, C., 1983. *The Sociology of Production in Rural Malay Society*, Kuala Lumpur: Oxford University Press.

Banks, D. J., 1983. *Malay Kinship*, Philadelphia: Philadelphia Institute for the Study of Social issues.

Barrett, M. & M. McIntosh, 1982. *The Anti-Social Family*, London: Verso.

Benhabib, S. and D. Cornell, 1987. *Feminism as Critique*, London: Polity.

Boserup, E., 1970. *Women's Role in Economic Development*, New York: St Martin's Press.

Cardoso, J. & Khoo, K. J., (n.d.) "Work and Consciousness: The Case of Electronics Runaways in Malaysia". Paper Presented to the Subordination of Women Conference, IDS, Brighton, 1978.

Chung, B. J. & Ng Shui Meng, 1977. *The Status of Women in Law: A Comparison of Four Asian Countries*, Singapore: Institute of Southeast Asian Studies.

Couillard, M.A., 1980. *Tradition in Tension: Carving in a Jah Hut Community*. Penang. Penerbit Universiti Sains Malaysia.

Couillard, M-A, 1987. "La Tendresse, Le Discours et le Pouvoir: Les Rapports Hommes-Femmes et les Transformations Sociales Chez les Paysans Malais Du Nord de la Peninsule Malais". Unpublished Ph.D. Thesis, Université Laval, Quebec.

Dancz, 1987. *Women and Party Politics in Peninsular Malaysia*, Singapore: Oxford University Press.

Dahlerup, D., 1987. "Confusing Concepts—Confusing Reality: A Theoretical Discussion of the Patriarchal State," in A. Showstack Sassoon (ed), *Women and the State: The Shifting Boundaries of Public and Private*, London: MacMillan.

Delmar, R., 1987. "What is Feminism?" in J. Mitchell and A. Oakley (eds), What is Feminism? Oxford: Basil Blackwell.

Djamour, J., 1965. *Malay Kinship and Marriage in Singapore*. London: Athlone Press.

Fan Kok Sim, 1982. *Women in Southeast Asia: A Bibliography*, Boston: Hall.

Fatimah Daud, 1985. *Minah Karan*, Kuala Lumpur: Berita.

Fett, I., 1983. "Women's Land in Negeri Sembilan," in L. Manderson (ed), *Women's Work and Women's Roles*, Development Studies Centre Monograph No 32. Canberra: Australian National University.

Firth, Raymond, 1966. *Malay Fisherman: Their Peasant Economy*, London: Routledge and Kegan Paul, 2nd edition.

Firth, Rosemary, 1966. *Housekeeping Among Malay Peasants*, London: Athlone.

Flax, J., 1987. "Post-modernism and Gender Relations in Feminist Theory". *Signs*. 12 (4).

Fox-Genovese, E., 1986. "The Claims of a Common Culture: Gender, Race and the Canon". *Salmagundi* 72, Fall.

Fraser, N. and L. Nicholson, 1988. "Social Criticism without Philosophy", in A. Ross (ed), *Universal Abandon? The Politics of Postmodernism,* Edinburgh: Edinburgh University Press.

Fujimoto, A., 1983. *Income Sharing Among Malay Peasants*, Singapore: Singapore University Press.

Gibbons, D. et al, 1981. *Land Tenure in the Muda Irrigation Area. Final Report*, Penang: Universiti Sains.

Gomes, A. G. 1986. *Looking-for-money. Simple Commodity Production in the Economy of the Tapah Semai of Malaya.* Ph.d Thesis. Canberra Australian National University.

Grossman, R., 1979. "Women's Place in the Electronic Circuit". *Southeast Asia Chronicle*, 66, pp. 2–17.

Harding, S., 1986a. The Instability of the Analytical Categories of Feminist Theory. *Signs*. Vol. 11, No 4, pp. 645–665.

——, 1986b. *The Science Question in Feminism*, Ithaca: Cornell.

—— (ed), 1987. *Feminism and Methodology*, Milton Keynes: Open University.

Heyzer, N. (ed), 1985. *Missing Women: Development Planning in Asia and the Pacific*, Kuala Lumpur: Asian and Pacific Development Centre.

——, 1987. *Women Farmers and Rural Change in Asia: Towards Equal Access and Participation,* Kuala Lumpur: Asian and Pacific Development Centre.

Hing Ai Yun, 1984. "Women and Work in West Malaysia". *Journal of Contemporary Asia*, 14 (2).

Hing Ai Yun et al (eds), 1984. *Women in Malaysia,* Kuala Lumpur: Pelanduk.

Hing Ai Yun and Rokiah Talib (eds), (n.d.) *Women and Employment in Malaysia*, Dept of Anthropology and Sociology, Kuala Lumpur: University of Malaya Women's Association of the Asia and Pacific Development Centre.

Hong, E. (ed), 1983. *Malaysian Women,* Penang. Consumers Association.

Hooker, M. B., 1972. *Adat Laws in Modern Malaya,* Kuala Lumpur: Oxford University Press.

hooks, b., 1984. *Feminist Theory: From Margin to Center*, Boston: South End Press.

Howell, S. 1983. *Chewong Women in Transition: The Effects of Monetization on a Hunter-gatherer Society in Malaysia.* Women and Development in Southeast Asia I, Occasional Paper No. 1. Centre of Southeast Asian Studies, University of Kent at Canterbury

——, 1984. Society and Cosmos: Chewang of Peninsular Malaysia. Singapore: Oxford University Press.

Husin Ali, S., 1975. *Malay Society and Leadership*, Kuala Lumpur: Oxford University Press.

Jamilah Ariffin, 1980. "Industrial Development in Peninsular Malaysia and Rural-Urban Migration of Women Workers: Impact and Implications". *Jurnal Ekonomi Malaysia*, 1.

Jamilah Ariffin and W. Smith, (eds.), n.d.). *Women Workers in Malaysia.* Singapore: Singapore Institute of Southeast Asian Studies. In press.

——, 1982. "Industrialisation, Female Labour Migration and the Changing Pattern of Malay Women's Labour Force Participation". *Southeast Asian Studies*. 19 (4), March; pp. 412–425.

Jomo K. S., 1986. *A Question of Class*, Singapore: Oxford University Press.

Jomo K. S. & Tan, (n.d.) *Not the Better Half: Malaysian Women and Development Planning*, Kuala Lumpur: Integration of Women in Development, Asian and Pacific Development Centre.

Jones, G. W. (ed), 1984. *Women in the Urban and Industrial Workforce: Southeast and East Asia*, Canberra: Australian National University.

Kanita, 1983. "Forum on the Development of Women in Malaysia". Universiti Sains Malaysia, Penang.

Khadijah binte Haji Muhamed, 1978. *Migration and the Matrilineal System of Negeri Sembilan*. Unpublished Ph.D. Thesis, University of Pittsburgh.

Keller, E. Fox, 1985. *Reflections on Gender and Science*, New haven: Yale University Press.

Kuchiba, M. et al, 1979. *Three Malay Villages: A Sociology of Paddy Growers in West Malaysia*, Honolulu: University Press of Hawaii.

Lai Ah Eng, 1986. "Peasants, Proletarians and Prostitutes: A Preliminary Investigation into the Work of Women of Chinese Origin in Colonial Malaya. Singapore: Institute of Southeast Asian Studies.

Lazreg, M., 1988. "Feminism and Difference: The Perils of Writing as a Woman on Algeria". *Feminist Studies*, 14, No 1, pp. 81–107.

Lebra, J. and J. Paulscn, 1980. *Chinese women in Southeast Asia*. Singapore: Times Books International.

Lee, R. L. M., 1979. "The Social Meaning of Mass Hysteria in West Malaysia and Singapore". Unpublished Ph.D. Thesis, University of Massachusetts.

Lewis, D., 1962. "The Minangkabau Malay of Negeri Sembilan: A Study of Social-Cultural Change". Unpublished Ph.D. Thesis, Cornell University.

Lim, L., 1978. *Women Workers in Multinational Corporations: The Case of the Electronics Industry in Malaysia and Singapore*. University of Michigan, Occasional Paper No 9.

——, 1983. "Capitalism, Imperialism and Patriarchy: The Dilemma of Third World Women Workers in Multinational Factories" in J. Nash and P. M. Fernandez Kelly (eds), *Women, Men and the International Division of Labour*.

Mascia-Lees, F. E. et al, 1989. "The Post-modern Turn in Anthropology". Signs, Autumn, Vol 15, No 1.

Maznah Mohamad, 1990. "The Malay Handloom Weavers: A Study of the Growth and Decline of Traditional Manufacture". Unpublished Ph.D. Thesis, University of Malaya.

McAllister, C. L., 1987. "Matriliny, Islam and Capitalism: Combined and Uneven Development in the Lives of Negeri Sembilan Women". Unpublished Ph.D. Thesis, University of Pittsburgh.

Manderson, L., 1979. "A Woman's Place: Malay Women and Development in Peninsular Malaysia", in J. C. Jackson and M. Rudner (eds), *Issues in Malaysian Development*, ASAA and Heinemann Educational Books (Asia).

——, 1980. *Women, Politics and Change: The Kaum Ibu UMNO Malaysia, 1945–1972*, Oxford University Press: Kuala Lumpur.

——, 1981. "Traditional Food Beliefs and Critical Life Events in Peninsular Malaysia". *Social Science Information*. 20, (6), pp. 947–975.

—— (ed), 1983 *Women's Work and Women's Roles*. Development Studies Centre, Monograph No. 32. Canberra. Australian National University.

——, 1987. "Blame, Responsibility and Remedial Action: Death, Disease and the Infant in Early Twentieth Century Malaya" in N. Owen (ed.), *Death and Disease in Southeast Asia*. Singapore. Oxford University Press.

Marcus, G. E. and M. J. Fischer, 1986. *Anthropology as Cultural Critique*, Chicago: University of Chicago Press.

Massard, J., 1983. *Nous Gens de Ganchong*, Paris: Editions du Centre National de la Recherche Scientifique.

Mohanty, C., 1988. "Under Western Eyes: Feminist Scholarship and Colonial Discourses". *Feminist Review*, No 30, 1988.

Moore, H., 1988. *Feminism and Anthropology*, Oxford: Basil Blackwell.

Moubray, G. A. C. de, 1931. *Matriarchy in the Malay Peninsula*, London: George Routledge and Sons.

Ng, C., 1984. "Production and Reproduction in a Padi Farming Community in Krian, Perak", *Ilmu Masyarakat:* 5.

——, 1985. "The Organisation of Gender Relations in Rural Malay Community (sic) with Special Reference to Semanggol and Pulau Tawar". Ph.D. Thesis, University of Malaya, Kuala Lumpur.

——, 1986. "Gender and the Division of Labour: A Case Study," in Hing Ai Yun and R. Talib (eds), *Women and Employment in Malaysia*, Kuala Lumpur: University of Malay Women's Association and Asian and Pacific Development Centre.

Nordin bin Selat, 1976. *Sistem Sosial Adat Perpatih*, Kuala Lumpur: Utusan Melayu.

Norhalim bin Haji Ibrahim, 1976. "Continuity and Change in the Matrilineal Society of Rembau". Unpublished M.A. Thesis, Hull University.

O'Brien, L., 1979. "Class, Sex and Ethnic Stratification in West Malaysia". Unpublished Ph.D. Thesis, Monash University.

Ong, A., 1983. "Global Industries and Malay Peasants in Peninsular Malaysia" in J. Nash and P. Fernandez-Kelly (eds), *Women, Men and the International Division of Labour*, Albany: State University of New York, pp. 426–39.

——, 1987. *Spirits of Resistance and Capitalist Discipline: Factory Women in Malaysia*, Albany: Suny University Press.

——, 1990. "Malay Families, Women's Bodies and the Body Politic". *American Ethnologist*. Vol 17 No 2, May.

Oorjitham, S., (n.d.) "Indian Women Workers" Paper presented to Conference on Women Workers in Malaysia, University of Malaya, 1985.

Pearson, R. & Elson, D., 1984. "The Subordination of Women and the Internationalisation of Production" in K. Young et al. (eds), *Of Marriage and the Market*, London: Routledge and Kegan Paul, pp. 18–40.

Peletz, M., 1981. *Social History and Evolution in the Interrelationship of Adat and Islam in Rembau, Negeri Sembilan*. Institute of Southeast Asian Studies, Discussion Paper No 27. Singapore: Institute of Southeast Asian Studies.

——, 1988. *A Share of the Harvest: Kinship, Property and Social History Among the Malays of Rembau*, Berkeley: University of California Press.

Ramazanoglu, C., 1988. *Feminism and the Contradictions of Oppression*, London: Routledge.

Rogers, B., 1980. *The Domestication of Women*, London: Kogan Page.

Rohanabihti Ariffin (1987), Women and Trade Unions in W. Malaysia. *Journal of Contemporary Asia*. Vol. 14, No. 4: 194–207.

Said, E., 1986. "Intellectuals in the Post-colonial World". *Salmagundi*. No 70–71, Summer.

Sanjek, R., 1982. "The Organization of Households in Adabraka: Towards a Wider

Comparative Perspective". *Journal of Comparative Studies in Society and History*. Vol. 24, No. 1: 57–103.

Scott, James, 1985. *Weapons of the Weak: Everyday Forms of Resistance*, New Haven: Yale University Press.

Scott, Joan, 1986. "Gender, A Useful Category of Historical Analysis". *American Historical Review*. Vol 91, No 5. Dec 1986.

Shamsul, A. B., 1986. *From British to Bumiputra Rule*, Singapore: Singapore Institute of Southeast Asian Studies.

Shamsul, A. B., (n.d.) "A Woman Politician". Paper presented to the Conference on Women Workers, University of Malaya, 1985.

Shaharil Talib, 1984. *After Its Own Image*, Oxford: Oxford University Press.

Spivak, G. C., 1987. *In Other Worlds*, New York: Methuen.

Stivens, M., 1985a. "The Fate of Women's Land Rights: Gender, Matriliny, and Capitalism in Rembau, Negeri Sembilan, Malaysia", in H. Afshar (ed), *Women, Work and Ideology, London*: Tavistock, pp. 3–36.

——, 1985b, *Sexual Politics in Rembau: Female Autonomy, Matriliny and Agrarian Change in Negeri Sembilan*. Occasional Paper of the Centre of Southeast Asian Studies, Kent: University of Kent.

——, 1987. "Family, State and Industrialisation: The Case of Rembau, Negeri Sembilan, Malaysia" in H. Afshar (ed), *Women, State and Ideology*, London: Macmillan, pp. 89–104.

Stivens, M., (n.d.) "Becoming workers: The Social Context of Female Migration in Rembau, Negeri Sembilan, Malaysia" in Jamilah Ariffin and W. Smith (eds), *Women Workers in Malaysia*, Singapore: Singapore Institute of Southeast Asian Studies (in press).

Stivens, M., Ng, C. and Jomo, K. S. (eds) (n.d.). *Malay Peasant Women and Land*, Boulder: Westview, in press.

Strange, H., 1981. *Rural Malay Women in Tradition and Transition*, New York: Praeger.

Strathern, M., 1985. "Dislodging a World View: Challenge and Counter Challenge in the Relationship Between Feminism and Anthropology", *Australian Feminist Studies*, 1 (1), pp. 1–25.

——, 1987. An Awkward Relationship: The Case of Feminism and Anthropology, *Signs*, 12 (2), pp. 276–292.

Swift, M., 1957. "The Accumulation of Capital in a Peasant Economy". *Economic Development and Cultural Change*. Vol V, 4.

——, 1963. "Men and Women in Malay Society" in B. Ward (ed), *Women in the New Asia*, Paris: Unesco.

——, 1965. *Malay Peasant Society in Jelebu*, London: Athlone Press.

Taylor, E. N., 1929. "The Customary law of Rembau". *JMBRAS* 7 (1), pp. 1–55.

——, 1948. "Aspects of Customary Inheritance in Negeri Sembilan". JMBRAS 21 (2), pp. 41–130.

Trinh T., Minh-ha, 1989. *Woman, Native, Other*, Bloomington: Indiana University Press.

10

Modernisation, Cultural Revival and Counter-Hegemony: The Kadazans of Sabah in the 1980s

Francis Loh Kok Wah

This is a study of the Kadazans of Sabah in the 1980s. After a brief introduction to the expectations and political fortunes of the Kadazans in the early 1960s, I will discuss the increasing incorporation of Sabah and the Kadazans into the modern Malaysian state. From this, it will be clear how modernization has also resulted in the emergence of a Kadazan intelligentsia which became increasingly disenchanted with an independent Malaysian state promoting Malay-Muslim hegemony. The last section focuses on Kadazan cultural revivalism, in particular the increasing symbolic significance of the Harvest Festival, promoted by the intelligentsia and which served as a catalyst for Kadazan political unity and the emergence of a counter-hegemonic movement in the mid-1980s. It is hoped that this specific study of the Kadazans will contribute to the general discussion of how culture and cultural distinctiveness gains political saliency.

The Kadazans and the "Twenty Points"

In the 1960 Census, indigenous Sabahans categorized as "Dusun" accounted for 32 percent of the state's population. In the 1970 Census, the estimated numbers of Kadazan (the name by then adopted to refer to the same group) amounted to 28.2 percent of the state's total. Due to the introduction of a new category, "Pribumi", in the 1980 Census (the significance of which will be discussed later), no details on the breakdown of specific indigenous ethnic groups are available after 1970. Nonetheless, it is clear that the Kadazans have been, and remain, the largest of the indigenous groups in Sabah.

In an important discussion of the "rise of Kadazan nationalism" in the 1950s Roff (1969) discusses how Donald (subsequently Fuad) Stephens, who became Sabah's first Chief Minister, and some other Kadazan leaders like Peter Mojuntin and Ganie Gilong, successfully united the non-Malay Muslim and non-Murut indigenous peoples of Sabah under one common umbrella.[1] This process involved two important steps; firstly, doing away with the name "Dusun" (literally "orchard" but implying "country hicks"), the term by which outsiders and the British referred to them and; secondly, imposing upon these various Dusun groups acceptance of the new category "Kadazan", (from the word Kakadazan, literally "town") which was actually the name by which only those who hailed from the Penampang area (just outside Kota Kinabalu) identified themselves. Quite apart from this, there was the related effort to promote usage of the "Kadazan language", standardised according to the dialect of the Penampang group, among the Dusunic speaking natives.

In part due to the fact that many of the non-Malay Muslim and non-Murut peoples speak variants of the same language, shared many similarities in their cultural practices and religious beliefs, Stephens and other Kadazan leaders from Penampang were apparently able to attract Dusun youths from Putatan, Papar, Inanam and other areas in the West Coast Residency to their cause. They also made some inroads into Kundasang, Ranau and Tambunan in the Interior Residency and Sandakan and Lahad Datu in the East Coast Residency. By emphasising the similarities among themselves and especially their common differences from the Malay Muslims and other groups, Roff suggests that a "Kadazan sense of nationhood" was ultimately forged (Roff 1969: 328–9).

The promotion of Kadazan identity was facilitated by the introduction of a "Kadazan Column" in the major daily, the "North Borneo News and Sabah Times which Stephens owned and edited. Likewise, the setting-up of Kadazan associations and clubs throughout the state, and the establishment of some 40 so-called "Native Voluntary Schools" where the Kadazan language was taught, also instilled a sense of Kadazan consciousness.

All these efforts culminated in the formation of the United National Kadazan Organisation (UNKO) in 1961 with Stephens as its leader. Following the district and town council elections held between December 1962 and April 1963, Stephens, with the support of the British, emerged as the first Chief Minister of Sabah. In his new capacity, he officially renamed the Dusun, as henceforth to be called Kadazan and British North Borneo, now called Sabah. On 16 September 1963 Stephens led Sabah into Independence as part of the new Federation of Malaysia.

Before supporting this incorporation, however, the Kadazan leaders acquired certain guarantees from Kuala Lumpur on the preservation of

---

[1] In fact, the initial attempt was to bring together all non-Malay Muslim indigenous people including the Muruts. However, this attempt failed to materialise when the Gunsanad brothers, the recognised leaders of the Muruts in Keningau, pulled out from a coalition with Stephens et al. One of their principal differences was over the formation of Malaysia to which the brothers objected (Lee 1976: 73–8).

their language, culture, and religion. For they feared these would be threatened by Sabah's incorporation into a Malay-Muslim dominated Malaysia. Stephens stated at that time:

> My people feel that if North Borneo joins Malaysia now as a state it would in fact mean that North Borneo would become not a state but a colony of the Federation of Malaya (Ongkili 1967: 36).[2]

This fear remained even after a visit by the Kadazan leaders to Malaya where they were particularly impressed with the latter's rural development success.

As I have pointed out, the Kadazan leaders sought a number of guarantees. Firstly, while Islam would be the official religion of the country, they insisted that this should not apply to Sabah. This was important since the majority of Kadazans and especially the Kadazan intelligentsia, were, and still are, Christians. Second, the leaders argued that while Malay was to be the national language, "English should continue to be used for a period of ten years after Malaysia Day". Other demands included the "Borneoization" of the public services as soon as possible; state control over immigration and land matters; special rights for the "natives" (including Sino-Kadazans); the channelling of development funds from Kuala Lumpur to Sabah; and "appropriate representation" to offset its smaller population in Parliament. These and other demands were finally formulated as the "Twenty Points": they were incorporated in amended form as part of the Inter-Governmental Committee Report, 1962 discussing the Independence arrangements and approved by the Sabah Legislative Assembly in March 1963. Subsequently, the Report formed part of the basis of the London Agreement paving the way for the formation of Malaysia in September 1963.

After these demands were incorporated into the new Sabah State Constitution, they, too, found their way through amendments, into the Federal Constitution of Malaysia (Ongkili 1972; Lee 1976 and Fung 1986: 94–7). In effect then, the "Twenty Points", though to a certain extent modified, were given official recognition. While this did not amount to according the "Twenty Points" legal status, an amicable settlement was nonetheless reached, principally because the Federal Government gave assurances to the Kadazan (and other Borneo) leaders that the spirit of the Twenty Points would be honoured.

Hence, Sabah (and Sarawak) were given special rights to which none of the other peninsular states were entitled. For this reason, many Kadazan and Sabahan leaders considered the status of Sabah to be different from that of the other states. Some harboured the opinion, still very much alive

---

[2] It should be clarified, however, that Stephens also feared domination by the Chinese whom he believed would become "the heirs when the British leave" (cited in Lee 1976: 91).

today, that Sabah had entered into the arrangement as an equal partner with the Federation of Malaya. Sabah was "one of three" signatories to the London Agreement and as such, should not be treated as "one of the thirteen" states, still less be dominated by Kuala Lumpur.[3]

The Demise of Kadazan Nationalism

Had Stephens and UNKO continued to govern and had the spirit of the Twenty Points been honoured by the Federal government, some measure of Kadazan political domination and cultural hegemony over the non-Kadazan people would have been likely. However, Stephens was forced to relinquish the Chief Ministership after only two years. His challenger was the governor, Tun Mustapha, a Suluk Muslim, who led the United Sabah National Organisation (USNO) which claimed to represent the "Malay-Muslims".[4] On his part, Mustapha had supported federation with Malaysia right from the start and favoured bringing Sabah more into line with the peninsular states, at least insofar as establishing Malay-Muslim hegemony in Sabah was concerned (Lee 1976: 104–5 and 122–33).

Stephens' close ties with Lee Kuan Yew and support for Lee's concept of a "Malaysian Malaysia" (when Singapore was still a part of the Federation) soured his relations with the Prime Minister, Tunku Abdul Rahman. When Singapore withdrew from Malaysia in 1965, and Stephens then expressed a desire to reexamine Sabah's continued participation in the Federation, he found himself under pressure from the Tunku as well. Stephens was subsequently forced to step down as the president of UNKO,

---

[3] See for instance the opinions of Pairin Kitingan, the present Chief Minister of Sabah in P. Kitingan (1986), and of Jeffrey Kitingan, the present chairman of the Institute for Development Studies, Sabah (J. Kitingan 1987). On parallel opinions among the Ibans of Sarawak, see Searle (1983).

In the present climate of heightened ethnic consciousness, these opinions have been extended to claims by the Kadazans that they are the "definitive" people of Sabah (J. Kitingan 1984: 236–7); a claim which takes after that by Malay leaders that they are the "definitive" people of the Malay peninsula if not Malaysia as a whole (Mahathir 1981: 126–7). It is on the basis of being definitive peoples that the Malays, Kadazans, Ibans and the other smaller indigenous groups are regarded as the "bumiputera" (sons of the soil) of Malaysia, which in turn results in certain "special rights".

[4] There is, of course, no cultural group that identifies itself as "Malay-Muslim". However, such a category is used increasingly in official, media and academic discourse to refer to the non-Kadazan non-Murut indigenous ethnic groups who are Muslims and who closely identify themselves with peninsular Malays who are invariably Muslims as well. These include the Suluk, Bajau, Illanun, Orang Sungai, Bisaya, Kedayan and Brunei Malays among other groups. Individually, all of them are numerically smaller than the Kadazans but together they constituted some 25% of the population in the 1960 Census.

at which point he charged the Federal government with not honouring the Twenty Points and treating Sabah as a "colony" (Ongkili 1972: 70 and Roff 1974: 86–118).

In the interim, Stephens had amalgamated UNKO with the National Pasok Momogun Organisation, led by the Dusun leader Gunsanad Sundang, to form the United Pasok-Momogun Kadazan Organisation (UPKO) in May 1964. In so doing Stephens abandoned his support for an exclusively Kadazan party in favour of a multi-ethnic party open also to Chinese. The change was in line with Stephens' own "flirtation" with Lee's concept of a "Malaysian Malaysia". However, most Chinese instead rallied behind the newly formed Chinese based party, the Sabah National Party (SANAP), which was subsequently reconstituted as the Sabah Chinese Association (SCA), which in turn entered into an electoral pact with USNO in the 1967 elections. With Kuala Lumpur's support, the USNO SCA alliance defeated UPKO and Mustapha came to power.

For a while, UPKO went into opposition. But when party members were lured to USNO, Stephens abandoned his attempt at multi-ethnic politics and called for "bumiputera unity" instead. Accordingly, UPKO was dissolved in December 1967, and its members were urged to join Mustapha's USNO. In 1968 Stephens became Malaysia's High Commissioner in Canberra where he remained until his return to Sabah in the mid-1970s (Roff 1974: 86–118).

Thus within a decade, there occurred what M. Roff has termed "the rise and demise of Kadazan nationalism". From being urged to identify themselves, first as Kadazans united behind UNKO, the non-Muslim Malay natives of Sabah were then urged to abandon their so called "distinctiveness" within the multi-ethnic UPKO. Still later, they were told to join USNO and to identify themselves as bumiputera in common with the Malay Muslims, their erstwhile enemies. The logic for these shifts lay in the Kadazan intelligentsia's bid for political power.[5] But they must certainly have created confusion among the ordinary villagers (Sta Maria 1978: 122–4; Jitilon 1985: 282; and Sator 1981: 56–7). The "demise" of Kadazan nationalism, presuming it had ever "risen" is not therefore surprising. On closer inspection, the process of "Kadazanization" in the 1950s and early 1960s was, at best, limited. Even in the 1980s, there are so-called Kadazan groups like the Rungus and Orang Sungai who consider themselves to be distinct ethnic groups. Additionally, many of the Lotud (of Tuaran), the Kwijau (of Keningau), the Bundu (of Kuala Penyu), and the Tambunuo and Kiulu of the interior areas continue to identify themselves as Dusun. It is essentially those from Penampang, Inanam,

---

[5] The first elected UPKO Assemblyman to cross over to USNO was appointed a Minister in Mustapha's government. Roff (1969: 342–3) also suggests that the dissolution of UPKO was probably related to the renewal of Stephen's timber concessions, the leases of which were due for reconsideration about that time.

Papar and Putatan—all in the West Coast region—who invariably identify themselves as Kadazan. And whereas the latter have since the early 1960s readily associated themselves with the Kadazan Cultural Association (KCA), some of the former prefer to participate in the United Sabah Dusun Association (USDA) formed in 1966 (Majihi 1979; Pung 1986; Tombung pers. comm. 1987; Topin pers. comm. 1987). From the foregoing, it can be seen that in spite of the efforts and wishes of Stephens et al, Kadazanization of the Dusuns was not completely successful. It was only in Penampang, Papar, Inanam, Putatan and certain other areas in the west coast that a sense of Kadazan identity emerged in the 1950s and 1960s. Confused, divided, leaderless and without their own party, the non-Malay Muslim people of Sabah were, by the late 1960s, "excluded from all political power" (Roff 1976).

Mustapha's Regime, 1967–76

Powerless, the Kadazans were soon subjected to Mustapha's USNO-dominated government (1967–76) and to his design for fostering "national unity" through *"satu bahasa, satu kebudayaan dan satu agama)"* (one language, one culture and one religion)—in effect a policy of Malayization and Islamization (Abdullah 1976: 95–6).

One of the early casualties of this policy was the Kadazan language as a subject of instruction in government schools. This occurred when the native voluntary schools run by local authorities were "up-graded" and made part of the national education system in the late 1960s.[6] The elimination of the Kadazan language in schools was in line with Mustapha's push to make Bahasa Malaysia the national and sole official language of the state. On 7 March 1972, a bill to this effect was introduced in the Legislative Assembly. However, because it contravened the State and Federal Constitutions (which, in line with the Twenty Points provided for a ten-year "grace period" in the use of English), the National Language Act did not come into effect in Sabah until September 1973. Thereafter, Bahasa Malaysia was used increasingly in the legislature, the bureaucracy and, to some extent, the courts. Beginning from 1 January 1974, Radio

---

[6] What occurred in Sabah contrasts markedly with the situation in neighbouring Sarawak where, despite the introduction of the same sort of policy, the Iban language has continued to be taught as a subject—the "Pupil's Own Language" (POL)—in government schools. Indeed, not only were POL classes taught in peninsula Malaysia government schools, but government-aided primary schools (which are privately-owned but adopt the Ministry of Education's curriculum including compulsory teaching of Malay as a subject of instruction) continued to teach most other subjects in Tamil or Chinese. Although many Christian missionary government-aided schools existed in Sabah, nonetheless, the Kadazan language was not taught in any of them either.

Malaysia-Sabah was ordered to broadcast only in Bahasa Malaysia and English. All broadcasts in Chinese, Kadazan, Murut, and other native languages were terminated (Abdullah 1976: 153–5 and 164; Jitilon 1985: 295).[7]

Beginning in 1968, Mustapha also embarked upon a programme to Islamize his state. Initially, he moved to consolidate religious practice among Muslims through the newly-established voluntary organisation, Pertubuhan Islam Seluruh Sabah or United Sabah Islamic Association (USIA) headed by Mustapha himself. USIA's initial role was to establish Islamic schools and standardise the teaching of Islam.[8] Soon, however, USIA began to propagate the faith among non-believers and successfully converted "tens of thousands" of Sabahans including prominent Kadazans (among them Stephens and Ganie Gilong) and Chinese during the early 1970s. During that time, foreign Christian missionaries serving the Kadazans and other non-Muslim Sabahans were expelled "causing much anxiety" for Christians (Tilman 1976).

Finally, Mustapha moved to amend the State Constitution to make Islam the official religion. This was achieved in 1973. With this important amendment, a State Mufti (Islamic jurisconsult) was appointed for the first time in Sabah's history and a new government body, the Majlis Ugama Islam Sabah (MUIS), funded by the government, was established. MUIS' role was to oversee the administration of Muslims and Islamic affairs in the state. To this end it worked closely with USIA. Funds for the promotion of religious instruction were also made available to USIA via MUIS.

These developments were regarded by many Kadazans as contrary to the Twenty Points and initiatives were taken to try to remove Mustapha. Because of the authoritarian nature of his rule and the weakness (in terms of numbers and resources) of the Kadazan middle-class, this was not achieved readily. It was only after he fell out of favour with Kuala Lumpur that he was finally ousted.[9]

Berjaya and Harris Salleh, 1976–1984

Despite the overthrow of Tun Mustapha's USNO-dominated government and its replacement by Berjaya in 1976, many of these policies were

---

[7] Such strident application of the National Language policy was contrary to its more relaxed implementation in Sarawak and the peninsula.

[8] USIA was established on 14 August 1969. It soon took over control of some 68 *madrasah* and *sekolah agama* (religious schools) in order to standardise the teaching of Islamic religious knowledge in them. Teachers were recruited from the peninsula for this purpose (Abdullah 1976: 98–9; Johari 1981: 25–32).

[9] Kuala Lumpur grew impatient with him as a result of his maverick ways which involved not only several attempts in by-passing the Federal government but also allegations of scandalous behaviour (Tilman 1976; Han 1979: 379–89).

not reversed. In fact, there occurred further erosion of the Twenty Points and the remaining provisions for the special treatment of Sabah as "one of the three" under Datuk Harris Salleh's Berjaya government.[10] Harris developed very close ties with the Federal Government during his nine year tenure from 1976 to 1984. Although this resulted in substantial federal funds being made available for development, it also led to further incorporation of Sabah into the Federation. This is perhaps best epitomised by Harris' controversial decision to cede the island of Labuan—without compensation or consultation with the people—to the Federal Government in 1984.[11]

The processes of Malayization and Islamization continued. In 1976, in line with national policy, all government-aided schools in Sabah were required to use Bahasa Malaysia as the sole medium of instruction. As during Mustapha's time, the Kadazan language was not officially taught anywhere at all. Federal government departments, and increasingly state ones as well, also more strenuously enforced the sole use of Bahasa Malaysia. The proportion of Bahasa Malaysia broadcasts over Radio Malaysia-Sabah broadcasts was also increased, though Kadazan programmes were re-introduced.

In 1978, when Islam had already been the official religion of the state for some five years, all government schools, including the Christian missionary government-aided ones, were required to organize Islamic religious instruction when at least 15 students in their schools so demanded (Johari 1981: 31). MUIS was entrusted with the role of placing religious teachers in these schools and the government colleges. As a corollary, Christian religious instruction was completely banned during school hours in all schools, including Christian missionary schools.

Another aspect of Islamization was increasing state sponsorship of Koran-reading competitions and the organisation of various dakwah (missionary) activities like the month-long annual dakwah campaign (Jitilion 1985: 289). Once the State Mosque initiated by Mustapha was completed in 1977, the construction began on a multi-million dollar MUIS complex. These and other efforts to promote Islam were further enhanced when Dr. Mahathir became Prime Minister in 1981 following which several other activities, like the introduction of "Islamic values" into government, Islamic religious instruction for Muslim civil servants, dress code, etc., were

---

[10] The new Berjaya government was first headed by Fuad Stephens. However, three months after coming to power, Stephens and other senior members of his cabinet including several Kadazans, were involved in a fatal air crash. At that point, Harris Salleh, a Muslim of mixed Malay-Pakistani parentage, took over as Chief Minister.

[11] When the Kuala Lumpur federal territory was acquired from Selangor, the state was paid $3 billion by the Federal government. For the allegation by the opposition party DAP that Harris, who owned much land in Labuan, had much to gain by its transfer to the Federal government, see Lim (1986: 420–35)).

also initiated (Mauzy and Milne 1986: 75–112).

But the most controversial move initiated by Harris' government was to reclassify all Sabahans of "Malay stock and related groups" as "Pribumi".[12] Introduced in 1980 to coincide with the census, the term "Pribumi" was to include not only the Kadazan, Murut, Bajau and other indigenous people of Sabah, but Indonesians, Filipinos, natives of Sarawak, and Cocos Islanders as well. The four latter groups had been categorised as "Others" in the 1970 Census. As a result of this re-definition, Pribumis accounted for 82.9% of Sabah's population in the 1980 Census (Malaysia 1983).

All this Harris considered to be in line with the promotion of "national culture", the core of which (as stipulated in the 1971 policy), is to be derived from Malay-Muslim elements. The Federal government believed this would help to promote national unity.

In addition to these cultural activities, incorporation was further promoted through the "federalization" of Sabah's state bureaucracy. Beginning in 1977, the Police Force and the education service were absorbed into their parent Federal departments, controlled from Kuala Lumpur. Over the next few years, an additional 20,000 other public servants in other State departments were also affected by federalization. By the early 1980s, only nineteen departments continued to be under the control of the Sabah government, while the number of departments under the control of the Federal government had increased from 13 in 1963 to 51 in 1981 (William 1981: 35–9). As a result, the State government lost almost all say in the appointment and promotion of employees in these federalized departments. Much anxiety resulted. As one Kadazan intellectual lamented. "Theoretically, it is possible for a Federal Department to be staffed entirely by recruits from Peninsular Malaysia" (ibid: 39).

In sum, under Harris and Mustapha, the Sabah state promoted both the further incorporation of Sabah into the Federation and the consolidation of Malay-Muslim hegemony over Sabah society. Though some of these policies were certainly excessive, most of them were tolerated, even encouraged, by the Federal government as well as some Kadazan leaders who were benefitting economically under the two regimes. Indeed, Mustapha's USNO, and Harris' Berjaya governments included several prominent Kadazan leaders as ministers while all of the amendments to the Sabah constitution were legally adopted by the Sabah Legislative Assembly.

The efforts of those in power to create a common political community within the territorial-state in the context of a plural Malaysia meant, in effect, the promotion of the cultural traditions of the politically dominant group and ultimately the cultural hegemony of Malay-Muslims over the Kadazans (and other minority groups). Inevitably, the result was a threat to the sense of identity and distinctiveness of the dominated. The project

---

[12] According to several informants, this notion of "Pribumi" originated from James Ongkili, a Kadazan who was Deputy Chief Minister to Harris.

of creating a political community amounted to their "encapsulation", that is, although they became incorporated they were not necessarily integrated (Strauch 1981).

Such a situation engendered the alienation of a group of young Kadazan intellectuals from the state. In the mid-1970s this group was still weak in numbers and resources and had to rely on Kuala Lumpur to help remove Mustapha. By the early 1980s, however, they had grown strong and were capable of taking the initiative by themselves. Ironically, the growth in strength of this group and the opposition that they mounted was a direct result of the incorporation process. For incorporation meant not only increasing interference of the Federal government in Sabah's affairs but increasing allocation of Federal funds for Sabah's development too, especially in the educational sphere.

The Emergence of the Kadazan Intelligentsia

Rapid economic growth occurred in Sabah throughout most of the 1970s and the early 1980s. Sabah's Gross Domestic Product (GDP) grew from $848 million in 1971 to $2177 million in 1983 (Malaysia 1981: 100; Malaysia 1984: 153).[13]

As was the case in the rest of Malaysia, the Federal government became deeply involved in the economy during this period. Under the Second Malaysia Plan (1971–1975), the Federal government allocated some $744 million for public development, an amount which increased to $1,453 million under the Third Malaysia Plan (1976–1980), and to $3,173 million under the Fourth Malaysia Plan (1981–85) (ibid; Malaysia 1976). The increasing involvement of the Federal government in the Sabah economy was directly related to the formulation in 1971 of the New Economic Policy (NEP) which, among other things, sought to eradicate poverty and eliminate the ethnic division of labour associated with colonialism.

To achieve these goals, a substantial proportion of the development funds was allocated for education and training. In Sabah these increased rapidly—from $35.6 million (4.2 percent of total public expenditure) under the Second Plan, to $202 million (13.9 percent of total) under the Third Plan, to $409.3 million (12.9 percent of total) under the Fourth Plan (ibid). Consequently, between 1971 and 1978 the number of students enrolled in secondary schools and pre-university classes increased by more than 100 per cent, from 30,632 to 68,982 students (Malaysia 1982). These figures underestimate the actual numbers of Sabahans attending upper secondary and pre-university classes since they do not include the large numbers sent to the peninsula and even overseas. Hence, it is not inconceivable that the total numbers attending both secondary and pre-university classes had

---

[13] Monies cited are in Malaysian ringgit which in the early 1980s was approximately the equivalent of US$1 to M$2.5. The GDP figures are in 1970 prices.

reached some 100,000 by the early 1980s. The 1980 Census (Malaysia 1983: Table 5.2) further reports that some 5,817 people, in contrast to 304 in 1960 (Rampasan 1989: 9), had attended universities and colleges. Meanwhile the number of indigenous graduates had increased dramatically from 2 in 1960 to 2,338 in 1980 (Rampasan 1989: 5). A further breakdown of these indigenous graduates according to smaller ethnic categories is not available. Nevertheless, it is clear that a substantial proportion included Kadazans.

Apart from the expansion of the bureaucracy which accompanied the increase in spendings on public development, the State also sought to fulfil its NEP goals by establishing various statutory authorities and quasi-government enterprises. Such bodies provided opportunities for bumiputera to involve themselves in the modern sector of the economy.

In 1971, there were only nine State statutory bodies and four other quasi-government bodies in Sabah. Only one of those, the Sabah Foundation, was actively involved in economic development activities. By 1980, however, there were 15 Federal statutory bodies, 16 State statutory bodies, and another 15 State quasi-government enterprises, most of which were involved in economic development. All of these, in turn, expanded and diversified their interests by creating numerous subsidiary companies.[14] By 1984, loans from the Sabah State Government alone to its 30-odd concerns totalled approximately $2 billion (*Star* 17.10.85).

The Sabah Economic Development Corporation (SEDCO) for instance, has received about $300 million from the State Government since its establishment in 1971. By the early 1980s, it had set up 25 other subsidiaries of its own with activities ranging from trading to property development including development of shop-houses and industrial estates, hotels, mining, and processing of raw materials (prawn, fish, flour, animal feed stuffs, and palm oil) to manufacturing (brickworks, paints, furniture, air-conditioner and vehicle assembling, etc.), ship construction and repair, and even to the film industry.

Likewise, the Yayasan Bumiputera Sabah, established in 1979, accumulated assets of over $500 million in about 5 years. By 1985 it was involved, through various subsidiaries, in banking, finance, insurance, publishing, agro-based industries, mining, hotels, and property development. One of its subsidiaries—Permodalan Bumiputera Sabah Bhd.—acting as the Yayasan's investment arm, ended up wholly or partially owning 20 other companies, involved in hotels, banking and finance, insurance, trading, property development, agro-based industries, mining and publishing. One of Permodalan's latest major activities has involved the investment of $100 million through two of these subsidiaries for the

---

[14] The following details on these bodies have been taken from Berjaya (1985) and Gudgeon (1981: 280–344) and supplemented with information gathered from numerous interviews with leading Sabahans conducted in April 1986 and January 1987.

construction of a $40 million office complex which would also serve as its headquarters.

Similar expansion and diversification programmes were also followed in the cases of the agencies set up to combat rural poverty. The Korporasi Pembangunan Desa (KPD), established as a cooperative in 1976 and reconstituted as a statutory authority in 1977, started off by venturing into small-scale agricultural projects in collaboration with smallholders. Through a subsidiary (Desa Cattle Sdn. Bhd.), it subsequently purchased more than a million hectares of grazing land in Australia for cattle ranching. Another subsidiary (Sabah Marketing Corp. - SAMA) went into trading activities, while others ventured into the processing of agricultural products, storage and shipping, furniture production, plantation agriculture involving cocoa, tea and other commercial crops, and hotels.

The expansion of the bureaucracy and the establishment of these statutory and quasi-government bodies and their numerous subsidiaries created not only a complex division of labour but also unprecedented employment opportunities for the emergent bumiputera middle class. Indeed, for some with the "right" political connections, there were also opportunities for appointments to high-paying directorships of these bodies and subsidiaries, and access to loans or other credit facilities from the Sabah Development Bank and the Sabah Bank, two other government institutions (established in 1977 and 1979 respectively).[15]

With the availability of such facilities, many politicians were able to set up their own private businesses, through which, at times, they entered into joint ventures with the subsidiaries of these government bodies, foreign investors, Chinese businessmen, or combinations of them. The New Economic Policy guidelines, which require bumiputera participation in such ventures, further facilitated such involvement by some members of the bumiputera intelligentsia.

---

[15] Details of some of these loans were first made public in May 1985, shortly after the Berjaya government was replaced by the new Parti Bersatu Sabah (PBS) one. Datuk Pairin Kitingan, the new Chief Minister, revealed in the Sabah State Assembly that various Berjaya leaders and their aides had been among the major borrowers of the Sabah Development Bank (SDB). For example, Berjaya Information Chief Datuk Majid Khan's Bena Group of Companies borrowed a total of $60 million from the bank while Selaseh Properties Sdn. Bhd., headed by Harris' aide, Hj. Ibrahim Merudin, borrowed about $6 million. Loans were also taken from the KPD and the Bumiputera Participation Unit (linked to the Yayasan Bumiputera Sabah) by the Berjaya leaders. According to another source, members of Harris' family borrowed some $3 million. Berjaya Youth leader, Datuk Yahya Lampong, borrowed about $11 million for his 12 companies, Berjaya secretary general Datuk Mohd. Noor Mansor borrowed some $1.5 million, and two other Berjaya leaders, Majid Khan and Abdul Malek Chua, borrowed, respectively, $284,000 and $135,000. (*Star* 21 May 1985; Chandran 1986: 75–7; and Tan 1986: 145–6). See Lim (1986: 239) for charges that some 800,000 acres of timber concessions were distributed to Berjaya party officials as well.

In summary, rapid economic growth occurred in Sabah during the 1970s and early 1980s. The Federal government began to play an increasingly instrumental role in the Sabah economy. Through its public spending on education, increasing numbers of secondary school and tertiary level graduates emerged. The expansion of the bureaucracy and the establishment of many statutory and quasi-government bodies and their subsidiaries created numerous employment opportunities for members of the emergent bumiputera intelligentsia. Those with the right political connections were even made company directors and/or gained access to credit enabling them to venture into business as well. Rapid economic growth was also accompanied by a growth in the system of patronage, bringing cronyism and nepotism to unprecedented heights in the state. The distinction between public and private funds became blurred. Conflicts of interests were ignored. In time, irregularities and mismanagement crept in and increasingly characterised the running of the statutory bodies, the quasi-government enterprises, and their subsidiaries (Chandran 1986: 76–82; F.E.E.R. 15 August 1985). The end result was an "absolute mess" in Sabah's financial position (Pairin in *Star* 21 May 1985).

Dissatisfaction Among the Kadazan Intelligentsia

As the economy continued to grow during the 1970s, the system of patronage expanded to cater for most of the needs of the bumiputera intelligentsia. The Chinese fraction of the intelligentsia also benefitted, though indirectly, from the patronage system. By the early 1980s, however, demands of the bumiputera intelligentsia had become more difficult to accomodate, a result of both an increase in their absolute numbers and their rising expectations. Catering for their needs posed a more complex problem for the Berjaya government in 1985 than it had in 1976, or for the Mustapha government of the early 1970s. Matters were made worse by the economic recession which began around 1982. Sabah's economy in particular, dependent as it is on external trade, was badly affected by the worsening international economic situation. Export commodity prices for its principal exports—timber, crude oil, palm oil, rubber and cocoa beans— were dropping rapidly. The result was a current account deficit totalling some $1 billion during 1981–1983. Both Federal and State governments resorted to foreign borrowing. But it also became necessary to revise the targets of the Fourth Malaysia Plan downwards. Funds were simply not available. Beginning in 1985, therefore, a total freeze on new positions and filling vacancies in the bureaucracy was declared. Similarly, the tightening up of funds from the state (coupled with nepotistic practices and mismanagement) caused many problems for the statutory and quasi-government bodies and their subsidiaries, many of which, as revealed in the Auditor-General's 1983 report (Malaysia 1985), were in the red.

The livelihoods of the working class were threatened by the recession. But at least, some members of the middle class were also affected. For the first time, Sabah graduates began to encounter difficulties in finding suitable employment. Young Kadazan intelligentsia, like their seniors, expected secure jobs, salaries that would allow them to purchase cars and maintain a high standard of living, rapid promotions, and loans and other credit facilities upon graduation. But these were not forthcoming. Neither had they access to positions of power in the bureaucracy commensurate with their educational training. With their hopes unfulfilled, they began to criticise the government.

Their major complaint was that "their Sabah" had been "colonised" by the Federal government and that Kadazans (in effect, themselves) were being discriminated against. These complaints were both cultural and socio-economic in nature. I have elaborated upon the rise of Malay-Muslim cultural hegemony above. I shall now discuss the socio-economic dimension of these complaints.

The "Colonisation" of Sabah

In 1971, the manufacturing sector's contribution to GDP for Malaysia as a whole was 14.7 percent while that for Sabah was only 2.5 percent. By 1983, the percentage for Malaysia as a whole had increased to 18.3 percent while that for Sabah was registering only 2.9 percent. Simultaneously, whereas the primary sector's (agriculture, forestry, fishing and mining and quarrying) contribution to Malaysia's GDP dropped from 37.1 percent to 27.2 percent over the same period, that for Sabah only dropped from 54.5 percent to 51.6 percent. The corresponding figures for the tertiary sector were 47.1 percent rising to 54.3 percent for Malaysia as a whole, and 43 percent rising to 45.4 percent for Sabah during the same period (Malaysia 1981: 100 and Malaysia 1984: 153). Accordingly, production workers as a proportion of the total labour force in the Peninsula rose from 27.3 percent to 33.3 percent between 1970 and 1980 (Malaysia 1981: 88). In the case of Sabah, however, they only rose from 3.3 percent to 4 percent between 1970 and 1978 (Sabah 1980: Table 11). Taken together, these statistics suggest that Malaysia's reputation as an emerging Newly Industrialised Country is principally a result of rapid industrialization in the Peninsula, not in Sabah. It appears, therefore, that a division of labour exists between the two regions.

This division between a more industrialized Peninsula and a Sabah specializing in the production of commodities is further reflected in the terms of trade between the two regions. While the total value of Sabah's trade had been increasing rapidly during the 1970s, certain unhealthy trends vis-a-vis that proportion of its trade with the Peninsula have developed.

Whereas in 1970 the value of exports to the Peninsula amounted to only $4.6 million, it increased to $360.2 million by 1984, some 6.6 percent of the total value of Sabah's exports. Over the same period, the value of imports from the Peninsula increased from $101.7 million to $1,340.7

million, some 36.6 percent of the total value of Sabah's imports. Consequently, Sabah's balance of trade with the Peninsula worsened some tenfold over the same period: from -$97.1 million to -$980.5 million (Soenarno 1986: 91). Not surprisingly, its major imports from the Peninsula comprised manufactured goods and articles, machinery and transport equipment, chemicals, beverage and tobacco, food and mineral fuels (*ibid*). As a result of the division of labour between the two regions, therefore, there has occurred a net outflow of funds from Sabah to the Peninsula.

In lieu of comparable data on income distribution between the two regions, we have to resort to statistics on the incidence of poverty to gauge how such a division of labour might have affected the corresponding wealth of the two regions. Although steadily declining since 1970, nonetheless, Sabah still registered some 33.1 percent of its population as poor in 1984. By contrast, the incidence of poverty in the Peninsula was down to 18.4 percent that year (Malaysia 1986: Table 3.2). There was, it would appear, some material cause for the Kadazans and Sabahans more generally to feel that they were being "colonised" by the Federal government.

Discrimination of Kadazans in the Services

The second complaint was that there was a preponderance of peninsular Malays and local Muslims especially in the upper levels of government and quasi-government bodies: specifically, that the Federal bureaucracy, statutory and quasi-government bodies and their subsidiaries were controlled by peninsular Malaysians, invariably Malays. In 1985, when Pairin Kitingan had replaced Harris as Chief Minister, he politely remarked in a forum on national integration that "the people in Sabah . . . have often complained that they are being deprived of economic and job opportunities because they are being swamped by people from the other side" (P. Kitingan 1986: 17). Additionally, it was claimed that local Muslims dominated the state government, its various parastatal bodies, and their subsidiaries.

No statistics are available to verify the Kadazan intellectuals' claim that Malay-Muslims dominate the Federal bureaucracy. However, informed observers have often noted that in the years following Sabah's entry into Malaysia, departing expatriates were invariably replaced by peninsular Malaysians on secondment to the state. The usual reason offered was that "there were insufficient local candidates to take over" (*ibid*). Although more Sabahans have since been appointed to the Federal bureaucracy, most top posts in the fifty-odd Federal departments continue to be filled by non-Sabahans.

However, some statistics are available for an assessment of the situation in the Sabah State bureaucracy. Statistics acquired from the Sabah Public Service Commission Annual Reports for the period 1970–1980 indicate that a majority of appointments, acting appointments and promotions to managerial and professional posts were given to non-Sabahans between

1970–1979. The figures available suggest that Sabahans were a minority in these upper divisions of their own State bureaucracy. In turn, Kadazans formed a percentage of this minority. Statistics made available by the Sabah Chief Minister's Office in 1985 for the "common pool services" further reveal under-representation of Kadazans (and Chinese) and over-representation of Malays and Muslims in Division A positions. The same was true for Division B positions. It was only in the lower Division C positions that Muslims and Malays did not predominate (Loh 1986: 5).

Although there are no statistics available to confirm the situation in the quasi government bodies and their subsidiaries it would appear, from the above discussion alone, that there was some basis to the complaints of the Kadazan intellectuals. Be that as it may, there was no automatic reason for urban working class and rural village Kadazans to be particularly concerned about how this group of educated middle class Kadazans were being discriminated. Yet, as I shall indicate in the next section, the former were ultimately mobilised into supporting the latter. How was this elite-mass gap bridged?

It is important to note that the Kadazan intellectuals did not voice their dissatisfaction in terms of their own socio-economic discrimination but in terms of the Federal and Sabah governments' neglect and discrimination of the Kadazan community as a whole. In this regard it is significant that they highlighted the problems of poverty confronting the rural Kadazan villagers. It was true, as they pointed out, that poverty was most acute among the Kadazans. In 1978, it was estimated that some 62 percent of all rural Kadazan households lived below the poverty line. This was clearly higher than the state's average of 42.6 percent for all rural households (Sabah 1980: 250).

The apparent failure on the government's part to cater to "Kadazan interests" was further attributed by one Kadazan intellectual to the formulation of the NEP in Kuala Lumpur without "direct input or participation from the Borneo states". Hence "regional interests and implications" were not adequately considered (J. Kitingan 1984: 153). As a result, Sabah Malays and Muslims were accorded similar benefits as their peninsular counterparts. In the Sabah context, however, this led, he stressed, to the relative neglect of a larger group of more needy bumiputera, namely, the Kadazans. The Federal government, therefore, was responsible for the Kadazan community's predicament.

Hence, the following discussion on how the Kadazan intellectuals began to promote a Kadazan cultural revival and successfully mobilised popular support for themselves, must be located within the context of increasing Malay-Muslim cultural hegemony during Mustapha's and Harris' governments, and against the background of the socio-economic problems I have just highlighted. These problems included acute poverty among the rural Kadazans; under-representation of the Kadazan middle class in the Federal and State bureaucracies, the parastatal bodies and their subsidiaries; "colonisation" of Sabah by the Peninsula; and the economic recession which began to set in around 1982.

The Kadazan Cultural Association and Cultural Revival

The Kadazan Cultural Association (KCA), launched in 1963, started off as an organisation geared towards the promotion of Kadazan culture and the standardization of the Kadazan language so as to foster Kadazan unity.[16] It took over these goals from UNKO when, with Independence, the party became part of the State government.

With UPKO's dissolution in 1967, and in the absence of a Kadazan based and led political party, the KCA emerged as the major organisation concerned with Kadazan affairs. Even so, it was not particularly active during Mustapha's years in office, reviving only after April 1976 when Berjaya came into power. In 1978, after several KCA branches were established throughout Sabah, a "Delegates Conference" was held for the first time. By early 1980s KCA emerged as a popular Kadazan organization; any Kadazan who aspired to lead the community could now not afford to ignore it. This explains why, since the late 1970s, KCA committee members have included Kadazan cabinet ministers, members of the State Assembly, Members of Parliament, top civil servants, professionals and business people. In 1982, its Patron was Datuk James Ongkili, then Deputy Chief Minister of Sabah; the President was Datuk Joseph Pairin Kitingan, and the Deputy President was Datuk Clarence Mansul (the latter two also members of the Berjaya cabinet).

In the early 1980s, the KCA entered a new phase. Increasing numbers of young educated Kadazans began to join the organization. It is probable that this was brought about by growing disillusionment with the ruling Berjaya party and its policies. As mentioned, these had resulted in increasing Malay-Muslim hegemony on the one hand, and, as a result of the recession and/or patronage system on the other, caused personal social, political and cultural ambitions to be thwart. Whichever the case, the new enthusiasm that they brought into the organisation resulted in a Kadazan cultural revival.

Under the auspices of the KCA, some of these young city-based Kadazan intelligentsia began to recover—and probably informed themselves too for the first time—some of the old oral myths of ancestry and historical memories of their people. These were written up, disseminated among themselves, and sometimes published.[17]

One such, which has been enthusiastically promoted, is the myth of *Nunuk Ragang*, the tree which is believed to have given Kadazans their deep tan. This myth recounts the way in which the different Kadazan tribes came from a single tree, the *nunuk* or banyan, commonly found along the Liwagu river in the Ranau region. In ancient days the children

---

[16] The following discussion is based on KCA (1986); Jitilon (1985: 72ff and 186–97); and Topin (personal communication 1987).

[17] See the collection in KCA (1983), from which the following two myths have been extracted.

of all the tribes played together in the river, after which they sunned themselves on the branches of the *nunuk*. Consequently, all Kadazans acquired a deep tan which distinguished them from the foreigners who later came to Sabah. Because of over-population, families began to trek outwards along the river in search of new land to farm. In these places they settled and over time began to speak variants of the same language. Likewise differences also emerged with regards to their other cultural and religious practices. Hence despite these differences, the Kadazan people, according to this myth, are in fact one.

Another popular myth, originating from Tuaran, recounts how the "Great Book of Knowledge", containing secrets for the solving of all problems and the resolution of all conflicts, was lost by the Kadazan "king" in a great flood. So long as the king himself continued to be around, however, there was still peace and order. The major loss was the script of the Kadazan language. To recover this treasure, the king set out to look for the book. He never returned. The elders or council of chiefs whom he had appointed took over. This explains why it is that no chief can pronounce a judgement on his own. Problems emerged within the community because even with the chiefs sitting in council, they were not as wise as the king. Moreover, the elders were often at odds with one another. Consequently, feuds and fights occurred causing some to move away. In time linguistic, cultural and religious differences developed amongst the various groups. Because such feuding continued the Kadazans became weak, and when the foreigners arrived were easily dominated by them. Since the Book of Knowledge was never found, the Kadazan system of writing was never recovered. This is why, the myth explains, the Kadazans have no literary texts and their language, first transcribed by Christian missionaries, is today written in the romanised script.

Recovering and retelling myths, such as the above, could not explain all aspects of the present Kadazan predicament. But they can and certainly did alert the Kadazans to certain dangers: for instance, these two (rather than other) myths were probably more enthusiastically promoted by the young intellectuals because they address the question of Kadazan disunity. The second myth also emphasizes the need for a new king or *Huguan Siou* (Paramount Chief). Such myths then have at least a moral value. At any rate, highlighting the myths allowed the intellectuals, who themselves were searching for their cultural roots, to reach down to the Kadazan villagers through a common medium, and so mobilise them more easily.

Aside from the recovery of myths, *kulitangan* and *sompoton* ensembles performing "traditional" (inverted commas around tradition and traditional are implied throughout) songs and tunes were also sought after and promoted. Recordings of their performances were made and sometimes cassettes and songbooks were marketed too. And of course, traditional—like the *sumazau* and *mongigol*—dances were also recovered and promoted. Often, however, this "recovery process" also involved a measure of reshaping what was the traditional. For instance, the songbooks and cassettes of traditional music included a few new tunes, composed by young intellectuals. At another level, traditional songs, tunes and dances were also divorced from their original ritualistic contexts. It was certainly also the case when the oral myths were creatively retold and re-presented to make them relevant to current issues and problems, or, when for the same purpose, two or three particular (rather than the other remaining stock of) myths were highlighted by the intelligentsia.[18] Nonetheless, the efforts did generate a Kadazan cultural revival. In the process, channels of communication were established between the urban-based intelligentsia and the villagers.

All this came together in the celebration of the annual Harvest Festival (*Tadau Tagazo Kaamatan*). Organized on a statewide basis as well since 1961, when the occasion was declared a public holiday, the Festival was becoming the KCA's major activity, and for increasing numbers of Kadazans their most important event of the year. As Kadazans, regardless of background, nowadays put it: "Just as the Malays have their *Hari Raya* and the Chinese their lunar New Year, we have our Harvest Festival" (Mianus 1983: 20; Noechaelisa 1983: 23). The Festival is no longer simply a traditional religious event related to the agricultural cycle but an event of major ethnic significance as well.

On this occasion, religious rites to *Bambaazon*, the Spirit of the Rice, are performed by various *bobohizan* (priestesses) who have come from different parts of the state. These rites are in thanksgiving and to secure good harvests for the following year. Apart from this, traditional (including the newly composed and arranged) Kadazan dances, music, songs and even the martial arts by various troupes are presented. During the two days of festivities, the Kadazans wear their traditional costumes and headgear while traditional Kadazan houses are constructed on the site of the Festival. Apart from much *lihing/montoku* (rice wine) drinking, the merrymaking includes competitive games like the buffalo-race, finger-wrestling, land-boat race, winnowing, and the making of *suki* (bamboo cups), all, according to one informant, related to various aspects of the "traditional Kadazan way of living". Hence, despite the inclusion of more universal games like tug-of-war, stilt-walking, egg-in-spoon, threading-the-needle and three-legged races; or the more spectacular Harvest Queen contest which for some is the highlight of the Festival, the occasion remains essentially a celebration and assertion of Kadazan-ness. In this regard it is significant that an important criterion in the selection of the Harvest Queen is the contestants' presentation of the traditional black costume of the Kadazans.

---

[18] On the process occurring elsewhere, see Hobsbawm and Ranger (1983). Anderson (1986) has also observed how genealogies of modern nations have been traced to mythic origins and how in the recounting of a nation's history the nationalist has often been very selective. The same is suggested in Smith's (1984) notions of "myths of origin" and "historical memories".

Thus the entry of the young and frustrated intellectuals into the KCA resulted in a Kadazan cultural revival which was manifested in particular by the growing significance of the annual Harvest Festival among increasing numbers of Kadazans throughout Sabah. Insofar as the modern incorporating state was viewed by the young intelligentsia to be discriminating against Kadazans and/or Sabah, in terms both of the division of the socio-economic cake and the drive for Malay Muslim cultural hegemony, these cultural activities were certainly counter-hegemonic in nature too. Indeed, following their participation in the KCA, the organization became a forum for debating important political issues, among them the neglect and erosion of Kadazan interests and the political direction Kadazans ought to take. Probably the first of these debates to have been aired publicly, and which sparked off more overtly political action against the government, pertained to official categorization of the Kadazans as one of the "Pribumi" groups. This exercise was vehemently criticised by the young intellectuals. They denounced as "puppets" the Kadazan representatives in the Berjaya government like James Ongkili, Clarence Mansul and Conrad *Mojuntin*, who supported Harris on the matter (Jitilon 1985: 302).

The Kadazan intelligentsia had two objections to this use of the term "Pribumi". First, they resented the fact that Indonesian migrants and Filipino refugees had been accorded the same status as themselves. They asked how it came to be that so many of the Indonesians and Filipinos were able to acquire identity cards, a step towards receiving citizenship papers. Second, they were concerned about the increasing proportion of Muslims among "Pribumi" in particular and in Sabah as a whole. (The vast majority of these refugees were Muslims). Whereas in 1960 Muslims constituted only 25% of the population, this had risen to 40% by 1970. With the inclusion of the Filipinos and Indonesians as Pribumi, the percentage of so-called Muslim Pribumis would have easily topped 50% in 1980.

For the Kadazan, the term "Pribumi" was an attempt to further consolidate Malay-Muslim hegemony.[19] They felt themselves under seige, their distinctiveness being "defined away" and their claim to be the "definitive people" of Sabah being made inconsequential as they came to be outnumbered. For them, the worst of Stephens' pre-Independence fears were being realised. They again claimed that the Twenty Points had not been respected, that Sabah was being treated as "one of the thirteen" or even "colonised", and, that the Kadazans were "second class Bumiputras".[20]

---

[19] In an interview in *Asiaweek*, 7 June 1985, Harris stated, "Muslims are multiplying faster and some of the refugees will become voters. In five years Muslims will hold the balance. Muslims will form the government." Such comments surely confirmed the worst fears of the non-Muslim Kadazan intellectuals.

[20] All these terms in parentheses, and the implications they convey were gathered from my conversations with some Kadazan intellectuals whose identities, it was requested, should not be revealed.

One leading young Kadazan intellectual has expressed these anxieties in the following way:

> The Kadazans consider themselves the true natives of Sabah and claim that they are the definitive people . . . [Yet] in reality, the Kadazans have found themselves to be subordinated to the Malays and discriminated against in favour of Muslim natives who also claim to be Malays by virtue of their religion (J. Kitingan 1984: 236–7).

Shortly after the debate over reclassification, the disenchanted young intelligentsia and the KCA openly broke away from Harris and the Berjaya government. This break was sparked off by government intervention in the Harvest Festival of 1982.

The Tambunan Harvest Festival, 1982

In late 1981, the Berjaya government decided to declare the Harvest Festival a *"Pesta Rakyat"* (People's Festival). All Sabahans, it argued, not only Kadazans, should be encouraged to join in the celebrations. This declaration was in line with the government's "Pribumi policy".[21] In view of the official visit of the Yang diPertuan Agong (King) to Sabah, the government also took over the organization and sponsorship of the event. This was necessary, it explained, to co-ordinate the holding of the Pesta with other events scheduled for the visit. James Ongkili, the Deputy Chief Minister would head the organizing committee for the Pesta.[22]

The state-sponsored Pesta held in Keningau in May 1982 differed in significant ways from those previously organized by the KCA. Security considerations prevented popular participation by ordinary Kadazans from throughout Sabah. In order to accommodate the tight schedule of the King, the festival was shortened from the usual two days to a single day, and with some of the religious events dropped. Yet the organisers found time to stage a ceremony to mark the conversion of some Kadazans to Islam during the King's visit. To the young KCA intellectuals, this was adding insult to injury.

Spurred on by pressure especially from the young Kadazan intellectuals but also the native chiefs, priests and priestesses who were concerned that the usual rites for that year had still not been conducted, Pairin and other KCA leaders consulted with their branches. With the support of the United Sabah Dusun Association (USDA), they decided to organize an additional Harvest Festival, to be held in Tambunan on the 26th and 27th of June.

---

[21] Harris first proposed celebrating the Festival as a Pesta Rakyat in 1978 but met with strong opposition from Kadazans. DE 23 May 1978.

[22] The following discussion has been gathered from numerous interviews with Kadazans during my visits to Sabah in April 1986 and January 1987.

This alliance of the KCA and USDA was a significant one. For up to that point, there was friction between the two.[23] Yet on this occasion the two "enemies" came together. KCA and USDA leaders explained that this second Festival was necessary to allow for the usual participation of people from throughout the state (DE 18 May 1982). This, of course, was only part of the truth. They feared that government intervention in the organization of their Festival was further leading towards a denial of their identity and the promotion of Malay-Muslim hegemony.

In response to the decision by KCA and USDA, Ongkili declared that anyone claiming that the Festival opened by the King had not been a state-wide celebration was insulting His Majesty. He made it clear that no government funds would be provided nor would the use of government facilities, including the community hall and the town *padang* (field), be allowed. And should the KCA still insist on holding its Festival, he ordered that the Festival not be declared a state-wide function. All Berjaya and government leaders were also ordered to boycott the event. There was also a media blackout. In these ways the government hoped to prevent the Festival occurring; should the KCA still go ahead, the government hoped to, at least, contain the event.

On both these scores the Berjaya government failed. The Harvest Festival of 1982, held on the outskirts of Tambunan in an open field by the river, turned out to be a state-wide affair. Kadazan and Dusun groups from all over the state and even Murut groups from the south turned out in force. Denied government funds and facilities, community efforts and self-help helped to make the Festival a success.

A few days before the Festival however, the Chief Minister announced the "resignation" of Pairin from the State Cabinet (*Star* 22 June 1982). It was clear that any other Kadazan leader in government, who dared to challenge the Berjaya government's ruling on the Festival, would be dealt with similarly. Thus with the exception of Pairin and Mark Koding (the leader of USDA) all Berjaya members of the Cabinet, State Assembly and Federal Parliament were absent. Only a handful of civil servants showed up. In the absence of Ongkili, who had been invited to open the celebrations, Pairin performed the opening ceremony.

---

[23] Although USDA was formed in 1966 it was inactive throughout most of the 1970s. It was only in the early 1980s that it was revived and began to gain support from Dusuns living in the more interior areas who refuse to identify themselves as Kadazan. More Islamic converts also tend to participate in USDA rather than the KCA. Nonetheless, compared to the KCA, it was a less popular organization.

It has been suggested that Harris was fearful of the increasing popularity of the KCA and was behind USDA's revival (J. Kitingan 1984: 239). Consequently, USDA began to sponsor a separate state-wide Harvest Festival as well. About the same time too, the Berjaya government re-introduced a radio programme in the Dusunic languages. Such developments contributed to the friction between the two organizations.

The Festival as Symbol of Kadazan Unity and Political Success

I have argued that the increasing importance of the Harvest Festival was due to the significant role it came to play in ethnic conflict. But it is important also for another reason, one which stems from the celebration of particular past Festivals on the occasion of Kadazan political success.

In the historical memory of the Kadazans, the Festivals of 1961 and 1976 are recalled with enthusiasm. The May 1961 Festival was special, for this was the first time that it was accorded the status of a public holiday after much lobbying by Stephens and the early Kadazan leaders. Because it was a public holiday, ordinary Kadazans from all over the state could travel to Penampang to celebrate the Festival together. This represents an important change, since in the past the "festival" was celebrated locally by the different groups, and at different times. The timing depended on the timing of local harvests (Jitilon 1985: 186). But when some of the older Kadazan villagers of Penampang described the 1961 Festival to me, it also conveyed, at least to me, the sense of a time when Kadazans felt themselves in control of Sabah and of their destiny. For the Festival marked the efforts by Stephens and others which ultimately led to Kadazan replacement of the British and their control of Sabah. Indeed, these older Kadazan villagers seem to recall the 1961 Festival more vividly and with greater enthusiasm than did they the 1963 celebrations marking the achievement of Independence. In the absence of a Kadazan political party, let alone a Kadazan Chief Minister between 1967 to 1976, this 1961 Festival probably also symbolised an early phase of Kadazan political success, a reminder of what could be.

Likewise, the May 1976 Harvest Festival also registers special significance with many Kadazans I spoke to. This Festival followed the defeat of Mustapha in the polls. Peter Mojuntin, the "Golden Son" of the Kadazans who had played an instrumental role in the overthrow of Mustapha, and was responsible for organising the 1976 Festival declared that his Committee's task had been to reinstal "the importance of the Harvest Festival in the Sabah calendar" and to restore to it the "honourable status which it had held until purged by the undemocratic USNO" government. It was also to be the "biggest ever" celebration (Sta Maria 1978: 239–42). Consequently, the Harvest Festival as a symbol of Kadazan political victory was further consolidated. It reminded them of the possibility of Kadazan political success.

For the older Kadazans therefore, the 1982 Festival was as important as the other two. For the young Kadazan intellectuals, including some who were not even in Tambunan, the 1982 Festival was, however, "even more important" because it led to Kadazan unity and ultimately a new Kadazan-dominated political party and government. In any case, the 1982 Festival marked yet another important turning point in the political history of the Kadazans.

The state-wide Kadazan Harvest Festival therefore has emerged as the most important symbol of Kadazan-ness. This is not simply because it is a traditional celebration providing meaning to an agricultural people, but also because it symbolises for the Kadazans their cultural identity in a multi-ethnic environment. But I have also argued that certain particular Festivals also mark important turning points in the historical memory of the Kadazans and therefore give the Festival political significance. In celebrating the Festival, there is always opportunity to recall how the Kadazans once stood up against the British, Mustapha and more recently Harris; of how there have been able leaders and heroes like Stephens, Mojuntin and now Pairin; and the need for Kadazan unity. Indeed, the Festival has taken on these emblematic representations because it was imagined by the young intellectuals as they began to promote a revival of Kadazan culture, in particular, popular celebration of the Harvest Festival.

However, we should not see the Festival and cultural revivalism as an outcome of ideological manipulation on the part of the intelligentsia to serve their own interests. The fact that the Festival takes on such symbolic significance is also due to the imagination by the rural villagers that both they, as well as the urban intelligentsia, belong to the same community. They believe that they not only share common myths, historical memories, and heroes but also a common experience of being "colonised" by the Federal authorities, subjected to Malay-Muslim cultural hegemony and discriminated against. In short, regardless of social differences, there emerged among lower and upper-class Kadazans a common imagination of themselves as a community. Although cultural difference may be considered a "given", imagining that others who share common cultural characteristics with one's self partake of a similar community is not; still less should the emergence of an ethnic community capable of united and sustained political action be assumed from cultural differences. Like Anderson (1983) says of the nation, such an ethnic community I maintain, is also a "cultural artefact" that has been created by the modern intelligentsia. Because the nation/ethnic community has popular connotations, it has successfully penetrated the imagination of the villagers as well. Hence "thinking ethnically" should not be considered as a manifestation of "false consciousness".

In Retrospect

The Harvest Festival, at first glance essentially a cultural event, has taken on new meanings in the minds and lives of the Kadazans, both villagers as well as intellectuals; a consequence of a conjunction of political, socio-economic and cultural developments coming together. It is only in this regard that the cultural should be seen as having important social and political effects. For instance, the KCA, responsible for organizing the Festival, became regarded as the pre-eminent Kadazan organization. Likewise KCA leaders who aspired to lead the Kadazans were seen to be legitimate in the eyes of the village Kadazans. And in obvious response to Harris' removal of Pairin from the State cabinet, the native chiefs and other Kadazans moved to confer upon Pairin the honour of *Huguan Siou* (Paramount Chief), implying both political and spiritual leadership of the Kadazan people as well as symbolizing their unity. This position had not been filled since the death of Fuad Stephens in 1976.

To further illustrate the point of how the "cultural" is imaginately created and can have important social and political effects, let us look at the way in which this honour was conferred on Pairin. Firstly, in conjunction with a Kadazan "Heritage Exhibition" held in Kota Belud in November 1983, the native chiefs invited Pairin to walk over seven heirloom gongs, according to my informants a "traditional" practice in that area, apparently reserved for warrior-chiefs returning from battle. In early 1984, the native chiefs in Menggatal then presented him with an old warrior's sword, apparently, another traditional way of conferring honour to a hero. Finally, due to what the KCA executive secretary described as "the people's demand" Pairin was "prayed over" and installed as *Huguan Siou* at the Third Annual Delegates Conference of the KCA held in Penampang on 3–4 March 1984 (DE 15 March 1984). Through these different steps therefore he was conferred the honour of Paramount Chief. Indeed, yet another ceremony was held in July 1984, at the Kadazan Society premises in Penampang where Fuad Stephens himself had been officially installed in the early 1960s. However, despite claims that this is a traditional title, it was not possible to clarify who, before Pairin and Stephens, had been similarly honoured. Considering that the category "Kadazan" is of recent creation, it is unlikely that there were *Huguan Sious* representing all of the Kadazans in pre-modern times, the myth of the Great Book of Knowledge notwithstanding. In fact then, this tradition seems to be of recent imagination. More pertinently, the installation of Pairin as only the second *Huguan Siou* indicates the successful political unification of the different groups of Kadazans for only the second time in the history of the modern state. It is not surprising therefore that one of my informants should have remarked: "there is no one agreed way on how to install the *Huguan Siou*". Consequently all known "traditional" ways were carried out to instal Pairin, including the obviously new one of being prayed over during the 1984 Conference of the KCA, a modern organization. Whichever the case, the installation of Pairin clearly marked dissatisfaction with Harris too, who, it was well known, was pushing for the appointment of Ongkili instead.

After the Tambunan Festival, the young KCA intellectuals became increasingly outspoken. At the KCA's 1984 Conference they called for the preservation and promotion of "people's cultures", in opposition to Ongkili's call on the same occasion for the creation of a "national culture" (DE 15 March 1984 and DE 26 April 1984). Their point of view prevailed and the KCA resolved that it would continue to promote Kadazan culture, especially among the young. Other resolutions called upon the Berjaya government to drop its use of the term "Pribumi", and to initiate the teaching of Kadazan in schools under the "Pupil's Own Language" programme. These demands were widely supported by Kadazans (*ibid* and DE 16 July 1985). Subsequently, when the State government attempted to merge all cultural organisations, including the KCA, into a single body— the Sabah Cultural Association, to which all government funds for private cultural activities would be channelled, Pairin and the KCA intellectuals also protested.

Pairin, a devout Catholic, also brought the existence of anti-Christian activities to the attention of the Berjaya party. These included reports of Muslim teachers who denigrated Christianity in their classes; "unqualified" Muslim missionaries who raised "sensitive issues" in rural areas; prohib ition by a lower-level official of the customary erection of crosses in the Tambunan hills during the Catholic season of Lent; and the like. Finally, he questioned Berjaya's mismanagement of public funds, nepotism in government, and the lack of development in rural areas (Chandran 1986: 124–5; *Star* 17 July, 1986; Topin 1985 personal communication).

His leadership of KCA, his defiance of Harris in the Tambunan Festival which resulted in his removal as a cabinet minister, his honorary title as *Huguan Siou*, and his continued challenge of Berjaya all contributed to his emergence as a folk hero of the Kadazan community. In that sense we can speak of the emergence of a counter-hegemonic movement under Pairin's leadership. Ironically, the movement was formalised with the formation of the multi-ethnic Parti Bersatu Sabah (PBS) headed by Pairin. Given the demographic realities of Sabah, however, working with Malay-Muslims and Chinese was the only way to achieve victory in the polls. Indeed, within a month of its formation, PBS defeated Harris Salleh's Berjaya party in the 1985 polls. Pairin then became Chief Minister, and some of the young Kadazan intellectuals were appointed ministers and assistant ministers. Before the year was up, still others were appointed to other top government posts, the statutory bodies and the myriad subsidiary companies. Pairin's new government immediately did away with the term "Pribumi", conducted an investigation into the presence of the Filipino refugees and Indonesian migrants, called for greater devolution of power and more development funds for Sabah, and, in late 1989, had essentially succeeded in acquiring Kuala Lumpur's approval for the teaching of the Kadazan language in Sabah schools again. However, tensions began to develop within the PBS between the Kadazan intellectuals and their non-Kadazan counterparts.[24]

---

[24] I have begun research on these tensions which ultimately led to the departure of several leaders from the PBS. These tensions arose because of allegations of corruption and nepotism in the PBS government, and of Kadazan discrimination of other ethnic groups. For a preliminary report see Loh (1989).

Bibliography

Abdullah Hussain, 1976. *Tun Datu Mustapha: Bapa Kemerdekaan Sabah*, Kuala Lumpur: M. F. I.

Anderson, Benedict, 1983. *Imagined Communities: Reflections on the Origins of Nationalism*, London: Verso.

———, 1986. "Narrating the Nation". *Times Literary Supplement*, 13 June 1986, p. 659.

Berjaya, 1985. "Progress and Development Under the Berjaya Government" (mimeo).

Chandran, Bala, 1986. *The Third Mandate*, Kuala Lumpur: Foong Tai Press.

Fung, Nicholas, 1986. "The Constitutional Position of Sabah" in F. Trindade and H. P. Lee (eds), *The Constitution of Malaysia: Further Perspectives and Development*, Kuala Lumpur: Oxford University Press.

Gudgeon, P., 1981. "Economic Development in Sabah, 1881–1981" in Sullivan and Leong, (eds), 1981, pp. 280–344.

Han Sin Fong, 1979. "A Constitutional Coup D'Etat: An Analysis of the Birth and Victory of the Berjaya Party in Sabah, Malaysia". *Asian Survey*, 19 (4), pp. 379–89.

Hobsbawm, E. and T. Ranger (eds), 1983. *The Invention of Tradition*, Cambridge: Cambridge University Press.

Jitilon, Kely, 1985. "Sejarah Perkembangan Politik Orang-orang Kadazan serta Peranan dan Implikasinya dalam Perpaduan Malaysia, 1961–1981", B. A. Hons Academic Exercise, History Department, Universiti Kebangsaan Malaysia, Bangi, Selangor.

Johari Hj. Alias, 1981. "Perkembangan Ugama Islam di Sabah" in *Pameran Hasil Sumbangan Islam Hingga Abad Ke-15 Hijrah*, Kota Kinabalu: Kementerian Kebudayaan, Belia dan Sukan, Sabah.

Kadazan Cultural Association (KCA), 1983. *Our Cultural Heritage*, Kota Kinabalu.

———, 1984. "Historical Background of the KKKS". Distributed at the Third Delegates Conference of the KCA of Sabah held in Tambunan, 3–4 March 1984.

Kitingan, J., 1984. "Political Stability and Economic Development in Malaysia". Ph.D. Thesis Tufts University, Boston.

———, 1987. "Thorny Issues in Federal-State Relations: The Case for Sabah and Sarawak" in *Reflections on the Malaysian Constitution*, Penang: Aliran Publications, pp. 149–68.

Kitingan, P., 1986. "Territorial Integration: A Personal View" in *The Bonding of a Nation: Federalism and Territorial Integration in Malaysia*. Petaling Jaya: Institute of Strategic and International Studies.

Lee, Edwin, 1976. *The Towkays of Sabah*, Singapore: Singapore University Press.

Lim Kit Siang, 1986. *Malaysia: Crisis of Identity*, Petaling Jaya: Democratic Action Party.

Loh Kok Wah, Francis, 1986. "Sabah: A Threat to Our Democracy". *Aliran Monthly* 6(4), pp. 2–5.

———, 1989. "A Return to Pre-1985 Politics for Sabah". *Aliran Monthly* 9(10), pp. 2–5.

Mahathir Mohamad, 1981. *The Malay Dilemma*, Kuala Lumpur: Federal Publications.

Majihi, F. Mathius, 1979. "The Question of Identity" in *Daily Express* 7–8 March.

Malaysia, 1976. *Third Malaysia Plan, 1976–80*, Kuala Lumpur.

——, 1981. *Fourth Malaysia Plan, 1981–85*, Kuala Lumpur.

——, 1982. *Lapuran Jawatankuasa Kabinet Mengkaji Perlaksanaan Dasar Pelajaran*, Kuala Lumpur: Kementerian Pelajaraan Malaysia.

——, 1983. *Population and Housing Census of Malaysia, State Population Report Sabah*, Kuala Lumpur: Department of Statistics.

——, 1984. *Mid-Term Review of the Fourth Malaysian Plan 1981–85*, Kuala Lumpur.

——, 1985. *Report of the Auditor-General Sabah, 1983*, Kuala Lumpur.

——, 1986. *Fifth Malaysia Plan, 1986–1990*, Kuala Lumpur.

Mauzy, D. and R. S. Milne, 1986. "The Mahathir Administration: Discipline Through Islam" in B. Gale (ed), 1986 *Readings in Malaysian Politics*, Petaling Jaya: Pelanduk, pp. 75–112.

Mianus, H. J., 1983. "Erti Perayaan Pesta Menuai Bagi Kaum Kadazan" in KCA, 1982, pp. 20–21.

Noechaelisa, 1983. "Apakah Pesta Hari Menuai bagi Suku Kadazan?" in KCA, 1983, p. 23.

Ongkili, James, 1967. *The Borneo Response to Malaysia 1961–1963*, Singapore: Donald Moore Press.

——, 1972. *Modernization in East Malaysia 1960–1970*, Kuala Lumpur: Oxford University Press.

Pung Chen Choon, 1986. "Kadazans or Dusuns, What's the Difference?" in *Daily Express* 21 December.

Rampasan, L. K., 1989. "Educational Opportunities for the Kadazans: A Preliminary Assessment", unpublished manuscript.

Roff, Margaret, 1969. "The Rise and Demise of Kadazan Nationalism" in *Journal of Southeast Asian History*, 10(2), pp. 326–43.

——, 1974, *The Politics of Belonging: Political Change in Sabah and Sarawak*, Kuala Lumpur: Oxford University Press.

——, 1976. "The Political Enculturation of Fringe Peoples: the Case of East Malaysia". *Review of Indonesian and Malaysian Affairs*, 10(2), pp. 103–112.

Sabah, 1980. *Sabah Regional Planning Study Final Report*, London: Hunting Technical Services Ltd.

Sabah Public Service Commission Annual Report (1970–1980).

Sator, M., 1981. "Kaum Dusun Kadazan dalam Politik Negeri Sabah", B. Soc Sc. Academic Exercise, Department of Politics, Universiti Kebangsaan Malaysia, Bangi, Selangor.

Searle, Peter, 1983. *Politics in Sarawak, 1970–1976: An Iban Perspective*, Kuala Lumpur: Oxford University Press.

Smith, Anthony, 1984. *The Ethnic Origins of Nations*, Oxford: Basil Blackwell.

Soenarno, Radin, 1986. "The Economic Dimension of Territorial Integration". *In The Bonding of a Nation: Federalism and Territorial Integration in Malaysia*, Petaling Jaya: Institute of Strategic and International Studies.

Sta Maria, Bernard, 1978. *Peter J. Mojuntin: The Golden Son of the Kadazans*, Seremban: Chang Litho Press.

Strauch, Judith, 1981. *Chinese Village Politics in the Malaysian State*, Cambridge: Harvard University Press.

Sullivan, A. and C. Leong (eds), 1981. *Commemorative History of Sabah, 1881–1981*, Kota Kinabalu: Sabah State Government Centenary Publications Committee.

Tan Chee Khoon, 1986. *Sabah: A Triumph for Democracy,* Petaling Jaya: Pelanduk.

Tilman, Robert, 1976. "Mustapha's Sabah 1968–1975". *Asian Survey,* 16(6), pp. 495–509.

Tombung, R. (USDA secretary-general), 1987. personal communication, Kota Kinabalu, 13 January.

Topin, B. (KCA executive secretary), 1987. personal communication, Kota Kinabalu, 10 January.

William, V. Gabriel, 1981. "The General State Administration of Sabah, 1881–1981" in Sullivan and Leong (eds), 1981.

Newspapers and Weeklies

Asiaweek	7 June 1985
Daily Express	1978–1988
Far Eastern Economic Review	1980–1985
Start	1980–1988

11

Ethnic Perspectives of the Left in Malaysia

Muhammad Ikmal Said

Either by design or by force of circumstance political organizations in Malaysia end up carving mass support along communal lines. Left and left-leaning political organizations have not been spared of this tendency. Thus, although avowedly non-communal, these political organizations, articulating both civil and communal interests, have appealed and organized mass support along communal lines. The distinction between civil and communal interests is impossible to make when they overlap.

The modern state is very often constructed upon the image, such as language and culture, of a dominant cultural group. Under such circumstances, the right of other groups to their language and culture, both a communal and civil right, poses a direct challenge to the identity of the state. In other words, the struggle for such rights inevitably challenges the dominant group's hold over the state. Such challenges are particularly formidable and wide in scope in territorially-defined nations such as those in the Soviet Union and Yugoslavia. "Simply dwelling within one's autonomous ethnic unit—no matter how circumscribed the authorities declare the unit's powers to be—instills a sense of possession of fundamental proprietary rights" Connor (1984: 501).

Civil and communal interests are often very difficult to separate even when they do not overlap. This is because the struggle for certain interests (say, the fight against poverty, for the right to one's language) is more often taken up seriously only by those who share similar experiences. For a wide variety of reasons (largely due to unequal development, different historical evolution), such causes are most often articulated by their fellow ethnic or national groups. In turn, the reallocation of resources brought about by the need to redress such problems would inevitably affect adversely the resources available for the better-endowed or favoured group. This is also often compounded further by the fact that

---

[1] I wish to thank Dr. Cheah Boon Keng and Dr. Syed Husin Ali for their comments. The usual disclaimer applies.

254

underprivileged ethnic groups also do not readily accept champions from other ethnic groups and that their own champions often discover that it is more efficacious to such causes in certain ethnic terms. As a result, the perception and articulation of civil interests in such societies take an ethnic or national form. In such circumstances, as Connor (1984: 496) argues so convincingly, form "becomes saturated with national content". Consequently, even the struggle for civil interests is defined in ethnic terms, and is perceived, organized and eventually articulated in such terms, making it very difficult for the parties concerned to forge a non-communal political line; an "ethnic trap" of sorts.

Like their comrades elsewhere in the socialist states, the left in Malaysia was also divided along ethnic lines. This was particularly evident in the forties and fifties[2], when the image of the state had yet to be established through civil politics. As a result, divisions among the left tended to differ little from the right *on matters relating to national identity and integration.* The split among the left along ethnic lines in Malaysia is by no means a unique one[3], nor, as we saw above, restricted only to capitalist social formations. Recent events in the socialist countries show quite clearly that ethnicity (or nationalism in other cases) continues to prevail even after capitalist class rule has been overthrown. Violent clashes between Armenians and Azerbaijans in early 1989 over, among other things, Nagorno-Karabakh, and increasing tension between Estonians, Kazakhs, Latvians, Lithuanians, Tajiks and Ukrainians on the one hand, and Great Russians on the other, underscore the continuing salience of ethnicity in Soviet Russia (Cockburn 1989; Connor 1984; Dragadze 1989). Yugoslavia is faced with a similar problem, as it has to meet the persisting conflict between the Serbs and the Croatians and Slovenes. The Chinese are also faced with mounting dissent by Tibetans (in Tibet) and Yugyur minorities (in Xinjiang Province) against the Hans.

These historically diverse cases raise several important questions. Foremost among these is why do left and left-leaning political movements fall back upon deep-seated ethnic symbols, fears, suspicions and interests? Is the appeal to narrow communal interests merely the machinations of contending ethnic elites seeking political support, or is this also a product of certain historical circumstances, where a large cross-section of each ethnic group develops mutually contradictory economic and political interests. Such a situation becomes particularly evident when, as in the case of Malaysia, the different ethnic groups occupy different locations in the

---

[2] The Federation of Malaya achieved its independence from British colonial rule in 1957. The aftermath of the Japanese Occupation during the Second World War offered both radical and conservative groups ample opportunities to usurp and establish state power. Both the Malay and non-Malay left-wing groups had their own version of the new state's identity.

[3] See, for example, Sithole (1980) for the Zimbabwean case.

social division of labour. Some sense of a "cultural division of labour" (Hechter 1976, 1978) is very much ingrained into the political system.

The "cultural division of labour" thesis proposed by Hechter is a highly useful one, for it is able to capture the class and status group dimensions of ethnicity, which Wallerstein (1972) had correctly emphasized. Viewed from this perspective, the conflict between the Chinese and Malay communities in Malaysia is largely due to the contradictory interests they developed arising from their different market positions. Under such conditions, cultural identity becomes an important medium through which the struggle against the inequities of the market is articulated and mobilized. The image of the exploiting immigrant middleman minority and the exploited indigenous peasant communities in Central and Latin America, East Africa and Southeast Asia has often been used to typify, in an ideal-typical way, the relationship between different ethnic groups.

This perspective may also be employed successfully to explain the divergent positions of the Chinese and Malay left-wing political organizations in Malaysia, for in order to secure support from their respective communities these organizations articulated the specific interests of their ethnic group. Thus, although the Chinese based Labour Party of Malaya (LPM) was, in many ways, more radical than the Malay based Partai Rakyat Malaya (PRM), its economic nationalization programme was restricted merely to the transport industry, which, at that time, was very largely state-owned. This, as the PRM argued, reflected the communal edge of LPM's politics, since Chinese capital had a significant stake in other sectors of the economy (Vasil 1971: 171). On the other hand, the PRM could call for a sweeping nationalization programme because there was hardly any Malay capital at that time.

The cultural division of labour thesis regards culture maintenance and expression only as a tool used by the different contending ethnic groups to strive for some form of equality. It is not considered as an important variable in itself. In other words, ethnic solidarity and political mobilization based upon it becomes salient only when cultural distinctions are related to inequalities in the social division of labour.

There are at least two major problems with such an approach. First, since ethnic conflict is viewed as arising from the struggle for economic equality, the source of such conflict is related to economic deprivation. However, as the problems facing Russian nationalities attest, conflict between different cultural groups may also be due to historical and political factors (Connor 1984; Dragadze 1989).[4] Furthermore, the Baltic nationalities, now in the forefront of the struggle for national autonomy/independence from the Soviet Union, are economically better-off than

---

[4] President Gorbachev underscores this point when he remarked at a special Supreme Soviet Presidium meeting on nationalities that "These were not just bursts from machine-guns but complete artillery salvoes from the past" (As quoted in Cockburn 1989: 170).

their Russian counterparts (Cockburn 1989). The Russians themselves are comparably better-off than most other Soviet nationalities, but also feel, like the Slovenes of Yugoslavia, that they are a deprived group (Connor 1984: 485–486).

If economic divisions alone are important in determining ethnicity then one would expect that ethnicity would decline as hitherto deprived ethnic groups are increasingly distributed more evenly in the division of labour. Quite apart from evidence to the contrary, such a view fails to appreciate the fact that the state is more than just a political instrument that expresses the relations between its economic constituents. It is also a highly tensed fusion of different and usually opposing cultural groups under one civil order; the "integrative revolution" as Geertz (1963) puts it. However, the contradiction in that process is not, as Geertz (1963) argues, between "primordial sentiments and civil politics", for such ethnic and national sentiments are neither primordial nor separate and apart from civil politics.

Ethnic sentiments are not primordial, because not all objective cultural groups, say Sri Lankan and South Indian Tamils in Sri Lanka, assume a strong common ethnic identity. Conversely, groups may also assume a common identity even while their objective cultural attributes are not quite similar (the Dayak identity in Sarawak, for example, incorporates such diverse and once rival groups such as the Bidayuh, Iban and the Orang Ulu). This last point illustrates very clearly that ethnicity is also a process in which narrow "primordial" loyalties are merged into a larger identity.

If such loyalties are not primordial, but are formed and reformed by the external environment (capitalism, colonization, modernization, the state), and, further, if ethnicity, as Geertz (1963) himself points out clearly, is an integral part of civil politics, then the contradiction facing such multi-cultural societies is not between "primordial sentiments and civil politics". Communal and civil interests continue to overlap, not just in new states, but also in old states which now have amongst its populace culturally different groups. Thus, as Smith (1988) argues, ethnicity is not an anachronism of the past that has somehow been unable to respond to the demands of the modern state. Rather, it is a contradiction of the basis of the modern state itself.

The modern state is a project which seeks to establish a particular cultural form. What that identity might be is a matter of acrimonious political debate[5], because the eventual identity it assumes would inevitably affect

---

[5] ". . . several African and Asian states which possess the 'civic' elements of nationhood far more effectively than did their late medieval European counterparts, are riven by ethnic cleavages at or very near the centre; typically, two or three main ethnic are engaged in a continuous competition for national power. Their task is to create, out of the often sharply defined ethnic cultures of their component communities, a single overarching culture. But this is not something

the rights of other groups and their development (Connor 1984: 289).
Thus, although cultural and political equality form important pillars for
the attainment of collective aspirations under the modern state, certain
ethnic groups painfully notice that their membership in the modern state
seriously threatens their own cultural and, for "old nations"[6], their historical identity as well. It is precisely the superimposition of the modern state
installed by colonialism upon long-established nations that form the basis
of conflict between the different ethnic groups we know today.

Thus, even while it is true that modern nations have emerged only
with the development of print capitalism (Anderson 1983), and that such
nations in the Third World came into being only with colonialism,[7] it
needs to be emphasized that modern nations that make up the state have
their own pre-modern ethnic histories, which remain relevant until this
day (Smith 1988). The modern Malay nation, for example, emerged clearly
in the forties, when its people rose against their Sultans to object to
the Malayan Union proposal (Cheah 1988), but their nationalist agenda,
that Malaysia's cultural and historical identity rests upon the genealogical
Malay nation (*"bangsa keturunan" Melayu*), will remain a potent source
of belief even after the Malays have attained an economic status comparable to the Chinese. Thus, the civic nation cannot be extricated from its
genealogical past.

The ethnic composition of Malaysia today is the product of colonialism
and the establishment of a new state whose basic structure and citizenry
includes immigrants who came with the colonial tide. Thus, upon independence and the grant of popular sovereignty to a wide cross-section
of the population, the disparate communities had to decide upon critical
questions relating to their respective rights and roles within the new
environment that was actually laid by colonialism. In the Malaysian case,
the long-established Malay cultural nation[8] was, through colonial domination, cut to size (numerically by the inflow of immigrants, and in terms
of power by the loss of political and economic control over their land) and

---

that can easily be manufactured in the classroom or even the peacetime barracks"
(Smith 1988: 11).

[6] "Old nations" refer to "those which had acquired national identity or national
consciousness before the formulation of the doctrine of nationalism" (Seton-Watson
1977: 7).

[7] "When print-capitalism arrived on the scene in a sizeable way after midcentury,
the [Indonesian] language moved out into the marketplace and the media. Used at
first mainly by Chinese and Eurasian newspapermen and printers, it was picked up
by inlanders at the century's close" (Anderson 1983: 121).

[8] This refers to "a community united by language or religion or historical mythol-
ogy or other cultural bonds" (Seton-Watson 1977: 4). An important point that is
left out in this definition is that this cultural bond may be space-bound, giving a
sense of legitimate claim over the sovereignty over that particular cultural area
even while no definite political boundary is attached to it.

transformed into an ethnic group. This meant that it was, from the colonialist's and the immigrant communities' point of view, no different from other ethnic groups; they all are ethnic groups with equal status before the laws of the modern state. Upon independence, all ethnic groups had to "fight it out" for their newly-acquired, but as yet undetermined rights and roles. In addition, they also had to fight against the very structures that inhibited their development while under colonial domination. Therefore, the process of integration had only just begun with independence.

The contradiction between old nations and new multi-national or multi-ethnic states is not something peculiar to the Third World. The First World is currently undergoing the same process as a consequence of its own designs. Europe's nation-states have, in the wake of drawing cheap labour into its borders from the Third World after decolonization, "trans nationalized" their own populations, who, by the grace of popular sovereignty, have as much right in asserting their respective cultural identities. In the process, cultural norms established upon relatively homogenous states are challenged. This last point underscores Smith's argument (1988) that nation-states, particularly those of Europe, are not a wholly modern construct, but are also constituted in the image of the older ethnic upon which they first emerged.

One other consequence of recognizing the importance of the historical dimensions of ethnic conflict is the realization that colonialism might, in other circumstances, also aggravate old animosities that continue to be perpetuated even while the contending communities are confronted with an external threat. This is predictably true for political movements that are dominated by the middle and upper classes. However, left-wing political movements have also found it difficult to distance themselves from ethnic considerations. As a result, recruitment and participation within these political movements, and, subsequently, the distribution of spoils after independence within these territories have an ethnic slant. Differences between the predominantly Chinese Malayan Communist Party and the Malayan People's Anti-Japanese Army on the one hand and the predominantly Malay Pembela Tanah Air during the Japanese Occupation are a case in point. The experience of the (ruling) Marxist Partido Africano de Independencia (PAIGC) of Guinea Bissau provides an equally good example.[9] It is evident, therefore, that history moulds the present in

---

[9] The PAIGC drew its supporters largely from the Balanta ethnic group. This was because the Balanta, the last to succumb to, but which suffered most under Portuguese colonial rule, could identify its interests with the PAIGC. On the other hand, the Fula, who in the 1800s forced their way into Guinea Bissau at the expense of the Balanta and the Mandinga, manned the commando units of the Portuguese colonial army and continued to resist PAIGC rule. As a result, the politics and distribution of the spoils of independence in socialist Guinea Bissau have also taken an ethnic form (Lyon 1980). See also Connor (1984: 287).

a surprisingly continuous way even though traditional Guinea Bissau had been transformed into a colonial capitalist enclave and, subsequently, a socialist republic.

Thus, left-wing political movements have often found it difficult, if not impossible, to disassociate themselves, implicitly or otherwise, from the cultural and even economic interests of a particular ethnic group. However, decisions over such critical issues often tend to perpetuate the ethnic basis of politics, and more important, make it difficult for these political organizations to isolate themselves from the demands of their supporters on other issues that might equally have an ethnic dimension to them. This fine line puts any political party in a difficult situation, and risks suffering further into the "ethnic trap" I referred to earlier. Thus, what issues are raised and how they are articulated determines the kind of support a political party gets. Likewise, the kind of support also determines the issues political parties pick to emphasize, and the way they are articulated. Decisions upon such issues are concretely difficult ones. It involves making concrete decisions regarding the ethnic composition of leaders and members, the target population, area of influence (where branch offices should be set up and what political and welfare activities ought to be carried out, etc.).

This paper examines only the record of left-wing political organizations regarding issues of national integration, and the consequences this might have had upon national integration and the development of left-wing politics in the country. No attempt is made here to deny that the Malay and Chinese left agreed and fought together on many other issues.

The first part of the discussion examines the extent to which left-wing political organizations in Malaysia may be regarded as communal. This will be followed by a discussion on the politics of that division. The final section traces the divergent positions of the different groups in their particular conception of national integration. A critical evaluation of these different approaches to the "national question" offers a preliminary attempt at redefining the agenda.

Ethnic Perspectives of the Left

Left-wing political organizations and parties are no less ethnically divisive than their right counterparts. The historical evolution of the Malays and the non-Malays are vastly different. Yet they have to evolve together. The perspectives they develop and the solutions they offer to resolve the contradictions of this process stem from their different historical experiences that cut across class lines. This appears to me as the great divide between the Malay and non-Malay communities. This is particularly because differences in their historical evolution also overlapped with their unequal stations in the social division of labour (Muhammad Ikmal 1980). The discussion below examines the socio-historical basis of differences between the Chinese and Malay left.

Like their rightist counterparts, the left is characterized by an absence of agreement on fundamentals about the nature of national integration. These fundamentals include the right to citizenship (which, due to the passage of time, no longer constitutes a critical problem), the right to equal representation, the right to one's culture and the preservation of vernacular schools, and the right to equal opportunities. It is basically a tussle over "*bumiputera*" and "minority" rights between the Malays on the one hand, and non-Malays on the other. Being "sons of the soil", Malays lay claim to "ownership" of the country. This means that only they can decide, alone or with consultation with other communities, what rights non-Malays can enjoy.

"This Land Belongs to the Malays"

It is fairly evident that the Malay claim to political superiority is based upon their claim to ownership of the country, where they have evolved historically in communities or states, with a fairly distinct civilization and culture (Ismail 1990; Rahman 1985). The process of colonial domination clearly arrested its development. However, the centralization of the state apparatus under the nominal direction of Malay Sultans acting upon the "advice" of British officials and the "pro-Malay" policies of the colonial administration appears to have provided an important smokescreen that the land remains under Malay sovereignty (Cheah 1983: 15–16; Roff 1967: 250). Furthermore, the problem of citizenship, and, by implication, equal rights never really emerged, for colonial domination rested upon the subjugation of a set of people under colonial rule. Even so, the threat posed by the two large immigrant communities was feared by the Malays. They were seen as "colonial parasites sucking away the wealth of their country hand in hand with British colonialism" (Cheah 1983: 16). Worse, they competed for the same resources, had little regard for the Malays and even demanded economic and political concessions from the British (Firdaus 1985: 58–59).[10] Such nominal control was no less important as it constituted the last bastion for any future claim to political power, which also forms their only defense against a slightly larger and economically more powerful non-Malay population. It was fully realized that the force of the free market and equal rights would have brought an irreversible process of decay upon the Malays in their own land.

---

[10] For example, Lim Ching Yan, a Chinese member of the Penang Legislative Council, was quoted to have retorted "Who said this is a Malay country? . . . This is ours, our country" (as quoted in Radin (1960: 11). Rahman (1985: 42–43) expresses Malay annoyance of the immigrant communities eloquently: "The process of Malayization that hitherto succeeded in containing the distinct differences of the foreigners was not effective. Foreigners, with their large numbers and sponsorship under British protection, are now capable of living independently of Malay society

The non-Malay threat became particularly real when the predominantly Chinese Malayan Communist Party (MCP) and the Malayan People's Anti-Japanese Army (MPAJA) imposed a "reign of terror" during the interregnum (between the middle of August and early September, 1945. Malays found themselves helpless and humiliated under the military might of the Chinese. They were subjected not only to armed attacks but also to public scorn and religious insults (Cheah 1983: 197, 231).[11] The second serious challenge to Malay sovereignty came from the Malayan Union Proposals, which was announced in October, 1945, just a few months after the violent Sino-Malay clashes. Basically, the Malayan Union Proposals wanted to do away with the sovereignty of the Malay rulers, the autonomy of the Malay states and the special position of the Malay community (Stockwell 1979: 17). Opposition from the Malay community was so widespread that the British withdrew the Malayan Union Proposals.[12]

The Malay left, including the Kesatuan Melayu Muda (Union of Malay Youth), the Partai Kebangsaan Melayu (Malay Nationalist Party) and Angkatan Pemuda Insaf (API, Conscious Youth Force) and even Pusat Tenaga Rakyat (PUTERA, Center of People's Power) also shared the view that Malays have a special claim to the country. The short-lived KMM, for instance, propagated *kemerdekaan Melayu* (Malay independence) from British rule within the context of *Melayu Raya* (sometimes interchangeably called *Indonesia Raya*), the Greater Malay nation-state, where "all Malays in one region should come together and see themselves as One Race, speaking One Language, and belonging to One Nation . . ." (Cheah 1983: 11). It was as Ishak Hj. Muhammad, a leading member of the KMM and later, the President of the MNP and Chairman of the Labour Party of Malaya (1957–58) as well, states, a call to "stop the Malays [from] being exploited by other races" (Roff 1967: 232).

Radical Malay political organizations of the Japanese Occupation (such as KRIS, PETA) and the post World War Two period (such as the MNP, API and PUTERA) subscribed consistently to the *Melayu Raya*

---

and practise, retain and promote their own customs within their own confines. Apart from the fine bonds, inclination and loyalty to their country of origin they also, for reasons related to British encouragement and sponsorship of their immigration, generally show more respect and sense of gratitude to the English" (My translation).

[11] A group of MPAJA guerillas was said to have slaughtered some pigs in a village mosque in Batu Pahat, Johor, after which Malays were forced to join them in the feast (Cheah 1983: 197). In Batu Pahat and Sungai Manik, Perak, members of the Malayan People's Anti-Japanese Union, the political and civil arm of the MPAJA, urged Malays there to change their Friday prayers to Sunday (Cheah 1983: 231).

[12] The Malays were economically and politically weak, but the fear of being submerged further as a nation brought about an unprecedented surge of anger on both occassions. Sovereignty, Stockwell (1979: 74) comments, "is often expressed the most vigorously when the authority it is seeking to justify is the least secure".

idea.[13] The KMM and, subsequently, the Pembela Tanah Air (PETA)[14] and Kesatuan Rakyat Istimewa (KRIS), actively collaborated with the Japanese with the hope of gaining independence and restoring Malay sovereignty within a federation of *Indonesia Raya*. Although this was initially aimed at toppling British colonialism, it also served subsequently as an important strategy against the possibility of a Chinese take-over through the MCP/MPAJA (Cheah 1985: 102–103, 119). Like the MCP's/MPAJA's approach to the Chinese community, the KMM and KRIS also rallied its cause through a united front of different sections of the Malay community, including members of the bureaucratic elite and aristocracy (Cheah 1983: 47, 105, 120).

In his analysis of the Malay nation, Dr. Burhanuddin Al Helmy, President of the MNP between 1945 and 1947, reiterated that it was through foreign trade that the Malay nation, once a singular entity under the Sri Wijaya and Melaka empires, came to be subjugated and divided by foreigners (Burhanuddin 1980: 31–35).[15] Therefore, the liberation of the Malays must be achieved via the formation of *Melayu Raya*. The highly romanticized *Melayu Raya* was based upon a glorious past. However, it probably simultaneously appealed to the uncertainties and fear of the Malays, who were outnumbered slightly by the Chinese and Indian communities in the thirties and forties (Cheah 1985: 101; Rahman 1985: 45). It was envisaged that this Malay nation would be comprised of a Malay nationality (*bangsa Melayu*), a national identity and citizenship that could be adopted by Chinese, Europeans and Indians who choose to make Malaya their home. What adoption of this nationality meant was not quite clear, as it tended to differ according to the different factions within the

---

[13] The MNP's platform contained in its 1945 constitution had eight items. The first of these was "To unite the Malayan races, to instil the spirit of nationalism in the hearts of the Malays and to aim at uniting Malaya within the larger family i.e. the Republic of Greater Indonesia" (Khoo 1981: 187). The remaining seven called for the observance of fundamental liberties, the upgrade of the Malays' economic position, the abolition of agricultural land tax and the freedom of farmers to market their produce, complete freedom for Malays to establish their national schools, encouraging the publication of books for the promotion of democracy and Malay nationalism, fostering friendly relations with other domiciled races to create a united and prosperous Malaya within the context of the Republik Indonesia Raya and support for the Indonesian nationalist movement. See also Firdaus (1985: 79–80).

[14] PETA was the Malay name for the Giyu Gun (Stockwell 1979: 12). It was a predominantly Malay volunteer army formed under the Japanese Military Administration which Ibrahim Yaacob, who had earlier requested the Japanese to establish a Malay army, hoped to transform into a real military force (Cheah 1983: 109).

[15] "... kedua-dua kerajaan Melayu inilah yang menjadi asas bentuk contoh Nasional Raya atau Kebangsaan Melayu Raya bangsa kita" (Burhanuddin 1980: 87).

MNP. Burhanuddin (1980: 115)[16] adopted an assimilationist attitude, which, for obvious reasons, was totally unacceptable to non-Malays. On the other hand, Ishak Haji Muhammad was much more moderate, and did not insist on assimilation by the non-Malays (Khoo 1981: 181). But the MNP leadership was very united as far as the Malay claim to ownership of the country was concerned. This was stated very explicitly by Ishak Hj. Muhammad, then Vice President of the MNP and Chairman of Pusat Tenaga Rakyat (PUTERA), the coalition of Malay progressive forces (including the MNP, API, Hizbul Muslimin, AWAS, GERAM) against the Anglo-UMNO collaboration in drafting an alternative constitution for post-war Malaya:

> The Pusat Tenaga Rakyat . . . though it holds that Malaya is fundamentally the country of the Malays, also holds that all foreigners who have permanently settled in our country are also Malay nationals, whether they are Chinese, Indians or Europeans. I must say plainly, however, that in the Chinese, Indian and European communities there will have to be a clear-cut division very soon as to those who wish to become Malay nationals and those who are to remain Overseas Chinese, Overseas Indians and Overseas Europeans. The MNP believes that there is no room in this world of the atomic age for small isolated countries and that the free Malaya of the future should become part of Indonesia as it was before.[17]

API was also very clearly a Malay political organization. The first item in its first manifesto strives for the establishment of a democratic government and "an open declaration of the sovereignty of the Malay people" (Means 1970: 96). Boestamam's endearing description (1972: 129–131) of Gerald de Cruz's willingness to mingle readily among the Malays and adapt to their culture suggests further that the Malay left, Burhanuddin's more extreme view notwithstanding, envisioned, or at least desired, some degree of assimilation of Malay culture on the part of non-Malays as an indication of Malay sovereignty.[18]

API was banned in 1948 and the MNP disbanded in 1950. Members of both organizations later regrouped in the *Kongres Pemuda* (Youth

---

[16] "Today the door to Melayu nationality is still open through a practice which has come to be termed "JADI MELAYU" or "MASUK MELAYU". This term is often used by foreigners such as the Chinese, the Indians, the Siamese etc. who have changed their nationality by adopting Malay culture, transforming their original identity in to Malay identity and thereafter have lived and died as Malays" (trans. by Khoo 1981: 179–180).

[17] *Malayan Daily News* 23 March 1947. As quoted in Stenson (1980: 124).

[18] Gerald de Cruz was a journalist and a leading member of the predominantly non-Malay Malayan Democratic Union. Boestamam (1971: 131) concluded his narration of de Cruz by raising a highly important and politically sensitive issue that is often hidden behind more formal principles: "I intentionally wrote at some length about de Cruz because I wish to pose a question to today's prominent

Congress), which was held in April 1955, along lines very similar to those of the MNP (Firdaus 1985: 153–154). Subsequently, this regroupment later led to the formation of the Partai Rakyat Malaya (PRM) in November, 1955. Although the PRM's idea of *Melayu Raya* was not formulated explicitly either in its conference resolutions or in its constitution and political manifesto, there is no doubt that the creation of the "Malay Homeland", consisting of Malaya, Singapore, Sarawak, North Borneo and Brunei (with strong links with Indonesia) formed an important object of its struggle (Vasil 1971: 171). The idea of *Melayu Raya* and "Malay Homeland" was partially revived with the creation of Maphilindo, which the Labour Party of Malay (LPM) rejected strongly as a "racial plot". Thus, the LPM and PRM again found themselves at odds with each other.

The lines drawn between the different left-wing political parties up till 1965 remain substantially similar today, although the Chinese left is no longer identifiable with any political party.

Equal Rights

Except for the brief but highly significant AMCJA-PUTERA[19] alliance between 1947 and 1948, the non-Malay left has consistently adopted a directly opposing view regarding their position *vis-a-vis* the Malays. The central rallying call of the non-Malay left revolves around their demand for equal rights within a liberated Malaya.

The earliest of these was the MCP, which grew out of the Kuomintang and the Nanyang Communist Party, both of which were oriented to China and matters Chinese. After its initial failure to mobilize Malay peasants and Indian workers, the predominantly Chinese MCP set the tone for subsequent non-Malay left-wing agitation by encouraging the different communities to "pursue their own separate racial or national struggles" (Cheah 1983: 57). This paved the way for its mobilization of the Chinese community through the anti-Japanese China Salvation Movement (1937–1941). This exacerbated further its identification with the Chinese community, which, even the MCP realized, had not yet developed a Malayan

---

non-Malay leaders of solidarity: 'Who among you would be willing to practice, not just theorize, such solidary behaviour as de Cruz did 27 years ago?'" (My translation). Ishak's speech quoted above also complained that "We realise that our hospitality has been too much taken for granted by some people. For instance, some of our guests have been allowed to own as much land as they desired to possess, to trade freely, to educate their children as they wish, to work in the service of our government and to exploit the wealth of this country to their heart's content. And these are the same people, who have countries of their own—rich, vast and beautiful—are demanding they should be given their due rights in this country" (*Malayan Daily News*, 24 March 1947; as quoted in Stenson (1980: 124).
[19] The AMCJA refers to the All-Malaya Joint Council for Action.

consciousness (Cheah 1985: 88–89). This and Japanese terrorization of the Chinese community between 1941 and 1945 reproduced specifically communal tendencies within the MCP/MPAJA.[20] This was particularly evident during the interregnum when MPAJA groups proclaimed that "the Chinese were going to rule Malaya and that the country would be liberated by the Chinese army" (Stenson 1980: 107).[21] Meanwhile, the Malay left collaborated with the Japanese with the hope of gaining independence and insure against a possible Chinese take-over. All these added to the mutual distrust between the Chinese and Malay left. Unfortunately, the turn of events was so rapid (the interregnum and proclamation of the Malayan Union were in the same year) that the distrust formed an important basis for Sino-Malay relations for many years to come.

In 1943, while Malaya was still under Japanese Occupation, the MCP proclaimed a nine-point programme, three of which indicate quite clearly its view regarding the position of non-Malays. The first of these concerns the establishment of a "National Organization composed of representatives universally elected from the different nationalities to govern our motherland". The second refers to the reorganization of the Anti-Japanese Army into the "National Army of Defence which will defend our territory", while the third states that "[f]ree education will be practiced universally in the various national languages by the different nationalities in order to develop National Culture" (Purcell 1967: 261). The first and third programmes were reiterated later in May 1946 (Hanrahan 1971: 93–94). Both these programmes, Hanrahan (1971: 95) observes, "were meant to appeal directly to the Overseas Chinese and Indians. . .". The former proposal was spelt in clearer terms in the later part of the year when it recommended "equal citizenship be granted to all peoples, and that the qualifications for gaining Malayan citizenship be simplified. . . only then, more Malayan Chinese and Malayan Indians would contribute their share in the work of rehabilitating Malaya".[22] In September, 1946 it organized a massive demonstration in Singapore, demanding self-rule and equal rights to all communities (Yeo 1973: 35). Thus, in contrast to the Malay left's

---

[20] "Throughout the war, the political orientation of the Chinese in Malaya towards China, especially to the more popular government of Chiang Kai-shek in Chungking, was growing stronger as many Chinese hoped for deliverance from the Japanese regime by Chiang's army" (Cheah 1983: 46). A significant proportion of the MCP's leaders were Overseas Chinese. Ninety-five per cent of the MPAJA's/MPAJU's membership was Chinese, many of whom were not communists. Mandarin was its *lingua franca*, and Malay cultural and religious sensitivities were hardly taken into account (Cheah 1983: 63–73; Hanrahan 1971: 76).

[21] See also Hanrahan (1971: 88). The MPAJA's arrogance is reflected in Cheah's paraphrase (1983: 72–73) of its attitude towards the Malays: "We can be victorious in our resistance struggle without the support of the Malays. We have done without them so far, we can continue to do without them".

[22] *Democrat*, 1 December 1946; as quoted in Hanrahan (1971: 96).

view of the special historical position of the Malays, the MCP insisted on equality of rights among all nationalities. As subsequent events were to show, this became translated to mean the right to Chinese rights. Competition against the conservative Malayan Chinese Association (MCA) under repressive conditions during the "Emergency" and its realization that "it was by attaching itself to national—i.e. Chinese—causes that the party had made most headway in the past" (Short 1970: 1082) pushed the MCP deeper into the communal end. It made considerable efforts to regain its previous strength by reverting to the rural areas, where Chinese had been resettled in "New Villages" and politicizing Chinese education under the "Defend Racial Culture" banner, which "in practice meant "Defend Chinese Culture" and, in particular, Chinese education" (Short 1970: 1085). The emphasis upon the struggle for Chinese rights continued right up till the late sixties, even if that meant risking "Malay progressive forces to leave us temporarily", and that "a bit of (racial) tension is not to be afraid of. In fact it will serve more effectively in educating and training the people".[23]

The basic sentiment underlying the MCP programmes was shared by the Malayan Democratic Union (MDU). Its leadership argued that the provisions for citizenship should be open to all communities, and not defined in terms that gave special preference to the Malays (Means 1970: 83). In turn, citizens of all communities above 21 years of age shall be given the right to vote. It was also perhaps in reference to "pro-Malay" British policies in government employment that the MDU's platform included in its eight-point manifesto the need for complete equality in employment for all races. The MDU played a central role in forging the multi-racial AMCJA-PUTERA alliance which drafted the historic "People's Constitution". Even so, the historic compromises between the Malay left and the non-Malay left still showed that "the major differences between the two groups were still ranged along communal lines" (Yeo 1973: 46).[24]

The MDU dismantled in 1948, partially as a result of the withdrawal of MCP support, following its disenchantment with the constitutional struggle and increasing British repression. It was not until the mid-fifties that the non-Malay left-wing began to assert itself again, this time under the Labour Party Of Malaya (LPM).

The historical evolution of the Labour Party is somewhat similar to the MCP. As for the latter, it too became increasingly communal in the process of articulating equal rights for the non-Malay communities. This became particularly evident when it "moved further to the left in an attempt to attract larger support among the working classes, particularly those of Chinese origin" (Vasil 1970: 111). A *putsch* by the Chinese-educated against the English-educated leadership in April 1956 subsequently

---

[23] Government Of Malaysia *The Path of Violence to Absolute Power*, K.L., as quoted in Short (1970: 1087).
[24] Means (1970: 86) shares this view.

consolidated this trend. Significantly, the Fourth National Conference demanded recognition of the MCP and liberal citizenship provisions (Vasil 1970: 114). Its memorandum to the Reid Commission, announced in late September 1956, categorically rejected "the false premise that Malaya belongs to any one race . . .". It further stated that all Malayan nationals should enjoy equal rights, and that the special position of the Malays should be abolished. Malay was recognized as the national language but English, Chinese and Indian languages should be taught in schools and spoken in the councils: "everything must be done to promote and foster the development of these cultures and languages in the Malayan context".[25] The Malay Rulers were to be made constitutional monarchs, but whose succession would have to be confirmed by a referendum (Vasil 1970: 115–117).[26]

The consolidation of Malay political supremacy within the Alliance government and, paradoxically, the LPM's alliance with the PRM within the Socialist Front pushed the LPM further into communal politics right up till its demise in 1966 (Vasil 1970: 119–121).

The Politics of Bumiputera and Minority Rights

The discussion above shows that both Chinese and Malay left-wing political parties have held fundamentally opposing views regarding national integration. Thus, although the MCP/MPAJA, PMCJA and the LPM on the one side and KMM, PETA, KRIS, MNP and PRM on the other were anti-colonial and socialistic, they could not agree to the rights of the different communities. This had far-reaching consequences upon their ability to forge any form of alliance and the direction such forms might take.

Let us first look at the MCP/MPAJA—KMM/PETA/KRIS situation. Each of the two parties had different enemies, and inevitably clashed in the process. There was hardly any dialogue between the two parties as they were fighting different "battles" before the War, which were subsequently transformed into a common one with the invasion of the Japanese. But they were on different sides. The KMM/PETA/KRIS collaborated with the Japanese with the hope of gaining independence. On

---

[25] The LPM's position on Chinese language and education, as indicated by its reaction to the Rahman Talib Report, was particularly opposed to the PRM's, which in 1960, led to Ahmad Boestamam's resignation from the Socialist Front's chairmanship. In 1966, it demanded that Mandarin and Tamil be made official languages.

[26] Its Sixth National Conference in August 1958 basically upheld the same political line. However, the special position of the Malays for economic upliftment was not contested, owing largely to its alliance with the PRM in the Socialist Front. It also did not insist its position on citizenship and language be contained in the Socialist Front Manifesto published in 1959.

the other hand, the predominantly Chinese MCP/MPAJA collaborated with the British against violent Japanese reprisals for their anti-Japanese activities beginning from 1941. A head-on political and military encounter was, therefore, inevitable, and rendered ineffective whatever tacit agreement they could have made to overthrow the imperialists (Cheah 1983: 72, 96–97). Although the failure of this agreement could be attributed to Lai Teck's (the MCP Secretary-General) double-agent activities, the violent post-war Sino-Malay clashes indicated that the gulf between the MCP/MPAJA and the KMM/PETA/KRIS was very real and deep-seated. Thus, the very process of identifying and actively supporting one colonizer against the other brought them into direct confrontation.

It is, of course, true that the MCP/MPAJA did not take Malay sensitivities into account. However, the driving wedge appears to be more fundamental than that, for as Cheah (1983: 299) concludes correctly,

Even if these were missed opportunities for the Malay nationalists in the KMM and the Chinese communists and guerrillas in the MCP/MPAJA to strike out their own paths to power and national independence, had either group made a definite move in that direction, it is doubtful if the other group or race would have accepted the *fait accompli*. There was bound to be Chinese resistance to *Indonesia Raya*, just as it was certain Malays would have resisted a [Chinese] communist republic. Neither the KMM nor the MCP had the vital ingredient—Malay-Chinese unity or multiracial unity as a whole—to forge a combined spirit of struggle for independence and national liberation.

As I have pointed out earlier, Chinese suspicion of *Indonesia Raya* stems from the fact that they would be far outnumbered by the Malays, while Malay fears of the predominantly Chinese MCP/MPAJA stems from their disrespect for Malay sovereignty.

The lack of effective co-operation between the MCP/MPAJA on the one hand and KMM/PETA/KRIS on the other is also due to the problem of leadership, as any decision to forge an alliance would have to take into account the possibility of assuming leadership for the joint movement. The problem of "leadership" predictably recurred in the AMCJA-PUTERA and Socialist Front alliance.

The AMCJA-PUTERA, was a fairly successful political alliance between the Malay left and non-Malays groups of various political shades, but led mainly by the left-wing MDU. Yet, fundamental differences between the two communities were evident. Like the problem of leadership offered by the MCP/MPAJA and the KMM, the tussle for leadership in the Pan-Malayan Council For Joint Action (PMCJA), the predecessor of the AMCJA-PUTERA coalition, was defined similarly in Malay—non-Malay terms. John Eber's letter to Tan Cheng Lock (Yeo 1973: 37) reveals the parameters of the issue:

... I am convinced that it would be a mistake to have the MNP
as chairman, because the Council needs an individual who is
MALAYAN as a focus.

The Malay-Malayan distinction was heavily ideological (Firdaus 1985:
95–96; Rahman 1985), and Eber was fully aware of its implications.[27] For
as Burhanuddin (1980: 108) was to articulate it later, "[t]he conflict between Melayu and Malayan will not end. Malayan follows the colonial
mould, it belittles and destroys the Malay nation or Malay nationalism,
that demands the return of its sovereign rights, that is wider than the
Malayan demand" (My translation). The MNP threatened to withdraw,
and subsequently withdrew from the PMCJA upon failing to secure its
leadership, and formed its own Malay left-wing coalition called PUTERA
(Yeo 1973: 39).[28]

The disagreement over leadership was resolved by the appointment of
the MNP to the chair of the Joint Working Committee of the AMCJA-
PUTERA. It opened up a wide area of agreement and co-operation hitherto unknown between Malays and non-Malays. However, the solution to
the problem of leadership subsequently laid bare the fact that it formed
only one dimension of the political agenda. Although the famous "People's
Constitution" produced by this coalition is a remarkable inter-communal
compromise, the coalition was actually very seriously divided over the
provisions of citizenship and the "Melayu" nationality, as it hung upon a
very simple majority—a tenous basis for sustained co-operation indeed
(Boestamam 1972: 135–136).[29] The demise of the AMCJA-PUTERA was
no doubt due partly to the bourgeois factions (particularly the Chinese
Chambers of Commerce and the Malayan Indian Congress) within the
AMCJA, which were weary of the left and predictably defected to the
British and the Malay conservative leadership. However, the MCP also
had an invisible hand, for it was not happy with the coalition's alternative
constitution, nor, by then, the constitutional struggle. For the MCP, the

---

[27] In another letter to Tan Cheng Lock, Eber wrote: "We want the Malay Rulers
to have full sovereignty, accepting the position of constitutional monarchs by
undertaking to accept the advice of their State Legislative Councils ... Such a
claim would, I think, not only avoid 'bloodshed' but would, on the contrary, bring
the Malay masses solidly in behind us, and, by proof of 'bona fides' wean them
to some extent off their fear of being called 'Malayans'" (As quoted in Yeo 1973:
38).

[28] Incidentally, except for two additional items, PUTERA's principles were ident-
ical with the PMCJA's. These include the stand that Malay should be the national
language and that the people of Malaya should have a national flag and a national
anthem. See Firdaus (1985: 93–93), Yeo (1973).

[29] The way Boestaman (1972: 136) described his decision to vote for the *jus soli*
citizenship principle must sound patronizing to non-Malays, or perhaps even to
Malays of today's generation: "a child adopted since birth is more loyal to his
adopted parents than one adopted when he/she has matured" (My translation).

"People's Constitution" was laid upon an incorrect basis (Cheah 1979: 89–90). A comparison of the MCP's line of 1943 and 1946 and the "People's Constitution" shows, its objection stems from its totally divergent view on "the national question". The withdrawal of its support, through the 300,000-strong Pan-Malayan Federation Of Trade Unions, was an important factor contributing to the eventual split of the AMCJA-PUTERA coalition. Thus, the split of the AMCJA-PUTERA was not just a class, but, more important, also a nationality issue.

The Socialist Front also failed on account of the inability of Malays and non-Malays to agree upon the same fundamentals. The diametrically opposed positions of the LPM and the PRM regarding the national language and the national system of education reflect this. The LPM consistently pursued a strongly "equal rights" line even while it was in the Socialist Front, although there were occasions when they were not insisted upon formally.[30] On the other hand, the PRM emphasized Malay as the national language and the institution of a national system of education based upon the national language. The government's 'Rahman Talib Report' (1960) reflected the PRM's sentiment but drew heavy criticisms from the LPM, for full government assistance would be given only to schools that conformed to the national-type system and that all official, national and public examinations would be conducted either in Malay or English. Both these recommendations meant that Chinese schools could receive aid only if they agreed to surrender their autonomy and that vernacular education would be restricted to primary schools only. Boestamam, the Socialist Front's Chairman, resigned in protest against the LPM's stance. Although a compromise was struck and Ahmad Boestamam resumed the chairmanship, the LPM issued a policy statement subsequently in 1961 which restated its original position. Thus, as Vasil remarks (1971: 139), "[t]he compromise was only a compromise of convenience among the leaders of the two member parties of the Front. It was never accepted by the rank and file".

Disagreement over fundamentals about national integration made it difficult for the Malay and non-Malay left to climb out of their respective communal moulds. Thus, although the nature of the AMCJA-PUTERA and Socialist Front coalitions progressed far beyond what the KMM/PETA/KRIS-MCP/MPAJA ever attempted to do, nonetheless, they

---

[30] At its Sixth National Conference, held in August 1958, the party called for (a) linguistic cultural autonomy (b) six years free and compulsory education in the vernacular language, and Malay be made a compulsory subject; secondary education ought to be run along the same lines (c) there should be equal citizenship for all. The LPM's position on non-Malay languages was not incorporated into the Socialist Front's election manifesto in 1959. Even so, its election campaigns relied considerably upon Chinese sentiments for multi-lingualism and the promotion of Chinese education (Vasil 1971: 132).

failed to articulate their respective communal interests from a broader perspective.[31]

It must be remembered also that the right-wing parties compete along the same lines, and were (and are) much more competent at it. For they can refer to the constituents' economic and political needs without threatening the *status quo*. On the other hand, the left can only harp on the communal line by questioning the *status quo* within their own communities. Therefore, their communal appeal appears to be directed only to certain sections of their respective communities, compromising their ideological image in the process. As a result, their "half-hearted" communalism and left-wing tendencies appeal to neither their community nor to their partners. They were, therefore, caught in a bind, as it was difficult to avoid the communal trap (that is, the incessant demand by their respective members for representation of their communal interests) while at the same time maintaining these class-based programmes.[32]

This "ethnic trap" has an internal dimension that subjects coalition partners to a continuous strain. As it can be expected, the basic party ("communal") line determines the ethnicity of its leadership and membership. In turn, the character of its leadership and membership determines the party line. This was clearly evident, for instance, when the PRM rejected a large number of applications from members of the deregistered, predominantly-Chinese National Union Of Factory And General Workers in 1958; as "a large number of Chinese in the party would change its racial balance" (Vasil 1971: 124). However, if the numbers are limited, recruitment could be considered without reference to ethnic considerations. Paradoxically, the relationship between the LPM and the PRM could be tested on such occasions. For instance, the *Annual Report of Socialist Front, 1958–59* noted:

> The Raayat attempted to enlarge itself on a non-communal basis. It began to take in Chinese non-Muslim members and in one or two cases there was a misunderstanding between the Labour Party and Raayat because of this, e.g. in Province Wellesley and in Salak

---

[31] The *Annual Report of Socialist Front, 1958–59* provides an insight into this: "Already the PPP and PMIP were threatening to tear the country apart by their dangerous [communal] propaganda, and this we found was also beginning to have some effect on the thinking of certain leaders of our party who began to question whether our non-communal stand could stand up against the strong emotional appeal of communalism in the forthcoming struggle and some were therefore inclined towards a certain degree of communalism for the purpose of the election campaign" (As quoted in Vasil 1971: 190).

[32] "The link-up had not helped the Party Raayat at all in the elections. In fact, the leadership of the party had a strong feeling that the association had done more harm than good. Being linked with an essentially Chinese party, controlled by Chinese chauvinists, it had found it extremely difficult to operate among the Malays" (Vasil 1971: 221).

areas. Since the problem of penetrating the *kampongs* is a much more difficult task, the Raayat began to develop in areas similar to that of the areas covered by the Labour Party, i.e. the Chinese suburbs and New Villages.[33]

The quotation above indicates further another important dimension of the great divide: there is a proprietary claim over ethnicity of following. In this case, it appears that there was a tacit understanding, as was true among communal parties in the Alliance, that each left party was to recruit members essentially along ethnic lines.

By so defining the "sphere of influence" along ethnic lines, the LPM became increasingly strapped to a communal belt. Following their poor showing in the 1955 general elections and particularly with the formation of the Socialist Front in August 1957, the LPM did not worry about the Malay constituency and decided to move further left (by including in its programme demands to do away with the Sultans, and granting recognition of the MCP)[34] and Chinese, particularly by emphasizing equal rights between the different ethnic groups.[35]

The entry of the Chinese-educated Chinese working class following these overtures (and disenchantment with the conservative Malayan Chinese Association) gradually transformed the character of the party into "an essentially Chinese communal and pro-Comminist (pro-Peking) party" (Vasil 1971: 158).

Similarly, an arguably "progressive" position was also compromised in order to seek support from an identifiable ethnic community. The PRM's economic programme boldly called for nationalization of the means of production, whereas the LPM restricted its nationalization proposal merely to the transport industry, which was largely already state-owned. This, the PRM argued, reflected the communal tone of LPM's politics (Vasil 1971: 171). However, upon coalition with the LPM, the PRM softened its radical line: its call for nationalization was to be restricted to all foreign-owned rubber estates, tin mines, transport companies and plantations" (Vasil 1971: 174).

It is clear from the discussion above that the absence of agreement upon the national question, that is, the rights of the different "nationalities", as it were, has institutionalized communal politics among the Malay and non-Malay left as well. This explains why they could only form inter-ethnic coalitions, which, by their very nature, thrived upon communal interests.

---

[33] As quoted in Vasil (1971: 190).

[34] Vasil (1971: 111–114).

[35] These were couched strongly in negative terms: it rejected "the false premise that Malaya belongs to one race . . .". It also strongly opposed the attempt by one race "to dominate other races or to maintain and extend its privileges over the others" (LPM, *Memorandum to the Reid Commission, 1956*; as quoted in Vasil (1971: 115–116).

Left-wing communal politics is a contradiction in terms and practice. The "ethnic trap" they got into tore them into irreconcilable directions. It might be argued that ethnic politics was actually institutionalized by the conservative political parties, and that the left were helplessly sucked into the same process. One need only be reminded that the different political positions of the Malay and Chinese left were made even before Independence. The experiences of socialist Eastern Europe also points out very clearly that communal politics is as much an integral part of the process of socialist reconstruction.

The "National Question"—Towards a Reformulation

The *bumiputera*—non-*bumiputera* conflict is arguably the most prominent, if not the principal contradiction in post-war Malaysian politics. Vasil (1980), for example, views this as the main internal contradiction of the Malaysian political system. With the Federation of Malaya Agreement (1948), Malaya no longer belonged to the Malays only, but to the Malays and non-Malays jointly: consequently, "[t]he non-Malays were now determined to convert their multi-racial nation of the Malaysian constitution into a genuine reality while the Malays began to look for more effective and lasting means to protect and promote Malaysia as Tanah Melayu" (Vasil 1980: 211). The centrality of the Malay—non-Malay conflict is evident from the involvement of the Malay and non-Malay left in communal politics and their inability to get out of the "ethnic trap". It also continually manifests itself in the continuing debate, political or otherwise, on the special rights of the Malays and the equal rights of minorities.

The compelling force of the political problem has even drawn some analysts into arguing along very crude and all too familiar lines. Hua (1983), for example, argues that in Malaysia communalism is a form of political domination perpetrated through the institutionalization of "*bumiputera rights*". "'Who was here first?' is still employed in order to deprive ethnic minorities of their political rights" (Hua 1983: 9–10). It was pointed out subsequently that Malays were immigrants themselves, and are, therefore, not entitled to special rights. Therefore "[t]he real basis of national unity rests fundamentally upon the recognition of equality of all nationalities" (Hua 1983: 193). It is very clear, therefore, that *bumiputera* and non-*bumiputera* rights form the center of Hua's analysis. However, there is hardly any historical appreciation of what constitutes the "*bumiputera* issue". It is cast aside in a very crude way, constricting the analysis in a familiar mould:

> Today, at the forefront of the struggle against communalism are the minority nationalities . . . who, in their demands for cultural rights, are furthering the democratic rights of the masses. Only through recognition of the rights of national minorities can the masses be united on a democratic and equal basis, and Malay workers and

peasants be freed from the ideology that ties it to its [sic.] own ruling class.[36]

Hua's reassurance (1983: 194)[37] notwithstanding, the implications of this mode of analysis are very far-reaching, for they bring us back into the "ethnic trap" I outlined earlier.

Neither is the *bumiputera*—non-*bumiputera* problem merely one of ruling elite manipulation (Cham 1975, 1977, 1980). This is because it involves the masses' interests as well. After all, sovereignty and the right to one's culture are not ostentatious objects of the elite, but are an integral part of social existence. It is probably this "common ground" that enables the elite to manipulate the masses continually along communal lines. That communal politics is not the preserve of the ruling elite, but also of the left-wing elite underscores further the need to define the problem from a broader perspective.

The seriousness of both Malay special rights and non-Malay minority rights makes it imperative for any analysis to consider them in relation to the contradictions of the historical development of the nascent nation-state. Only through such an undertaking can the left hope to redefine the "national question". I propose to outline a perspective which I believe provides a basis for such a mode of analysis.

For Malays, including the Malay left, Malaya/Malaysia is not a newly-founded social space, over which anyone can determine its character merely on the basis of the modern claim that everyone has a right to citizenship (and, by implication, the right to vote). In fact, it was a land of the Malays. The Malays as a cultural nation have been here over many hundred, if not thousand years, during which time they have developed a rich history, a distinct culture, civilization and sovereignty. British colonialism dealt a hard blow to its sovereignty, which was, nonetheless, respected, even if only formally. However, with imminent decolonization, the Malays suddenly found that their anti-colonial struggle could also, through the development of popular sovereignty (including "immigrants" who actually formed an inextricable part of the colonization process), deny their historical identity and challenge their sovereignty.

On the other hand, the non-Malay left assert that the sovereignty of the people is based upon equal rights, not only to vote, but also to (practise) their culture, language and to equal economic opportunity. These are, by any measure, totally acceptable democratic principles. However, this notion of popular sovereignty arose from the contradictions of colonialism, the very process that subjugated the indigenous population. Therefore, the

---

[36] Hua (1983: 2).

[37] "The democratic demand for the cultural aspirations of the nationalities is not a defence of segregation, for in the process of the struggle for greater (genuine) democracy, the masses will, without doubt, come into contact with those from the other cultures".

rebuttal from the Malay left would be that such democratic principles cannot be used to legitimize the further subjugation of a people, nor the denial of its historical character. From this perspective, therefore, non-Malays may belong to Malaya/Malaysia, but it does not follow that it belongs to them, in the sense that they have the right to ignore Malay sovereignty and character of the country.[38]

These opposing positions arose from the contradictions of change in Malaya. By destroying the basis of traditional Malay society, colonialism freed the people from traditional bondage, made possible by the development of popular sovereignty and destruction of colonialism itself.[39] The development of popular sovereignty implied, as it was clear to all, that power relies ultimately upon the people. In England or France, this meant the English or the French. However, in post-colonial societies, whether popular sovereignty should be based solely upon the colonized indigenous population or include the immigrant communities as well is an open question and is an object of struggle. Such a struggle, of course, would not occur if the immigrant communities in question are small, as they could be accommodated, that is, "controlled", easily. On the other hand, if they form a large proportion of the population, an economically stronger majority as in the Malayan case, then the implications are very different. For if popular sovereignty, which implies equal rights, is pursued, it could result in the subjugation of the colonized indigenous population. In other words, popular sovereignty can simultaneously threaten their historical identity and original sovereignty. This phenomenal contradiction, of civilizational proportions, unfolded very rapidly and under very uncertain conditions in the forties and fifties in the Malay peninsula.

The process of development of the nation-state in Malaya (and other similarly colonized countries) is therefore burdened with at least two contradictions simultaneously. The first refers to the process mentioned above, where the acquisition of popular sovereignty threatened the historical continuity and historical sovereignty of the Malay nation. Basically, this refers to the transformation of the Malay nation into an ethnic community. Herein lies what I consider to be Burhanuddin's (1980: 107–108) most significant contribution to the debate, for as he pointed out:

> These foreign nationals want to be Malayan but yet do not become one, for they still retain their original nationality, such as Malayan

---

[38] The LPM's recommendation regarding the status of the Malay rulers, the symbol of Malay sovereignty, contained in its memorandum to the Reid Commission in 1956, is a good case in point. It recommended that Malay rulers ought to be retained only as constitutional monarchs, and that their succession should be confirmed through a referendum. In other words, Malay sovereignty could be put to a vote. Most of the small number of Malays in the party resigned as a result.

[39] Cheah's fine essay (1988) provides a very good and interesting account of the development of popular sovereignty among the Malays.

Chinese, Malayan Indian and so on. The more the word "Malayan" is associated with each foreign national the secrets and fear of communalism, community and factionalism will arise. And since then the Malay nation and Malay nationalism (anything with a Malay trait) is viewed by the divide and rule policy as an ethnic group or community only. More specifically, it transforms the Malay nation that seeks to become a sovereign nation among a community of nations into any other ethnic group in this country.[40] (My translation).

The Malay community's resistance to the Malayan Union and the citizenship proposals, its struggle for Bahasa Melayu as the national language, and the medium of instruction and Malay culture as the basis of the national culture must be seen in this light.

However, the pioneers in the Malay left conceptualized this contradiction within the context of an idealized past that appears to have exceeded beyond Malay consciousness at that time (Ismail 1990; Khoo 1981).[41] The idealized past was based upon the Sri Vijaya and Malacca empires; two distant, probably highly decentralized empires, whose links with the present were largely restricted cultural considerations. The tremendous forces of British and Dutch colonialism were definitely recognized[42], but the pioneers appear to have underestimated the ability of European colonialism to create new and more important, different economic and political realities. One such redefined reality was expressed by Sukarno himself.[43]

As a result, a modern political nation based on the Malay cultural nation could not be realized. Additionally, this idea of Melayu Raya which attempted to bridge the contemporary with the past was also thwarted by the fact that the "flow of traffic" was actually only one-way, from the Dutch colony to the British one. Thus, the idea of recreating *Melayu Raya*

---

[40] Rahman's interesting essay (1985) has attempted to analyze the development of Malay nationalism from this perspective.

[41] "Kesedaran Melayu sesungguhnya satu lagi warisan nikmat dari penjajahan. Dalam period prakolonial, perasaan yang seperti itu barangkali tidak pernah wujud, malah istilah Melayu pun barangkali jarang digunakan. Ribuan sukubangsa Melayu-Polinesia yang menghuni sesuku muka bumi itu jelas tidak punya nama yang khusus bagi sukunya sendiri, apalagi punyai nama umum untuk semuanya" (Ismail, 1990: 16).

[42] "Dalam masa berpuluh tahun dan beratus tahun dalam keadaan begitu sempadan-sempadan koloni menyekat perhubungan di antara Melayu Raya bertambah-tambah renggang dan menyebabkan lupa dan terbiar. Perasaan bertempat-tempat dan bernegeri-negeri itu makin bertambah melarat dan besar pertalian dengan saudara sebaka di seberang pula beransur-ansur renggang tambahan dengan beberapa nodaan mendesak" (Burhanuddin, 1980: 37).

[43] "The union idea including Malaya is not convenient, as we would have to fight both the British and Dutch at the same time" (A. H. Nasution *Sekitar Perang Kemerdekaan*, 1977; as quoted in Cheah (1983: 123)).

did not find strong support among the main Indonesian nationalists.[44]

The second contradiction refers to the complement of this process; although the development of popular sovereignty absorbs the immigrant communities into the historical evolution of the new nation-state, it does so only partially, denying them the very fruits of popular sovereignty. The relative autonomy accorded to immigrant communities (the Chinese particularly) to generate their own economy, establish their own schools and cultural organizations under colonial rule is suddenly, and paradoxically, upon the acquisition of popular sovereignty, monitored to be streamlined, resulting in a continuous struggle for "equality".

Both these two processes of change are of great historical significance; the first has to do with Malay sovereignty (*bumiputera* rights) and the second with equal rights for the non-Malay communities. Malay special rights and non-Malay minority rights are not irreconcilable contradictions. The national language issue, for example, accords a special position to the Malay language, without necessarily undermining, in principle, the right of other communities to their languages. However, the demand for the two rights has been fought so acrimoniously even among the Malay and Chinese left that it became very difficult to come to terms with each other.[45]

Conclusion

The discussion above argues that the left has been divided along ethnic lines. This is because the civil state is also a cultural project; it was therefore important that each community strives to have a say in that project. As a result, both the Malay and non-Malay left have tended to be communal, even when their programmes were fairly "universal" in nature. The consequences of being communal is very far-reaching, for it not only distanced them further away from each other but, more important, deflected whatever mass support they had for communal rather than for particular class objectives.

The inability of the Malay and non-Malay left to unite is attributed to their failure to come to terms with the fundamental contradictions between the formation of the new state and the cultural basis upon which it has to evolve. The first of these is the transformation of the Malay nation

---

[44] The one-way migratory flow into the Malay Peninsular was pointed out by Rahman (1985: 45), a potentially important indicator of the flow of ideas and consciousness at that time. Interestingly, Ismail (1990), who argued for the existence of a Malay cultural nation, observed that Malay consciousness was restricted to the elite in the Philippines. It was of limited import among the Indonesian nationalists.

[45] The disagreement of the PRM and the LPM over the Rahman Talib Report and the division between Malay and non-Malay members of the PSRM over the Merdeka University issue fairly recently are two good examples.

into an ethnic group; the scale of which has yet to be appreciated fully. The second refers to the integration of the immigrant communities within the historical evolution of Malay society and the new state. The previous leaders did not have the benefit of history to ponder independently over the tremendous changes that were unleashed before them. This explains partially why the earlier left-wing Chinese and Malay movements could not forge any real dialogue between them. This later evolved into a popular inter-ethnic united front (AMCJA-PUTERA) and later, between 1957 and 1966, into a loosely organized but specifically left-wing inter-communal coalition (the Socialist Front). Their evolution has improved mutual understanding between the Malay and non-Malay left. But the gulf between them remains wide and along similar lines. Boestamam once said that a merger between the LPM and the PRM was not possible; and this was due to "the traditional antagonism by the Malays towards the Chinese" (Gamba 1958: 129). He was a sign of his times.

The non-Malay left have, since the LPM, either moved into the right-wing parties or remained dormant on the side lines, while the Malay left-wing (PRM) has yet to make any impact upon the Malaysian political scene. Unlike Boestamam and his contemporaries, the present generation enjoys the benefit of learning from history. Some serious reflection of this history is now necessary.

Bibliography

Abdul Aziz Mat Ton, 1988. "Sekitar Penubuhan Partai Kebangsaan Melayu Malaya", in Adnan Hj. Awang (ed), *Perak: Dahulu dan Sekarang, Kuala Lumpur:* Persatuan Muzium Negara.

Abdul Rahman Ismail, 1985. *"Takkan Melayu Hilang Di Dunia: Suatu Sorotan Tentang Masionalisme Melayu"*, in R. Suntharalingan and Abdul Rahman Ismail (eds).

Ahmad Boestamam, 1972. *Merintis Jalan ke Punchak*, Kuala Lumpur: Pustaka Kejora.

Burhanuddin Al Helmy, 1980. Kamarudin Jaffar (ed), *Politik Melayu dan Islam*, Kuala Lumpur: Yayasan Anda.

Carnell, F., 1953. "Communalism And Communism in Malaya", *Pacific Affairs*, Vol. 16, pp. 99–117.

Cham B. N., 1975. "Class and Communal Conflict in Malaysia", *Journal Of Contemporary Asia*, Vol. 5 (4), pp. 446–61.

——, 1977. "Colonialism and Communalism in Malaysia" *Journal Of Contemporary Asia*, Vol. 7 (2), pp. 178–199.

——, 1980. "Colonialism, Communalism, and Class in the Third World: The Malay-Chinese Conflict in West Malaysia", Paper Presented at the UNITAR International Conference on *Alternative Development Strategies And The Future Of Asia*, New Delhi, March 11–17.

Cheah Boon Kheng, 1979. *The Masked Comrades: A Study of the Communist United Front in Malaya, 1945–48*, Singapore: Times Books International.

——, 1983. *Red Star over Malaya: Resistance and Social Conflict during and after the Japanese Occupation, 1941–1946*, Singapore: Singapore University Press (Second Edition).

——, 1985. "Asal-Usul Dan Asas Nasionalisme Malaya" in R. Suntharalingam and Abdul Rahman Ismail (eds).

——, 1988. "The Erosion of Ideological Hegemony and Royal Power and the Rise of Postwar Malay Nationalism, 1945–46", *Journal Of Southeast Asian Studies*, Vol. 19 (1), pp. 1–26.

Connor, W., 1984. *The National Question in Marxist-Leninist Theory and Strategy*, Princeton: Princeton University Press.

Dragadze, T., 1989. "The Armenian-Azerbaijani Conflict: Structure and Sentiment", *Third World Quarterly*, 11 (1), pp. 55–71.

Firdaus Abdullah, 1985. *Radical Malay Politics: Its Origins and Early Development*, Kuala Lumpur: Pelanduk Publications.

Gamba, C., 1958. "Labour And Labour Parties In Malaya", *Pacific Affairs*, Vol. 21 (2), pp. 11–130.

Geertz, C., 1963. "The Integrative Revolution: Primodial Sentiments and Civil Politics in the New States" in C. Geertz (ed), *Old Societies and New States*, New York: The Free Press.

Hanrahan, G. E., 1971. *The Communist Struggle in Malaya*, Kuala Lumpur: University Of Malaya Press.

Hechter, M., 1976. "Ethnicity and Industrialization: On the Proliferation of the

Cultural Division of Labour", *Ethnicity,* Vol. 3, pp. 214–223.
——, 1978. "Group Formation and the Cultural Division of Labour", *American Journal of Sociology,* Vol. 84 (2), pp. 293–318.
Hua Wu Yin, 1983. *Class and Communalism in Malaysia,* London: Zed Press.
Ismail Hussein, 1990. *Antara Dunia Melayu dengan Dunia Kebangsaan,* Bangi: Penerbit Universiti Kebangsaan Malaysia.
Khoo Kay Kim, 1981. "The Malay Left 1945–1948: A Preliminary Discourse", *Sarjana,* Vol. 1 (1), pp. 167–191.
Kua Kia Soong, 1987. *Polarisation in Malaysia: The Root Causes,* Kuala Lumpur: Malaysian Chinese Research And Resource Centre.
Lim Mah Hui, 1980. "Ethnic and Class Relations in Malaysia", *Journal Of Contemporary Asia,* Vol. 10, (1/2), pp. 130–154.
Means, G., 1970. *Malaysian Politics,* London: University Of London Press.
Purcell, V., 1967. *The Chinese in Malaya,* Kuala Lumpur: Oxford University Press.
Radin Soenarno, 1960. "Malay Nationalism, 1896–1941", *Journal of Southeast Asian History,* Vol. 1, (1), pp. 1–28.
Roff, W., 1967. *The Origins of Malay Nationalism,* Kuala Lumpur: University Of Malaya Press.
Seton-Watson, H., 1977. *Nations and States,* London: Methuen.
Short, A., 1970. "Communism, Race and Politics in Malaysia", *Asian Survey, Vol. 10 (12), pp. 1081–1089.*
Smith, A. D., 1988. "The Myth of the Modern Nation", *Ethnic and Racial Studies,* Vol. 11 (1), pp. 1–27.
Stenson, M., 1980. *Class, Race and Colonialism in West Malaysia: The Indian Case,* St. Lucia: University Of Queensland Press.
Stockwell, A. J., 1979. *British Policy and Malay Politics during the Malayan Union Experiment,* 1942–1948, Kuala Lumpur: Malayan Branch of the Royal Asiatic Society Monograph No. 8.
Suntharalingam R. and Abdul Rahman Ismail, 1985. *Nasionalisme: Satu Tinauan Sejarah,* Petaling Jaya: Fajar Bakti Sdn. Bhd.
Tan Liok Ee, 1987. "Bangsa And Minzu: Preliminary Notes on Political Concepts in a Multi-Ethnic Society", Paper Presented At The *Malaysian Social Science Association—Malaysia Society (ASAA) Coloquium,* Penang, 29 June–3 July.
Vasil, R. K., 1971. *Politics in a Plural Society: A Study of Non-Communal Political Parties in West Malaysia,* Kuala Lumpur: Oxford University Press.
——, 1980. *Ethnic Politics in Malaysia,* New Delhi: Radiant Publishers.
Yeo Kim Wah, 1973 "The Anti-Federation Movement In Malaya, 1946–1948", *Journal Of Southeast Asian Studies,* Vol. 4 (1), pp. 31–51.

12

Counterpoints in the Performing Arts of Malaysia

Tan Sooi Beng

After the coup in 1973, the Chilean military banned all cultural activities associated with the Allende government they had just overthrown. Musicians were imprisoned for their *nueva cancion*, the new songs with political texts. Some singers like Victor Jara were murdered while many others went into exile (Márquez 1983).

The works of Richard Wagner have been forbidden in Israel ever since the state was created. The official reason given is that Wagner was anti-semitic and his music would violate the sanctity of those killed during the Holocaust (Uscher 1983).

After the 1949 revolution, the Chinese Communist Party transformed the performing arts in order to propagate socialist ideals. During the Cultural Revolution, model operas which portrayed class struggle directly were created. Popular music was censored because it was "reactionary" (Mackerras 1981).

In South Africa, anti-apartheid songs are banned today. Records such as Peter Gabriel's "Biko", Sonny Okosun's "Fire in Soweto" and Peter Tosh's "Equal Rights" have been disallowed (Street 1986: 19).

Government control of the performing arts exists in all societies at one time or another although the degree of control varies. The above are but

---

[1] This paper is based on research and personal involvement in the various performing arts of Malaysia from 1980–88. During this period, I studied the Chinese *er-hu* (2-stringed fiddle) and performed with the Chinese orchestra of the Penang Philharmonic Society; learnt how to play the musical instruments of the *wayang siam* (shadow play) with dalang Hamzah from Kelantan and performed with the Universiti Sains Malaysia (USM) student troupe; studied the *rebana* (framed drum) and *gong* with Pak Mat, a veteran bangsawan and ronggeng musician and performed with the *Bangasawan* Sri USM. I attended organizational meetings of the Chinese musical associations of Penang and the Ministry of Culture, Youth and Sports Music Sub-Committee of Penang; and participated in bangsawan workshops organized by the Ministry and USM. I also conducted interviews with musicians and dramatists, looked through Malay and English newspapers, and surveyed the cassettes and records produced by the music industry in Malaysia. I would like to thank Khoo Kay Jin and Loh Kok Wah for their critical comments.

a few examples. This paper looks at how the Malaysian state has tried to centralize and control the performing arts and how individuals and groups involved in the arts have responded. Even though the state has promoted what it approves of and censors and bans what it finds "undesirable", independent, alternative and oppositional performing arts groups continue to resist and challenge the state's attempts to control them.

National Policy and the Support of Approved Arts

Following the 1969 racial riots in Malaysia, the task of creating "a national and common culture for purposes of national unity" (Ismail 1977: 1) was given greater priority.[2] The state began to centralize cultural activities. A Director of Culture, "charged with the responsibility of promoting cultural activities consonant with the needs of the nation", was appointed in the Kementerian Kebudayaan Belia dan Sukan (KKBS) or Ministry of Culture, Youth and Sports[3] (Taib Osman 1984: 283). Under his leadership, a nationwide congress was organized in 1971 where the national culture policy based on the following principles was formulated (KKBS 1973: vii):

1 the national culture of Malaysia must be based on the cultures of the people indigenous to the region;
2 elements from other cultures which are suitable and reasonable may be incorporated into the national culture; and
3 Islam will be an important element in the national culture.

Following this congress, the infrastructure to implement the new national culture policy was created. The cultural division of KKBS was expanded and reorganized into three sections: (i) research into indigenous culture; (ii) promotion and training of the arts; and (iii) a cultural

---

[2] As well, policies for "restructuring society" and the "inculcation of loyalty to the nation" were introduced (Taib Osman 1984: 281–282). The New Economic Policy (NEP) which emphasized the creation of a Malay commercial and industrial community was implemented. The *Rukunegara* (Principles of the Nation) was formulated to promote unity among the various ethnic groups. Beginning from 1971, the medium of instruction in former English national-type primary schools was changed to Bahasa Malaysia.

[3] Prior to 1969, culture was planned and managed as an extension of youth activities under the Ministry of Social Welfare (1953–57) and later the Ministry of Information and Broadcasting (1957–64) (Ismail Zain 1977: 9–10). Although the Ministry of Culture, Youth and Sports was established in 1964, it was headed by an assistant Minister. At that point, the major cultural activity of KKBS revolved around "performances for state guests" (Taib Osman 1984: 281). In 1989, the cultural division was moved from KKBS to the Ministry of Tourism so that a new Ministry of Culture and Tourism was formed.

production unit based at the National Cultural Complex (Ismail Zain 1977: 10–13). The National Art Gallery and The National Museum were also placed under the aegis of KKBS. A network of state and district level offices of KKBS and local cultural committees covering the main towns was established to build up a widespread organization for cultural administration.

The government then began to support cultural activities it deemed desirable. Since the introduction of the national policy, competitions and festivals which present short items by local performing groups have been organised to promote the "traditional" Malay performing arts as well as to attract tourists. These include the annual *pesta budaya* (cultural festival) in Kuala Lumpur and the *Pesta Pulau Pinang* (Penang Festival).

Seminars and workshops which bring performers, academics and administrators together to discuss the state, documentation and preservation or revival of the performing arts have also been held. Some examples include the national music seminar in 1974, a seminar on boria in 1974, a *bangsawan* workshop in 1977, a *wayang kulit* workshop in 1979, and a three-day folk poetry and music seminar in Kota Kinabalu in 1986 (*BH* 4 November 1974; *NSunT* 4 April 1986).

"National" styles of performing arts based on selected Malay folk and popular arts have been created and presented as the "traditional" arts. Two of these include the *bangsawan* and the *boria*. *Bangsawan* (a type of Malay popular commercial theatre which combined Malay, Western, Indian, Chinese, Javanese and Middle Eastern elements) has been gradually "Malayized" in the 1970s and 1980s with Malay court elements and the glories of the Malay kingdoms of the past emphasized (Tan 1988)[4]. The *boria*, a popular Malay theatre of Penang (consisting of a farcical comic sketch and a song-and-dance sequence), once performed during awal Muharram (the first day of the first month of the Muslim calendar) and later introduced at weddings and other social functions as well, has done away with elaborate costumes and stories (Rahmah Bujang 1987). These days, performers wear batik and sing about national development in competitions and television appearances (*NST* 31 March 1973).

As Islam is an important component of the national culture policy, *nasyid* (a type of Arabic cantillation of *syi'ar* [poetry] with noble and Islamic themes) is promoted.[5] Through Radio Televisyen Malaysia (RTM), the government has organized *nasyid* contests at the national and state

---

[4] This "national" form of *bangsawan* is performed during festivals (eg. Penang Pesta), for tourists (*NSunT* 20 Aug 1986), on television (*NST* 31 December 1986) and to entertain the rural FELDA settlers (*NST* 26 Nov 1972, 1 April 1973).

[5] Throughout the centuries, writers of Islamic works have debated the benefits or dangers of certain genres of art especially *musiqa* (Arabic term for music) to the performance of Islamic religious duties and Muslim society in general. Different regions of the Muslim world have put restrictions on the performance of certain genres while supporting and cultivating others. Many of the encouraged

levels (Kumpulan Noor El-Kawakib Paper (nd): 1–2). These contests and other *nasyid* performances are also televised. During such contests and performances, Malay texts praising Allah as well as offering advice to Muslims to serve Allah and abide by the Quran are sung. As in other forms which have been streamlined, verses often emphasize national development through Islam.

As it was decided at the National Culture Congress that the western orchestra should also be promoted (KKBS 1973: 212) in a "modern" nation, the Orkes RTM (formed in 1961) has been developed into the country's national orchestra (Star 23 April 1986). Today, the Orkes RTM performs Malay traditional tunes and Malay popular songs (with an intermingling of some Western, Chinese and Indian pop songs).

In 1982, KKBS started a symphonic orchestra called the Orkestra Simfoni Muda (OSM). Under the baton of Abdul Fatah Karim, this orchestra comprises children and teenagers who attend music camps (*kem muzik*) and music classes at the Kompleks Budaya Negara. Performances include Malay folk and pop songs, western popular songs and classical pieces (*UM* 1 March 1983; 22 February 1984).

Censorship of Disapproved Arts

Besides setting up the infrastructure to implement the national culture policy and promoting approved arts, the police and other authorities began to make use of existing laws to curb cultural activities that are considered "politically subversive" or "retrograde". For instance, under the Police Act (1967)[6] which deals with unlawful assembly, police permits must be obtained before any theatre, music or dance concert can take place. To acquire a police permit, all scripts of productions and names of actors/ actresses must be submitted to the police for censorship and approval before the show. Additionally, licences are required to open theatres as

---

genres which include the Quranic Chant (*qira 'ah*); religious chants (*adhan*); chanting of poetry with noble themes (*syi'ar*); family, celebration and occupational songs and military music; are not designated as musiqa in case they are confused with unsanctioned types of musiqa (Al Faruqi 1985: 7–9). *Nasyid* is considered permissible as it is a type of chanting of poetry with noble themes. In the case of Malaysia, the gambus, bass, drum and organ are sometimes used to accompany the *nasyid*.

[6] Under the Police Act (1967) which was amended in 1987, mainly to curb the activities of the Islamic Party, PAS, applications for police permits to hold public gatherings (including theatre, music or dance concerts) must be made by an organisation of three persons acting jointly, compared to the present single applicant. An assembly of four or more persons without a police permit is deemed unlawful. Being "found in the vicinity" of such an illegal assembly becomes a criminal offence with a one-year jail sentence and ignorance of the illegality will no longer be an allowable defence (*FEER* 10 December 1987).

well as for the sale of tickets. Before a licence to open a theatre or place
of public amusement is given, the licensing officer "may require the
applicant to furnish to him the script . . . the particulars of persons . . .
concerned in the promotion of the theatrical production . . . particulars of
the persons who have agreed to participate . . . and the purposes to which
any profits are intended" (Laws of Malaysia Act 182, 1977: 6–7).

Some states have also introduced their own set of regulations regarding the performing arts. For example, any overseas performing group
that wishes to perform in the Federal Territory has to seek approval
from the Ministry of Culture, Youth and Sports, City Hall, the Police, the
Ministry of Home Affairs and the Immigration Department. In Penang,
Chinese operas have to get permits from the Police, Fire Brigade, and the
Departments of Health, Building and Engineering before they can perform
during celebrations of Chinese deities (See for instance "Syarat-syarat
daripada jabatan-jabatan berkenaan untuk pertunjukan masa Phor Tor").

Moreover, KKBS has introduced a set of guidelines on the types of
shows to be encouraged and those to be banned (NST 14 May 1983). Both
the Ministry of Culture, Youth and Sports and the Ministry of Home
Affairs have the power to instruct the police not to award permits. Thus,
in September 1986, after declaring a ban on all open air rock concerts, the
Ministry of Home Affairs ordered the police not to issue permits for such
concerts throughout the country (UM 8 September 1986).

All programmes played on radio and television also have to be passed
by the censors. They have to be in accordance with the objectives of Radio
Television Malaysia (RTM) which are predominantly "to explain . . . the
policies and programmes of the government", "to assist in fostering national
unity . . . through the use of Bahasa Malaysia", and "to provide suitable
elements of popular education, general information and entertainment"
(Ministry of Information 1975: 2).

All stories and scripts are vetted (NST 22 June 1983). Music which is
considered to be "retrograde" in the eyes of the government is censored.
For instance, following a government ban on open air rock/heavy metal
concerts in 1986, the Information Ministry banned heavy metal rock music
over radio and television (BH 9 September 1986). In the same year, in line
with the government's campaign to fight dadah (drugs), RTM also banned
"music by known dadah-addicted artistes on radio and its television shows"
(NST 31 December 1986).

Conflicts and Bureaucratic Problems

While the state has attempted to control the arts through various policies, laws and institutions, and sponsored and streamlined selected "traditional" and "popular" Malay forms, complete control has not occurred.
Before discussing the challenges to these policies and guidelines by various groups, we need to highlight that the government's own efforts have
fallen short of its stated objectives because of internal problems.

Firstly, there is the problem of KKBS working under the constraints of a limited budget. For the duration of the Fifth Malaysia Plan (1986–1990) for instance, allocations to KKBS amounted to only 0.03% of the total development budget (Malaysia 1986: 553). Additionally, there is a short‍age of trained personnel to initiate programmes for the Ministry. Only a few are sent to the Arts Centre at Universiti Sains Malaysia annually and only for a one-year non-degree training course. Further, the priority of the trained personnel seems to be the preparation of the national troupe for performances at festivals and fairs locally and overseas where short excerpts of "traditional" performing arts are performed.

Secondly, inspite of existing policies, bodies and guidelines, KKBS itself does not seem to have a clear direction about the promotion and management of certain forms of Malay arts. In particular, there is the dilemma of how to "deal with forms that are "Malay" and yet pre-Islamic?" (*NST* 14 April 1984). Stalwarts of "traditional" folk theatre like Ghulam Sarwar (a lecturer at USM) have observed that even though the government considers the Malay *wayang kulit*, *makyong* and other theatre forms as "national heritage", it has "provided very little inspiration, encouragement or assistance to *makyong* or to any other Malay theatre form" (*NST* 14 April 1984). Although "lip service continues to be paid at all levels to our 'national heritage', almost nothing is being done to help preserve these art forms," Ghulam asserts. Thus, whereas in 1970 there were a hundred-odd *wayang Siam* troupes, today there are a mere dozen or so. It has been suggested that one of the reasons for this decline is criticisms from purists and orthodox Muslims (from within and outside the Ministry). To the Islamic purists, "traditional" Malay theatre forms are *haram* (forbidden) because they are performed for spiritual occasions including healing. Moreover, spirits are invoked during performances while non-Islamic stories (Hindu-Indian epics like Ramayana and Mahabharata) are used. Also, the making of *wayang kulit* figures and their use in performances raise objections from purists who do not wish to see any kind of human representation even if it is stylised and non-naturalistic. Worse still, idolatory is promoted on state by humans and puppets (*NSunT* 4 June, 1984).[7]

Thirdly, as a result of competition from TV3, the commercial channel set up in 1985, RTM has been forced to change its programmes in order to attract viewers and advertisers. "Inform, educate and entertain" has made way for RTM's new keywords "variety and entertainment".

---

[7] Similary, it is interesting to note the following comment by Azmil Mustafa, "Best Actor for 1985" who also thinks that there is a lack of direction in government cultural policies. He says that "being a Muslim nation, we have our limitations with regards to moral values depicted in films. We cannot have scenes that are too steamy nor too violent. So we have a little of this, a little of that, and what do we end up with? Half-baked, tawdry films" (*NST* 24 June 1988).

Documentaries which have limited appeal have been removed while foreign dramas, miniseries, sitcoms, sports and shows that appeal to a wider
audience have taken over prime time spots. RTM has also ventured into
selling transmission time to a private media company so that Cantonese
serials are shown on RTM daily (*Star* 26 February 1990). To further
compete with TV3, RTM even airs foreign music video clips which
sometimes have violent and suggestive images. This turn that has occurred
in RTM's programming, it could be suggested, is contrary to the
government's stated policy and guidelines.

Independent Groups

More importantly, the government has not been able to completely control
the performing arts because private and independent groups (including
groups which perform the dominant Malay forms) continue to resist
government control and innovate and extend the arts beyond the terms of
governmental or bureaucratic directions.[8] These groups are able to maintain their independence for artistic innovation and even for some social
comment. This section describes some of these groups in peninsular
Malaysia, in particular how they have responded to government intervention and control.

Chinese Cultural Associations

Amateur Chinese cultural organisations and martial arts and lion dance
troupes have existed in Malaysia since the Chinese arrived in the late
nineteenth and early twentieth centuries. These organisations were first
organised as part of larger voluntary associations such as clan associations
(*hui guan* or regional societies and *kongsi* or surname societies). Later,
other amateur cultural clubs attached to Chinese schools, old boys' associations, political parties and religious groups were also formed (Tan
1983). These Chinese cultural organisations provide a place for Chinese
educated youth and working class Chinese to socialize and to learn new
cultural skills. Activities within the cultural clubs include drama, dancing,

---

[8] It should be noted that many private groups which promote Malay culture and
which adhere to government terms also exist. They include Teater Suasana and
Yayasan Seni which produce big theatre events involving huge sums of money.
Because Teater Suasana has been able to combine traditional Malay court and folk
dance with technological professionalism, it has represented Malaysia on several
occasions as at the Indian Ocean Festival in Perth and the Tenth Festival of Asian
Arts in Hong Kong. The patron of Yayasan Seni is the Prime Minister of Malaysia
while the board of trustees is chaired by Mahani Daim (wife of the Minister of
Finance).

singing, playing Chinese musical instruments, and the martial arts, including the lion dance. They survive on annual dues from members and occasional contributions from rich patrons and the general public during the annual concerts they organise.

In the 1950s, 1960s and 1970s, these amateur cultural clubs identified themselves either as organizations promoting "art for the people" or "art for art's sake". Although most of the dances and music scores were "imported" from China, some of the local groups did develop their own dances, music and plays with Malaysian content too. In general, those groups which advocated "art for the people" promoted art which portrayed social reality with the aim of inculcating political and social values in audiences. Those who advocated "art for art's sake" on the other hand, viewed art essentially as a form of artistic and aesthetic activity. Although there existed this major difference in outlook, nonetheless both groups were concerned with promoting and preserving Chinese culture.

However, by the late 1970s and 1980s, this distinction between Chinese cultural groups became less important for two reasons. First, many of the "art for the people" organizations found it increasingly difficult to function. It was difficult to put on performances as police permits were often not given till the eve of the performance. There were also occasions when performances had to be cancelled because the number of pieces allowed to be performed had been cut down by one-half or more.[9] As a result, programmes could not be printed and enough tickets sold in time. Concerts could not be publicised adequately too. Some cultural activists of the "art for the people" organizations were also arrested in the early 1970s because of their alleged political ties with the underground Communist Party.[10] The crackdown led some individuals to join the "art for art's sake" associations instead. Meanwhile, in the aftermath of the Indochina war, changes in China itself and the influence of video culture from Hong Kong and Taiwan on the younger generation, all of which led to a general decline in leftist influences, some "art for the people" groups became transformed into "art for art's sake" associations.

Secondly, the national culture policy which is perceived by the Chinese cultural groups as assimilationist has further brought previously ideologically-opposed groups together.[11] Chinese cultural groups have

---

[9] Interview with an officer of the Han Chiang Old Boys' Association (8 March 1982, Penang), an officer of the Pei Fong Old Boys' Association (6 June 1982, Malacca) and Lee Soo Sheng, conductor and composer of the Keat Hwa Old Boys' Association (Alor Star, 22 May 1982).

[10] For example, some performers of the Chinese Language Society in Universiti Malaya and Universiti Sains were arrested for alleged links with the underground Communist Party of Malaya. Similar groups operating in Singapore had begun to be arrested from the 1960s.

[11] For the same reason, many Chinese cling on to "traditional" emblems as forms and means of resistance and to assert their identity. These emblems include festivals

consolidated to preserve the cultural rights of the Chinese and to assert their identity.[12]

According to them, since the government does not recognize Chinese culture as part of national culture (even when it is Malaysian in content) and does not offer any encouragement or financial support, it is up to the Chinese to take care of themselves and to promote their own culture. Consequently, most cultural groups today have common objectives: to promote "healthy culture" (*jiankang wenhua*) as opposed to "yellow culture" (*huangse wenhua*)[13]; to promote Chinese culture; and to promote close friendship among its members. These cultural groups often share scores and musicians and even put on joint productions.

Aware of the need for local relevance, the Chinese cultural groups have consciously incorporated Malay and Indian folk music, dances and Malaysian dramatic themes into their performances. Some folk songs such as "Tanah Air Ku", "Air Didik" and "Inang Cina" (arranged by Lee Soo Sheng) and new compositions incorporating local dance rhythms like "Malay Dance" based on the *ronggeng* rhythm (by Saw Yeong Chin) are commonly played. Conscious efforts have also been made to learn Malay and Indian dances which have been performed in recent concerts. Plays with local social themes like increasing consumerism in Malaysian society have been promoted. For example, in Qiong Qing's play "Lucky Draw" performed in Penang in 1981, a lower income city dweller drinks fizzy bottled drinks, and eats instant noodles everyday in order to collect enough tokens to take part in the "Lucky Draw" of a supermarket. What did he win at the end? Gastritis.

Perhaps taking a cue from the government, Chinese cultural activists have also started their own competitions to promote Chinese culture. For example, there is an annual Singapore—Malaysian Art Song Competition whose winners then "represent Malaysia" at the South-East Asian Art Song Contest held in Hong Kong (*Star* 10 April 1986, *NST* 15 April 1985).

Moreover, state-wide associations like the Penang Chinese Martial Arts Association (with about 40 lion and dragon dance troupes as members)

---

like the Hungry Ghost Festival, Chinese opera, Chinese instrumental music, dance and folk songs (Tan 1980 and 1988a).

[12] Indian organisations like the Temple of Fine Arts in Kuala Lumpur have also attracted many Indians as members. The Temple of Fine Arts' six-day "Festival of Arts" (performed each year since 1981) can be seen as an assertion of Indian identity. For six days, the Malaysian Indian community comes together to watch a combination of Indian classical and modern dances - bharatanatyam, Gujerati folk dance etc. (*NSunT* 2 March 1986). The Temple of Fine Arts has also set up a branch in Penang.

[13] "Yellow" culture includes local, Hong Kong and Taiwanese pop rock that has permeated every strata of Chinese society. Their condemnation places cultural groups in the same category as the state vis-a-vis heavy metal rock music.

have been formed in order to promote the sharing of musicians, performers and skills. Additionally, such an organization has been able to offer the troupes some form of protection against unnecessary harassment by police especially when applying for performance permits. And should it be necessary, a state-wide organization can protest more effectively too. For example, in 1985, the Penang Chinese Martial Arts Association pulled out about 40 troupes and boycotted the Chingay procession at the Pesta Pulau Pinang (Penang Festival) when its representative was not included in the Pesta sub-committee subsequent to which various restrictions were insisted upon in the performance of the lion dance (*NST* 27 December 1985). Likewise, when then Home Affairs Minister, Tan Sri Ghazali Shafie, declared that the lion dance be changed to a "tiger dance" ("the tiger, unlike the lion is found in Malaysia") accompanied by music from the gong, flute, tabla or gamelan, a widespread protest from the martial arts associations and other Chinese cultural organizations was easily mounted (Ghazalie Shafie 1979: 7).

Despite the lack of government support and harassment by the authorities, nonetheless, these associations have grown. There is at least one cultural association in each town in Malaysia today. Bigger towns like Penang and Kuala Lumpur have more.[14] In addition, a sense of solidarity seems to be emerging among them.

Modern Theatre (Teater Moden)

Modern theatre is the term used to describe English and Malay language plays which are performed in theatres mainly in the urban areas. At such productions, audiences are overwhelmingly middle-class and educated. Modern theatre usually uses symbolism making it difficult to attract those who are not educated in it. Some current and social issues may be raised in modern theatre but its main role is to entertain. The term has also been used to include dance-dramas and dance productions in the 1980s.

In the 1950s and 1960s, modern theatre using both English and Bahasa Malaysia developed separately. Local plays which were "Malaysian" in content were written in both languages. Some Malay playwrights wrote in both languages too. Most of these plays were realistic plays which portrayed prevalent social issues such as the rifts between the town and

---

[14] In Penang, these include the Jit Sin Old Boys' Association, Hui Yin Se, Nightingales Penang Art Society, Han Chiang Xiao You Hui, Xiao Fan, Penang Philharmonic Association, Penang Arts Chorus, Chinese Language Society of USM. The Penang Philharmonic has a membership of 200 (*NST* 15 April 1985) while the Penang Arts Chorus has 250 members ranging from 8 years to 57 years old (*Star* 10 April 1986). Apart from the big eight, there are many other smaller ones.

country and the young and old. Some commented on social norms, social injustice and imbalance of wealth.[15]

The introduction of the national culture policy was an important turning point for both Malay and English playwrights since at the Congress of National Culture in 1971, it was agreed that "national literature is to be defined as works written in Bahasa Malaysia and the contents of which reflect the background of Malaysian society" (KKBS 1973: 526). Under the circumstances, writing in the English language was regarded by some as inhibiting the development of a national culture. As a result of the policy, the number of plays written in English dropped considerably (Chee 1982). Malays who used to write in English concentrated their efforts in the Malay language[16]. A divide emerged between those who wrote in Malay and those who wrote in English.

While English plays were not encouraged or supported, the government organised competitions (*pesta drama*) to promote Malay modern theatre. The *Hadiah Sastera* (Literature Prize) was awarded to the best works in Malay literature, including plays.

Shaken by the 1969 racial riots and influenced by the national culture policy, Malay modern theatre went through many changes. Heightened by the need to develop a Malay identity in theatre, playwrights of the 1970s introduced Malay folk idioms[17] into their plays (*NE* 8 May 1979, *NST* 1 April 1979). For example, Noordin Hassan combined Malay poetry, music, *boria* and *dikir barat* in his "Bukan Lalang di Tiup Angin" which also made references to 13 May 1969.[18] In the late 1970s and 1980s, co-inciding with the resurgence of Islam in Malaysia, a few Malay playwrights "began searching for an Islamic theatre" (Krishen 1984: 127). This search was led by Noordin Hassan who staged plays like "1400" (1981) based on Islamic themes. These plays "evoked Islamic iconography and imagery" while spirits were "mounted as false gods" (*ibid.*: 135).

Though local English plays are not encouraged[19], there remain playwrights who continue to write them. With the growth of the middle class

---

[15] Some of these plays include Ghulam Sarwar's "Halfway Road", Dorall's "There is a Tiger in Our Community", Lee Joo For's "Nero Has Arisen in Malaysia" (Chee 1982), Mustapha Kamal's "Atap Genting" and Usman Awang's "Tamu Di Bukit Kenny" (*NSunT* 19 May 1974).

[16] Syed Alwi was one example. His first two plays "Going North" and "The More We Are Together" are in English.

[17] Earlier Malay modern theatre writers tended to believe that "traditional" theatre and art forms were feudalistic and promoted apathy (*NST* 1 April 1979).

[18] At the same time, other playwrights like Dinsman began to produce "anti-realistic" plays. Dinsman experimented with "absurd" techniques and "shocking" characters. In one of his plays, Hang Jebat was portrayed as a hippie. In another play "Ana", he sowed "doubts about the worth of language as an effective means of human communication" (*NST* 8 April 1979).

[19] Occasionally, if these plays are critical, they have also been banned. For example, Chin San Sooi's "Refugee: Images" (a play about the plight of the

in the 1970s and 1980s, these English plays have been well supported. For example, Kee Tuan Chye's "1984 Here and Now" (presented by the Five Arts) touching on race relations in Malaysia and revamping George Orwell's novel "1984" drew a capacity audience for 5 nights. Chin San Sooi's "Yap Ah Loy" (also presented by Five Arts) and K S Maniam's "Breakout" presented by LIDRA are other examples of success (*NSunT* 5 January 1986).

At the same time some Malay dramatists, who are of the opinion that the government is not doing enough to promote modern Malay theatre, have symbolically declared their independence from the Ministry. In 1983, a few leading troupes conducted their own state and inter-state festivals when KKBS cancelled the Pesta Teater which it considered "extravagant" and "of dubious value in the development of the nation's theatre" (*NST* 1 January 1984). To these groups, the Ministry's priority seems to be the promotion of selected "national" Malay forms for state functions and for tourism. They further drew attention to the fact that after nearly twenty years since the idea was first raised, a National Theatre has yet to be built.[20]

To attract audiences and so earn enough to maintain themselves, both Malay and English modern theatre enthusiasts have begun to promote greater professionalism. Polished productions are emphasized. Some examples include the Crown Players' "Servant of 2 Masters" (by Goldoni) and the 80s Drama Centre's "Pandanglah Lihatlah" and "Gerhana" (by Ramli Ibrahim) (*NST* 1 January 1984).

Because these groups are independent, they are able to innovate beyond the constraints of government policy. Theater expressing a multi-cultural viewpoint has become more common in the 1980s. Fusion is taking place. Ramli Ibrahim's productions of the three-act "Kalau Kau Mau" (featuring "Gerhana", "Baris" and "Sutrarasa") during the Second KL Arts Festival showed the merging of the "traditional" with the "modern" and drew from Malaysia's multi-cultural background (*NST* 16 August, 30 December 1986). Mohd Ghouse also interpreted the various dance forms in Malaysia in his choreography of "Melayang Di Angkasa" while Marion d'Cruz's "Solo '86" featured many fusion pieces. In fact, renditions of classical Indian dances have been performed by professional Malay performers like Ramli Ibrahim (*NSunT* 5 January 1986).

Vietnamese refugees and the reactions, insecurities and lack of humanitarian values shown by the Malaysian public and government towards them) was not granted a permit for performance in Kuala Lumpur in 1980 because it touched on "sensitive issues".

[20] After its temporary resurrection in 1981 by Datuk Mokhtar Hashim, Minister of Culture, Youth and Sports (sentenced to life imprisonment for murder shortly after that) (*Star* 25 November 1981), the ideal fell victim to the economic stringency cuts in 1983 (*NST* 1 January 1984).

Despite government censorship, a few Malay playwrights have been able to touch on sensitive political issues in their plays. Noordin Hassan's "Anak Tanjung" (1987) used abstract images and symbolism to raise the issue that Malaysia not only belongs to the Malays but is "Ah Heng's country too". This statement stimulated other Malays to condemn the play as "selling the Malay race" (*jual bangsa*) (*UM* 27 and 28 February; 5, 27 and 28 March 1987). In a more recent production "Cindai" (1988), Noordin Hassan portrayed the conflict within the ruling party UMNO.

However, unlike the Chinese cultural groups, there is still a lack of co-operative spirit among theatre groups. There is little attempt to come together to shape scheduling, discussion of techniques, expectations or trends. Most of these groups operate quite independently of one another.

Alternative Theatre

Alternative or people's theatre is theatre that seeks to point out the social problems in society and to offer alternative solutions to the problems using creative means. Emerging first in Latin America in the 1960s, its activities are related to the ideas of the Brazilian educator, Paulo Freire who was particularly concerned about designing educational processes that could enable the illiterate or semi-literate adults in the Third World to better themselves.[21] Freire's ideas stress the necessity of a new type of teacher, one who believes in and appreciates the creativity and wisdom of the ordinary people. When applied to the world of theatre, Freire's ideas imply that a new kind of actor is needed. This actor does not go to the community simply to teach but rather to learn from and with the people (Freire: 177–178). The task of the actor is not to perform for the people but to help them perform their own plays themselves. This theatre emphasizes group process rather than performance. Consequently, the play is created through the collective cultural action of the community. In so doing, the people become increasingly aware of their social situation, their creativity, their ability to express themselves and their strength as a group.[22]

Alternative theatre emerged in Malaysia in tandem with the rise of social movements in Malaysia in the 1970s. (It must be stressed however, that only small numbers of people are involved in this type of theatre in

---

[21] In general, Freire's pedagogy confronts "banking" concepts of education in which knowledge "is a gift bestowed by those who consider themselves knowledgeable upon those whom they consider to know nothing" (Freire 1983: 54).

[22] People's theatre differs from "political theatre" which also seeks to create social awareness but emphasizes production and the artist as performer. The spectator is not involved in the creation and production of the play. Similarly, although Chinese cultural associations of the "art for the people" type also seek to heighten political consciousness and emphasize group process, the audience remains separate from the performers.

Malaysia). Organizations like Aliran, Insan (Institute of Social Analysis), Environmental Protection Society, CAP (Consumers Association of Penang), Civil Rights Committee, Selangor Graduates Society and a few church groups were concerned with raising the consciousness of the people through forums, publishing, and various other legal means of action.

After attending a few workshops run by the People's Theatre Network of the Philippines or PETA (the leading people's theatre proponent in Asia), some of the social movements began to use alternative theatre as a means of developing among their target groups both a critical consciousness of the reality that surrounds them, and confidence in speaking out for social change. Some groups promoted alternative theatre among squatters and workers with the hope of providing them with the tools for creative self-expression and an analysis of their predicament. Some groups within the Catholic Church began to use theatre to educate its members about poverty and social justice. For example, a video of the theatrical piece "The Christmas Play" (about the "true meaning" of Christmas)[23] was shown to parishioners of many Catholic churches in Malaysia.

An amateur theatre group, Pentas Drama Kreatif, was incorporated in 1986 "to create and stage plays that are Malaysian in every sense and through that, play a part in the growth of a distinct Malaysian theatre". The group has produced two plays thus far—"A Thousand Planks" (staged in July 1986) which focused on the plight of squatters and "Inch by Inch" on the overcrowded public transport system, reckless driving, bad road conditions and problems faced by commuters (*NST* 1 November 1987). The group has also conducted workshops for students and performed a sketch on the effects of radiation. This was in solidarity with the people of Papan who are protesting against the dumping of radio-active waste in the vicinity of their small town.

Some of the social activists involved in alternative theatre were accused of being Marxists and of being threats to "national security" and were arrested under the Internal Security Act[24] in late 1987. Nonetheless, alternative cultural activities continue. In 1988, a special program was performed by various groups and individuals in conjunction with an exhibition of "Violence Against Women" organised by the Women's Development Collective. On this occasion, some of the individuals

---

[23] In this play, Mary and Joseph are depicted as illegal immigrants arriving by boat to Malaysia. The pregnant Mary is not welcomed by the authorities, the wealthy or the church. A poor boy befriends the couple and invites them to his squatter-home where Mary delivers the baby Jesus.

[24] The ISA allows for detention of any person "for activities that have been or may be detrimental to national security." Section 73 (1) of the ISA empowers the police to detain a person for up to 60 days without a detention order. The detention can then be extended for another two years. In the past, some of the cultural activists associated with the "art for the people" organizations had been arrested under the same Act.

involved in modern theatre cooperated with the social activists. The items presented included a *dikir barat*, poetry recital, the dance "Arise" by Marion de Cruz and a sketch by Jit Murad from the play "Caught In The Middle" (*NST* 14 March 1988). On August 11, 1988, a concert entitled "Hiroshima – Never Again" was produced by Krishen Jit, a well-known Malaysian playwright, director and critic of modern theatre. This event was held to commemorate Hiroshima Day and was organized by the Malaysian Physicians for the Prevention of Nuclear War (MPPNW) "to educate the public on the threat of nuclear war". Local poets and performers such as Usman Awang, Ramli Ibrahim, Dinsman, Marion d'Cruz and Vijaya Samarawickrama read poems and performed sketches, dances and songs (*NSunT* 21 August 1988).

Popular Music and the Entertainment Industry

Popular music has a larger audience than any other performing arts and is the genre that is most often performed. The audience cuts across ethnic, class and age groups. Malaysians of all ethnic origins take part in its composition, performance and production. It is not only played on the radio but in live concerts, nightclubs, discotheques, show lounges and even supermarkets.

Popular music emerged in Malaysia through the *bangsawan* in the early twentieth century in Malaysia (Wan Kadir 1988, Tan 1988b). These *bangsawan* songs incorporated Arabic, Western, Hindustani, Latin American, Javanese and Chinese elements and were accompanied by dance style orchestras combining strings, trumpets, trombones, clarinets, drum set, maraccas and sometimes tabla and harmonium.

Popular music has always adapted to the latest trends in other parts of the world. In the 1930s and 1940s, the swing, mambo and fox-trot rhythmic patterns were added to Malay folk songs like "Sri Mersing". In the 1950s, with the emergence of rock'n'roll in America, electrically amplified stringed instruments like guitars were introduced in Malaya. "Rock Around the Clock" and "It's Now or Never" were sung in Malay by stars like P Ramlee and Samad Harun.

In the 1960s, with the Beatles craze in the west, a phenomenon called "pop yeh yeh" emerged in Malaya. Bands or *kugiran* (comprising 3 guitars and a drum) such as "The Siglap 5", "The Hooks", "Mutiara Timur" and others regularly performed concerts not only in big but small towns and even kampungs. These bands played the "twist", "blues", "country and western" and "a-go-go". When *dangdut* (using *gendang*, *gambus*, bass, harmonium, bamboo flute or *suling* and guitar) was created in Indonesia in the mid-1960s, bands in Malaysia began to adapt it as well.

Beginning in the 1970s, an important new development occurred in the popular music scene in Malaysia. Giant conglomerates like CBS (USA), EMI (UK), Polygram-Philips (German Federal Republic-Holland), and

WEA (USA)[25] moved into Malaysia in search of markets. Since they command vast resources which allow them to launch massive marketing campaigns involving films, TV programmes, records and merchandizing (such as John Travolta T shirts, Boney M buttons, ABBA posters and so on), they have quickly gained control over the popular music scene (Wallis and Malm 1984: 300). Since then, a type of "transnationalized culture" or "transculture" has been popularized throughout Malaysia. But this is not simply a result of the music of Michael Jackson, Boney M, ABBA and the like which they efficiently promote. It is also a result of the promotion of local versions of similar music by these giant conglomerates. It is important, therefore, to note that the most famous local bands and singers in Malaysia today are the ones promoted by the subsidiaries of these foreign companies. Some examples include The Alleycats [Philips], Sudirman [EMI], Sharifah Aini [EMI], The Blues Gang [WEA], The Search [Philips] and Asiabeat [CBS].

With the introduction of cassettes and cheaper cassette recorders and transistor radios, this transnationalized popular music has become easily accessible even to those in remote villages. Through "pirating", even the poor can afford cassettes.[26]

Concerned that transnational corporations can create conflicting cultural trends among youths, the government has begun to promote Malay popular songs that it approves of. Annual national talent programs like "Bintang RTM"[27], "Bakat TV", "Juara Kugiran" and "Pesta Lagu Malaysia" have been organized by RTM. Popular songs about love of the nation ("Cintailah Malaysia"), loyalty ("Setia"), national pride ("Thanks for the Memories") and progress ("Sing a Song of Progress/Show How Much You Care") have been commissioned and broadcasted several times a day over radio and television.

Besides promoting the kind of popular music it approves of, the government has also attempted to restrict what it deems "undesirable". For example, RTM bans songs with words that can "stimulate one to violence" and/or "heavy metal" or other "music that is too westernised". In 1986, it banned the title song of Sahara Yaacob's new album because of the allegedly offensive phrase "Ustazah Blues" (Ustazah of the Blues). To RTM there was a contradiction between the image of an Ustazah and a nightclub

---

[25] The country shows where these companies originated. Today, these corporations are transnationals and are active all over the world. They are part of even bigger concerns. EMI for example, is owned by Thorn Electrics while WEA is part of the Kinney group of companies. Each of them issues records on many different labels (Wallis and Malm 1984: 49).

[26] In contrast to the originals which might cost M $8–$10, the pirated versions might cost only M $2–5.

[27] Stars like Sudirman Haji Arshad and Jamal Abdillah were first promoted through Bintang RTM. Winners have a contract with RTM for a year. They cannot sign up with private recording companies during that time.

singer—a good Muslim should not be singing Blues and definitely not in a nightclub[28] (*NST* 5 December 1986).

As mentioned earlier, a set of "guidelines" on the types of shows to be encouraged and those that should be banned was introduced in 1982 (14 May 1983). According to the Assistant Director of the Ministry, some shows needed to be banned because they promoted "undesirable influences" like "violence", "obscenity", and "long and unkempt hair" (*NST* 14 May 1983). Commenting on the Rock Summit held at Stadium Merdeka, the same official declared that:

> it was an undesirable event and should not be encouraged . . . The performers behaved wildly and so did some sections of the crowd. The audience . . . were dancing and some of them even removed their shirts. Now, this is unruly beheviour and it should be stopped . . . . This pattern will catch on, and soon, everybody who attends a concert will be dancing. It's not the proper place to dance. If they want to dance, they can go to the discos . . . Anyway, that's not the sort of thing our youths should indulge in. What will the foreigners think of our society dancing and behaving wildly?. What's more, dancing at concerts is the way of the west. We are supposed to be a gentle society, rich in tradition and culture.[29]

Subsequently, the government banned open-air rock concerts for a few months. This came after the rock concert "Battle of The Bands" in Penang. On that occasion, the Pasukan Polis Simpanan Persekutuan (FRU) in charge of riot control was called in when the audience "acted wildly because they were too influenced by the heavy metal band." Some of the reasons for the ban are given below:

> "Why do we need entertainment that is wild [*liar*]? Why do we allow our lives and way of thinking to be influenced by yellow culture [*kebudayaan kuning*]? . . . Datuk Haji Mohd Zaman Khan (Director, Department of Security and Public Order, Kuala Lumpur) (*MM* 7 September 1986).

> "Rock music is not the culture of Malaysia . . . The audience acts as though they have lost their minds [*hilang akal*] . . . this does not reflect the code of ethics of the people of Malaysia . . . The time has come for us to ban matters that are nonsensical [*perkara yang bukan-bukan* . . ." . . . Datuk Sri Dr. Mahathir Mohamad (Prime Minister of Malaysia) (*UM 9* September 1986, *BH 9* September 1986).

---

[28] Sahara Yaacob spent a few months at the Darul Arqam Islamic commune but left because of disillusionment. Nonetheless, she still considers herself a "good" Muslim.

[29] When the interviewer cited examples like "Joget Lambak" and what happened once at Panggung Anniversari when some youths got up and danced to the *asli* tunes of SM Salim, the same official replied "that's different, that's a cultural event."

Despite the banning of rock concerts and various other efforts to control popular music, some musicians have been able to innovate and adapt beyond the terms set down by both the government as well as the transnational companies to which they are contracted.

New musical styles inspired by internationally distributed popular music and local music of various ethnic origins have emerged. For example, The Blues Gang's "Apo Nak di Kato" combines rambling rocking rhythm of American blues with the dialect (loghat) of Negri Sembilan. The Alleycats incorporate local dance rhythms like *masri* and *inang* with Western folk and pop elements. The Streetlights blend rock and Punjabi vocal style in their "Punjabi Rock" (*NST* 31 August 1984). Asiabeat fuses Asian percussion instruments (like *gamelan*, *tabla*, Chinese drums and *kompang*), *shakuhachi* and *nagaswaram* with western jazz elements.

Smaller locally owned recording companies and studios have also promoted the works of musicians ignored by the government and disregarded by the big foreign companies[30]. These companies include Suria Records Co, Iramanada Musical Industries (IMI), Warnada, Guntur Records, AB Records, Josal Music, Omry, Titra, Jansen Records and Suara Cipta Sempurna (SCS). Local recording studios like Redifusion, Sun Recorders, Betarees, The Booty Boys, and Estee Sound have also been set up. One of the most interesting of the musicians promoted by small independent companies is Hang Mokhtar. Hang Mokhtar combines Chinese, Indian and Malay tunes and manner of speech in his songs. The example below is one of his most popular songs which uses *bahasa pasar* (market Malay) and is sung to the theme song from the Hong Kong serial "The Bund":

Kepala peninge hati susah	[My] head ache, I am distressed
Ta'lak air con balan semua basah	Without air-conditioning, my body is all wet
Kaki kili atak penatlah	[My] left leg is tired
Tiap kali gua mesti tekan "kelak".	Everytime I have to press the clutch.
Lobanglah, kolek	Digging holes
Talikom tampal, LLN nanti kolek	Talikom [Department of Telecommunication] patches up [one hotel], LLN [National Electricity Board] digs another
Hali-hali tampal kolek	Everyday [someone] is patching or digging holes

---

[30] Big companies determine styles through sales and promotions. With the spread of a selection of synthetic rhythms to every market, all performers have to relate to these pre-determined rhythms. Usually big companies are "not willing to take on anything away from the beaten track" (*Star* 30 April 1983).

Balu tampal besok atak kolek [x2]	What has been patched up is dug up the next day [x2]
[Aya jua-a, banyak susah hati loh!]	[Aya, it is hot, I am distressed loh].

[1 verse and chorus from "Korek Tampal"; lyrics by Hang Mokhtar; album "Kocik Kocik Jago Kobau"; produced by Segar; distributed by Suara Cipta Sempurna]

Some of the singers have also incorporated various topical issues including complaints against the government in their lyrics. These songs are invigorated by humour in the tone of voice and the lyrics. As shown in the example above, Hang Mokhtar sings about the perpetual digging of roads to the frustration of commuters. Another of his songs "Ayo-yo Sami" (Sami refers to Samy Vellu, the Minister of Transport in Malaysia) describes how the people are being increasingly subjected to the collection of highway tolls. "Ayo-yo Sami" became so popular that it was adopted as the theme song at the opposition Democratic Action Party's demonstrations against tolls.

Ayo-yo Sami Ayo-ayo Sami	Ayo-yo Sami Ayo-yo Sami
Sekarang orang ada susah hati	People are distressed at this moment
Tol di sana, tol di sini	[There's] toll here, [there's] toll there
Di Penang orang suka naik feri	In Penang people prefer to take the ferry
Ayo-yo Sami Ayo-yo Sami	Ayo-yo Sami Ayo-yo Sami
Tak boleh kasi tol kurang lagi	Can't you lower the cost of tolls
Hari-hari bayar tol lagi	Everyday we have to pay tolls
Nanti saya habis duit gaji.	Soon, I will have used up all my pay.

[chorus and 1 verse of "Ayo-yo Sami"; lyrics by Hang Mokhtar, album: "Kocik Kocik Jago Kobau"; produced by Segar; distributed by Suara Cipta Sempurna].

In addition to the emergence of a new type of pop music which blends Western and local elements and which comments on social problems, a Malaysian brand of "heavy metal" has also flourished. Even though the government has placed severe restrictions on this type of rock and banned such rock concerts before, rock bands such as Search, Lefthanded, Bumiputera Rockers, Bloodshed and Wings remain very popular.[31] In the city of Kuala Lumpur, thousands of fans gather at rock concerts weekly to listen to these bands. In fact, since the banning of open-air rock concerts

---

[31] Local bands were first influenced by heavy metal bands such as Uriah Heep and Deep Purple which visited Malaysia and recordings of such music imported from overseas. The bands have since established identities of their own.

in 1986, a type of rock community comprising mainly male, Malay youths has emerged (*ibid.*). These youths hang around shopping complexes, record shops and attend rock concerts. They can be distinguished by their long frizzy hair, corduroy or leather pants, T-shirts, leather jackets, boots and big motorbikes.[32]

An argument can be made here as it has been made for situations elsewhere (Hebdige 1979) that this rock subculture challenges the dominant culture and social norms defined by the state and moral guardians such as Islamic purists. "Heavy metal" rock music, with its loud drums and electric guitar bass pounding the beat, and aggressive electric lead guitars repeating riffs, provides outlets for youths to air their discontent and criticisms of society. The Wings, for example, criticize those who are "mad over status, name, power and wealth" in their song "Hukum Karma" ("Condemn Fate"):

Oh dalam dunia, oh kita raja	Oh in this world, oh we are kings
Oh jangan lupa, oh jangan gila	Oh do not forget, oh do not be mad
Gila darjat, gila nama	Mad over status, mad over name
Gila kuasa, gila harta.	Mad over power, mad over wealth

[chorus and verse of "Hukum Karma"; lyrics and tune by Wings; album "Hukum Karma"; produced and distributed by Antartic Sound Production (ASP), an independent local company.]

Above all, loud rock music helps youths escape from the problems of everyday life. The Rusty Blade, for instance, invites its fans to "rock" away their "sufferings":

Hey kawan jangan kau bermuram saja	Hey friends don't be gloomy
Luputkanlah terpendamnya cinta lama	Get rid of and conceal your old love
Mari teman lupakanlah dukacita	Come friends forget your sadness
Tiada guna menambahkan merana	It is of no use to increase your sufferings in life
Marilah semua dendangkan bersama	Let us sing together
Iringan wirama rock kita (metal)	Accompanied by our rock beat (metal)
Rock! Rock! Rock! Rock!	Rock! Rock! Rock! Rock!
Yang sudah tu sudah lupakanlah saja	Forget what has happened

---

[32] On the other hand, Chinese youths gather at discos and are more attracted to pop music from Hong Kong, Taiwan and the West. These youths follow the fashions of pop stars shown on videos from Hong Kong and Taiwan.

Tak perlu kutahu cerita gundahmu.   It is not necessary to let me know
your hesitating stories.

["Rock"; lyrics by Yantzen; tune by Rusty Blade; album "Rintangan Hidup
Dunia"; produced by Razzi M; distributed by Life Rekod, an independent
local company.]

Fringe singers and composers further provide an alternative flow of
musics. During the KL Arts Festival of 1986, a concert called "Statements
from the Musical Fringe" was organized (*NSunT* 16 August 1986). Some
of the items presented include Rafique's "Lobotomy", Kit Leee's avant
garde "Opus 8" and Julian's "Fred The Mutant" (a "mutation" of joget),
all of which would not have been considered "desirable" by the government or of marketable value by the big companies. In 1988, some of these
self-declared fringe singers combined their efforts to produce an album entitled "Suara" (Voices) to commemorate the 40th anniversary of the United
Nations Universal Declaration of Human Rights (1948–1988). It is noteworthy that four major recording companies turned down the album—
apparently because it was "lacking in . . . commercial value"—before it
was accepted by a small concern called "Jiwa" (*Aliran* 1988: 20). Equally
noteworthy is the fact that despite the government's crackdown on social
activists and alternative theatre a year ago, these singers released songs
like "kebebasan":

Kalau mau dibebaskan	If you want to be free
dari segala cengkaman	from all forms of repression
jangan dikeretalembukan	don't be left behind
terus teguhkan keinsanan.	stand up for your humanity.

[chorus of "Kebebasan"; album: "Suara"; produced by Jiwa; distributed
by Warnada]

Lastly, musicians involved in popular music have begun to come
together to encourage solidarity and to highlight the common problems
they face via revival of The Musicians' Union of Peninsular Malaysia
(MPUM) which was set up some three decades ago (*Star* 31 August 1984).
Since this revival, MPUM has protested against the government's ban on
open-air rock concerts (*NST* 16 October 1986) and organized "Showcase
sessions" for musicians to "jam" with one another (*NST* 19 June 1984).
MPUM has also voiced opinions about the protection of local musicians
against the influx of foreign ones in places of entertainment (*Star* 15
March 1987). Acting together, the musicians were able to gain approval
for certain concerts shortly after the government ban on open-air rock
concerts. For instance, the open-air "Resolution '87 Concert" was held in
Kuala Lumpur on New Year's Eve night, 1986. In January 1987, permission was granted to "heavy-metal" rock bands like Search and dR Sam
and Musafir to perform indoors at the "Konsert Rozana Search" (*Star* 25
December 1986). Even though only "approved" bands like Zurah II (singing

nostalgic songs of the 60s) and Headwind (singing commercial pop) were featured in the "Resolution '87 Concert" and rock groups had to hold the "Rozana Search Concert" indoors and adhere to strict rules regarding their repertoire, dress and facial make-up, the concerts did mark "breakthroughs" on the part of the musicians against the government's stringent rulings on popular music (*NST* 30 December 1986).

Conclusion

By introducing various policies, guidelines and institutions in the 1970s and 1980s, the government has tried to centralize and control the performing arts. Those art forms which are in line with the national culture policy and performances which adhere to the stipulated guidelines have been promoted and encouraged. However, those which are considered "anti Islamic", those which are alleged to stimulate "violence" and those which are generally "undesirable" have been banned or censored. Additionally, the performing arts which are "political" in content have been harshly treated. By using the Internal Security Act, some social activists involved in creating an "alternative Malaysian culture" have also been detained. Even the popular music industry, dominated by transnational companies and show promoters, has been subjected to the same intervening institutions and restrictions.

Government control of the arts, however, has not been complete. This is partly because there remain unresolved differences among officials and within government institutions charged with the responsibility of overseeing the arts. For example, KKBS does not yet know how to deal with art forms that are Malay and yet pre-Islamic. Moreover, not only does KKBS suffer budgetary constraints, it is also prone to bureaucratic inefficiencies including a serious shortage of trained personnel in the performing arts. Censorship and programming in RTM seem to have been relaxed as a result of competition from the commercial channel TV3.

More importantly, independent individuals and groups continually evade government control and directions. Even as the government continually passes new laws, introduces new guidelines and appropriates particular forms that it cannot control or ban completely (such as popular music), their challenge persists. In this way, new ideas, themes and forms are experimented with and developed in the performing arts by these independent (though financially poor) individuals and groups. Although they share common problems (financial, official harassment and others) and, to varying degrees, disagree with the government's national culture policy and/or its attempts to control the performing arts, nonetheless, they do not subscribe to a common notion of an alternative Malaysian culture. Instead, the vision is extremely fragmented. And there is little possibility of the emergence of any sort of alternative or counter-hegemonic movement. In this regard they may be regarded as "counterpoints" to the government's cultural policy.

Bibliography

Books and Articles

Al-Faruqi. Lois Ibsen, 1985. "Music, Musicians and Muslim Law." *Asian Music*, 17 (1).

Chee Moon Leng, 1982. "The English Language Drama in Malaysia: A Study of its Development, Themes and Styles." BA Thesis, Universiti Sains Malaysia, Penang.

Freire, Paulo, 1983. *Pedagogy of the Oppressed*, New York:

Ghazalie Shafie, 1979. "Keperibadian Nasional Belum Lahir." *Dewan Masyarakat*, 17 (8), 15 August.

Hebdige, Dick, 1979. *Subculture: The Meaning of Style*. London and New York: Methuen.

Ismail Zain, 1977. "Cultural Planning and General Development in Malaysia." Siri Kebudayaan Kebangsaan 17.1. Kementerian Kebudayaan, Belia dan Sukan Malaysia [KKBS].

KKBS [Ministry of Culture, Youth and Sports Malaysia], 1973. *Asas-Kebudayaan Kebangsaan*, Kuala Lumpur.

Krishen Jit, 1984. "Toward an Islamic Theatre for Malaysia: Noordin Hassan and 'Don't Kill the Butterflies'". *Asian Theatre Journal* 1 (2), pp. 127–146.

Kumpulan Noor El-Kawakib Papar, (nd). "Lagu-lagu Nasyid", Sabah,

Mackerras, Colin, 1981. *The Performing Arts in Contemporary China*, London: Routledge and Kegan Paul.

Malaysia, 1977. *Laws of Malaysia, Act 182, Theatres and Places of Public Amusement (Federal Territory) Act 1977*. Kuala Lumpur: Government Printers.

——, 1986. *Fifth Malaysia Plan, 1986–1990*. Kuala Lumpur: National Printing Department.

Márquez, Andrés, 1983. "When Ponchos are Subversive." *Index on Censorship* 12 (1).

Ministry of Information, 1975. *Inilah Radio/TV Malaysia*. Kuala Lumpur: Government Printer.

Mohd. Taib Osman, 1984. *Bunga Rampai: Aspects of Malay Culture*. Kuala Lumpur: Dewan Bahasa dan Pustaka.

Penang (Police, Fire Brigade, Departments of Health, Building and Engineering), (nd). "Syarat-syarat daripada jabatan-jabatan berkenaan untuk pertunjukan masa Phor Tor." (Stencilled sheets).

Rahmah Bujang, 1987. *Boria: A Form of Malay Theatre*, Singapore: Institute of Southeast Asian Studies. Local History and Memoirs.

Street, John, 1986. *Rebel Rock*, New York: Basil Blackwell.

Tan Sooi Beng, 1980. "Chinese Opera in Malaysia: Changes and Survival." *Review of Southeast Asian Studies*, 10, pp. 29–45.

——, 1983. "Alat-alat Orkestra Cina Moden Malaysia: Satu Pengenalan." *Masakini* 1 (4).

——, 1984, *Ko-tai: A New Form of Chinese Urban Street Theatre in Malaysia*. Singapore: Institute of Southeast Asian Studies. Research Notes and Discussions Paper, 40.

——, 1988a. *"The Phor Tor* Festival in Penang: Deities, Ghosts and Chinese Ethnicity."* Melbourne: Centre of Southeast Asian Studies, Monash University. Working Paper, 51.

——, 1988b. "From Popular to 'Traditional' Theatre: The Dynamics of Change in Bangsawan of Malaysia." *Ethnomusicology* 33 (2), pp. 229–274.

Uscher, Nancy, 1983. "Wagner, Strauss and Israel." *Index on Censorship* 12 (1), 1983.

Wan Abdul Kadir, 1988. *Budaya Popular Dalam Masyarakat Melayu Bandaran.* Kuala Lumpur: Dewan Bahasa dan Pustaka.

Wallis, Roger and Malm, Krister, 1984. *Big Sounds from Small Peoples,* London: Constable and Co. Ltd.

Newspapers and Magazines

Aliran
Berita Harian (BH)
Dewan Budaya
Dewan Masyarakat
Far Eastern Economic Review (FEER)
Mingguan Malaysia (MM)

National Echo (NE)
New Straits Times (NST)
New Sunday Times (NSunT)
Star
Utusan Malaysia (UM)

Index

Apart from a few authors whose work is discussed in detail in the text, the index does not include references to secondary authors and sources.

Contributors

CHEEK, Ahmad Shabery was with the Faculty of Economics and Administration, Universiti Malaya and is now an independent researcher specialising in Malaysian politics and Islam. He has edited *Warisan Shariati* (Shariati's Heritage, 1987) and *Cabaran Malaysia Tahun* 1980an (Malaysia's Challenges in the 1980s, 1989).

CROUCH, Harold is a Senior Fellow in the Department of Political and Social Change, Research School of Pacific Studies, Australian National University. He taught political science at the National University of Malaysia between 1976 and 1991 and is the author of *The Army and Politics in Indonesia* and co–editor of *Malaysian Politics and the 1978 Election.*

JOMO K S is with the Faculty of Economics and Administration, Universiti Malaya. He has studied and taught at Yale, Harvard, Universiti Sains Malaysia, Universiti Kebangsaan Malaysia, Universiti Malaya and Cambridge. His book publications include *A Question of Class: Capital, the State and Uneven Development in Malaya* (1986) and *Growth and Structural Change in the Malaysian Economy* (1990).

KAHN, Joel S was born in the United States, and studied Anthropology at Cornell University and then the London School of Economics. He taught anthropology at University College London before taking up the Chair of Anthropology at Monash University in 1986. He has carried out research in West Sumatra, Indonesia and in different parts of Malaysia and published books and articles on the peasantry, economic anthropology, culture and ideology and the history of anthropological theory.

KESSLER, Clive S is Professor of Sociology at the University of New South Wales, Sydney, Australia. He has been researching Malaysian culture and politics for the past twenty–five years and is author of *Islam and Politics in a Malay State: Kelantan 1838–1939* (1978) and numerous essays analysing contemporary Malaysian society.

KHOO, Kay Jin studied Anthropology in Columbia University and now lectures in the School of Social Sciences, Universiti Sains Malaysia. He has published on a wide variety of topics and recently edited *Whose War? What Peace? Reflections on the Gulf Conflict* (1991).

LOH, Francis Kok Wah studied Politics and Southeast Asian Studies in Cornell University. He is author of the Politics of Chinese *Unity in Malaysia* (1982) and *Beyond the Tin Mines* (1988). He taught in Monash University from 1986–1989 and is now with the School of Social Sciences,

Universiti Sains Malaysia. He is completing a book on Sabah's recent politics.

SAID, Muhammad Ikmal is Associate Professor in the Department of Anthropology and Sociology, Universiti Malaya. He is author of *The Evolution of Large Paddy Farms in the Muda Area, Kedah* (1985) and co–edited Images of Malaysia (1991). He is currently engaged in a comparative study of ethnic relations in Sabah, Sarawak and the Peninsula.

SALLEH, Halim is a graduate of Monash University and the Institute of Development Studies, Sussex University. He lectures in Development Studies in the Universiti Sains Malaysia, Penang. He is the author of *Bureaucrats, Petty Bourgeois and Townsmen* (1981) and has recently been published on rural development in Malaysia, particularly on land matters.

STIVENS, Maila was born in Australia and studied Anthropology at Sydney University and the London School of Economics. She has carried out research in Sydney on kinship in a middle class suburb, in Negeri Sembilan, Malaysia, on gender and underdevelopment, and more recently on the formation of the urban Malay middle class. She taught at University College, London for some years before returning to Australia to teach in the Women's Studies Programme at Melbourne University.

TAN, Liok Ee is a graduate in Philosophy from the University of Singapore and in History from the University of Malaya. She is Associate Professor in History at Universiti Sains Malaysia, Penang. Among her publications are the *The Rhetoric of Bangsa and Minzu* (1988) and articles on Chinese education in Malaysia in various books and journals.

TAN, Sooi Beng is an Ethnomusicologist in the Arts Centre, Universiti Sains Malaysia, Penang. She studied in Cornell, Wesleyan and Monash Universities and is author of *Ko–tai: Chinese Urban Street Theatre in Malaysia* (1984), *The Phor Tor Festival, Penang* (1989) and various other articles on the performing arts in Malaysia. Her study on *bangsawan* will be published by Oxford UP in 1991.